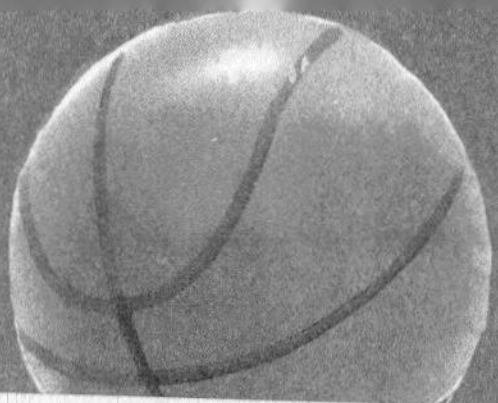

TAKEHIKO INOUE

REAL 3

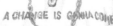

A CHANGE IS GONNA COME

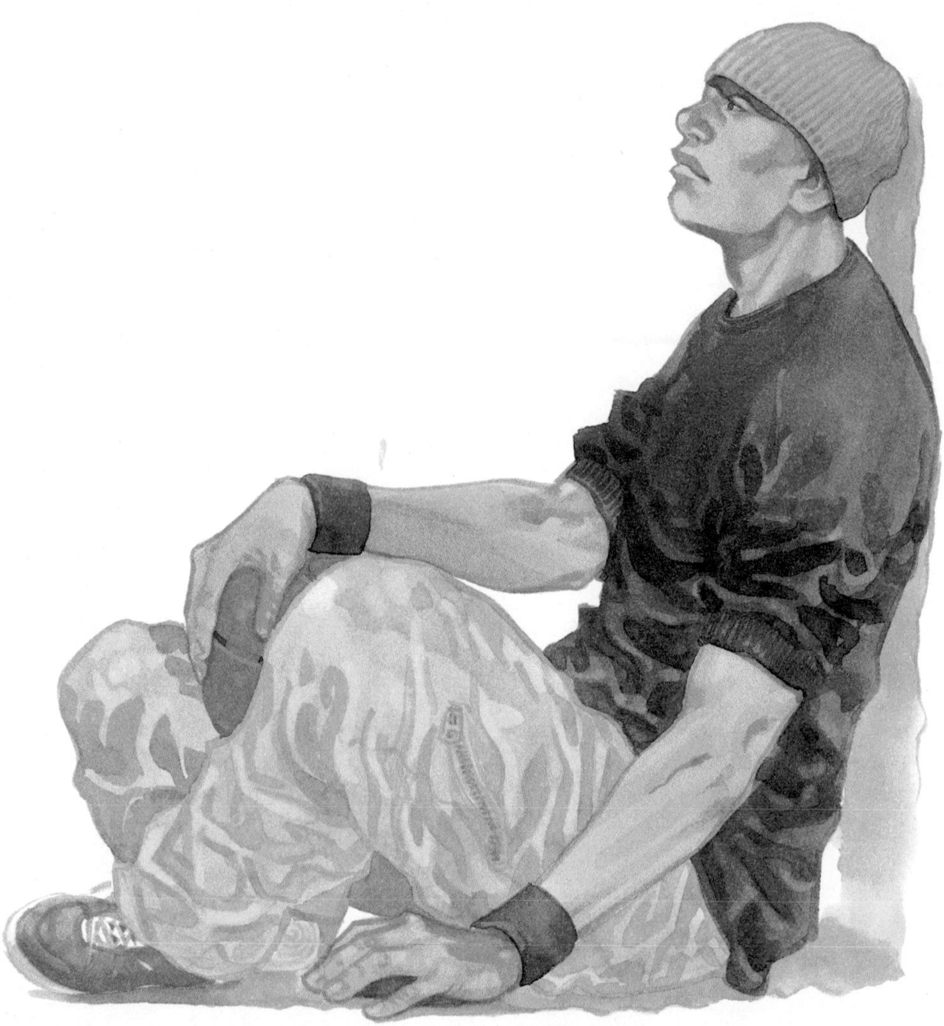

GRAPH
INOUE
V. 3

c o n t e n t s

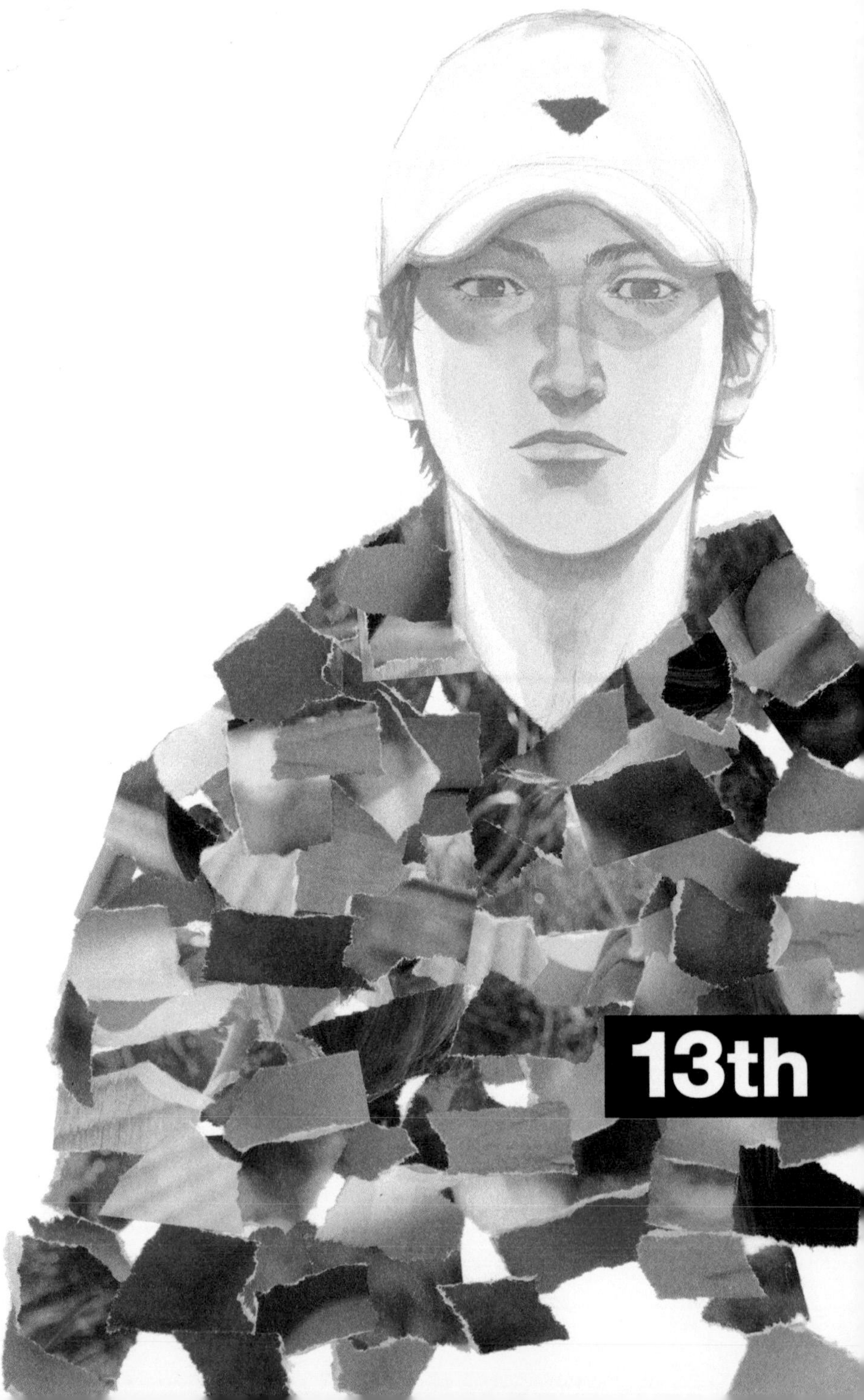
13th

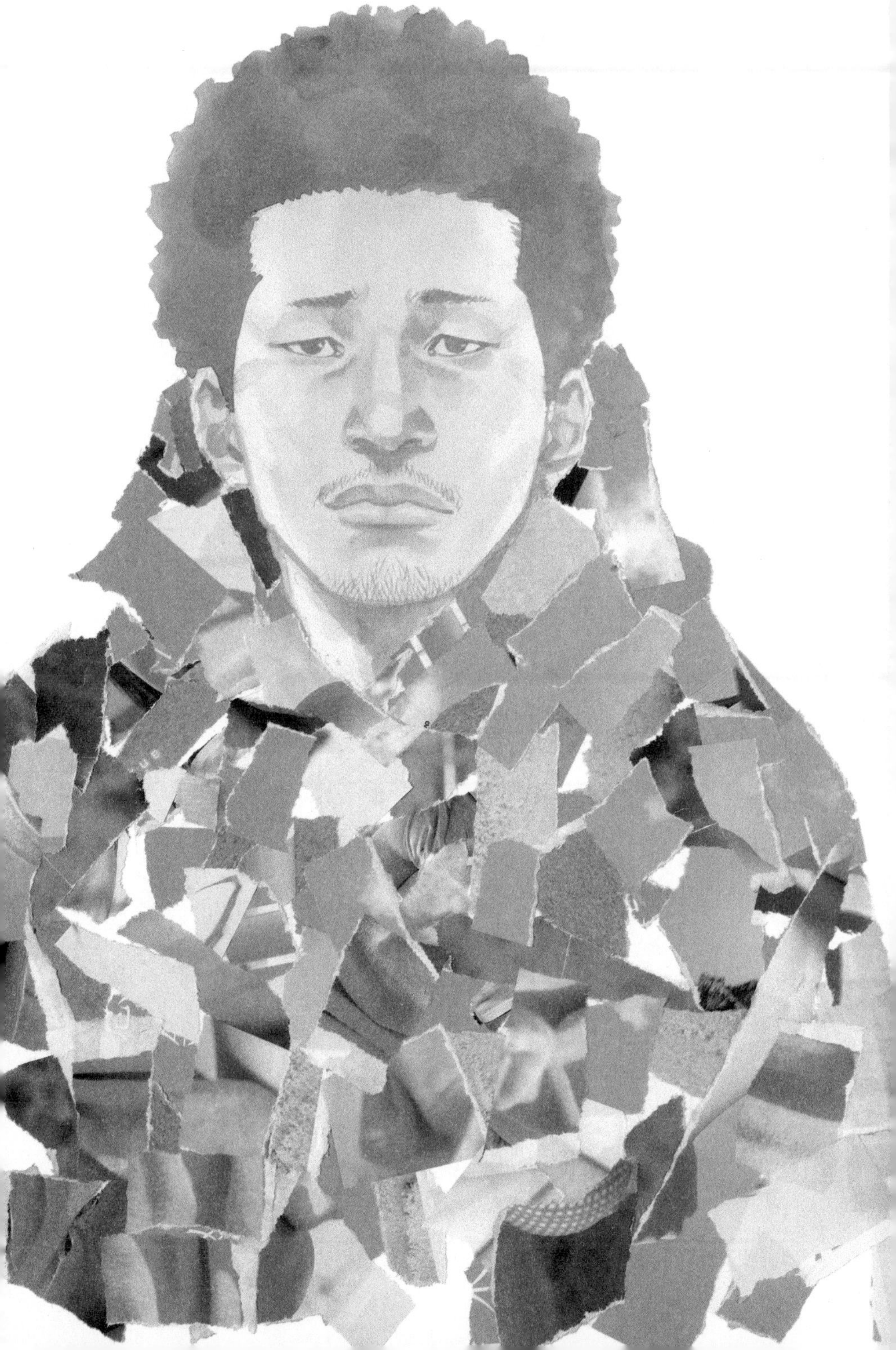

TROD
TROD
VROOM
SCRCH
TAMURA

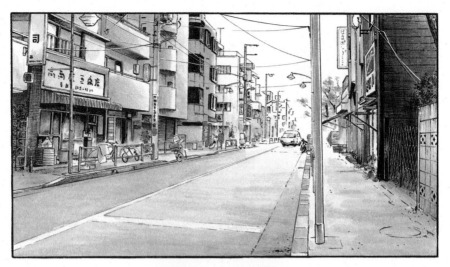

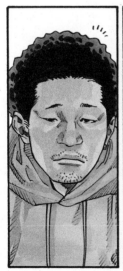

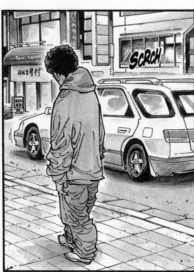

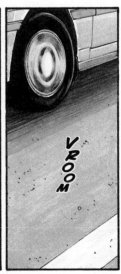

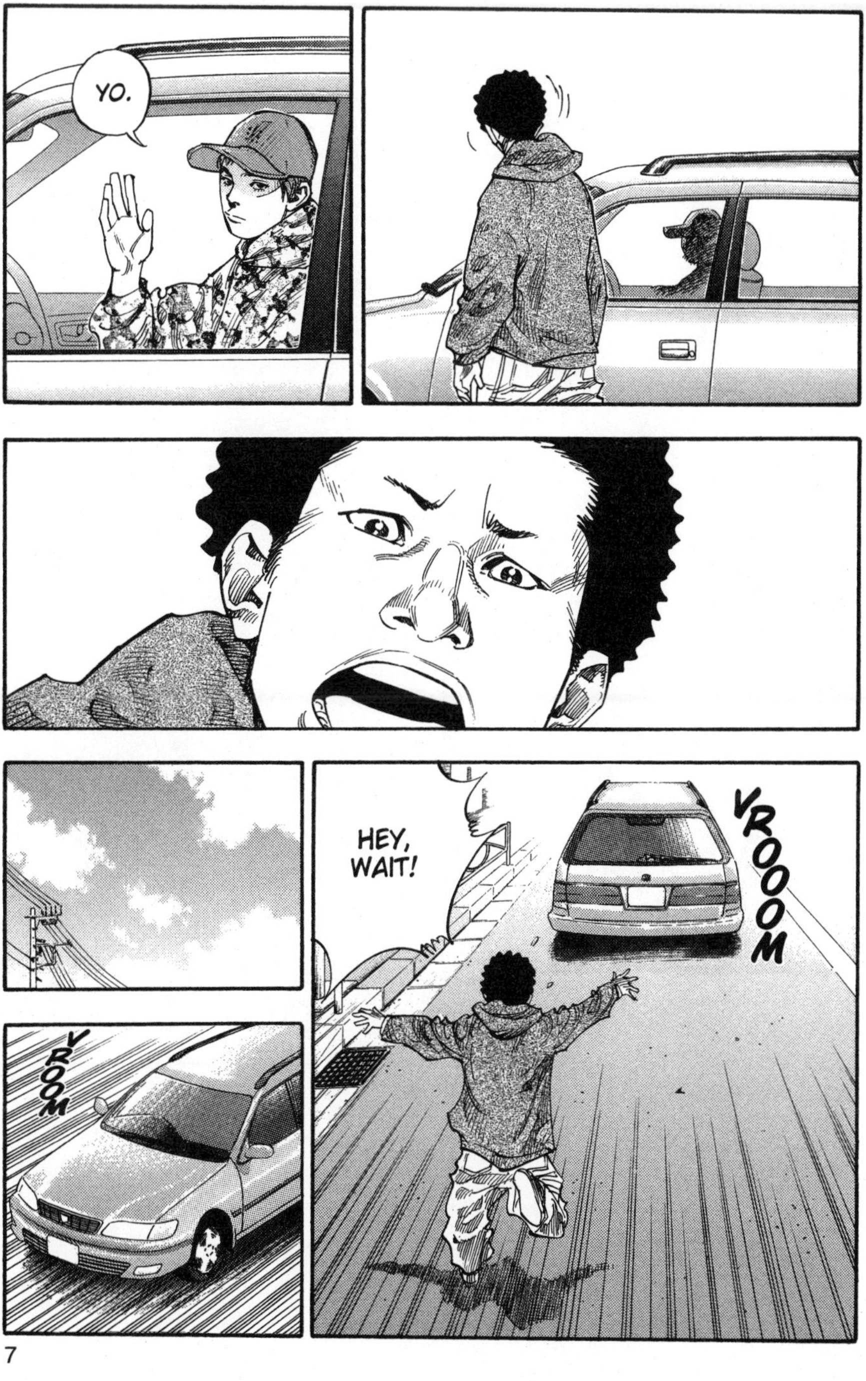
YO.
HEY, WAIT!
VROOOOM
VROOM

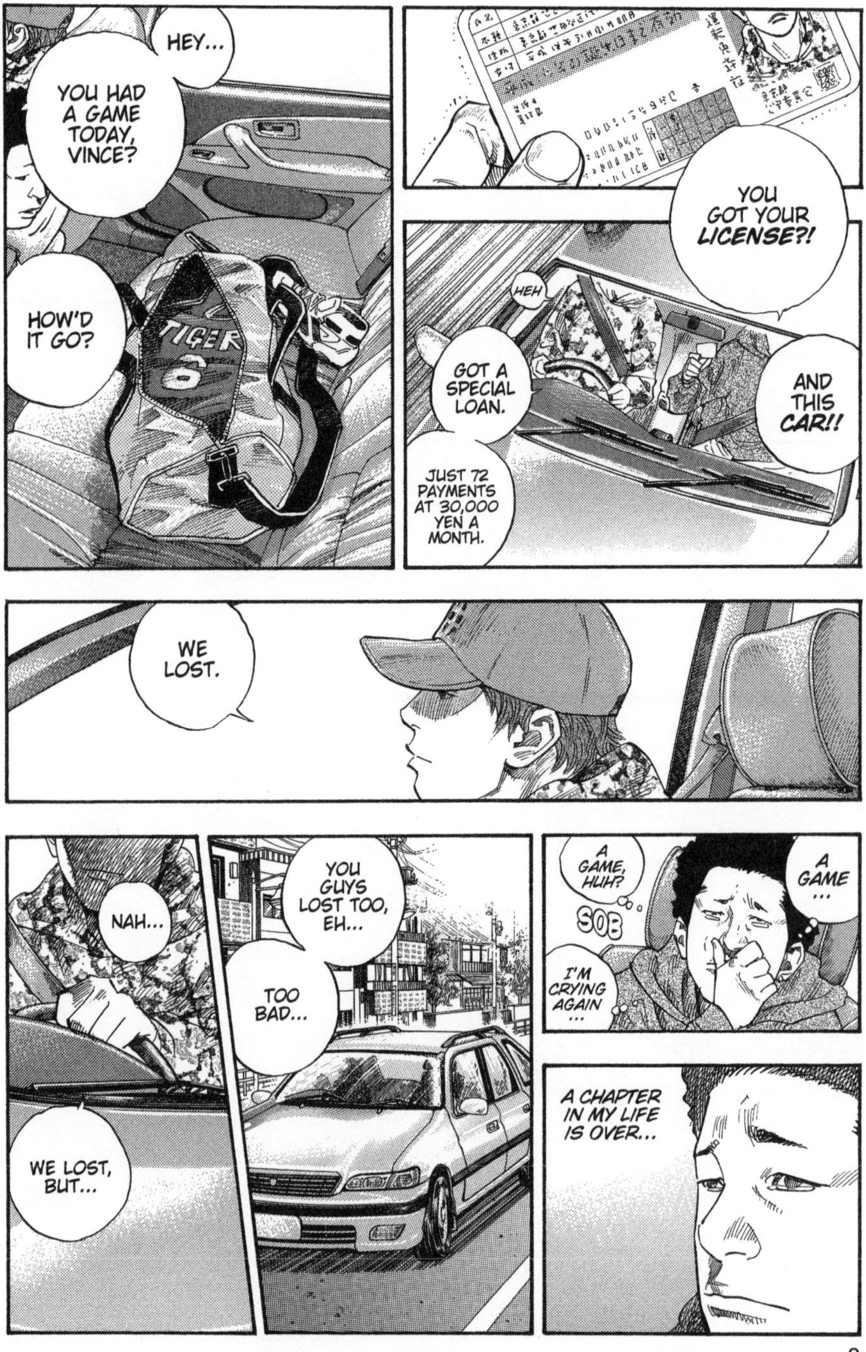
YOU GOT YOUR LICENSE?!
AND THIS CAR!!
HEH
GOT A SPECIAL LOAN.
JUST 72 PAYMENTS AT 30,000 YEN A MONTH.
HEY...
YOU HAD A GAME TODAY, VINCE?
HOW'D IT GO?
WE LOST.
A GAME...
A GAME, HUH?
SOB
I'M CRYING AGAIN...
A CHAPTER IN MY LIFE IS OVER...
YOU GUYS LOST TOO, EH...
TOO BAD...
NAH...
WE LOST, BUT...

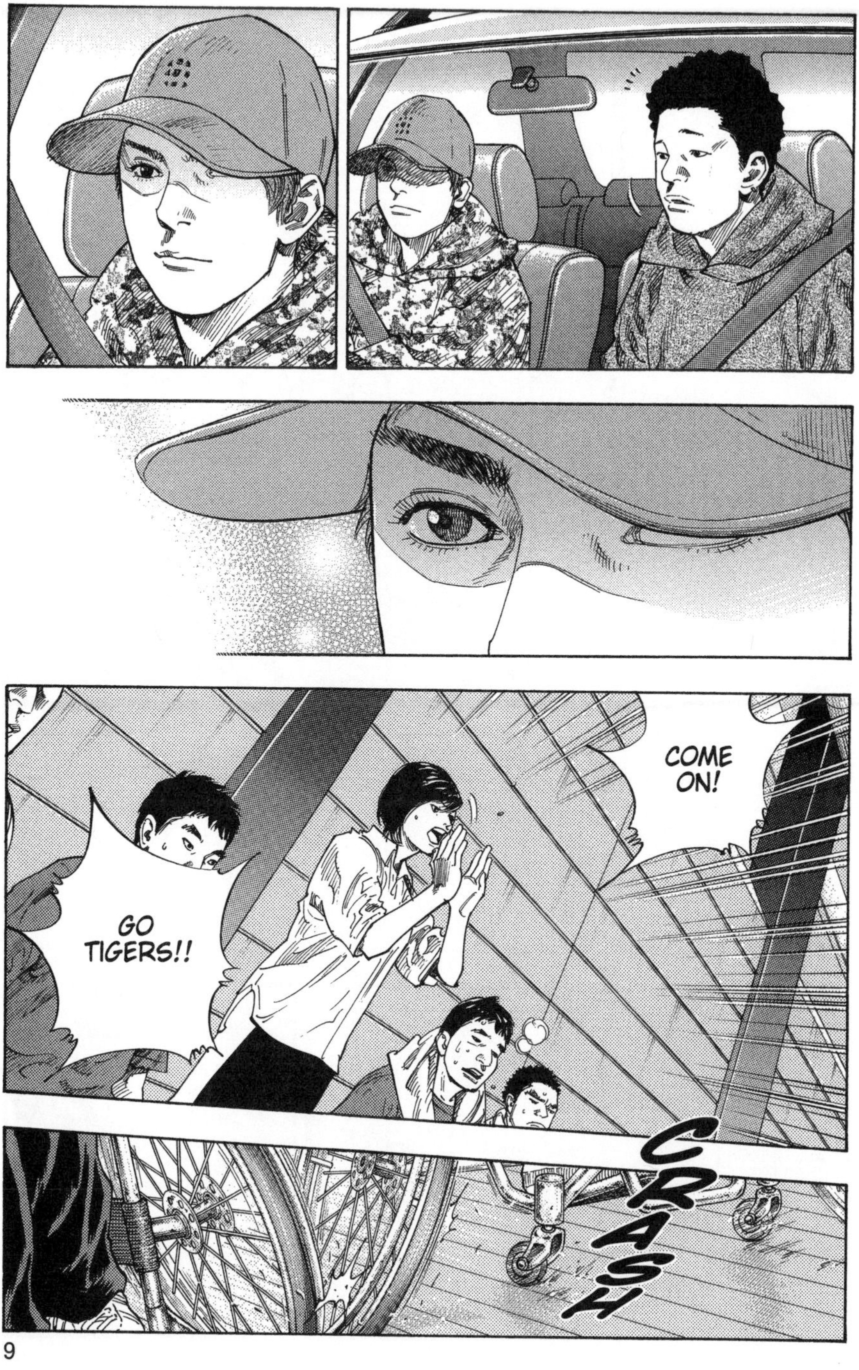
COME ON!
GO TIGERS!!
CRASH

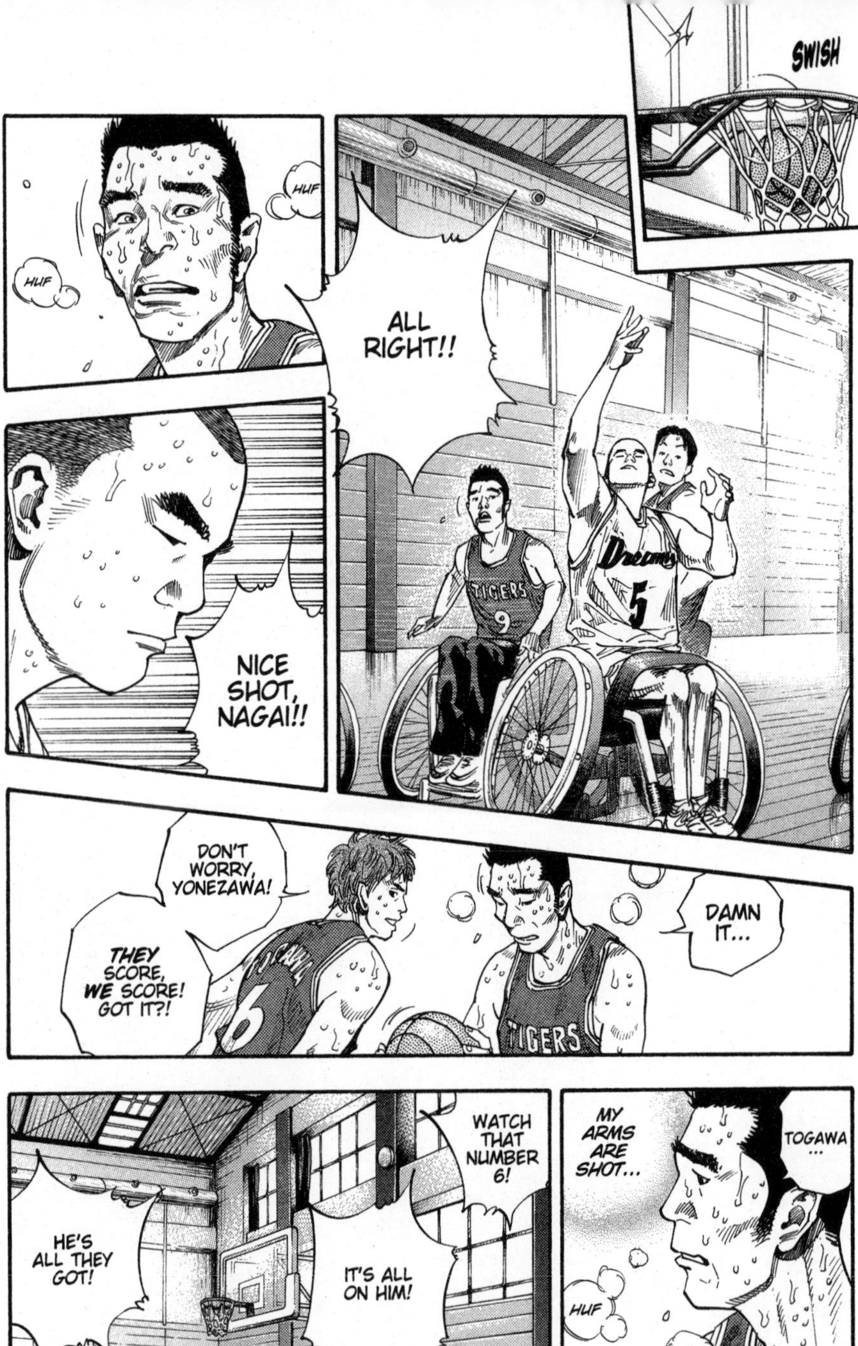
SWISH
ALL RIGHT!!
HUF
HUF
NICE SHOT, NAGAI!!
DAMN IT...
DON'T WORRY, YONEZAWA!
THEY SCORE, WE SCORE! GOT IT?!
TOGAWA...
MY ARMS ARE SHOT...
HUF
HUF
WATCH THAT NUMBER 6!
IT'S ALL ON HIM!
HE'S ALL THEY GOT!

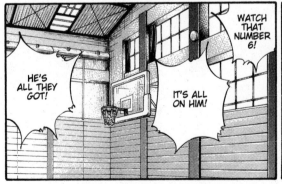

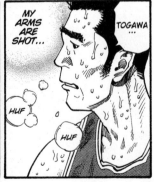

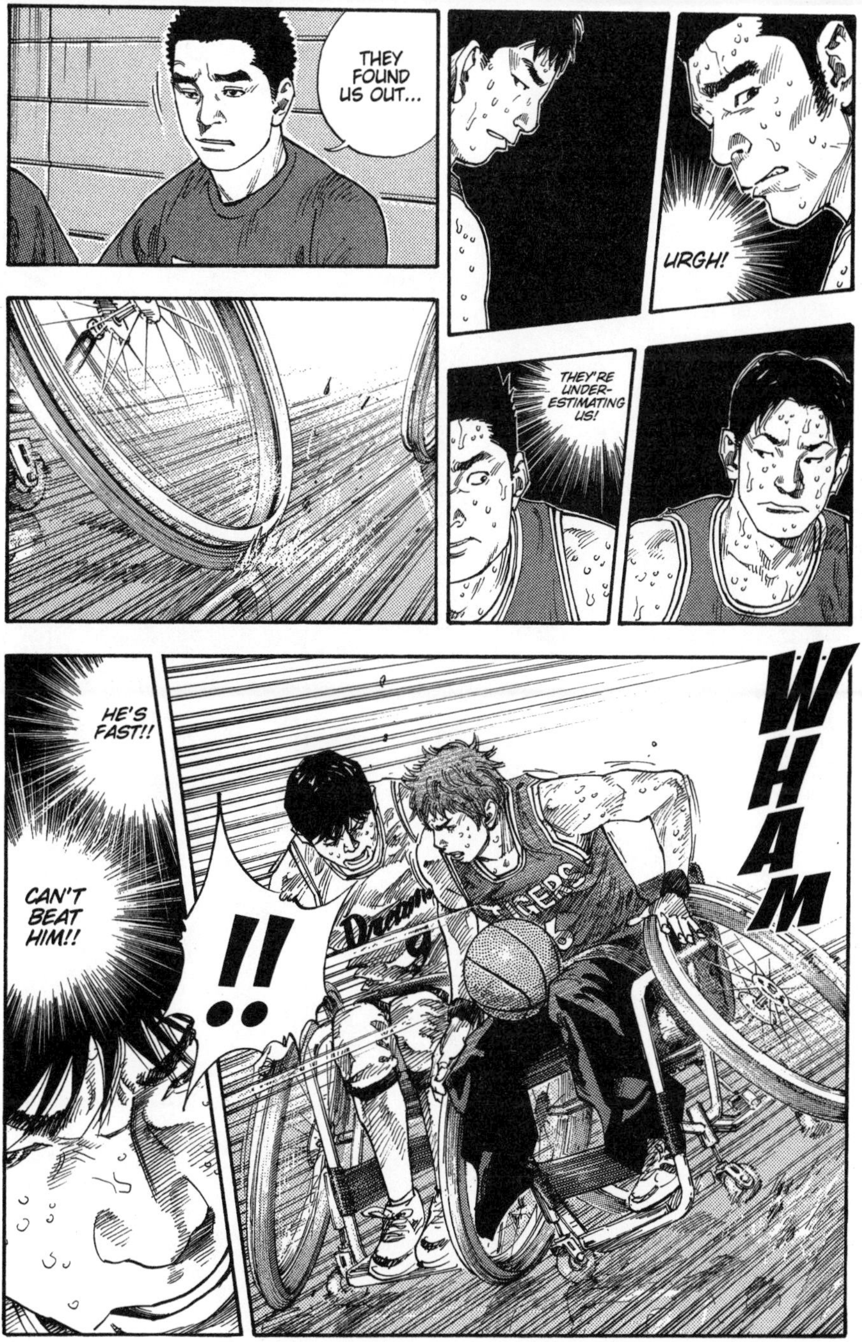
URGH!
THEY FOUND US OUT...
THEY'RE UNDER-ESTIMATING US!
WHAM
HE'S FAST!!
CAN'T BEAT HIM!!
!!

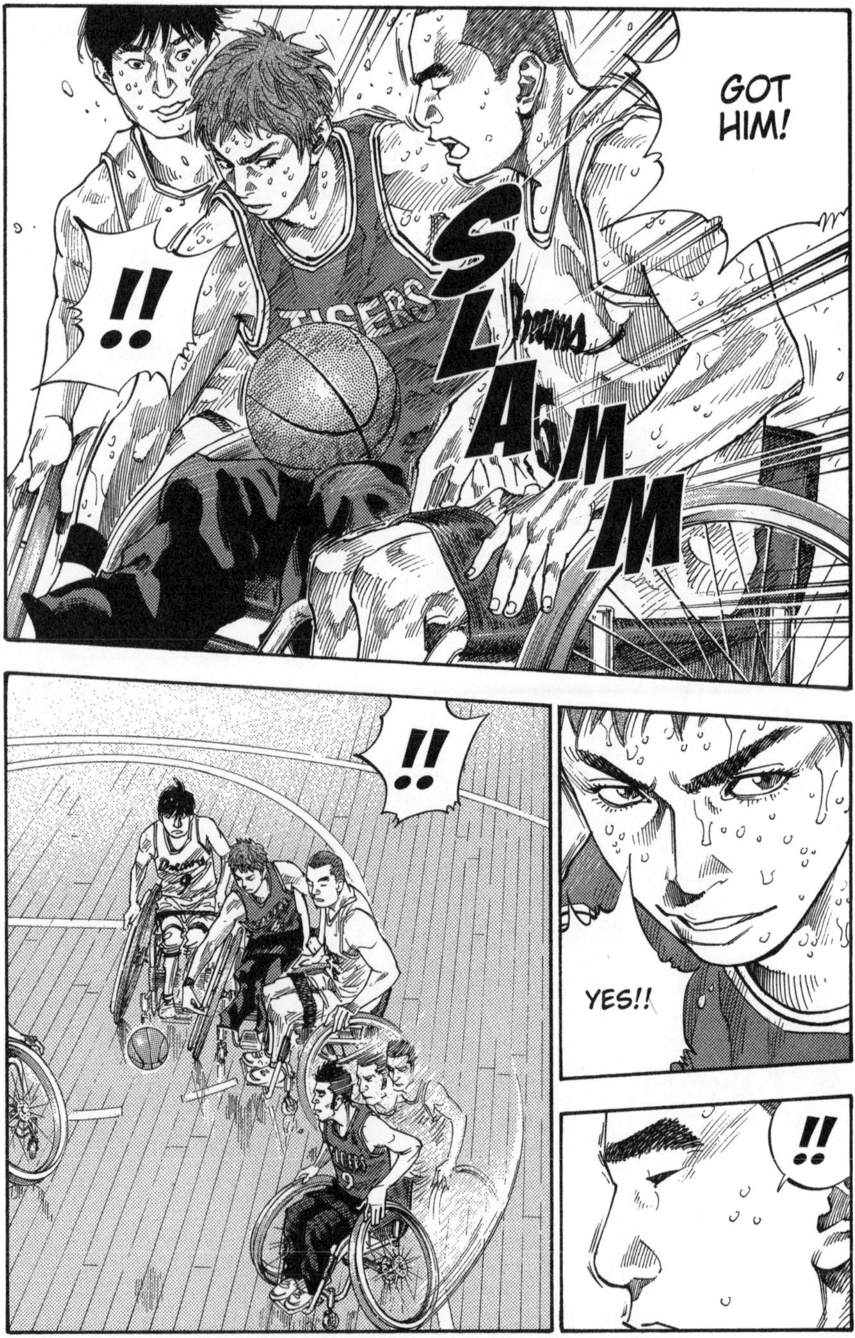
GOT HIM!
SLAMM
!!
YES!!
!!
!!

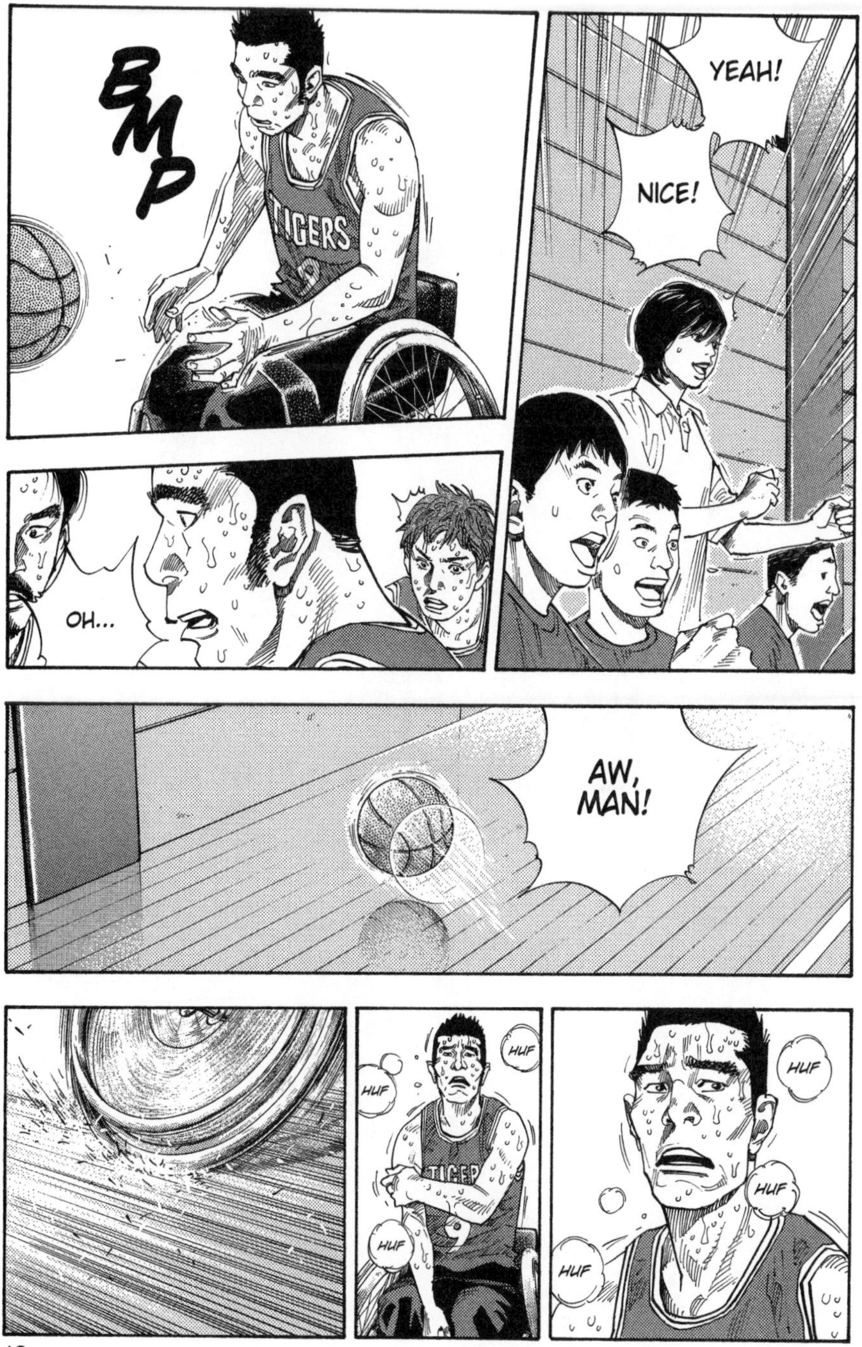
YEAH!
NICE!
BMP
OH...
AW, MAN!
HUF
HUF
HUF
HUF
HUF
HUF
HUF

CRAP!

TIGERS 41 : DREAMS 54

IT'S NO USE.

IT'S OKAY IF HE BEATS YOU...

...JUST DON'T LET HIM GET BY AT BASELINE!!

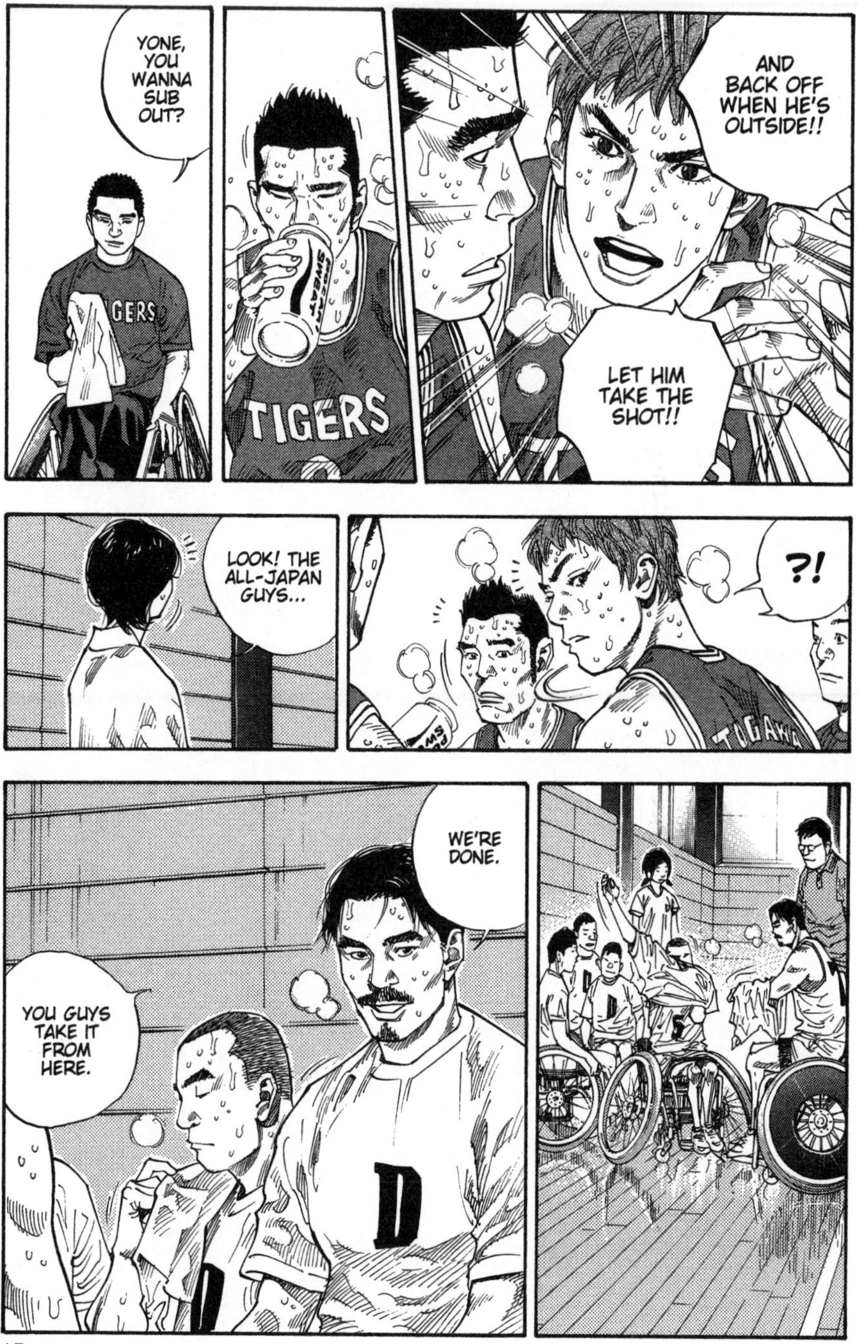
AND BACK OFF WHEN HE'S OUTSIDE!!
LET HIM TAKE THE SHOT!!
YONE, YOU WANNA SUB OUT?
?!
LOOK! THE ALL-JAPAN GUYS...
WE'RE DONE.
YOU GUYS TAKE IT FROM HERE.

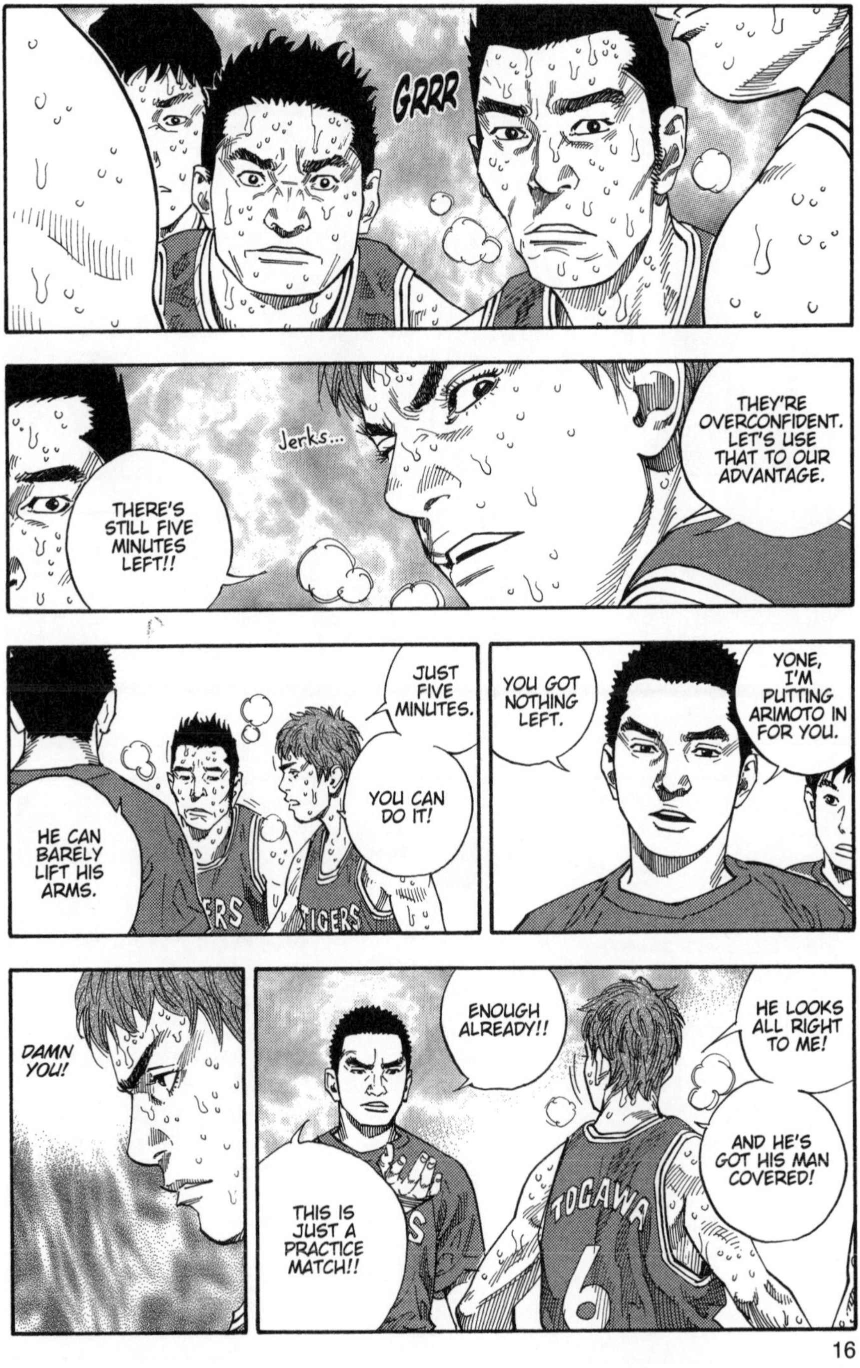
GRRR
THEY'RE OVERCONFIDENT. LET'S USE THAT TO OUR ADVANTAGE.
Jerks...
THERE'S STILL FIVE MINUTES LEFT!!
YONE, I'M PUTTING ARIMOTO IN FOR YOU.
YOU GOT NOTHING LEFT.
JUST FIVE MINUTES.
YOU CAN DO IT!
HE CAN BARELY LIFT HIS ARMS.
TIGERS
HE LOOKS ALL RIGHT TO ME!
AND HE'S GOT HIS MAN COVERED!
ENOUGH ALREADY!!
THIS IS JUST A PRACTICE MATCH!!
TOGAWA
6
DAMN YOU!

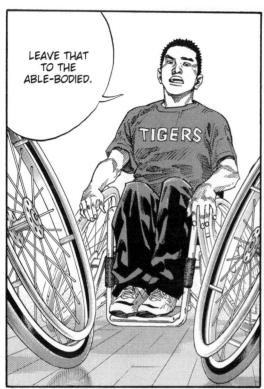

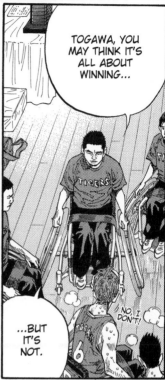

TOGAWA, YOU MAY THINK IT'S ALL ABOUT WINNING...
TIGERS
NO, I DON'T!
...BUT IT'S NOT.
LEAVE THAT TO THE ABLE-BODIED.
TIGERS
WHAT THE HELL ?!
THAT'S NOT FOR US.
TELL ME...

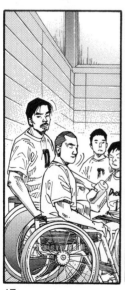

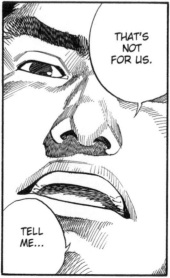

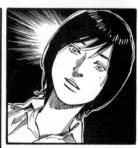

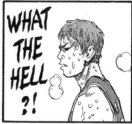

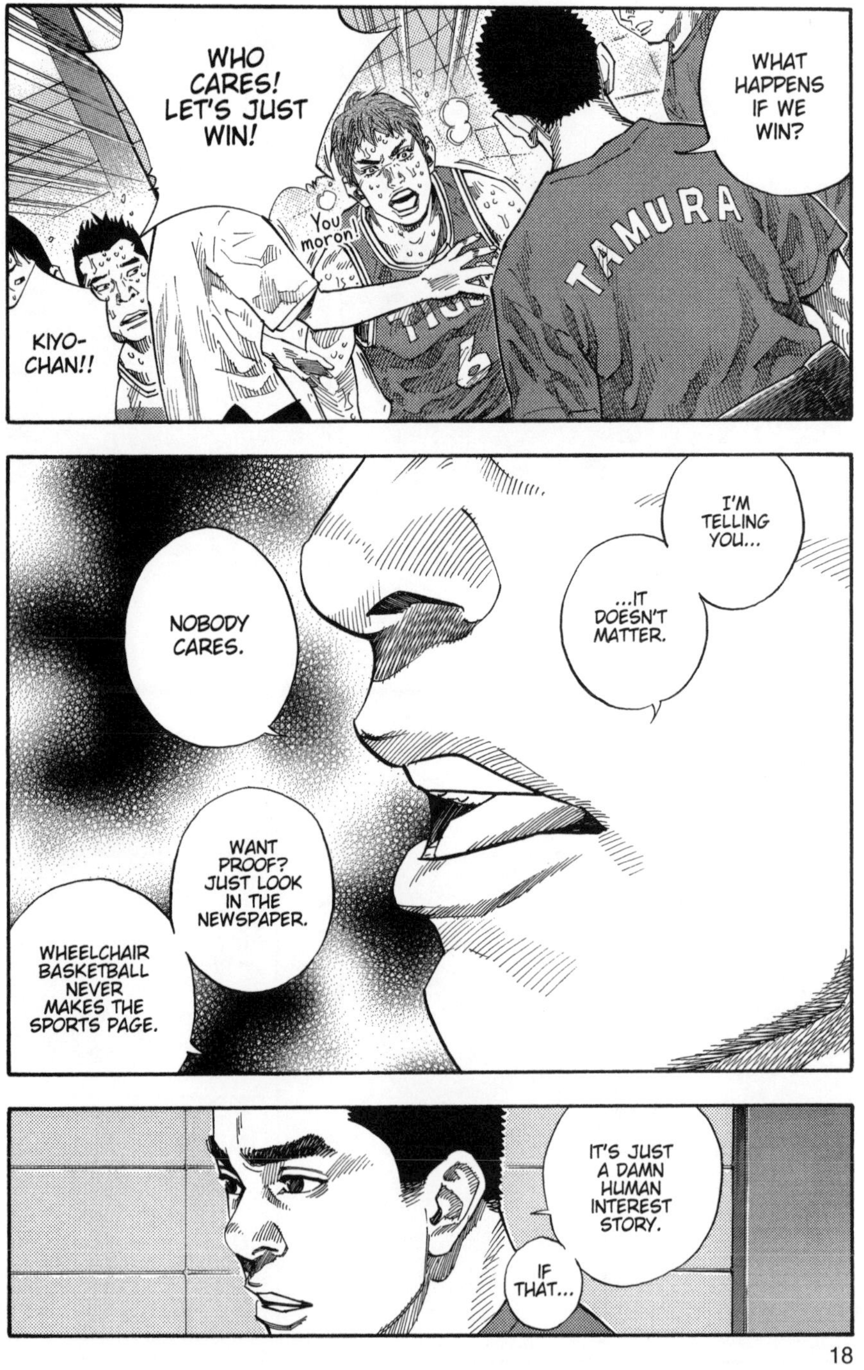
WHAT HAPPENS IF WE WIN?
WHO CARES! LET'S JUST WIN!
You moron!
KIYO-CHAN!!
I'M TELLING YOU...
...IT DOESN'T MATTER.
NOBODY CARES.
WANT PROOF? JUST LOOK IN THE NEWSPAPER.
WHEELCHAIR BASKETBALL NEVER MAKES THE SPORTS PAGE.
IT'S JUST A DAMN HUMAN INTEREST STORY.
IF THAT...

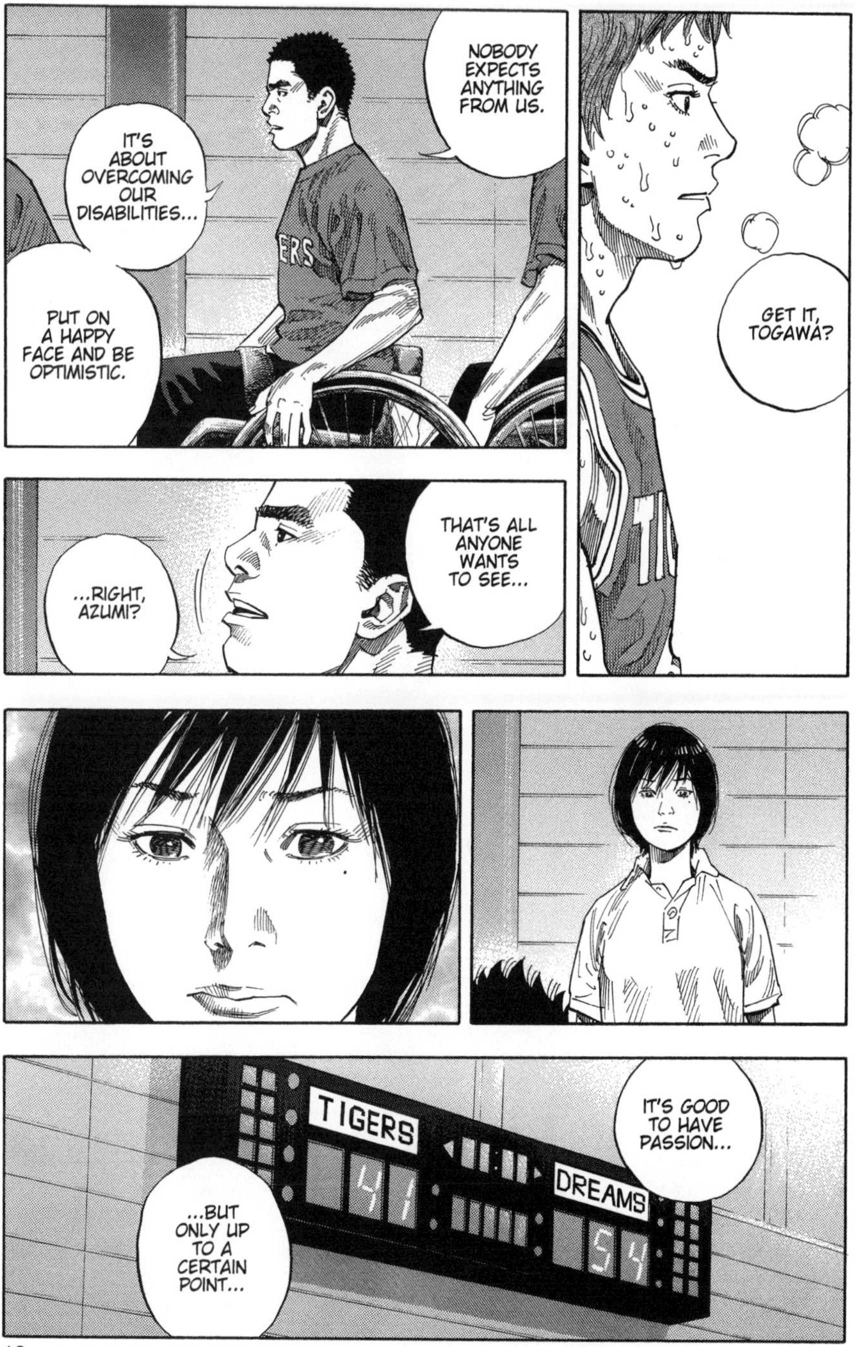
GET IT, TOGAWA?
NOBODY EXPECTS ANYTHING FROM US.
IT'S ABOUT OVERCOMING OUR DISABILITIES...
PUT ON A HAPPY FACE AND BE OPTIMISTIC.
THAT'S ALL ANYONE WANTS TO SEE...
...RIGHT, AZUMI?
IT'S GOOD TO HAVE PASSION...
TIGERS
41
DREAMS
54
...BUT ONLY UP TO A CERTAIN POINT...

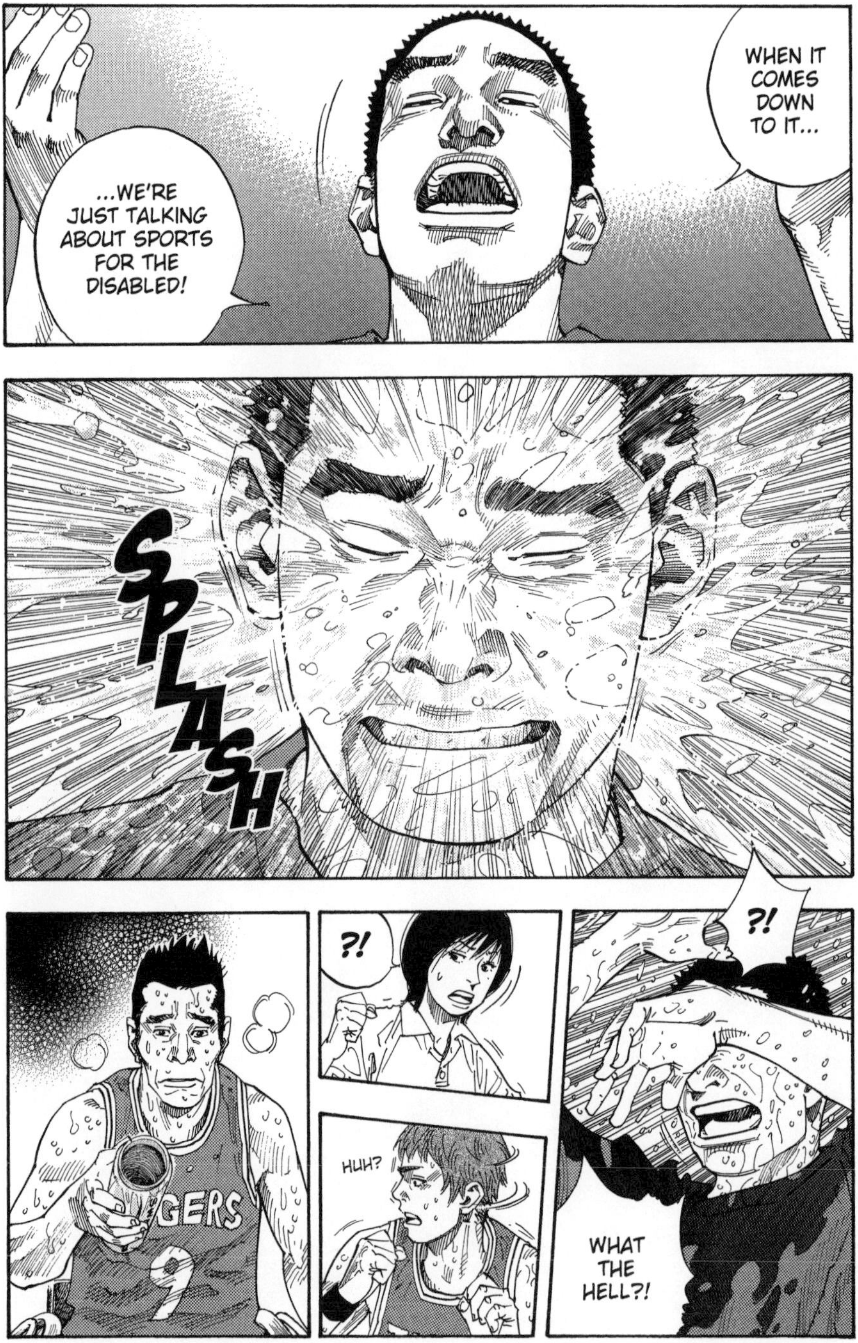
WHEN IT COMES DOWN TO IT...
...WE'RE JUST TALKING ABOUT SPORTS FOR THE DISABLED!
SPLASH
?!
WHAT THE HELL?!
?!
HUH?
GERS
9

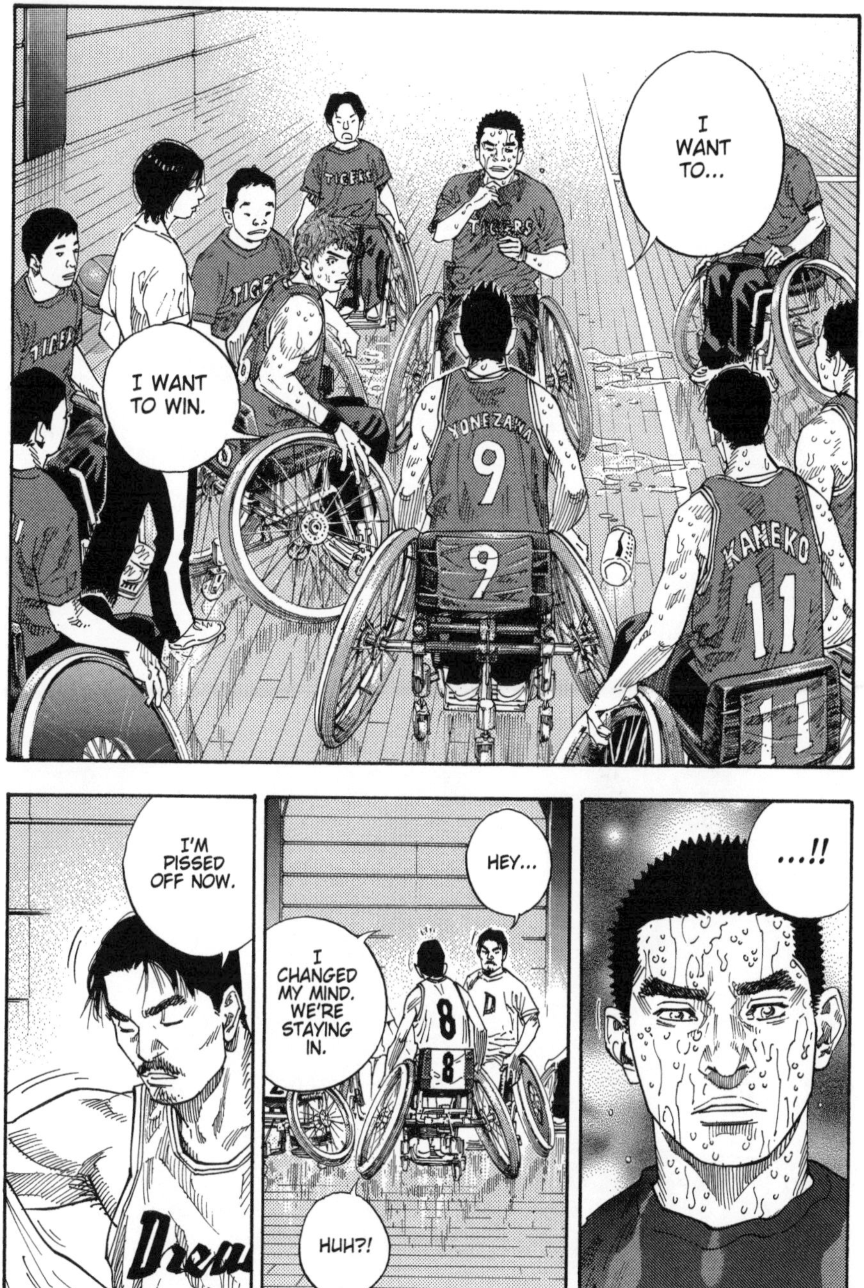
I WANT TO...
I WANT TO WIN.
...!!
HEY...
I CHANGED MY MIND. WE'RE STAYING IN.
HUH?!
I'M PISSED OFF NOW.

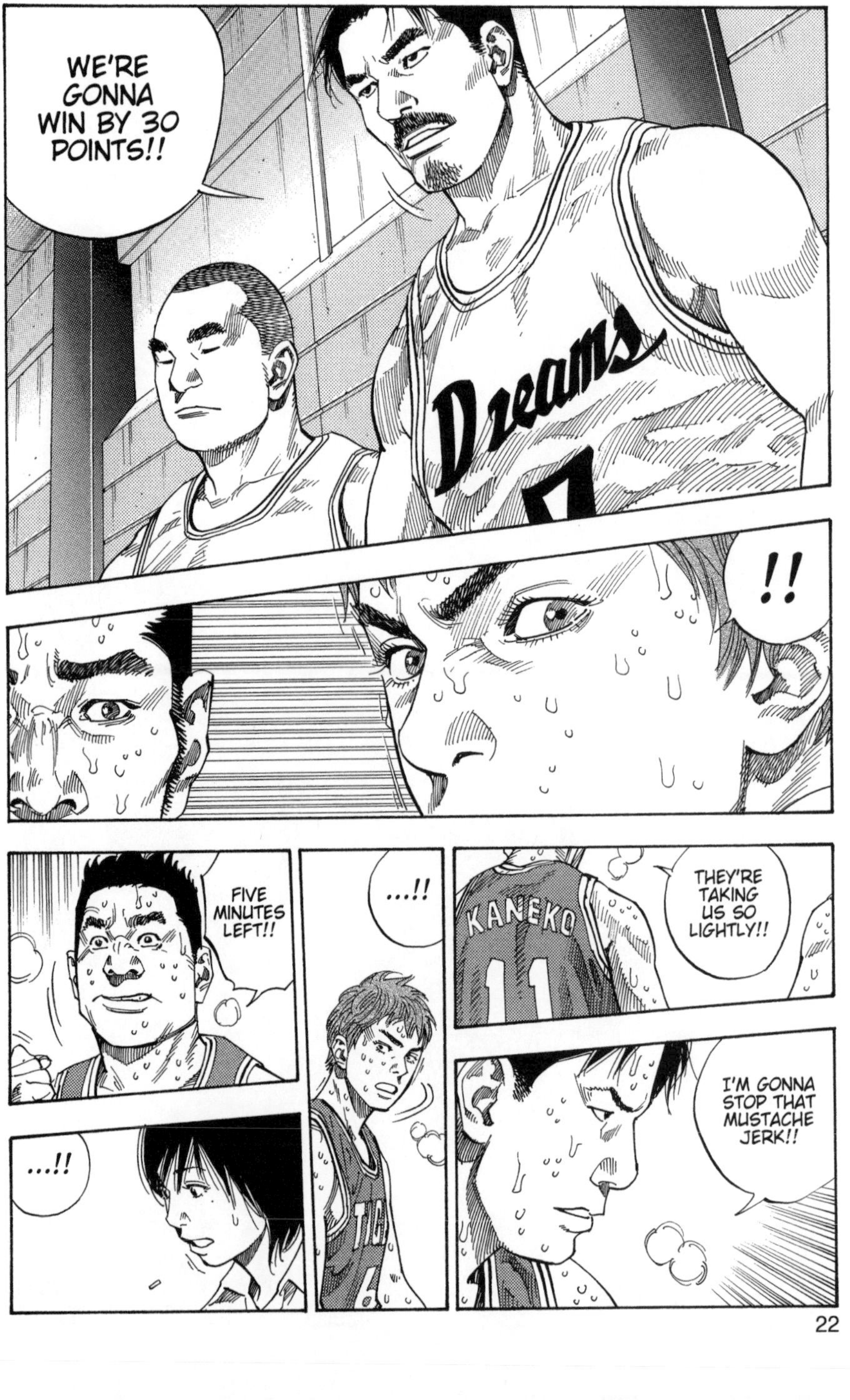
WE'RE GONNA WIN BY 30 POINTS!!
Dreams
!!
KANEKO 11
THEY'RE TAKING US SO LIGHTLY!!
I'M GONNA STOP THAT MUSTACHE JERK!!
...!!
FIVE MINUTES LEFT!!
...!!

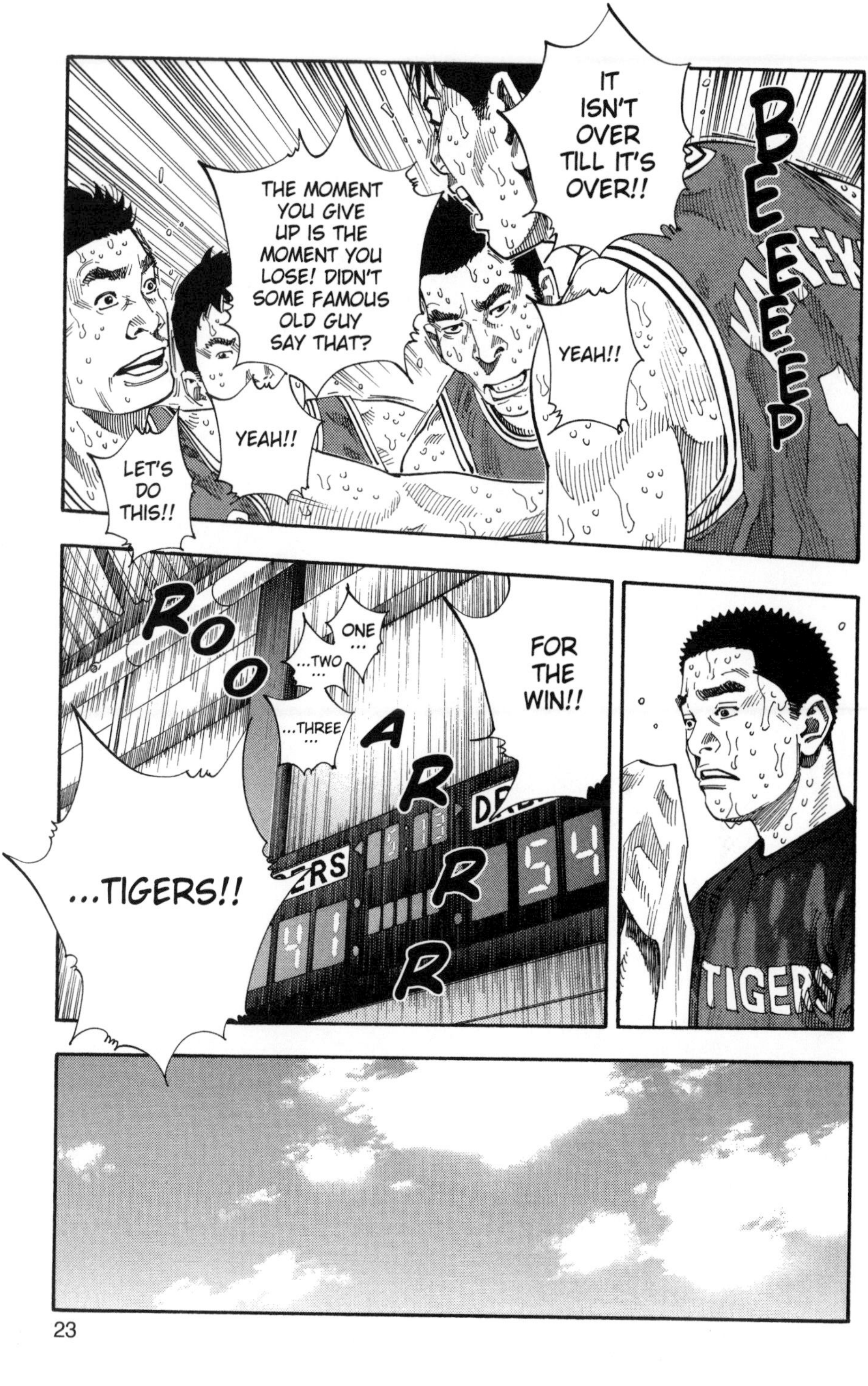
BEEEEEP
IT ISN'T OVER TILL IT'S OVER!!
YEAH!!
THE MOMENT YOU GIVE UP IS THE MOMENT YOU LOSE! DIDN'T SOME FAMOUS OLD GUY SAY THAT?
YEAH!!
LET'S DO THIS!!
TIGERS
FOR THE WIN!!
ONE...
...TWO...
...THREE...
ROOARRR
...TIGERS!!

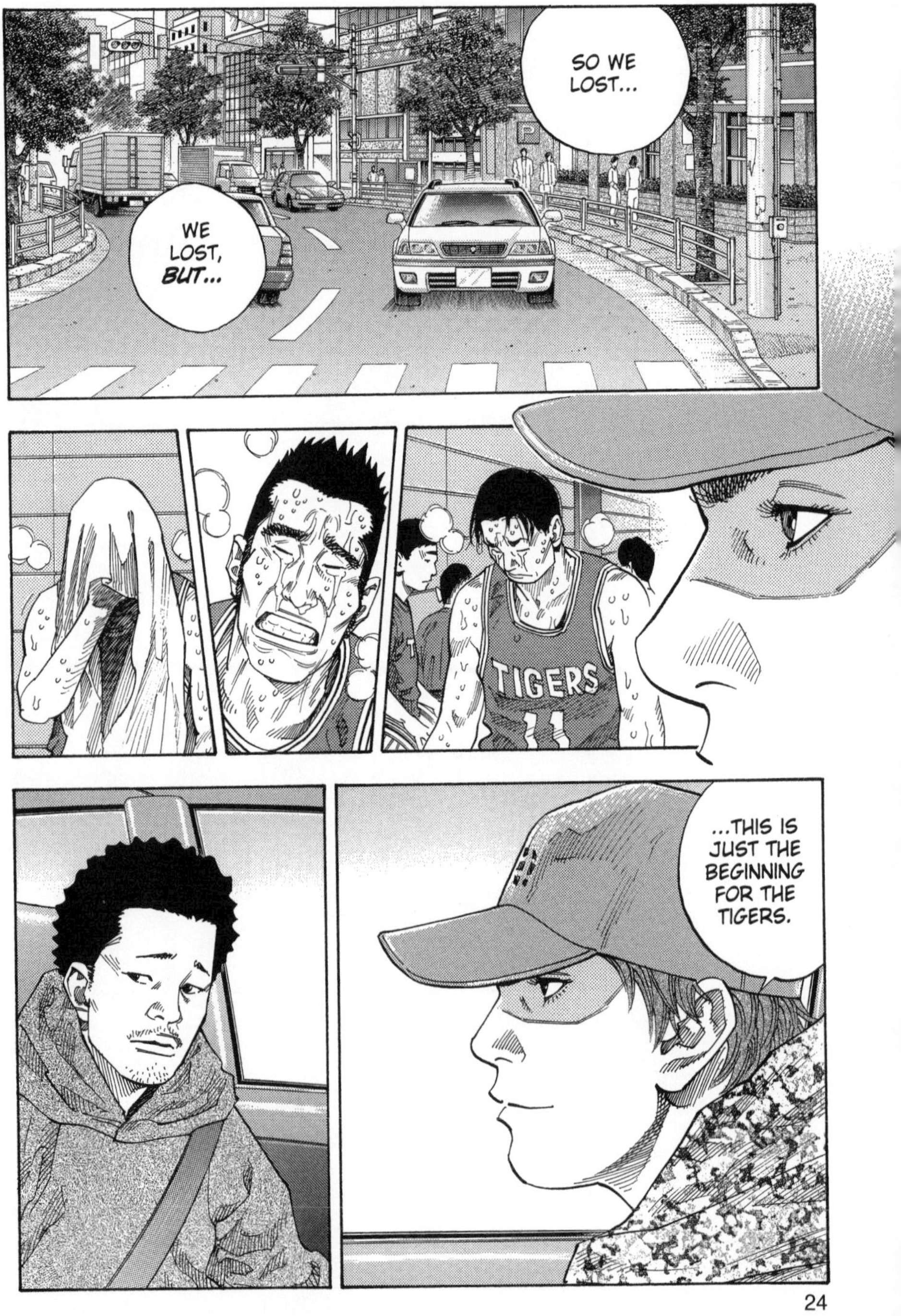
SO WE LOST...
WE LOST, BUT...
TIGERS
...THIS IS JUST THE BEGINNING FOR THE TIGERS.

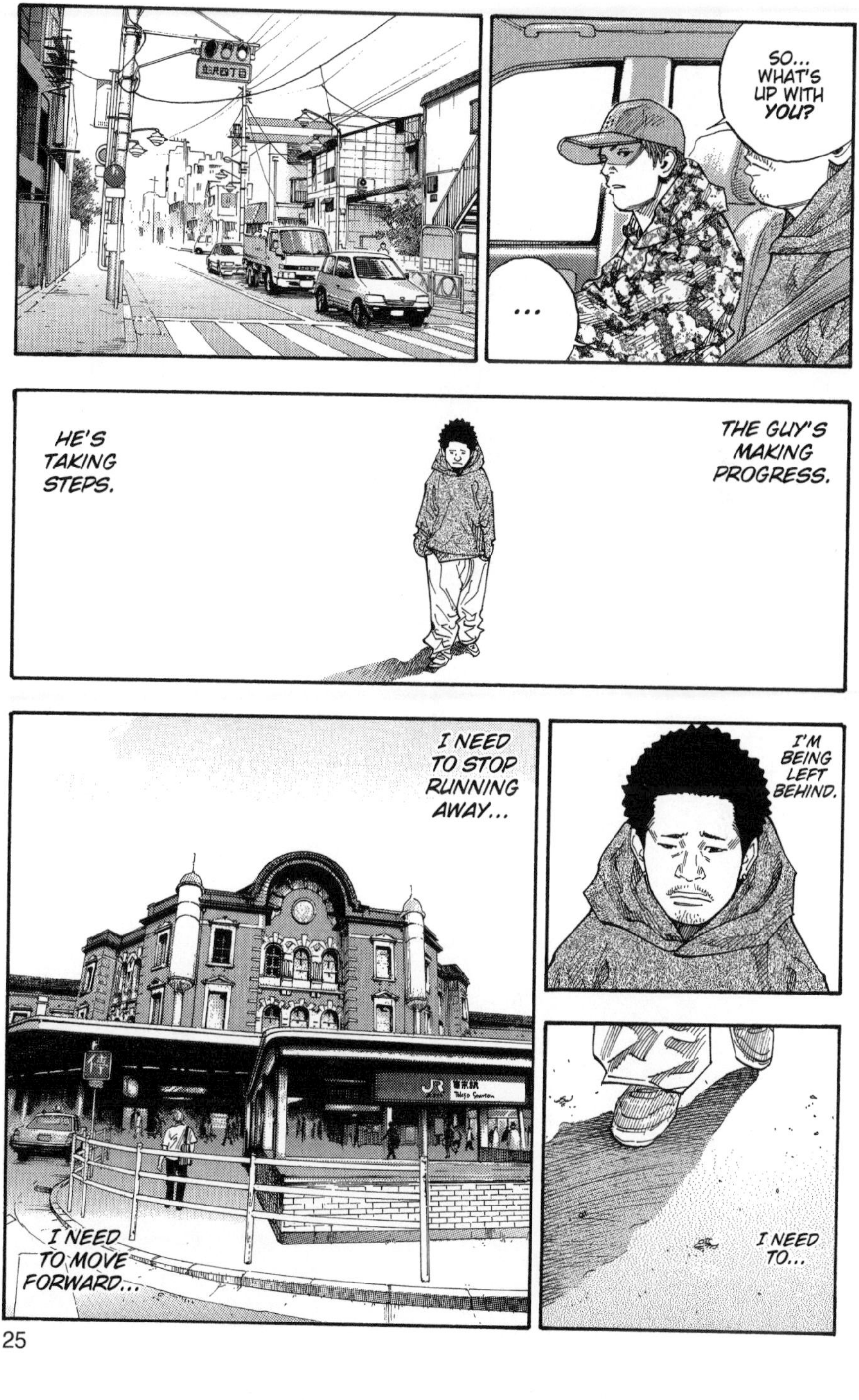
SO... WHAT'S UP WITH YOU?
...
THE GUY'S MAKING PROGRESS.
HE'S TAKING STEPS.
I'M BEING LEFT BEHIND.
I NEED TO...
I NEED TO STOP RUNNING AWAY...
I NEED TO MOVE FORWARD...

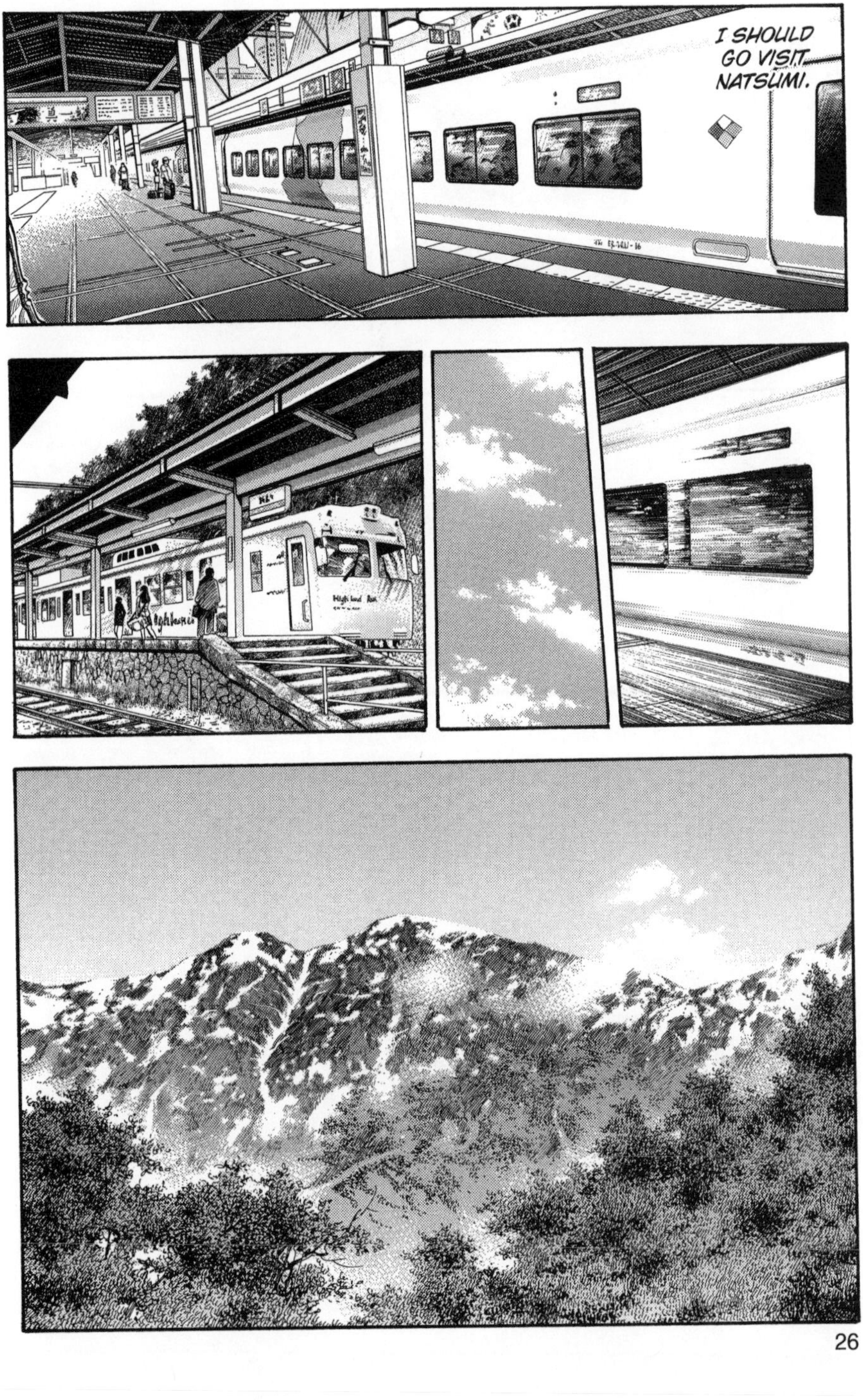
I SHOULD GO VISIT NATSUMI.

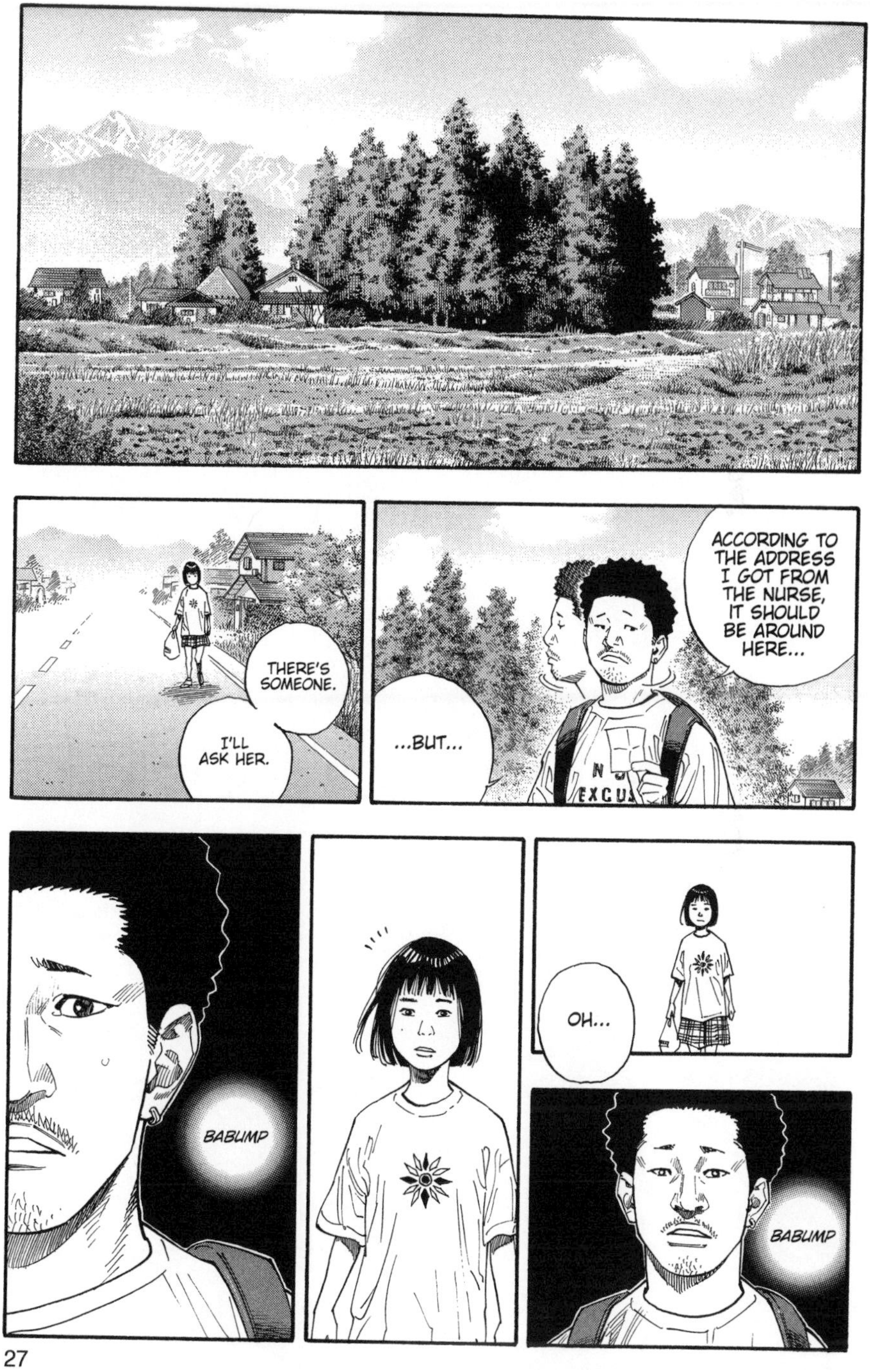
ACCORDING TO THE ADDRESS I GOT FROM THE NURSE, IT SHOULD BE AROUND HERE...
...BUT...
THERE'S SOMEONE.
I'LL ASK HER.
OH...
BABUMP
BABUMP

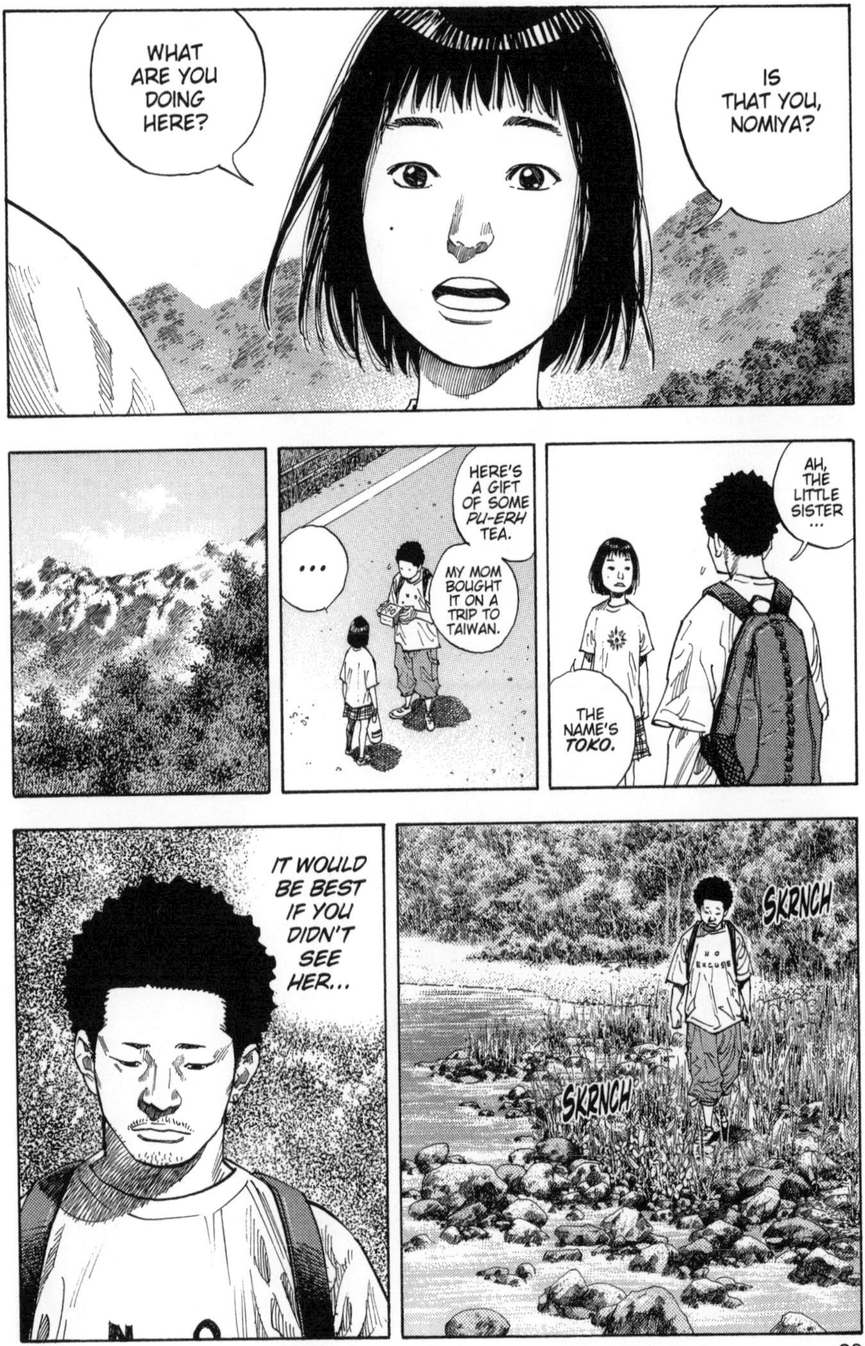
IS THAT YOU, NOMIYA?
WHAT ARE YOU DOING HERE?
AH, THE LITTLE SISTER...
THE NAME'S TOKO.
HERE'S A GIFT OF SOME PU-ERH TEA.
MY MOM BOUGHT IT ON A TRIP TO TAIWAN.
...
SKRNCH
SKRNCH
IT WOULD BE BEST IF YOU DIDN'T SEE HER...

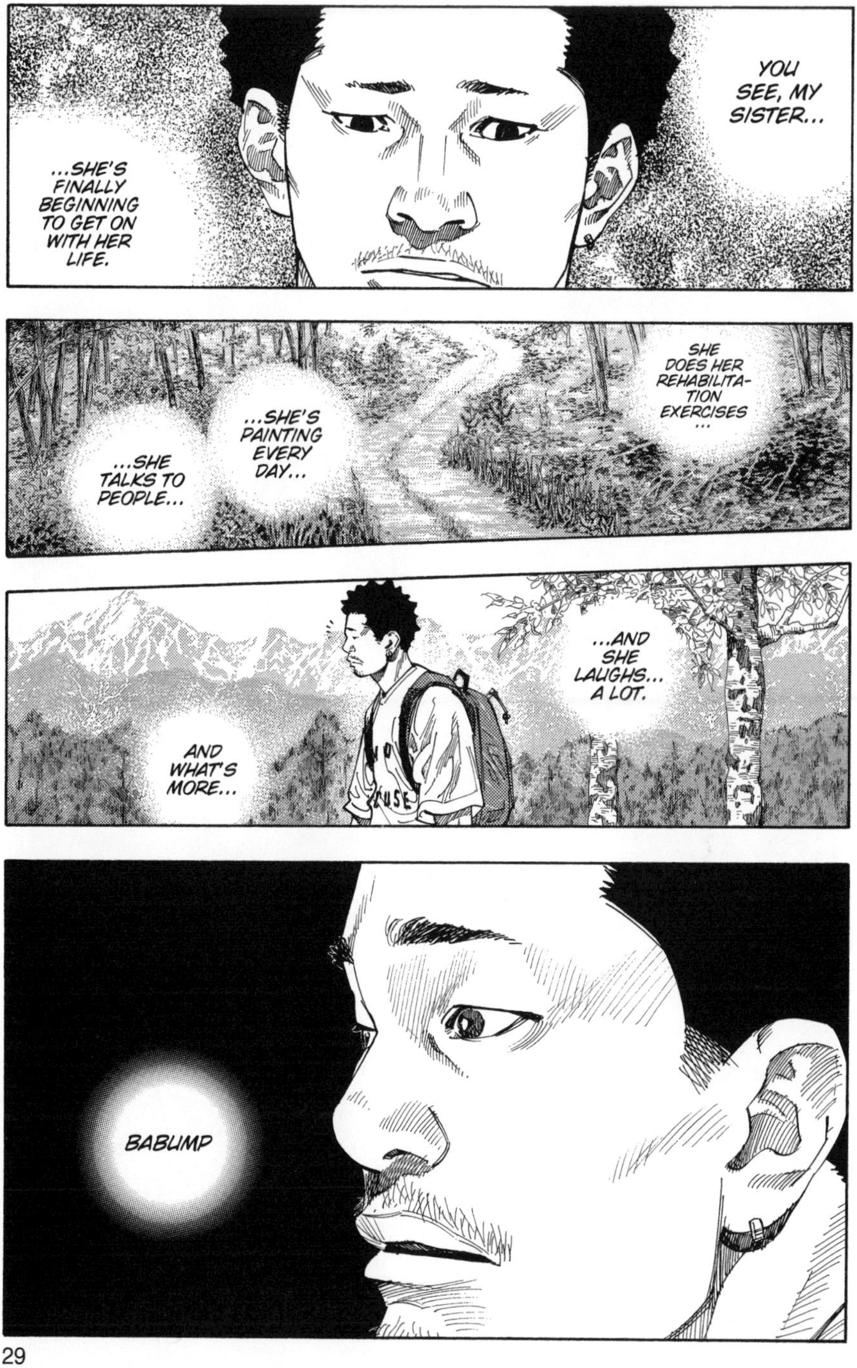
YOU SEE, MY SISTER...
...SHE'S FINALLY BEGINNING TO GET ON WITH HER LIFE.
SHE DOES HER REHABILITATION EXERCISES ...
...SHE'S PAINTING EVERY DAY...
...SHE TALKS TO PEOPLE...
...AND SHE LAUGHS... A LOT.
AND WHAT'S MORE...
BABUMP

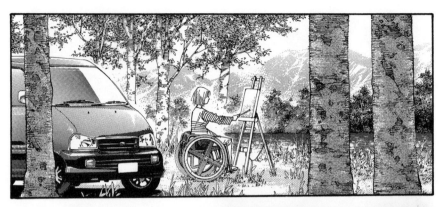

BABUMP

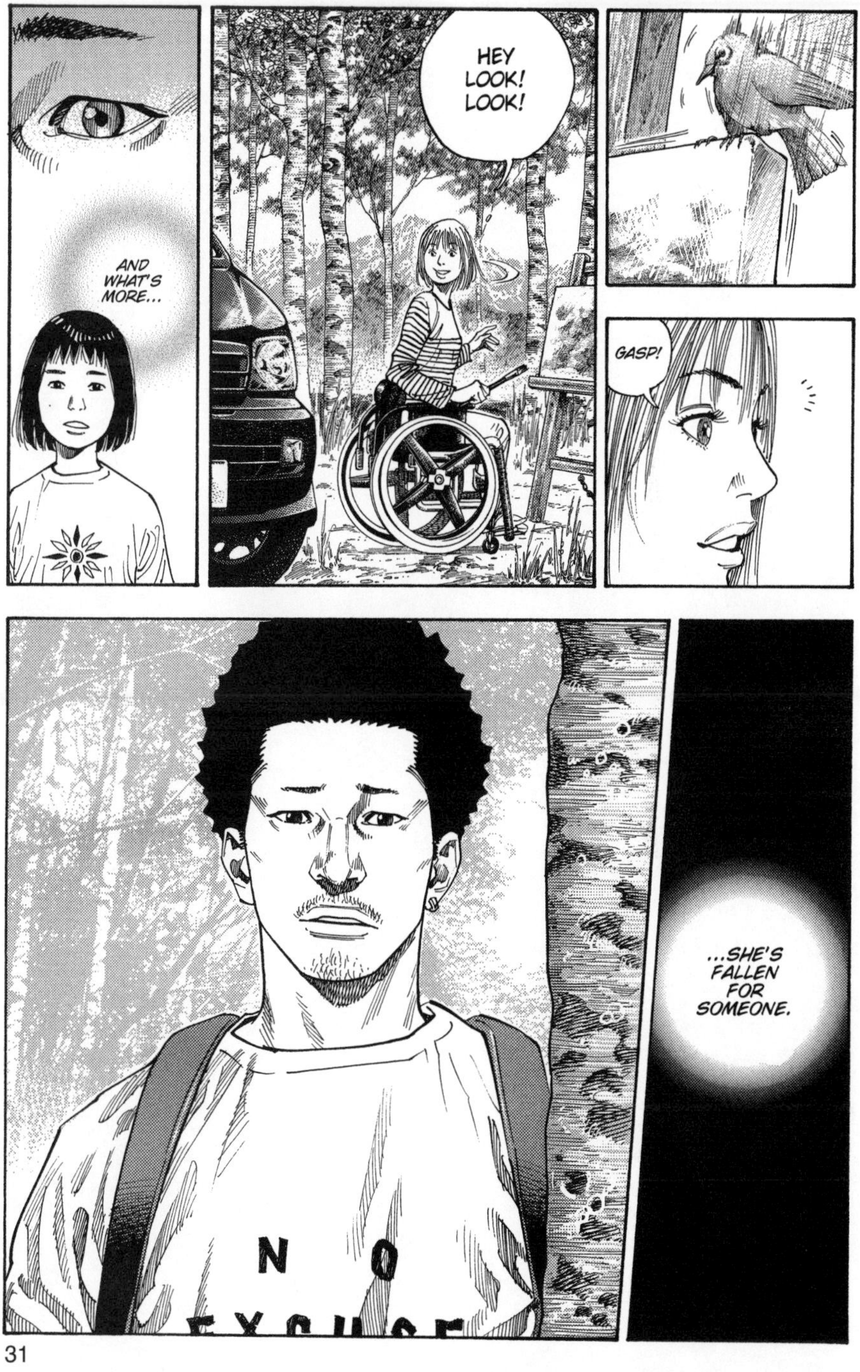
GASP!
HEY LOOK! LOOK!
AND WHAT'S MORE...
...SHE'S FALLEN FOR SOMEONE.

REAL

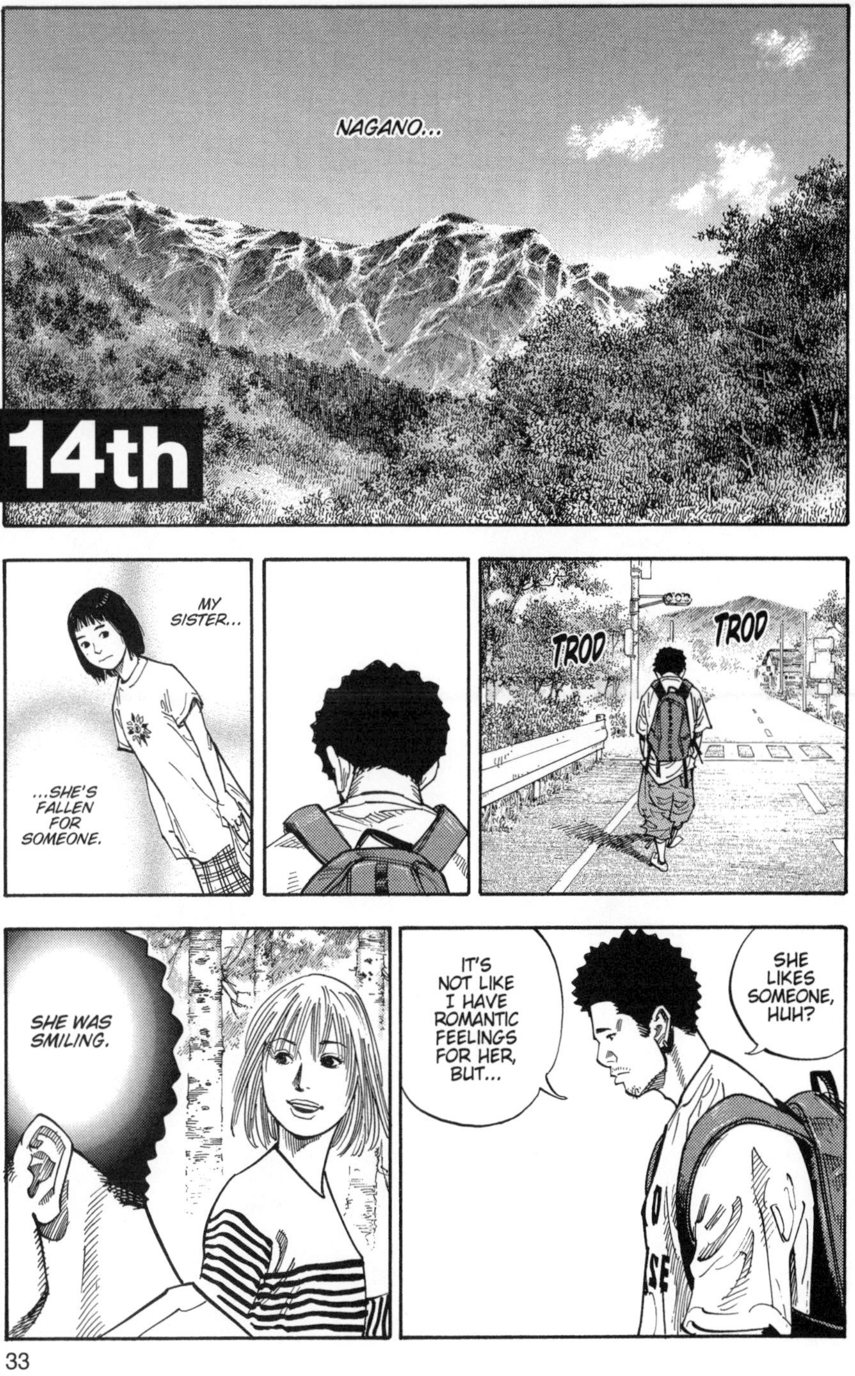
NAGANO...
14th
TROD
TROD
MY SISTER...
...SHE'S FALLEN FOR SOMEONE.
SHE LIKES SOMEONE, HUH?
IT'S NOT LIKE I HAVE ROMANTIC FEELINGS FOR HER, BUT...
SHE WAS SMILING.

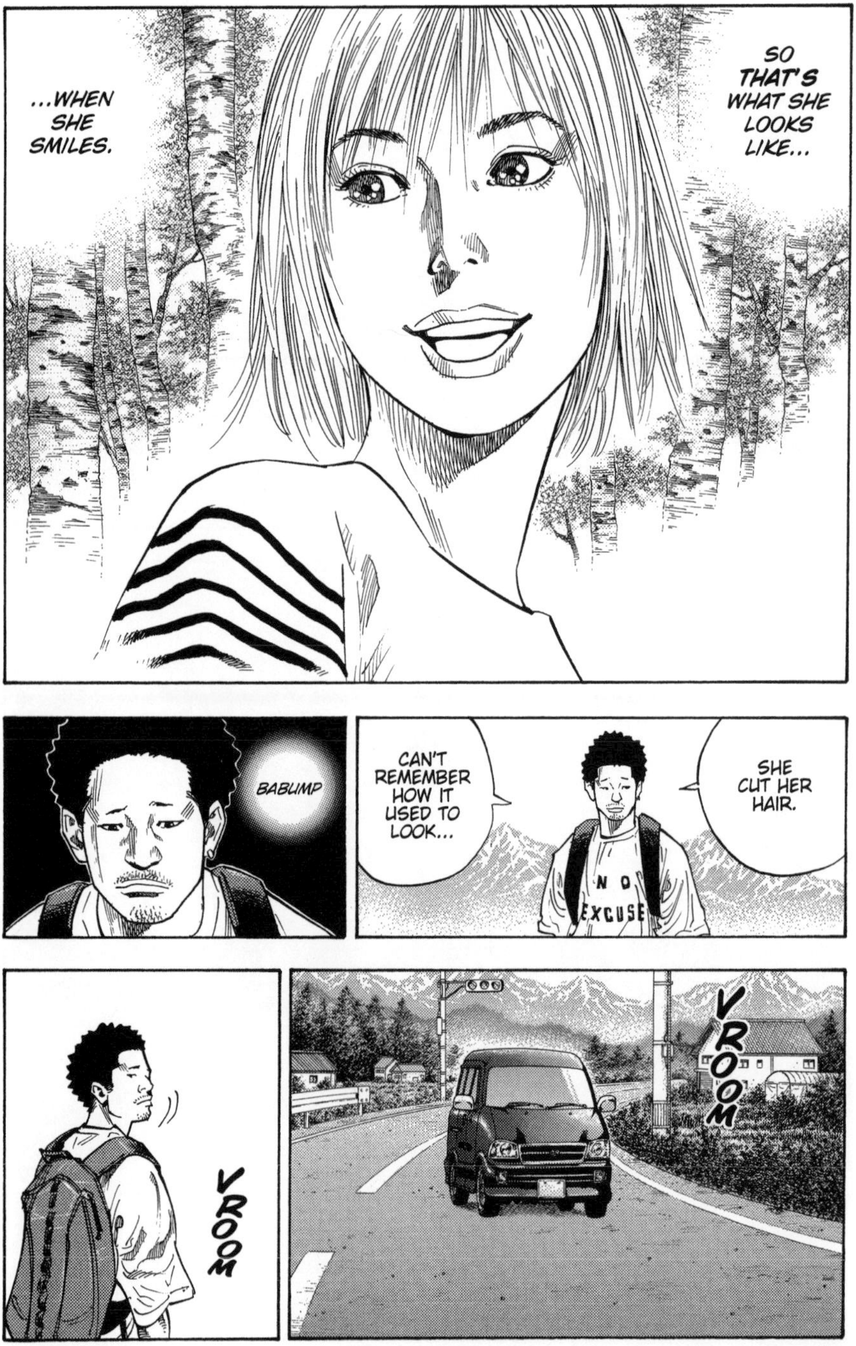
SO THAT'S WHAT SHE LOOKS LIKE...
...WHEN SHE SMILES.
SHE CUT HER HAIR.
CAN'T REMEMBER HOW IT USED TO LOOK...
NO EXCUSE
BABUMP
VROOM
VROOM

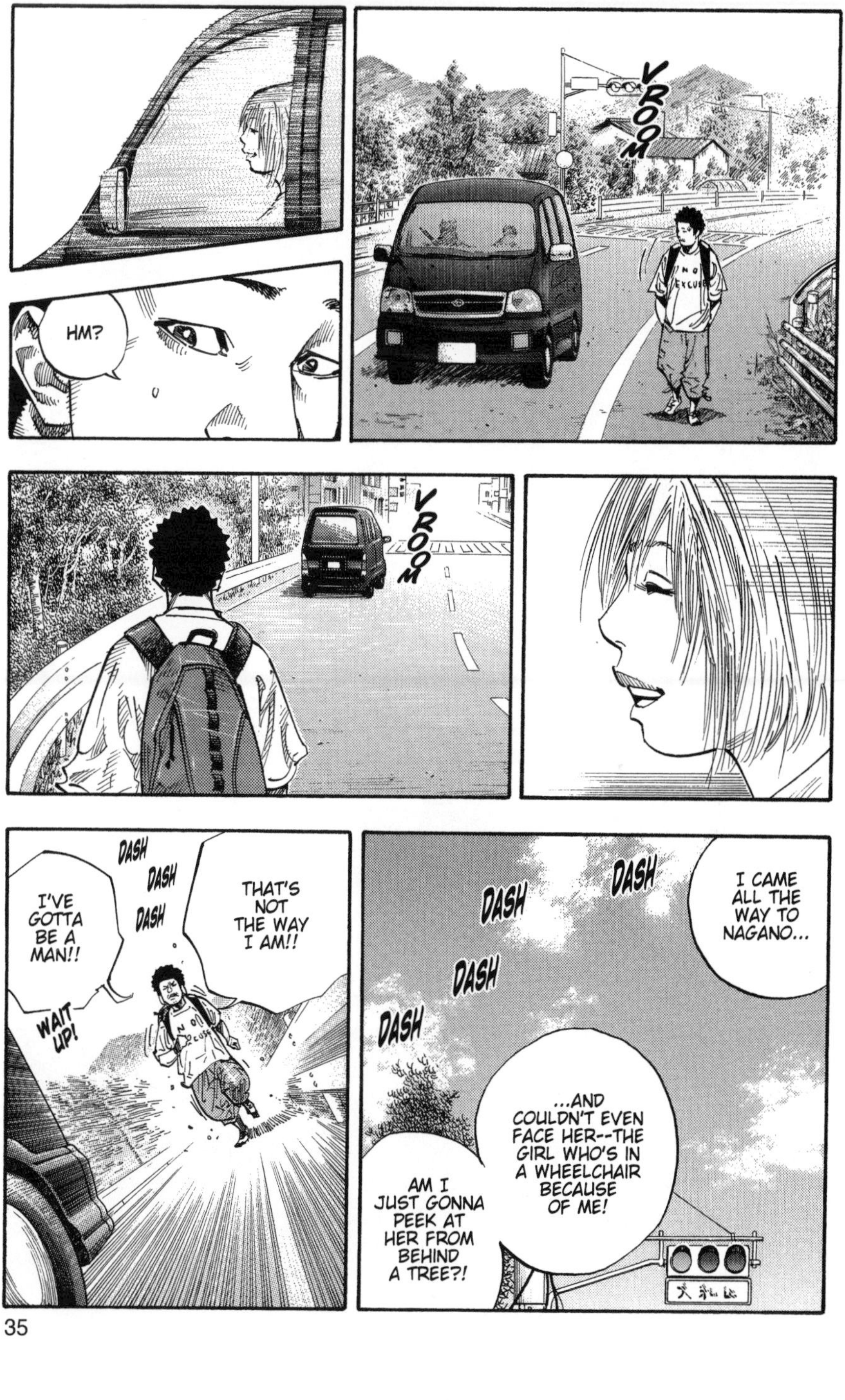
VROOM
HM?
VROOM
DASH
DASH
DASH
DASH
I CAME ALL THE WAY TO NAGANO...
...AND COULDN'T EVEN FACE HER--THE GIRL WHO'S IN A WHEELCHAIR BECAUSE OF ME!
AM I JUST GONNA PEEK AT HER FROM BEHIND A TREE?!
DASH
DASH
DASH
THAT'S NOT THE WAY I AM!!
I'VE GOTTA BE A MAN!!
WAIT UP!

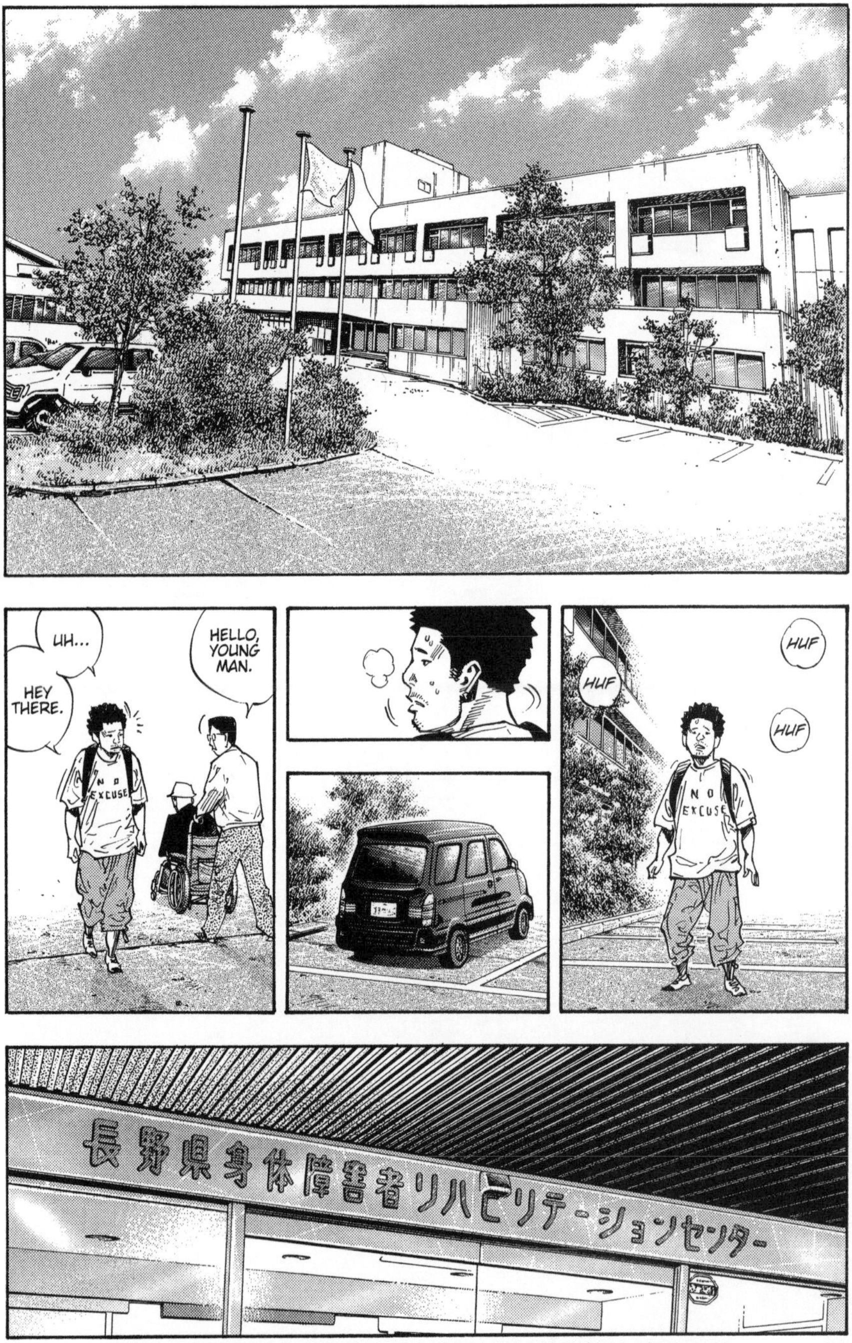
HUF
HUF
HUF
HELLO, YOUNG MAN.
UH...
HEY THERE.
NO EXCUSE
NO EXCUSE
長野県身体障害者リハビリテーションセンター

*NAGANO PREFECTURAL REHABILITATION CENTER FOR THE PHYSICALLY DISABLED

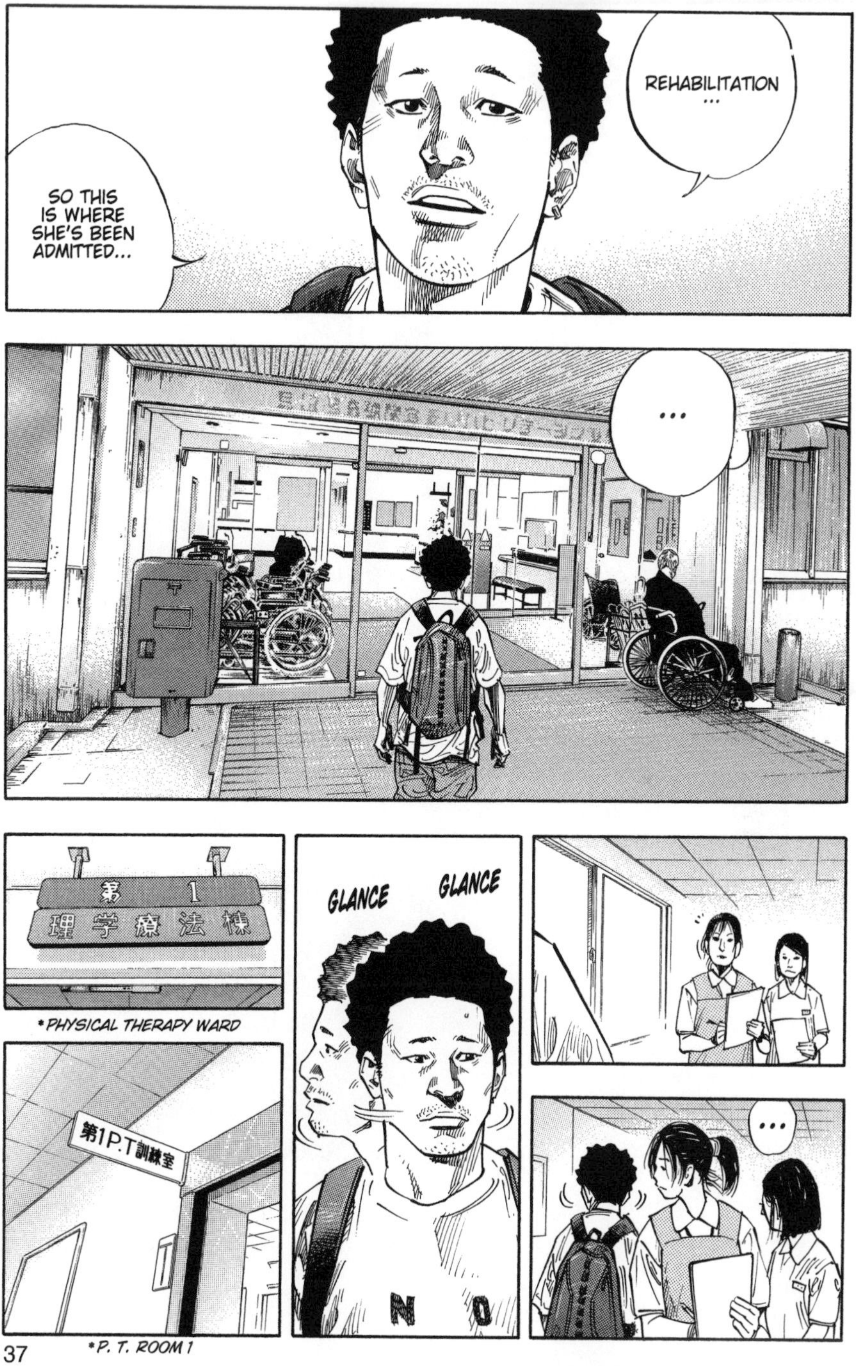
REHABILITATION ...
SO THIS IS WHERE SHE'S BEEN ADMITTED...
...
...
GLANCE GLANCE
第1
理学療法棟
*PHYSICAL THERAPY WARD
第1P.T訓練室
*P. T. ROOM 1

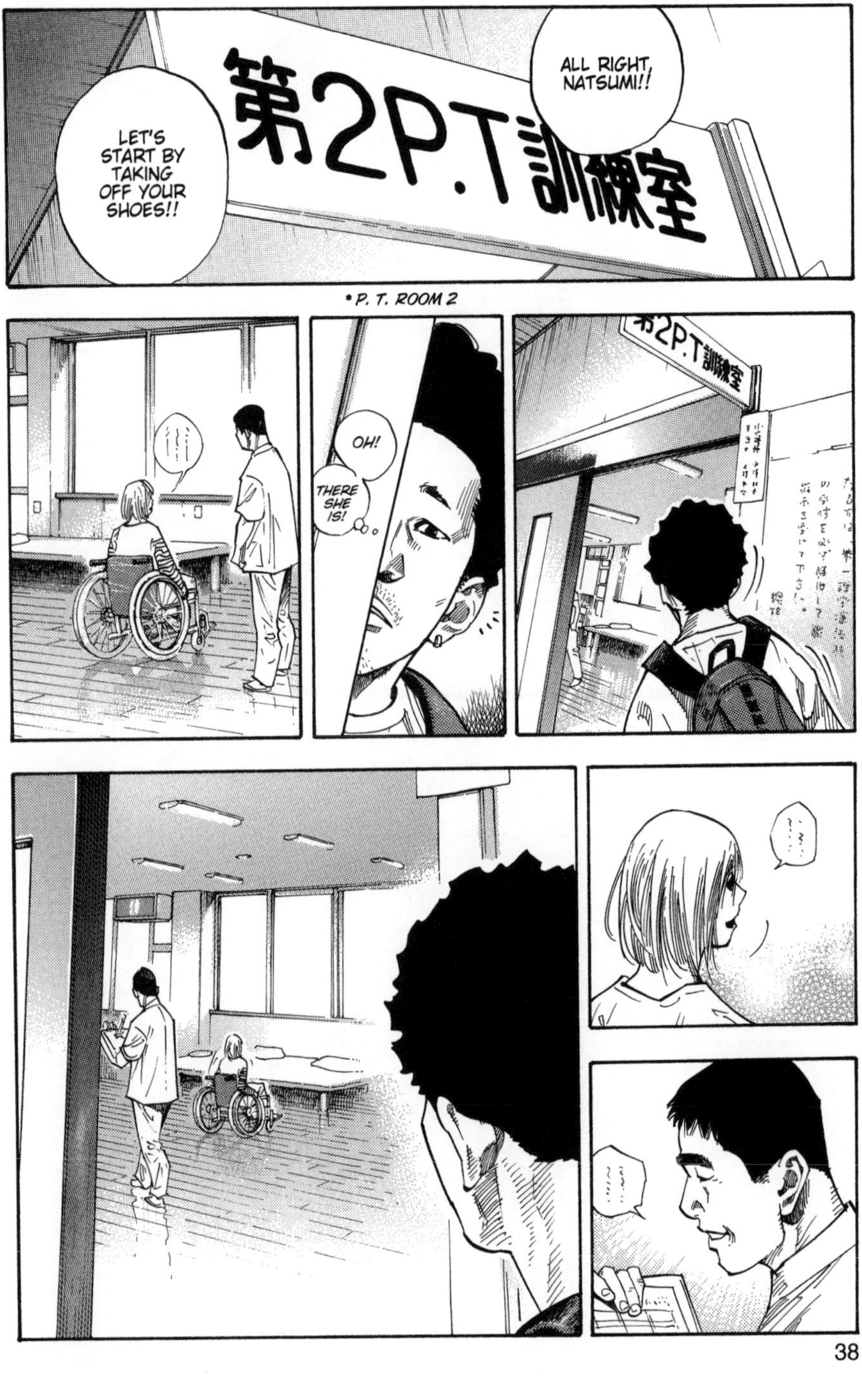

ALL RIGHT, NATSUMI!!
LET'S START BY TAKING OFF YOUR SHOES!!
*P. T. ROOM 2
OH!
THERE SHE IS!

NNGH!
SKWIK

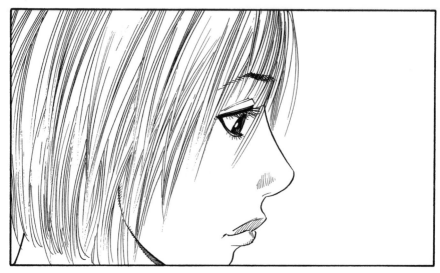

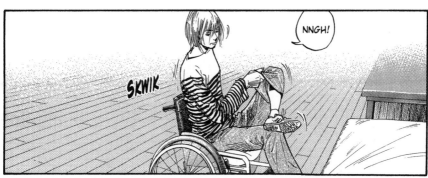

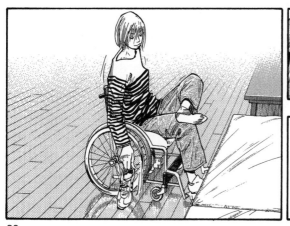

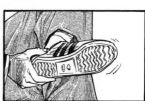

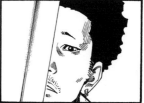

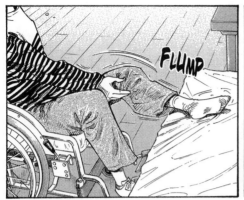
FLUMP

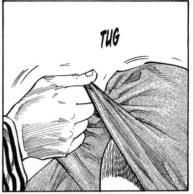
TUG

PHEW!

SKWIK

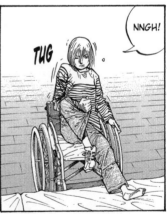
TUG

NNGH!

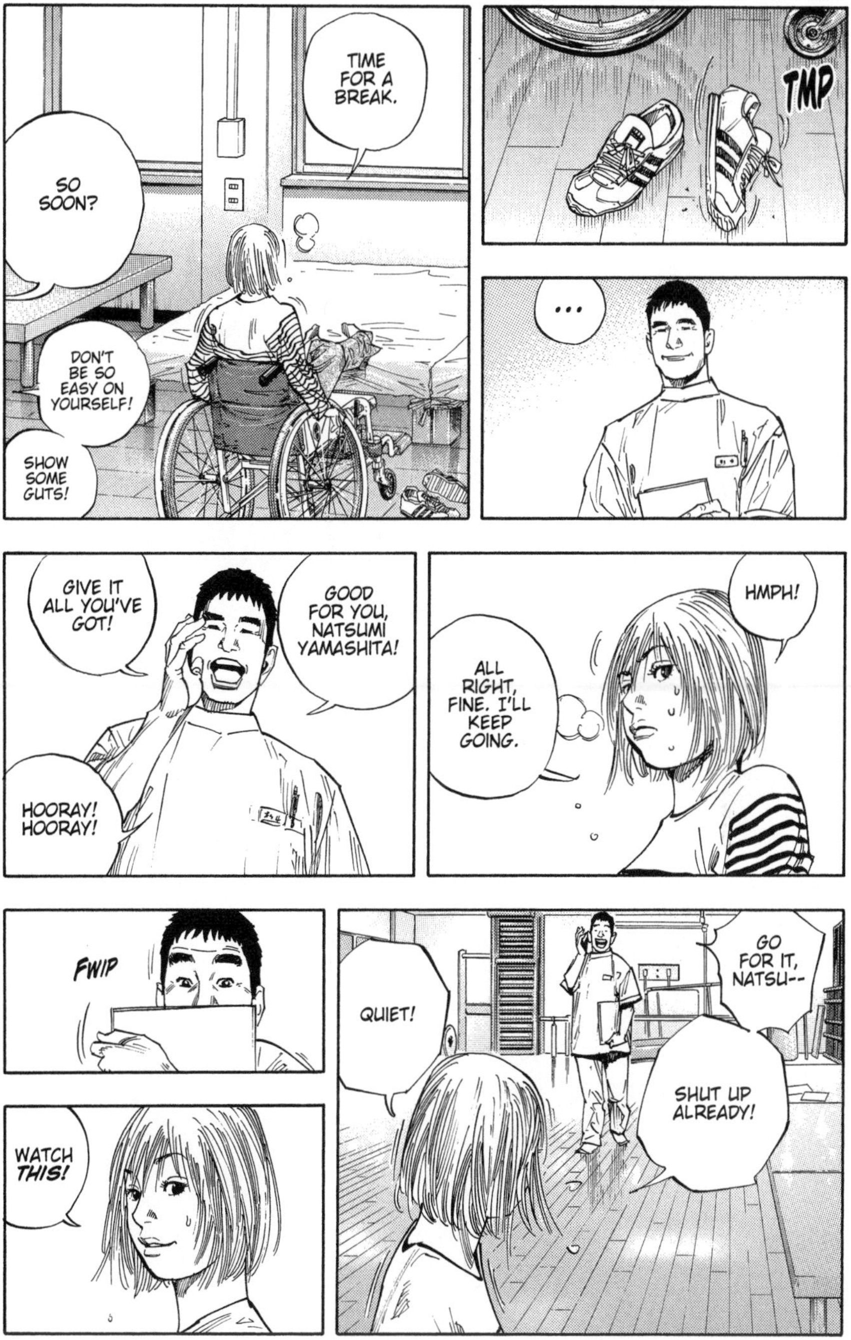
TMP
...
TIME FOR A BREAK.
SO SOON?
DON'T BE SO EASY ON YOURSELF!
SHOW SOME GUTS!
HMPH!
ALL RIGHT, FINE. I'LL KEEP GOING.
GOOD FOR YOU, NATSUMI YAMASHITA!
GIVE IT ALL YOU'VE GOT!
HOORAY! HOORAY!
GO FOR IT, NATSU--
QUIET!
SHUT UP ALREADY!
FWIP
WATCH *THIS!*

UMF!
SKWIK
SKWIK
FLUMP
HUF
HUF
HUF

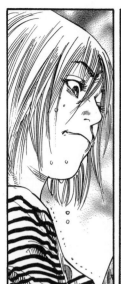

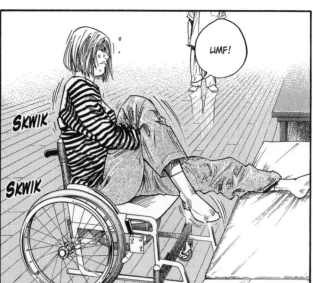

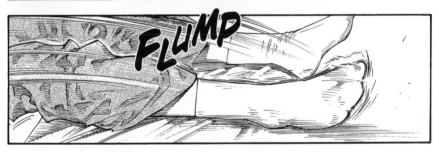

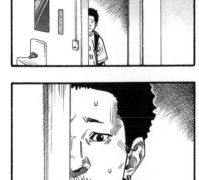

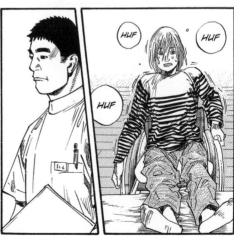

I SEE...

...SHE'S TRYING TO MOVE FROM THE CHAIR TO THE PLATFORM!!

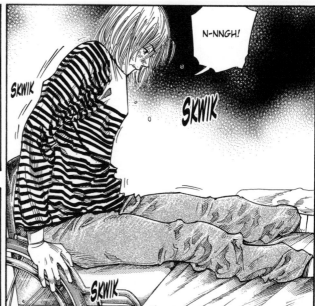

N-NNGH!

SKWIK

SKWIK

SKWIK

SKWIK

SKWIK

HUF

HUF

NNGH!

ARGH!

SHFF

UMF!

...

43

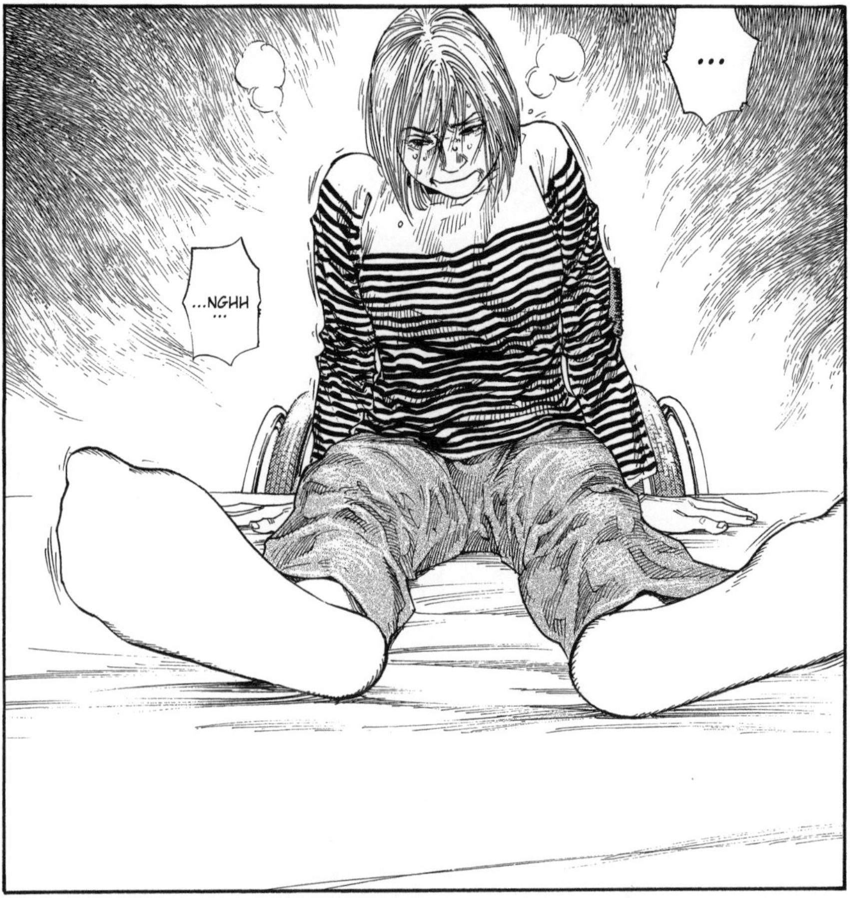
...
...NGHH
...

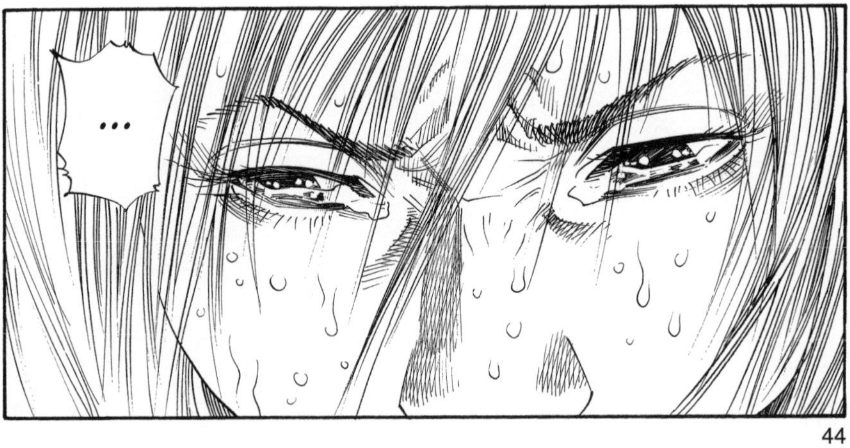
...

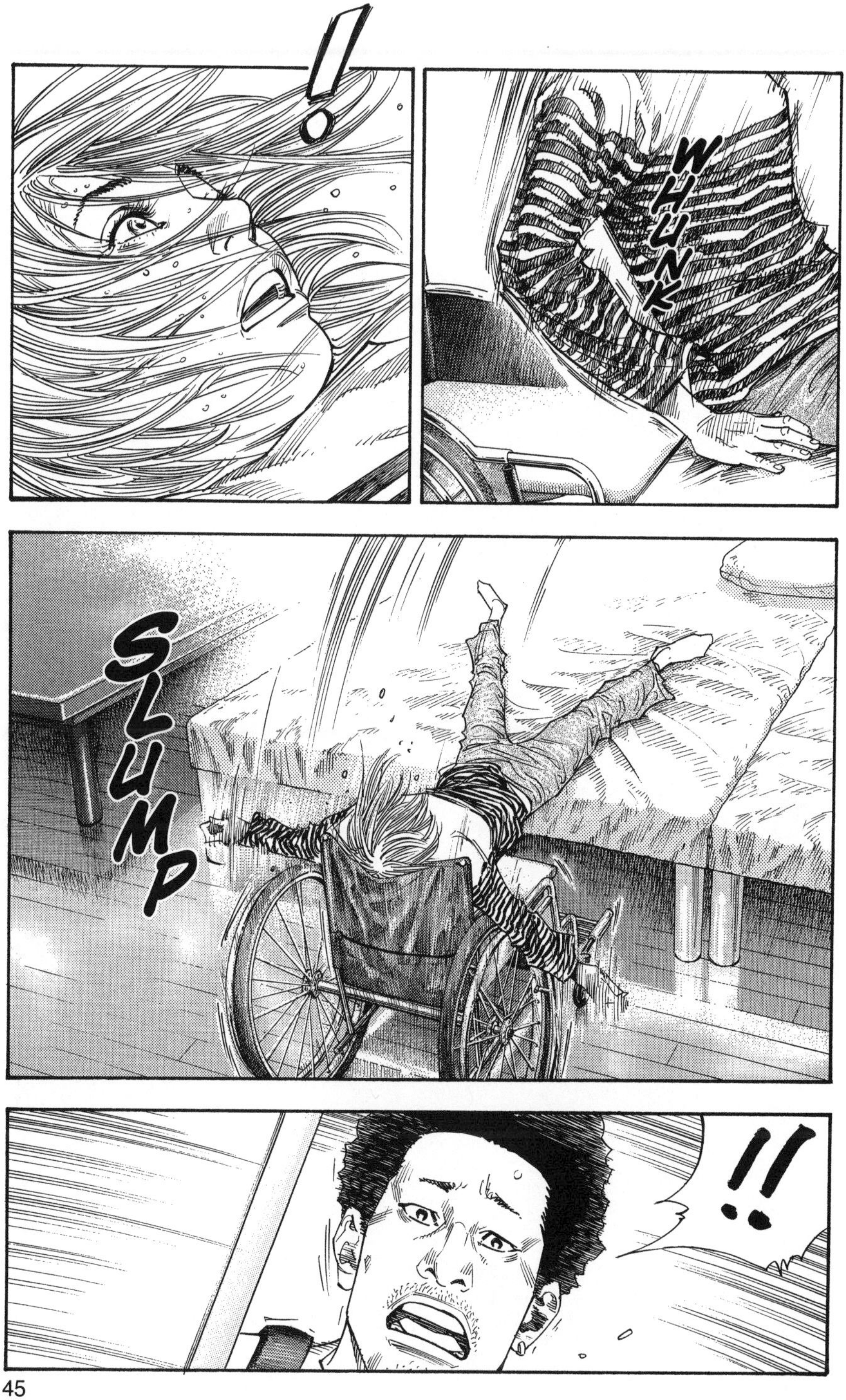
WHUNK
!
SLUMP
!!

NATSU! ARE YOU ALL RIGHT?
SKWIK
SKWIK
GO AWAY.
DON'T LOOK AT ME.
SOB
SOB
SOB

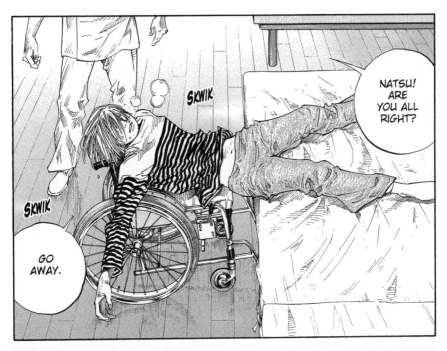

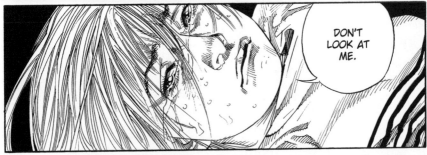

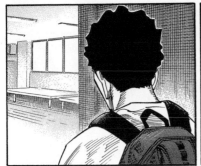

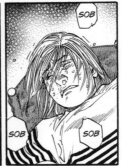

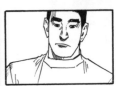

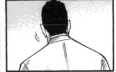

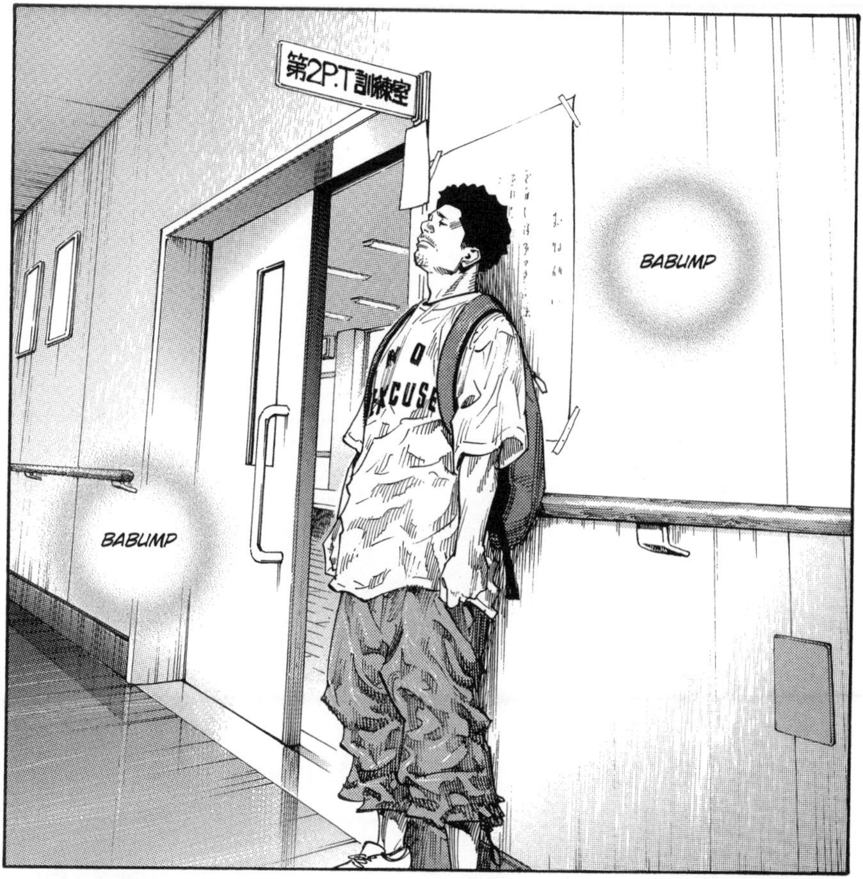
第2P.T訓練室
BABUMP
BABUMP

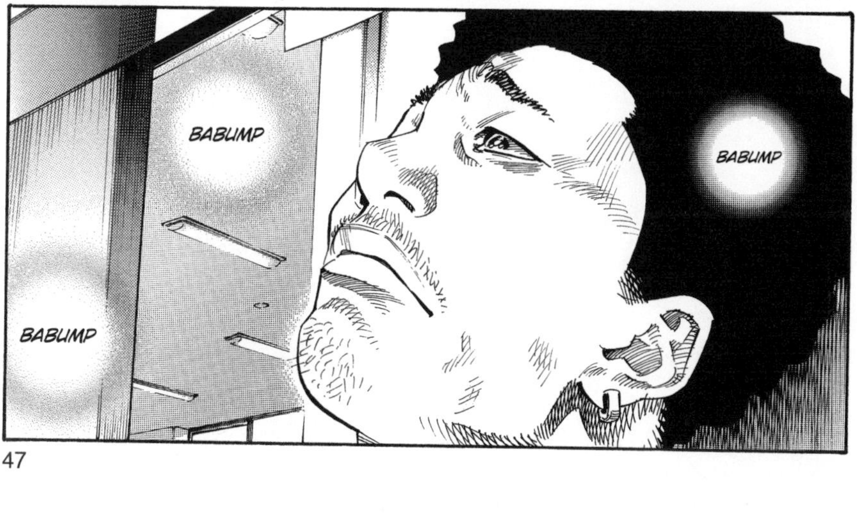
BABUMP
BABUMP
BABUMP

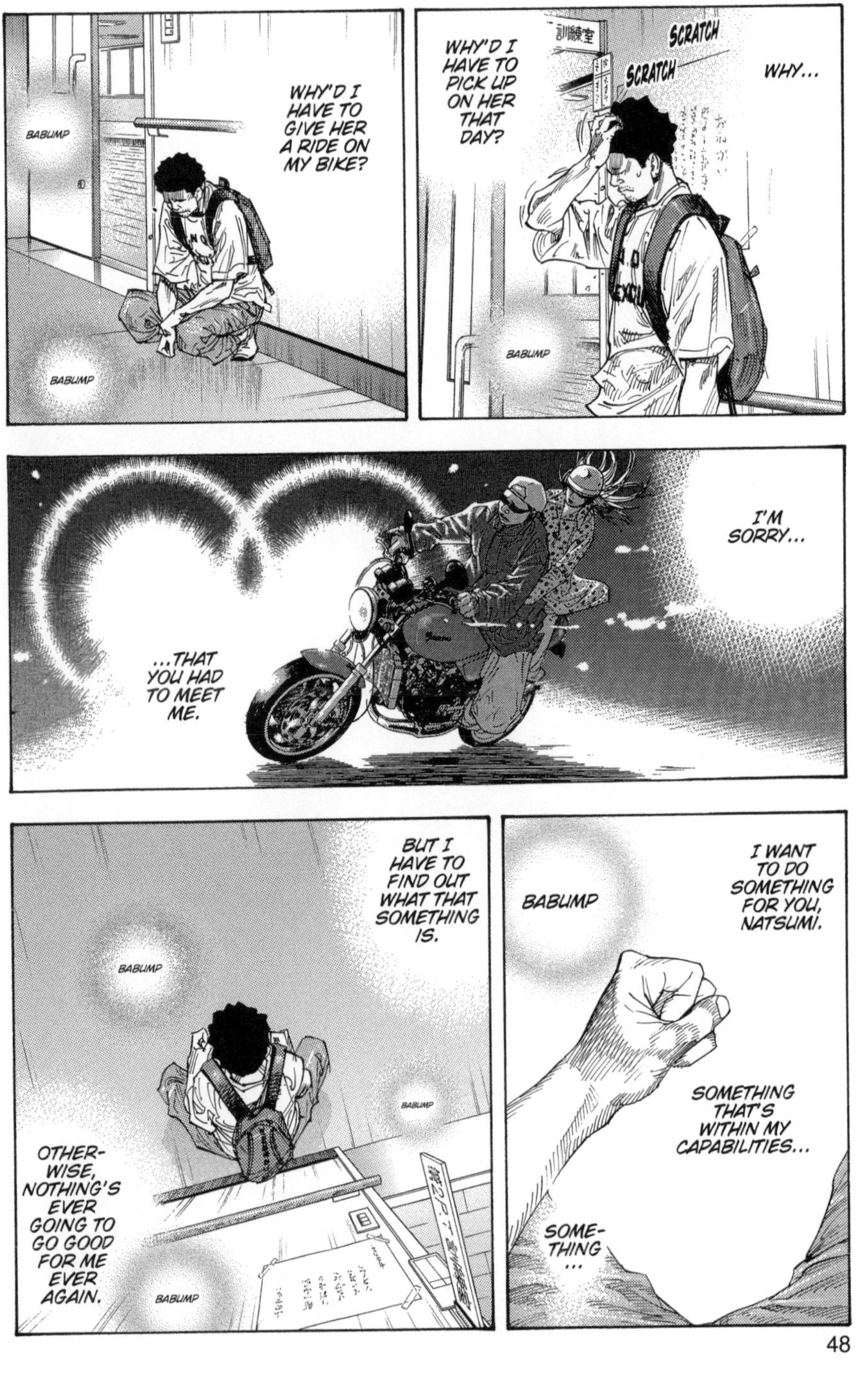
SCRATCH
WHY...
SCRATCH
訓練室
WHY'D I HAVE TO PICK UP ON HER THAT DAY?
BABUMP
WHY'D I HAVE TO GIVE HER A RIDE ON MY BIKE?
BABUMP
BABUMP
I'M SORRY...
...THAT YOU HAD TO MEET ME.
I WANT TO DO SOMETHING FOR YOU, NATSUMI.
BABUMP
SOMETHING THAT'S WITHIN MY CAPABILITIES...
SOME-THING ...
BUT I HAVE TO FIND OUT WHAT THAT SOMETHING IS.
BABUMP
BABUMP
OTHER-WISE, NOTHING'S EVER GOING TO GO GOOD FOR ME EVER AGAIN.
BABUMP

HELP ME UP.

SNIFF

SIGH

YES!

I'M GOING TO DO IT THIS TIME.

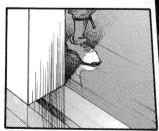

49

SHE
DOESN'T
NEED
ME...

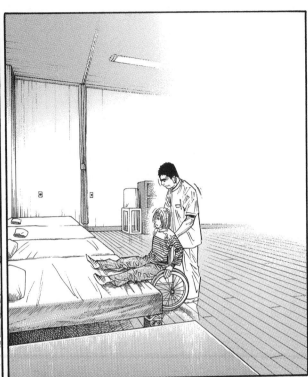

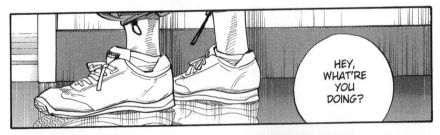

HEY,
WHAT'RE
YOU
DOING?

第2P.T

50

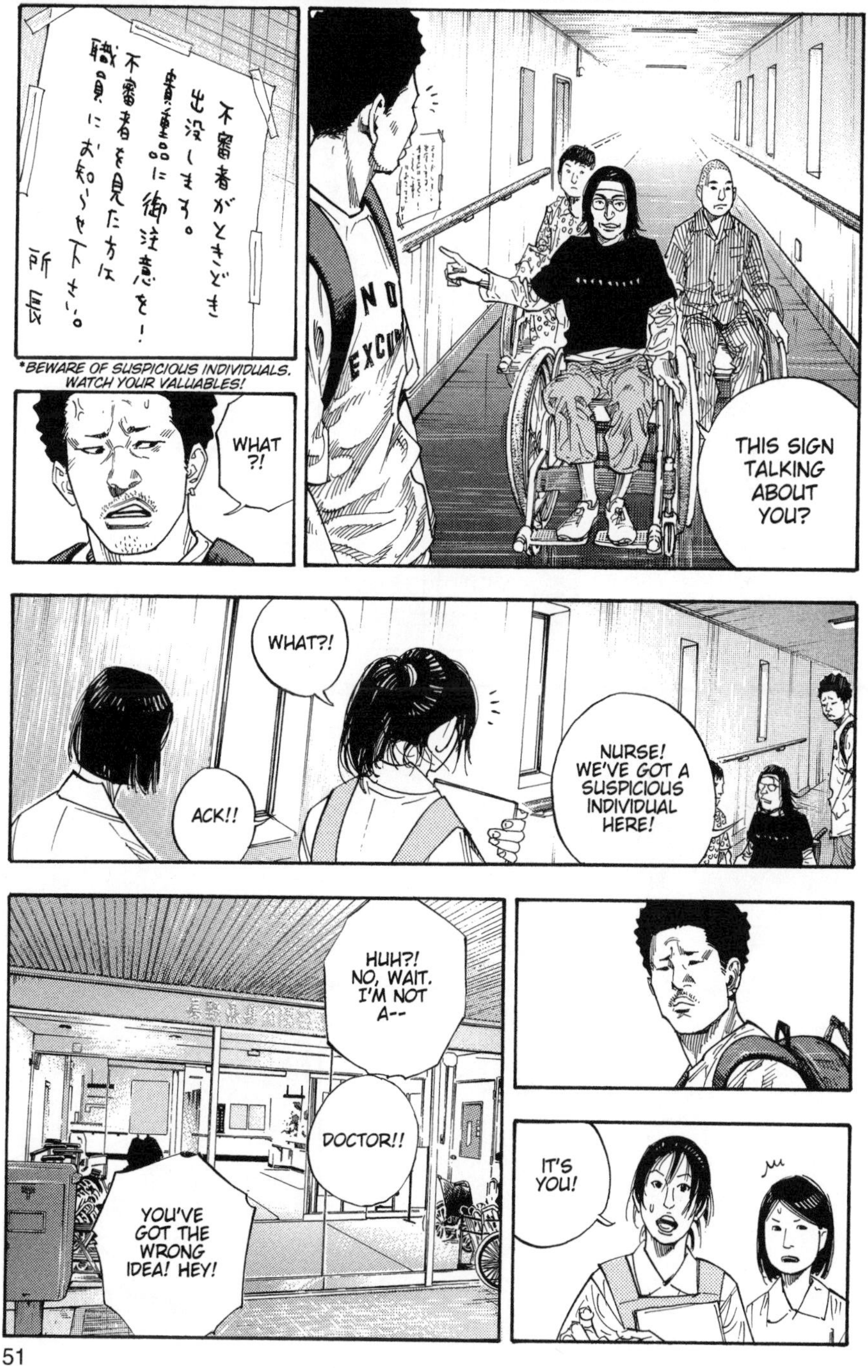
THIS SIGN TALKING ABOUT YOU?
不審者がときどき出没します。貴重品に御注意を！不審者を見た方は職員にお知らせ下さい。所長
*BEWARE OF SUSPICIOUS INDIVIDUALS. WATCH YOUR VALUABLES!
WHAT?!
NURSE! WE'VE GOT A SUSPICIOUS INDIVIDUAL HERE!
WHAT?!
ACK!!
IT'S YOU!
HUH?! NO, WAIT. I'M NOT A--
DOCTOR!!
YOU'VE GOT THE WRONG IDEA! HEY!

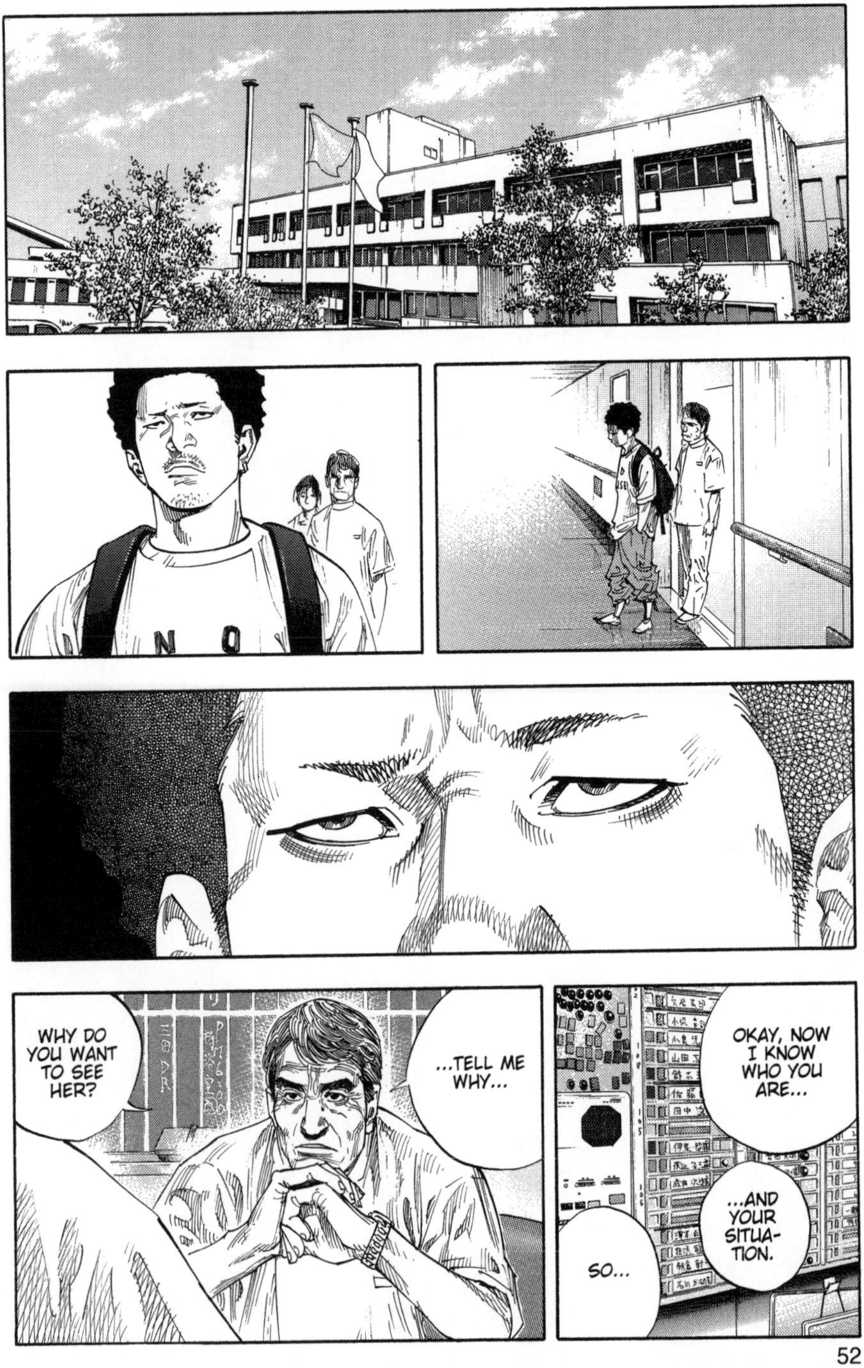
OKAY, NOW I KNOW WHO YOU ARE...
...AND YOUR SITUATION.
SO...
...TELL ME WHY...
WHY DO YOU WANT TO SEE HER?

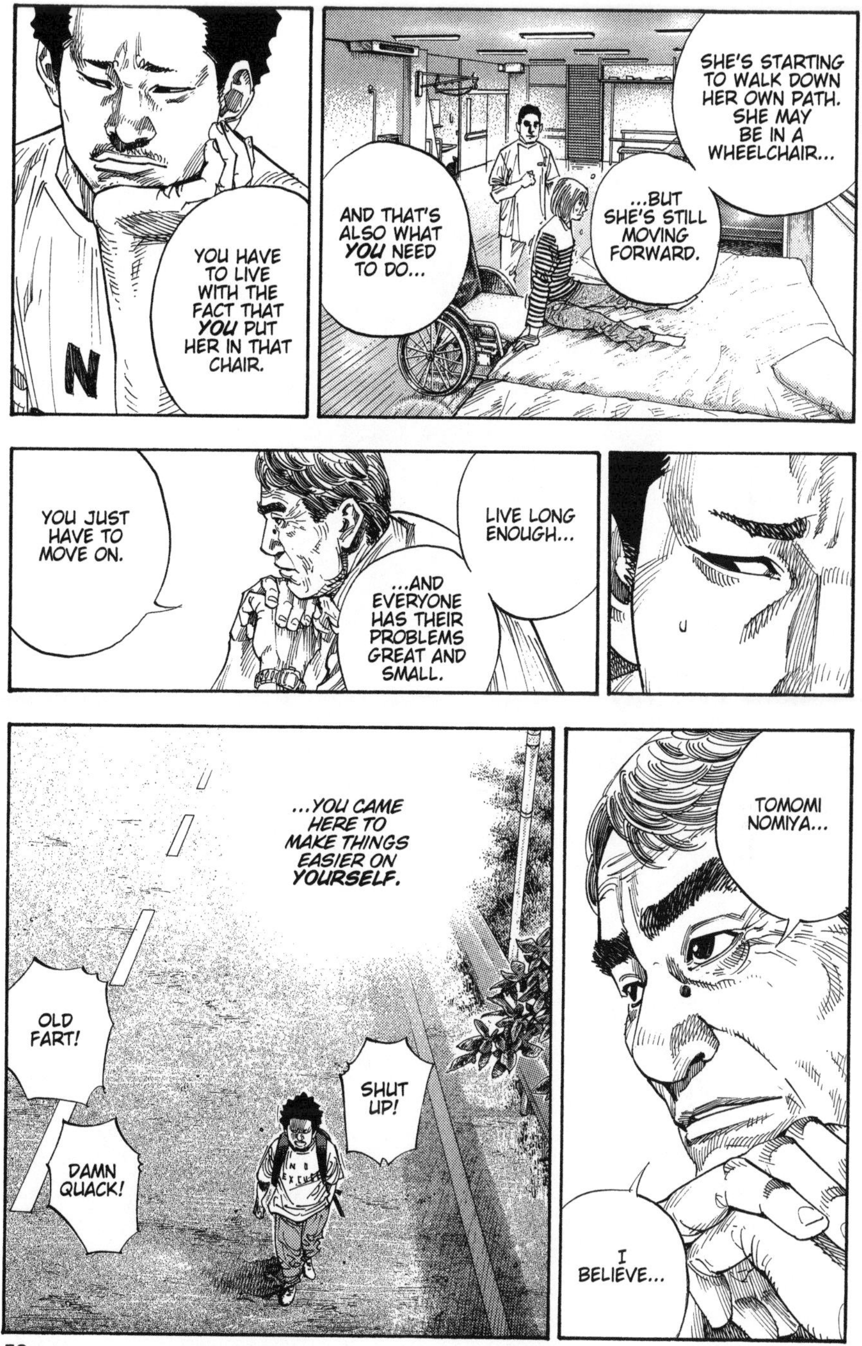
YOU HAVE TO LIVE WITH THE FACT THAT *YOU* PUT HER IN THAT CHAIR.
SHE'S STARTING TO WALK DOWN HER OWN PATH. SHE MAY BE IN A WHEELCHAIR...
...BUT SHE'S STILL MOVING FORWARD.
AND THAT'S ALSO WHAT *YOU* NEED TO DO...
YOU JUST HAVE TO MOVE ON.
LIVE LONG ENOUGH...
...AND EVERYONE HAS THEIR PROBLEMS GREAT AND SMALL.
TOMOMI NOMIYA...
I BELIEVE...
...YOU CAME HERE TO MAKE THINGS EASIER ON *YOURSELF*.
OLD FART!
SHUT UP!
DAMN QUACK!

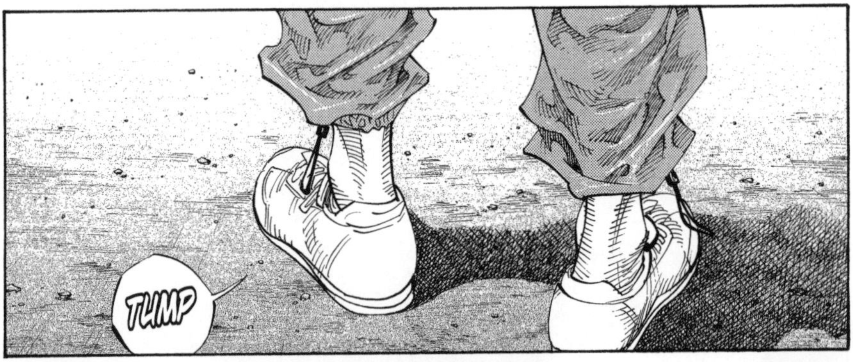
TUMP

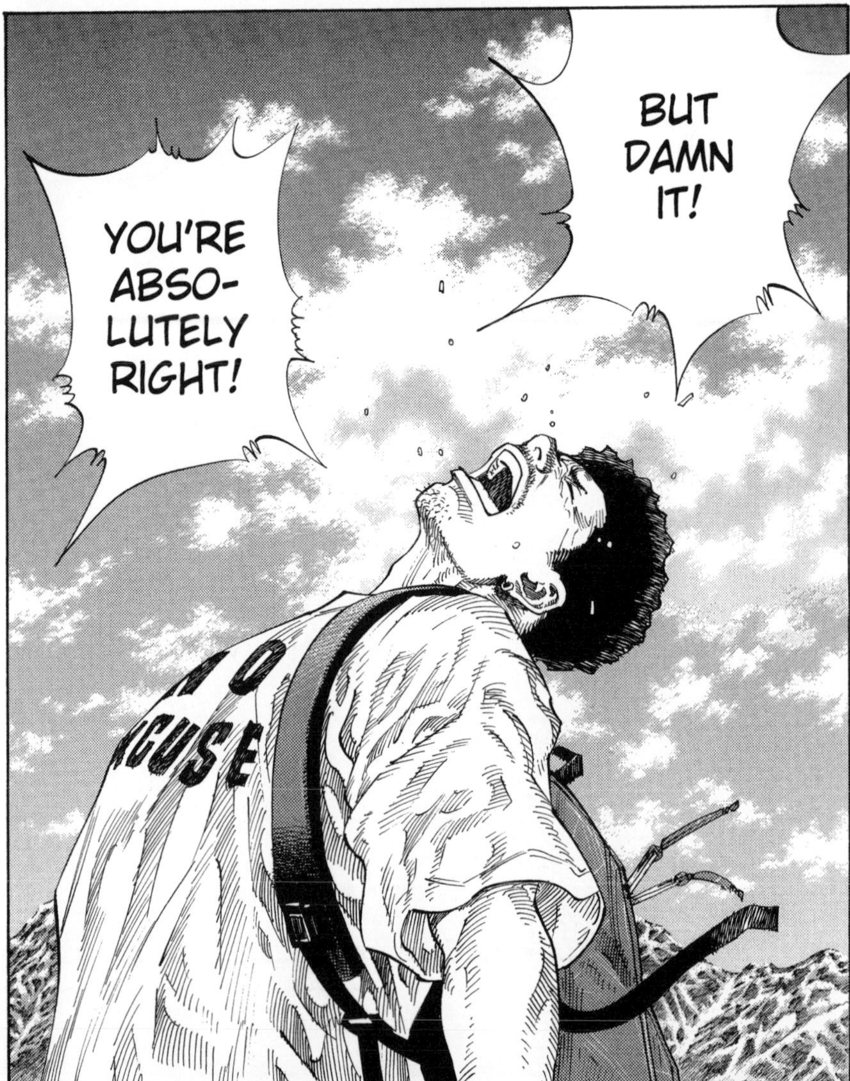
BUT DAMN IT!
YOU'RE ABSO-LUTELY RIGHT!

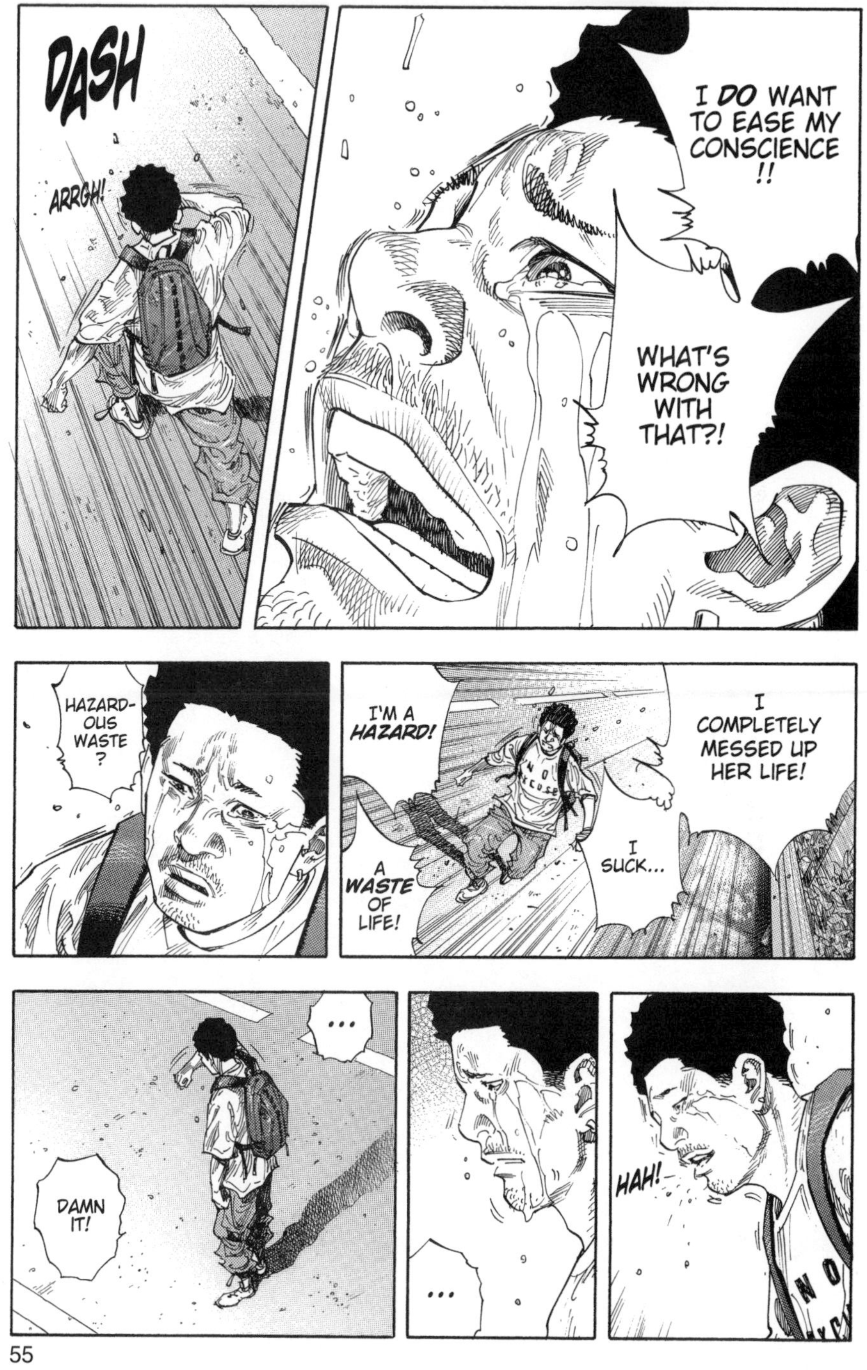
I DO WANT TO EASE MY CONSCIENCE !!
WHAT'S WRONG WITH THAT?!
DASH
ARRGH!
I COMPLETELY MESSED UP HER LIFE!
I'M A HAZARD!
I SUCK...
A WASTE OF LIFE!
HAZARD-OUS WASTE ?
HAH!
...
...
DAMN IT!

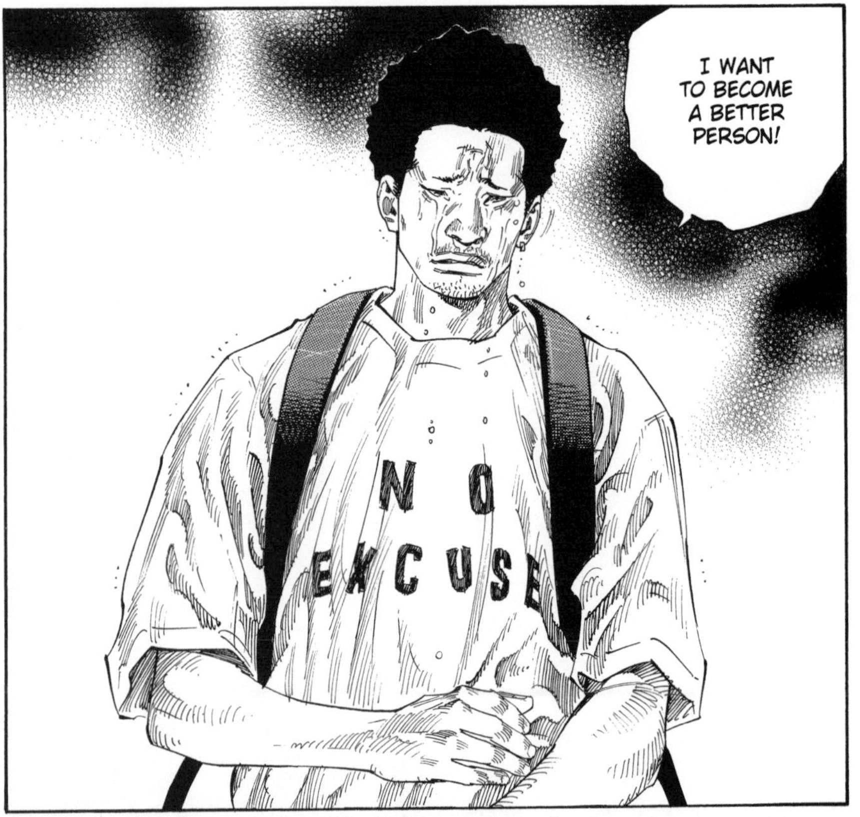
I WANT TO BECOME A BETTER PERSON!
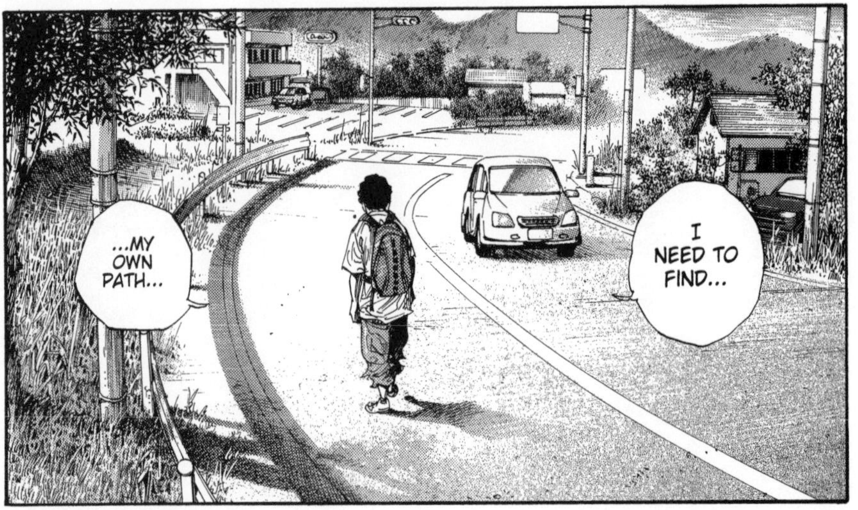
I NEED TO FIND...
...MY OWN PATH...

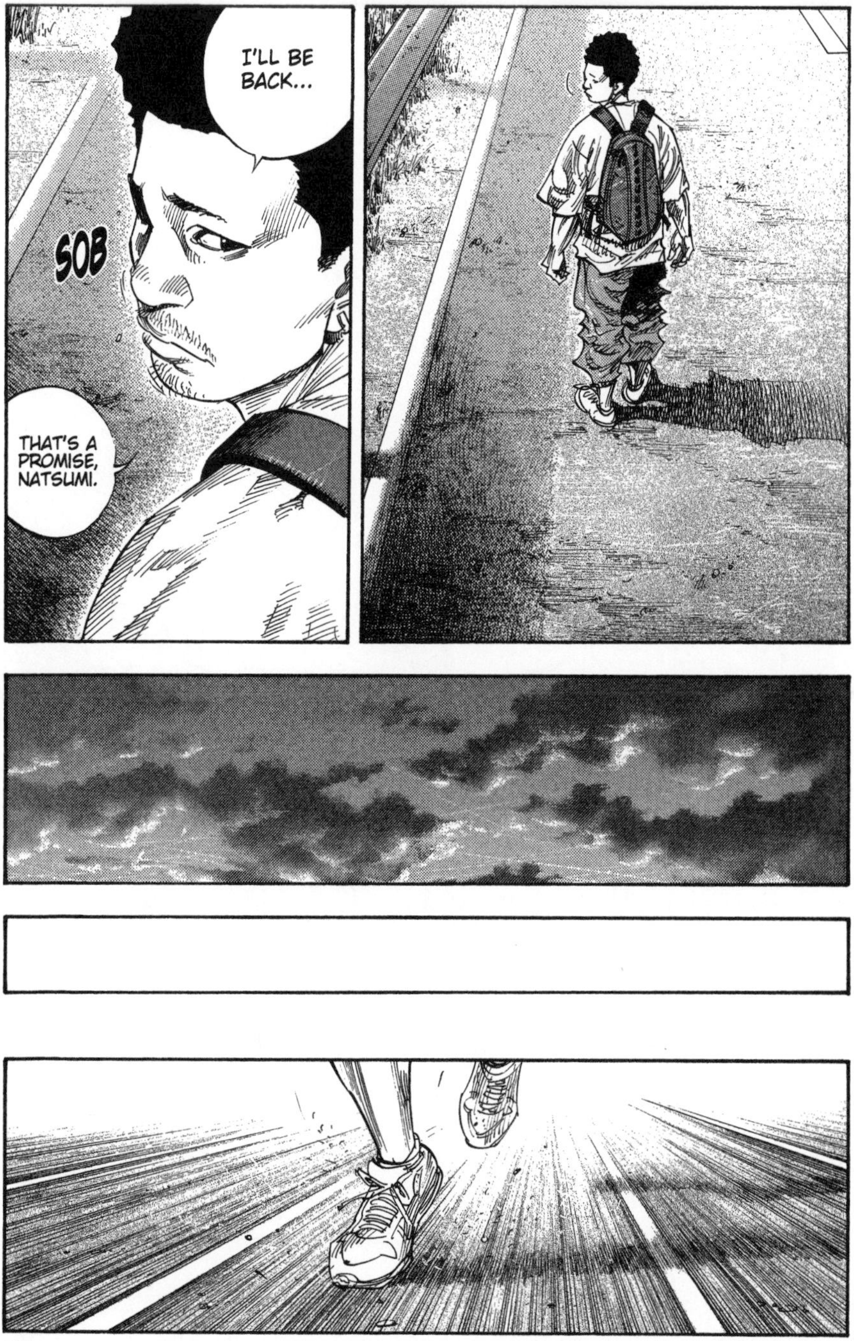
I'LL BE BACK...
SOB
THAT'S A PROMISE, NATSUMI.

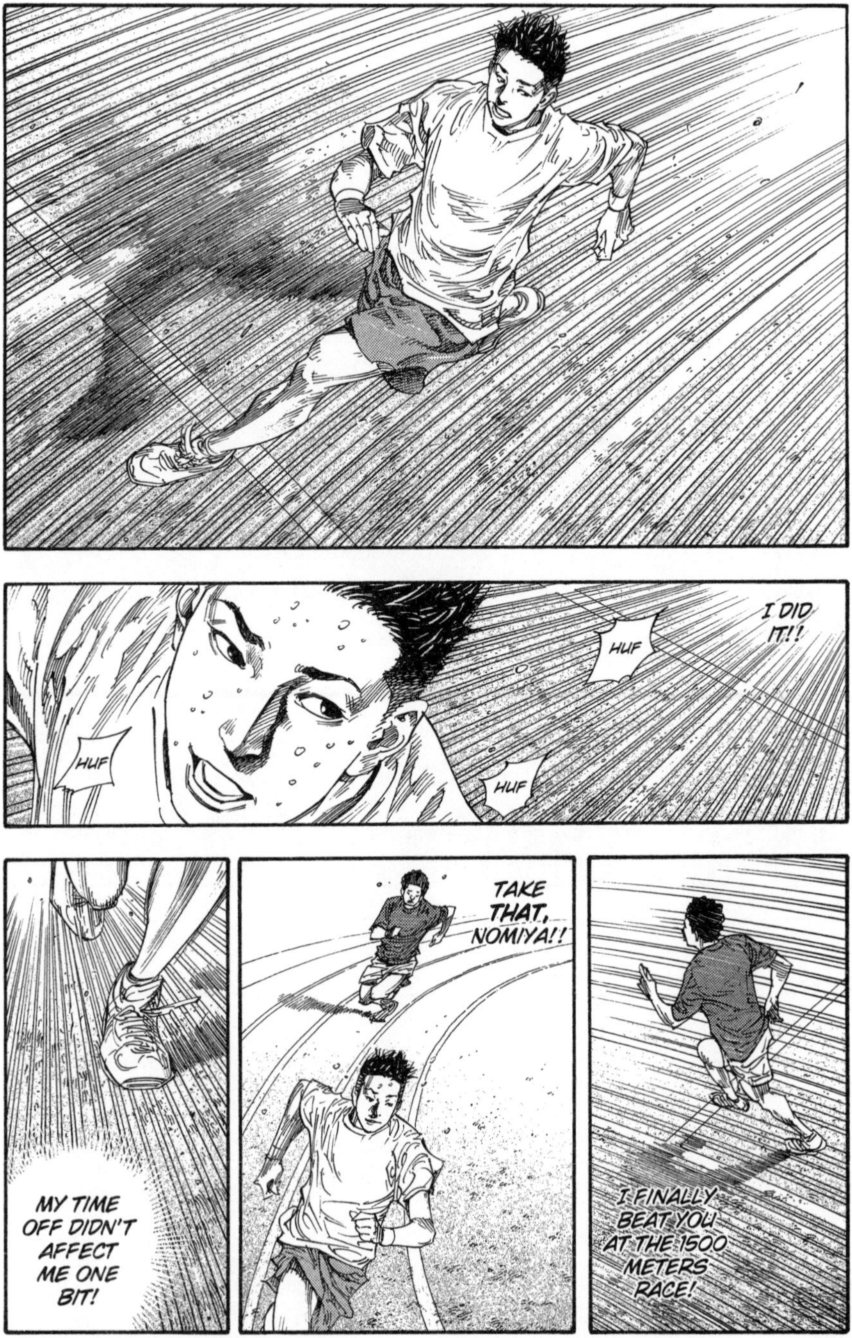
I DID IT!!
HUF
HUF
HUF
I FINALLY BEAT YOU AT THE 1500 METERS RACE!
TAKE THAT, NOMIYA!!
MY TIME OFF DIDN'T AFFECT ME ONE BIT!

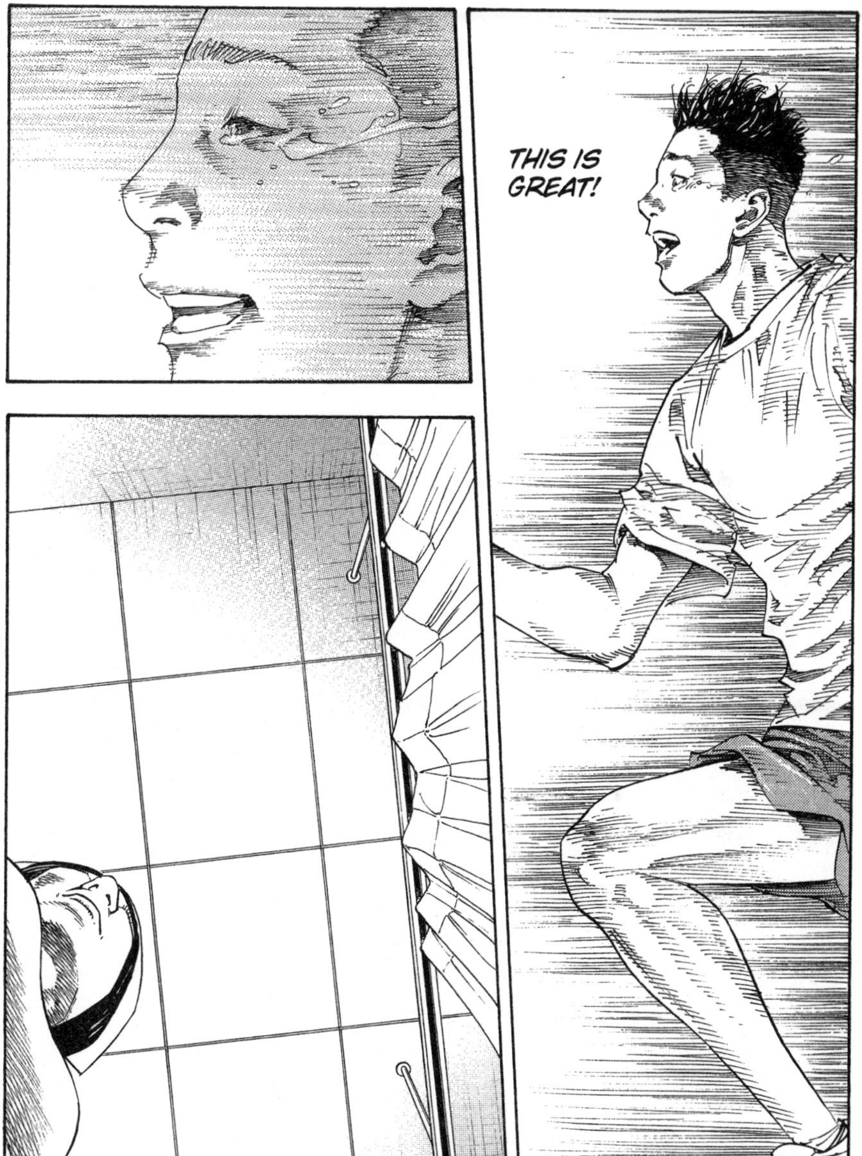
THIS IS GREAT!

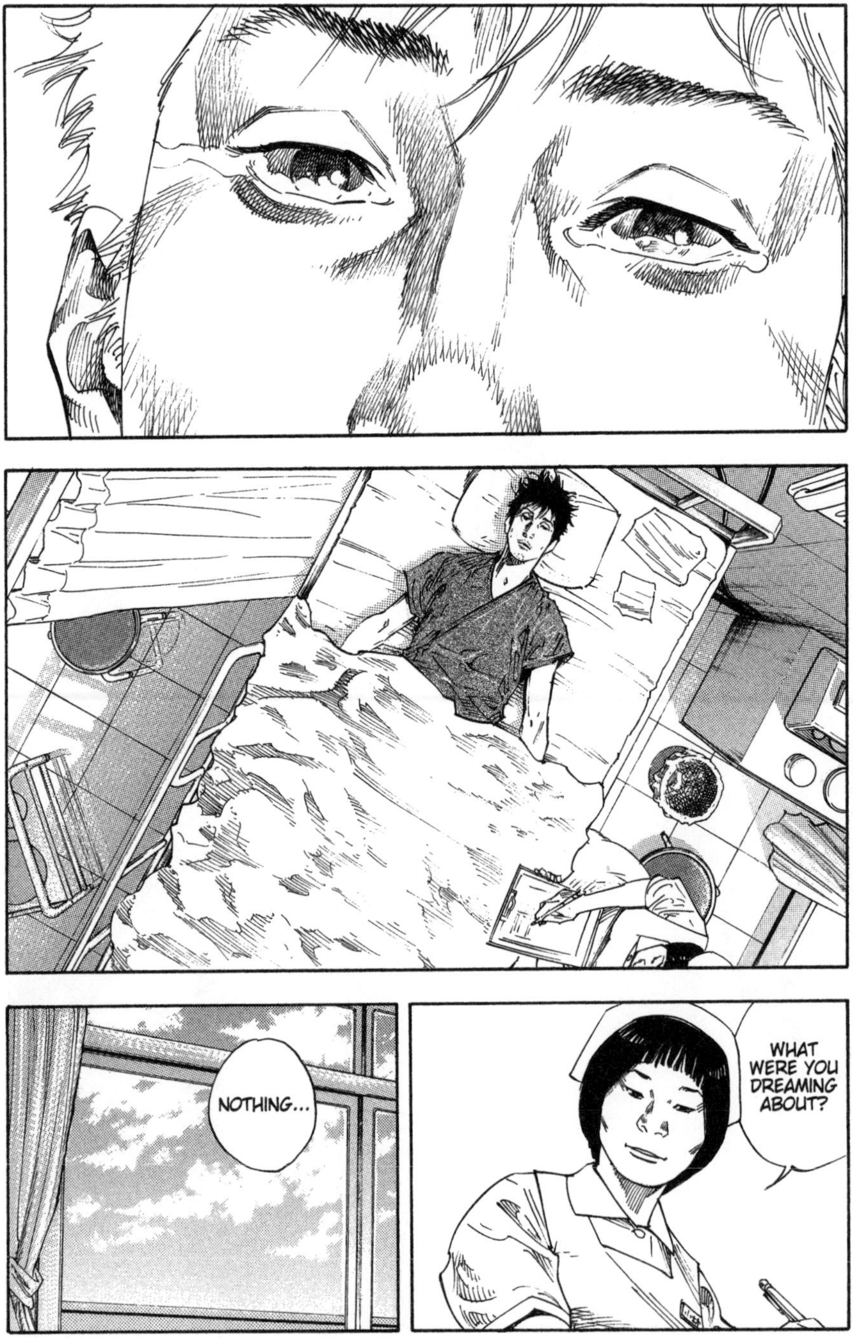
WHAT WERE YOU DREAMING ABOUT?
NOTHING...

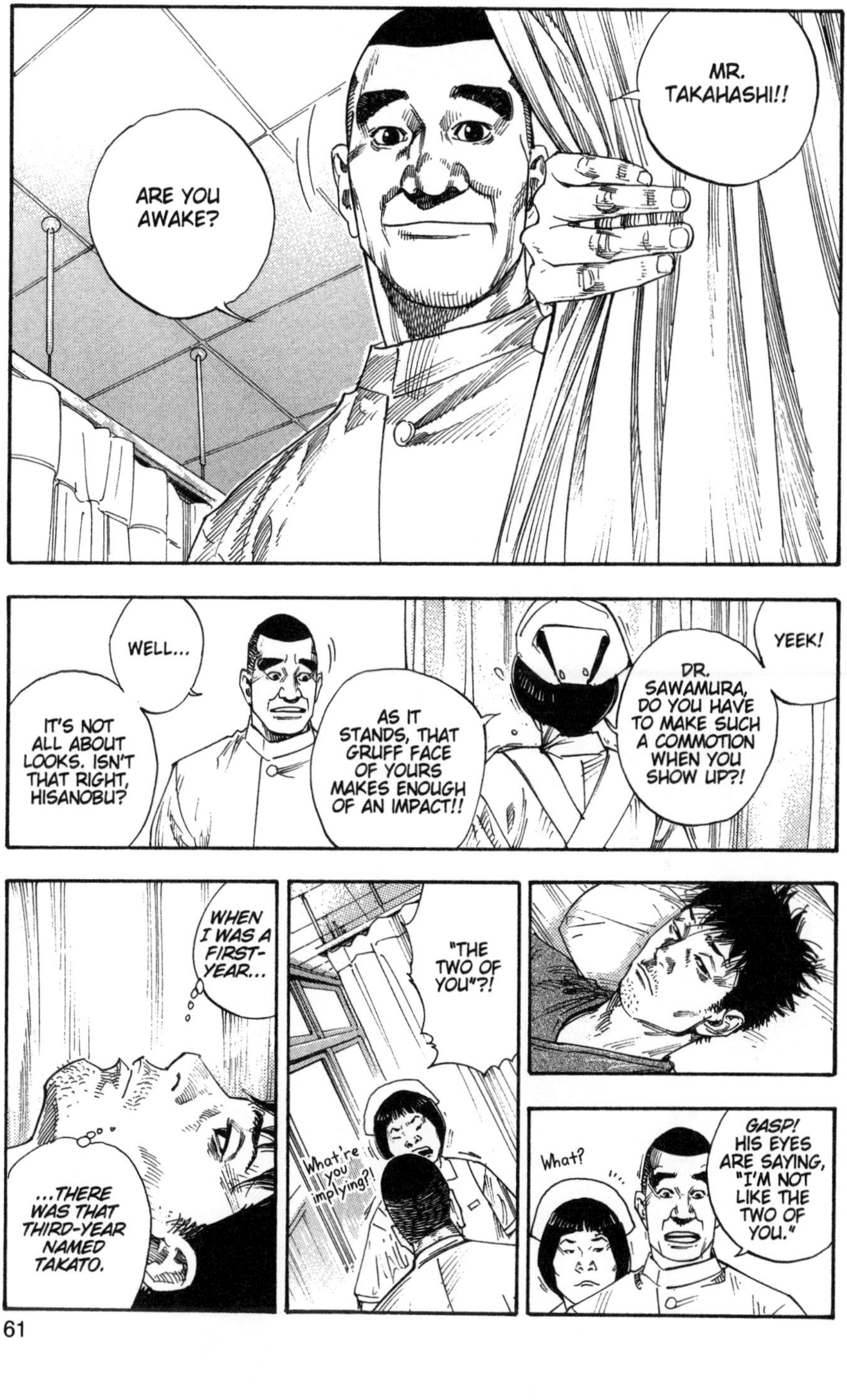
MR. TAKAHASHI!!
ARE YOU AWAKE?
YEEK!
DR. SAWAMURA, DO YOU HAVE TO MAKE SUCH A COMMOTION WHEN YOU SHOW UP?!
AS IT STANDS, THAT GRUFF FACE OF YOURS MAKES ENOUGH OF AN IMPACT!!
WELL...
IT'S NOT ALL ABOUT LOOKS. ISN'T THAT RIGHT, HISANOBU?
GASP! HIS EYES ARE SAYING, "I'M NOT LIKE THE TWO OF YOU."
What?
"THE TWO OF YOU"?!
What're you implying?!
WHEN I WAS A FIRST-YEAR...
...THERE WAS THAT THIRD-YEAR NAMED TAKATO.

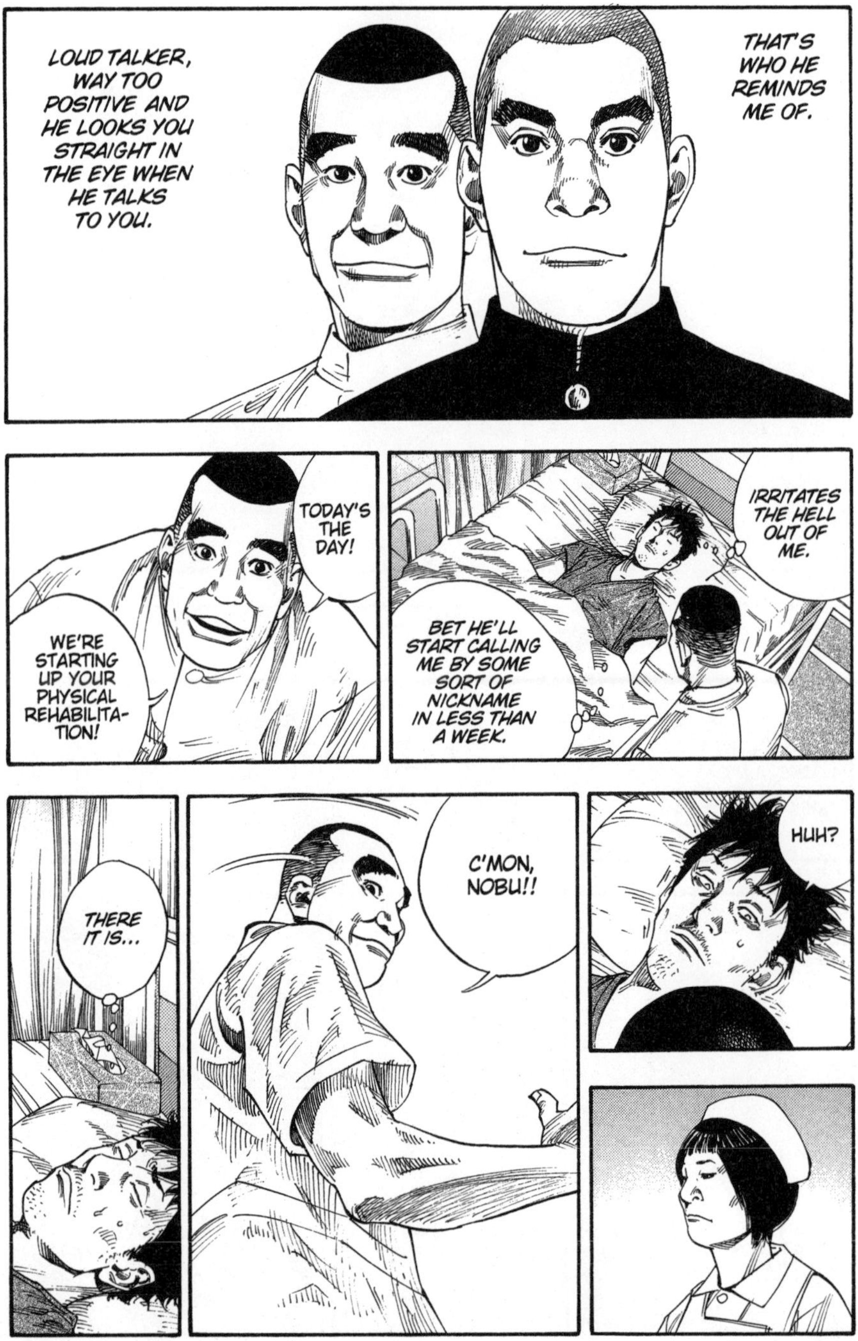
THAT'S WHO HE REMINDS ME OF.
LOUD TALKER, WAY TOO POSITIVE AND HE LOOKS YOU STRAIGHT IN THE EYE WHEN HE TALKS TO YOU.
IRRITATES THE HELL OUT OF ME.
BET HE'LL START CALLING ME BY SOME SORT OF NICKNAME IN LESS THAN A WEEK.
TODAY'S THE DAY!
WE'RE STARTING UP YOUR PHYSICAL REHABILITA-TION!
HUH?
C'MON, NOBU!!
THERE IT IS...

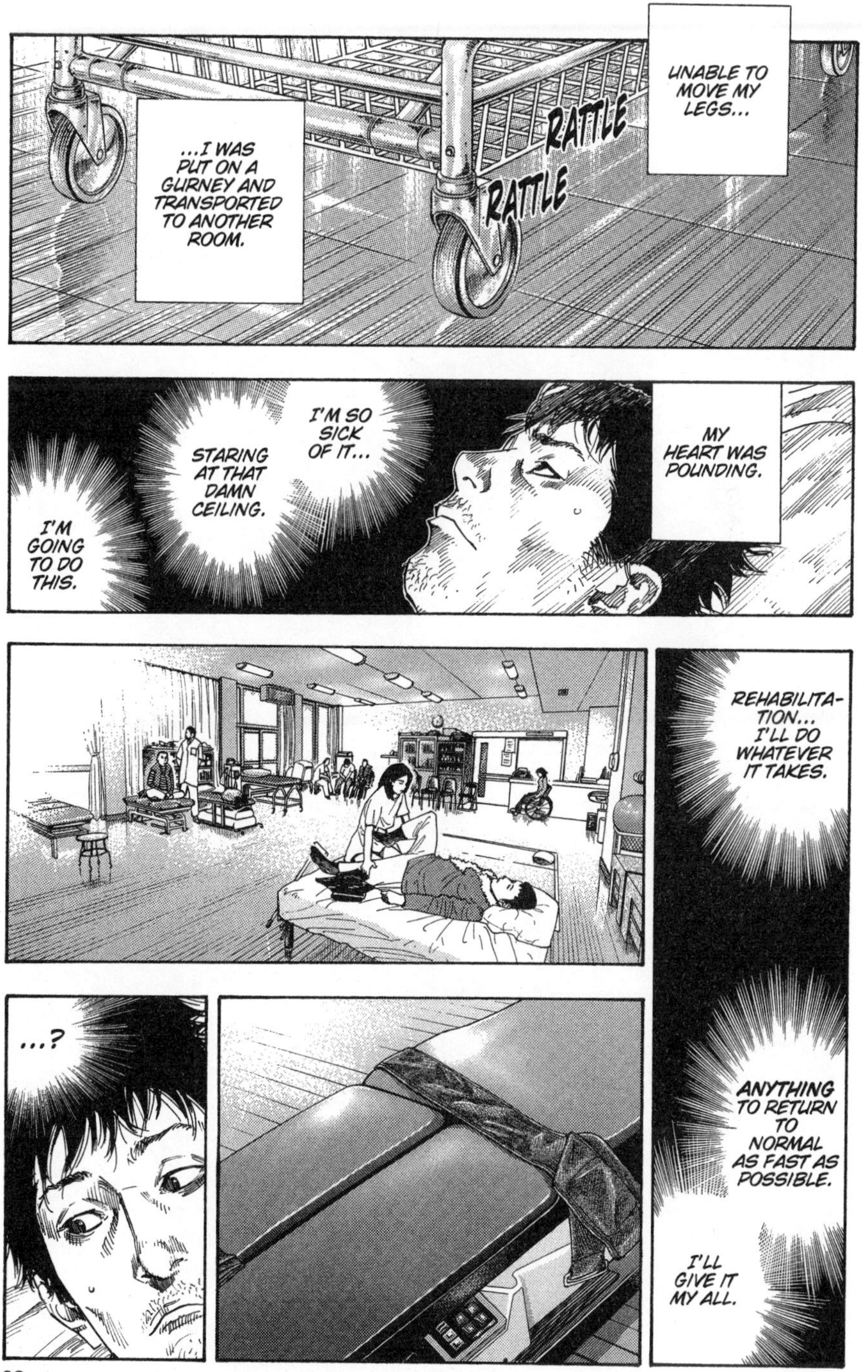
UNABLE TO MOVE MY LEGS...
RATTLE
RATTLE
...I WAS PUT ON A GURNEY AND TRANSPORTED TO ANOTHER ROOM.
MY HEART WAS POUNDING.
I'M SO SICK OF IT...
STARING AT THAT DAMN CEILING.
I'M GOING TO DO THIS.
REHABILITATION... I'LL DO WHATEVER IT TAKES.
ANYTHING TO RETURN TO NORMAL AS FAST AS POSSIBLE.
I'LL GIVE IT MY ALL.
...?

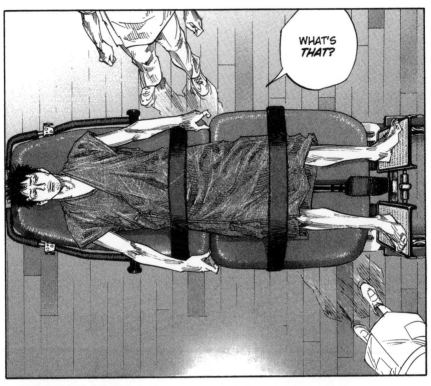

WHAT'S *THAT?*
AN INCLINE TABLE!
THIS CONTROL BOX ADJUSTS THE ANGLE!
WHAT...?
...
YOU CALL THIS REHABILITA-TION?
YOU GOTTA BE KIDDING ME.

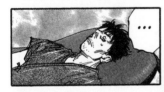

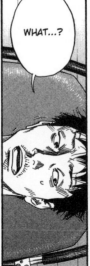

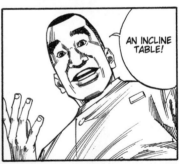

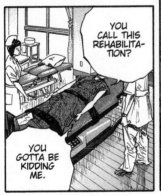

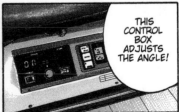

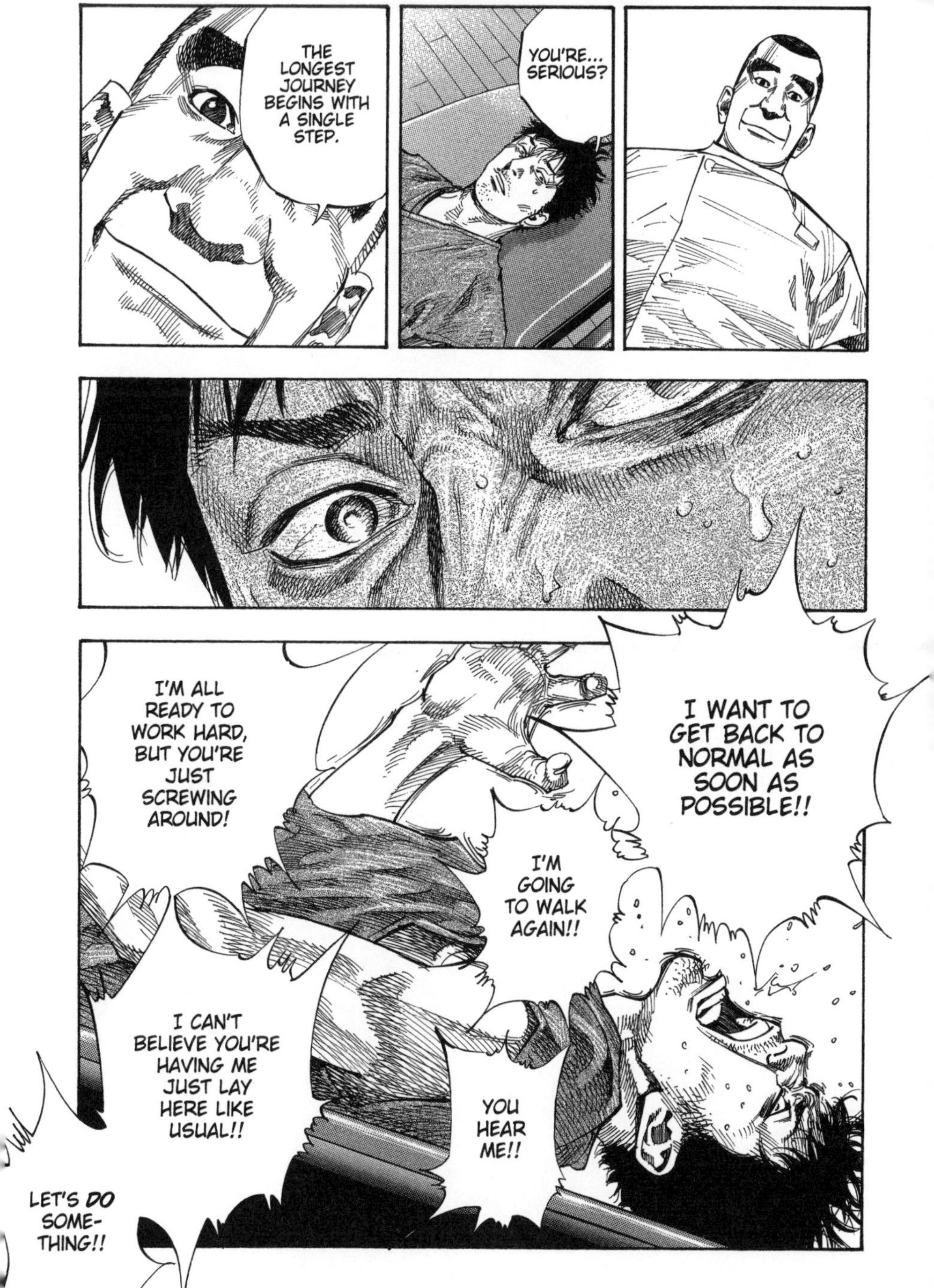
YOU'RE... SERIOUS?
THE LONGEST JOURNEY BEGINS WITH A SINGLE STEP.
I WANT TO GET BACK TO NORMAL AS SOON AS POSSIBLE!!
I'M ALL READY TO WORK HARD, BUT YOU'RE JUST SCREWING AROUND!
I'M GOING TO WALK AGAIN!!
YOU HEAR ME!!
I CAN'T BELIEVE YOU'RE HAVING ME JUST LAY HERE LIKE USUAL!!
LET'S *DO* SOME-THING!!

GRIN

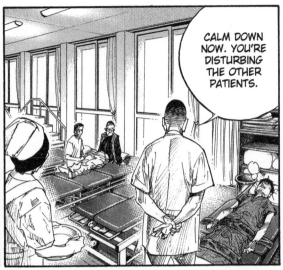

CALM DOWN NOW. YOU'RE DISTURBING THE OTHER PATIENTS.

GRIN

!

OKAY, UP YOU GO.

BIG DEAL.

I'M MOVING UP.

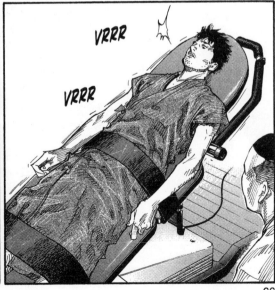

VRRR

VRRR

...!!

VRRR

VRRR

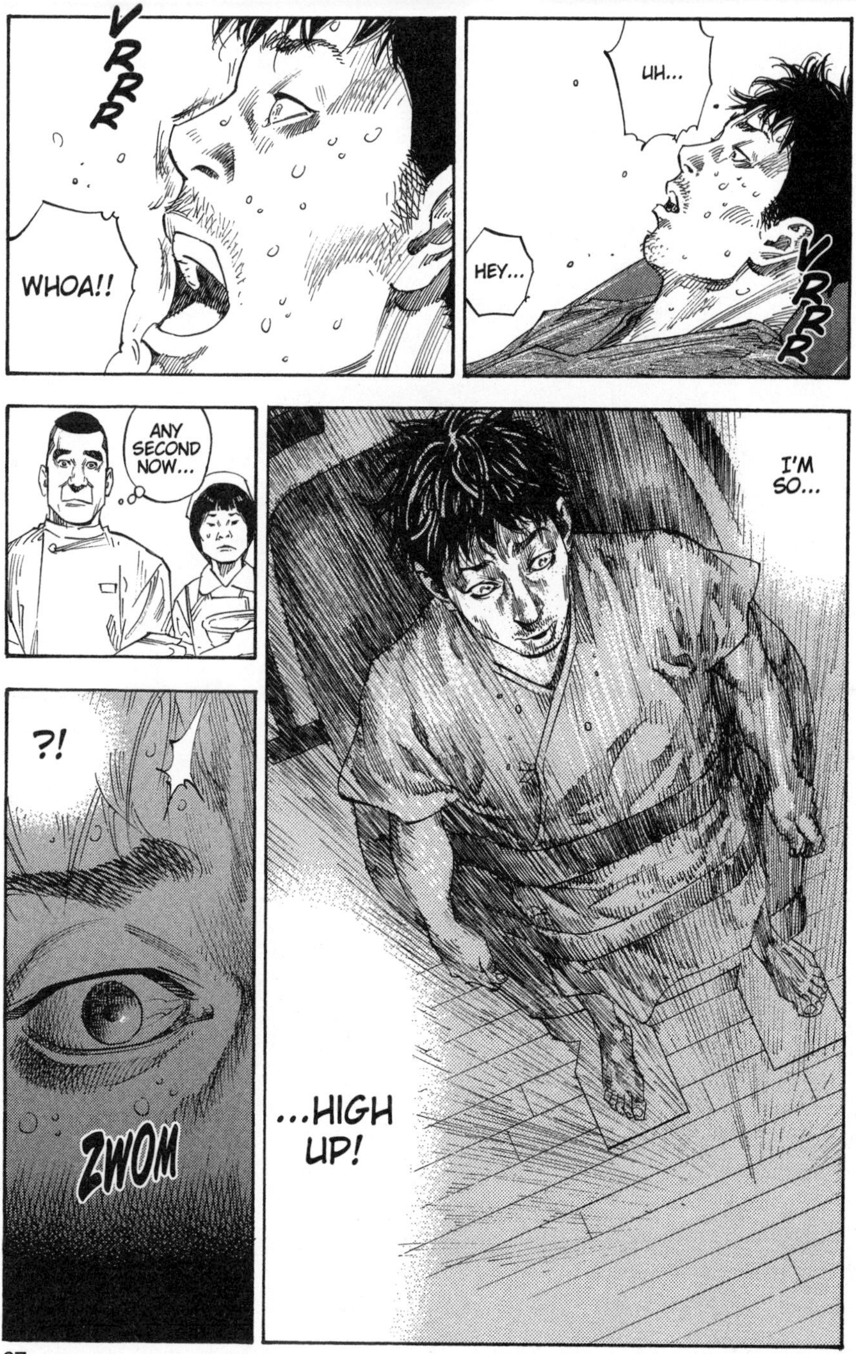
UH...
HEY...
VRRR
VRRR
WHOA!!
I'M SO...
...HIGH UP!
ANY SECOND NOW...
?!
ZWOM

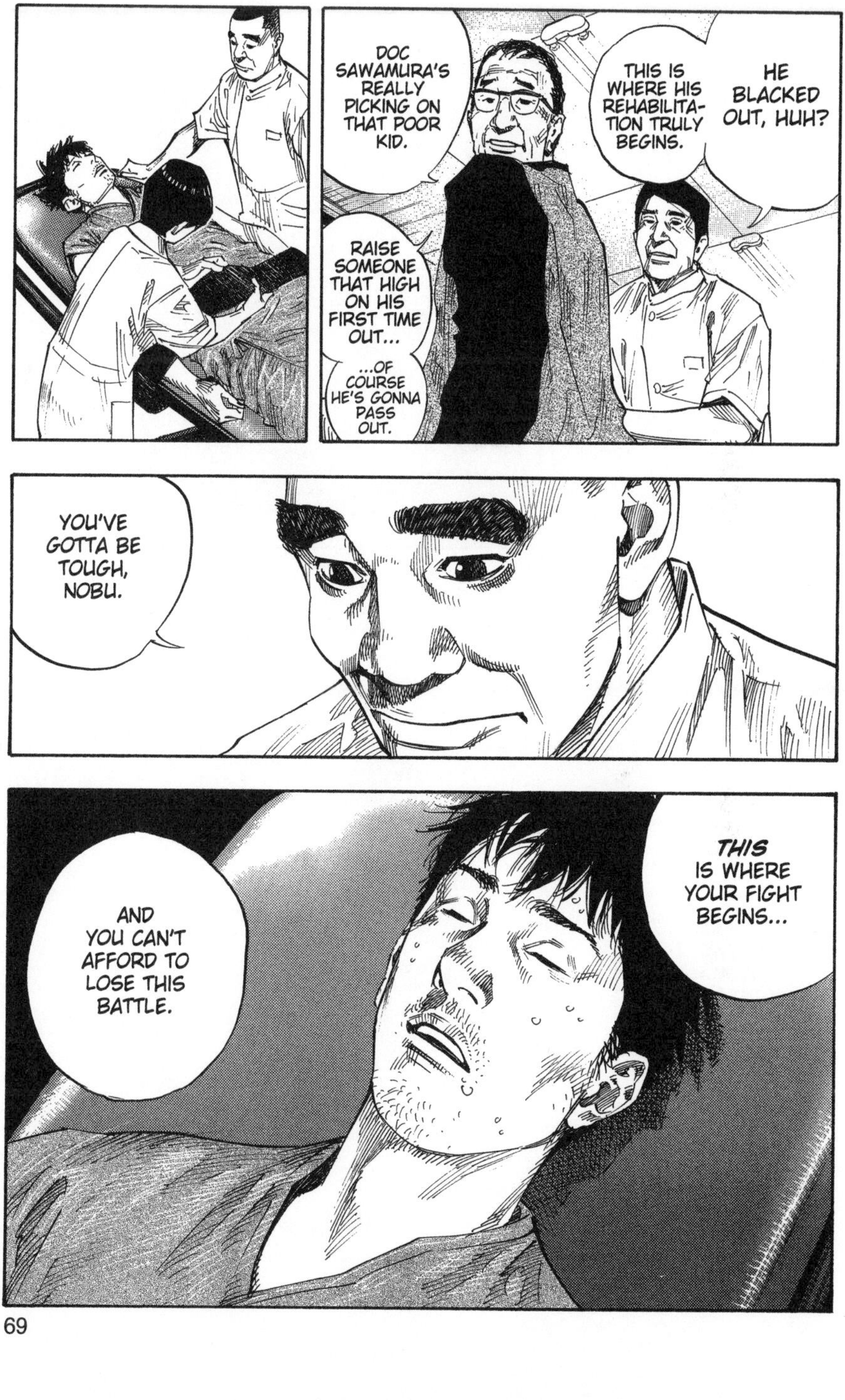
HE BLACKED OUT, HUH?
THIS IS WHERE HIS REHABILITA-TION TRULY BEGINS.
DOC SAWAMURA'S REALLY PICKING ON THAT POOR KID.
RAISE SOMEONE THAT HIGH ON HIS FIRST TIME OUT...
...OF COURSE HE'S GONNA PASS OUT.
YOU'VE GOTTA BE TOUGH, NOBU.
THIS IS WHERE YOUR FIGHT BEGINS...
AND YOU CAN'T AFFORD TO LOSE THIS BATTLE.

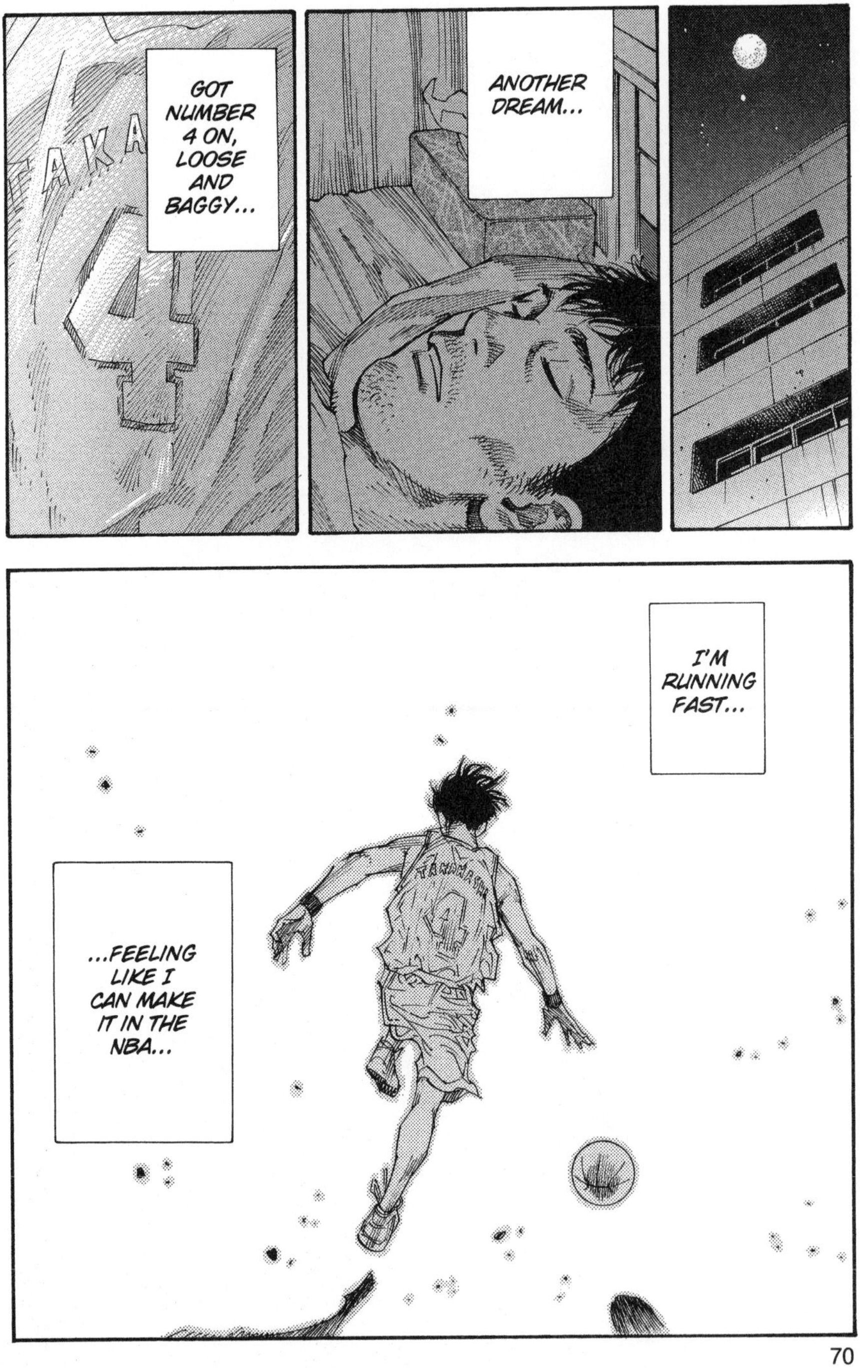
ANOTHER DREAM...
GOT NUMBER 4 ON, LOOSE AND BAGGY...
I'M RUNNING FAST...
...FEELING LIKE I CAN MAKE IT IN THE NBA...

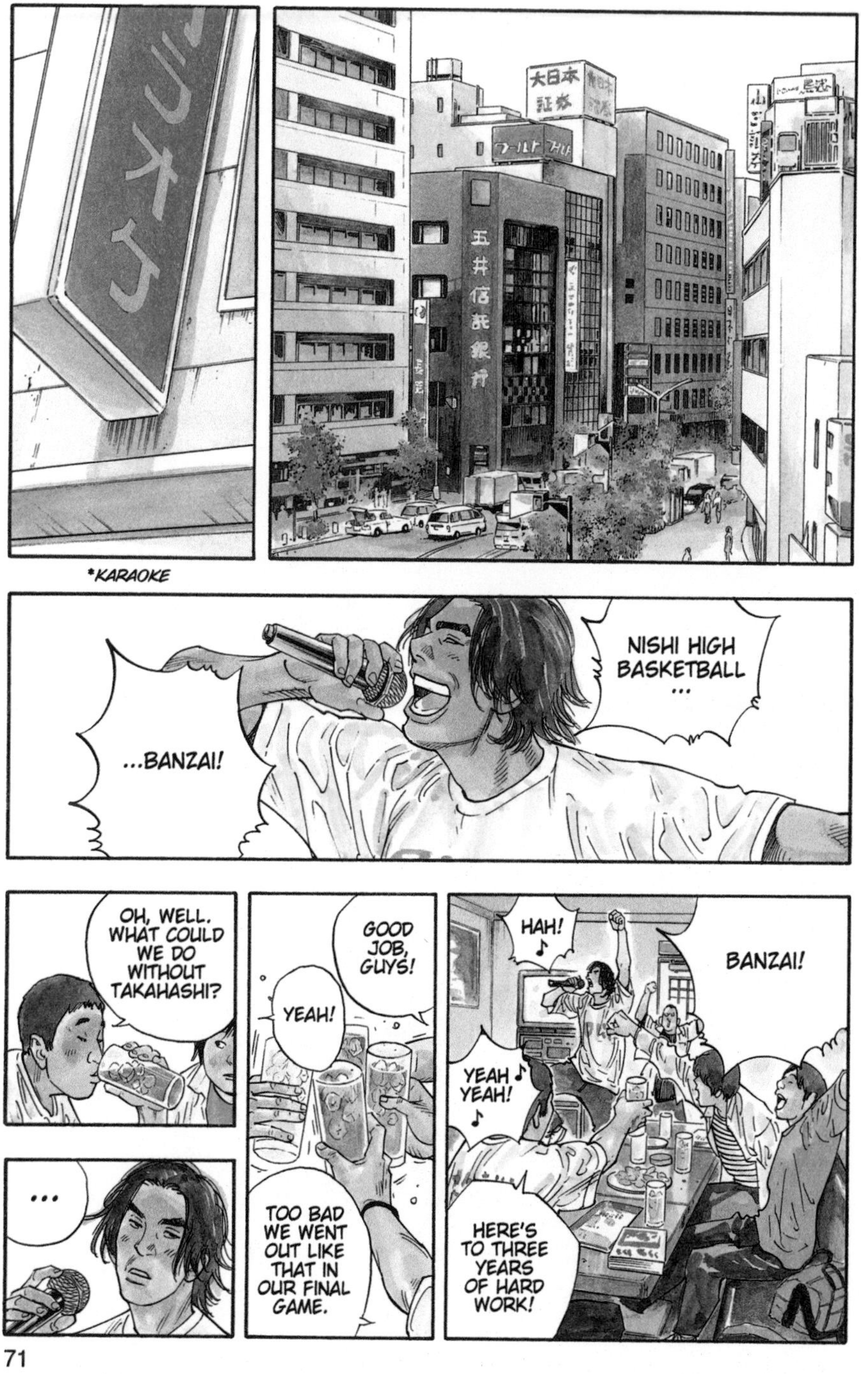
大日本 証券
五井信託銀行
*KARAOKE
NISHI HIGH BASKETBALL ...
...BANZAI!
BANZAI!
HAH! ♪
YEAH YEAH! ♪ ♪
HERE'S TO THREE YEARS OF HARD WORK!
GOOD JOB, GUYS!
YEAH!
TOO BAD WE WENT OUT LIKE THAT IN OUR FINAL GAME.
OH, WELL. WHAT COULD WE DO WITHOUT TAKAHASHI?
...

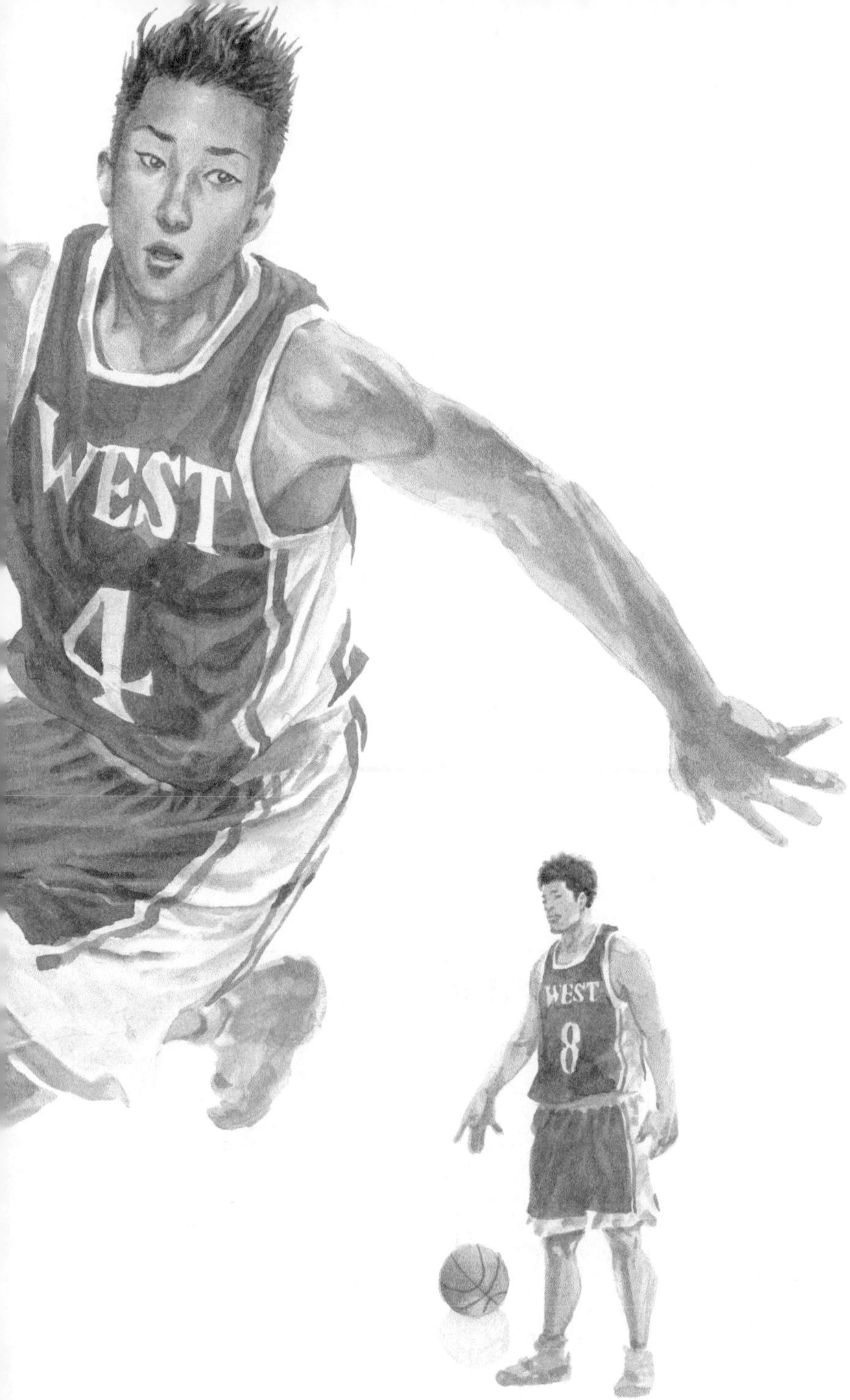
WEST
4
WEST
8

15th

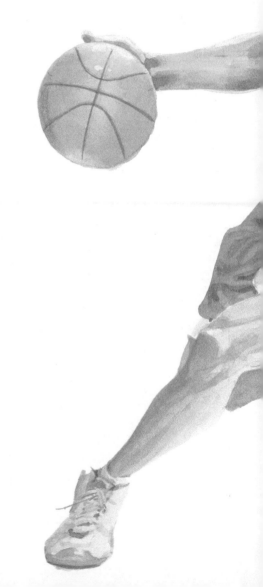

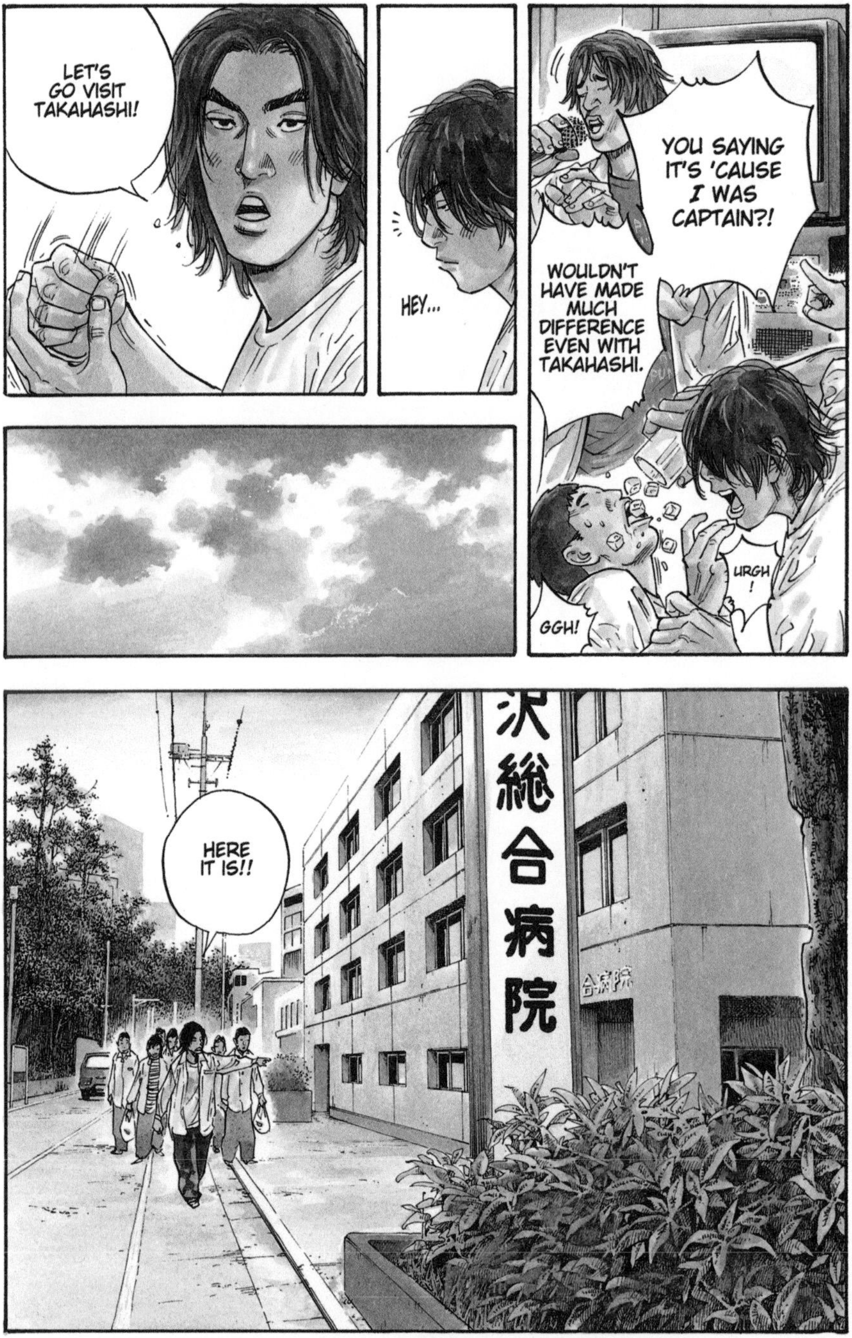
YOU SAYING IT'S 'CAUSE I WAS CAPTAIN?!
WOULDN'T HAVE MADE MUCH DIFFERENCE EVEN WITH TAKAHASHI.
URGH!
GGH!
HEY...
LET'S GO VISIT TAKAHASHI!
沢総合病院
合病院
HERE IT IS!!

*TACHIZAWA GENERAL HOSPITAL

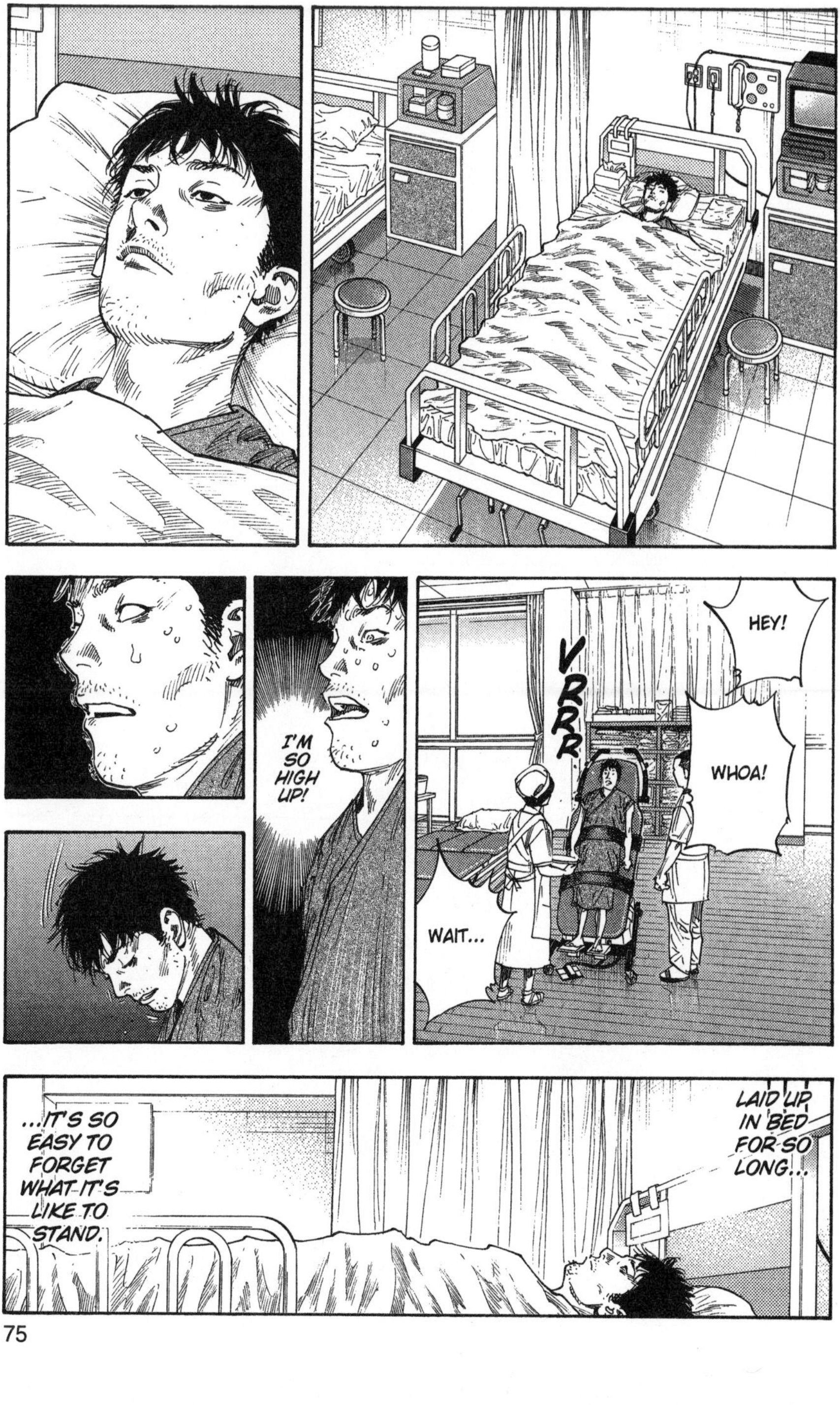
HEY!
VRRR
WHOA!
WAIT...
I'M SO HIGH UP!
LAID UP IN BED FOR SO LONG...
...IT'S SO EASY TO FORGET WHAT IT'S LIKE TO STAND.

I GUESS I'M GETTING USED TO BEING LIKE THIS.
...
I CAN'T EVEN STAND...
NOT EVEN A SIMPLE THING LIKE THAT.
I'M MORE HELPLESS THAN A BABY.
WERE THEY SERIOUS...
...ABOUT ME NEVER WALKING AGAIN?

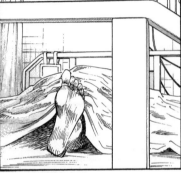

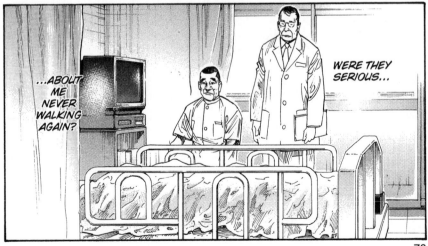

NO WAY.

THAT JUST CAN'T BE...

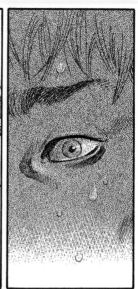

I'M GOING TO WALK JUST LIKE BEFORE.

HUH?

GUESS WHO'S HERE?

SHUF

SHUF

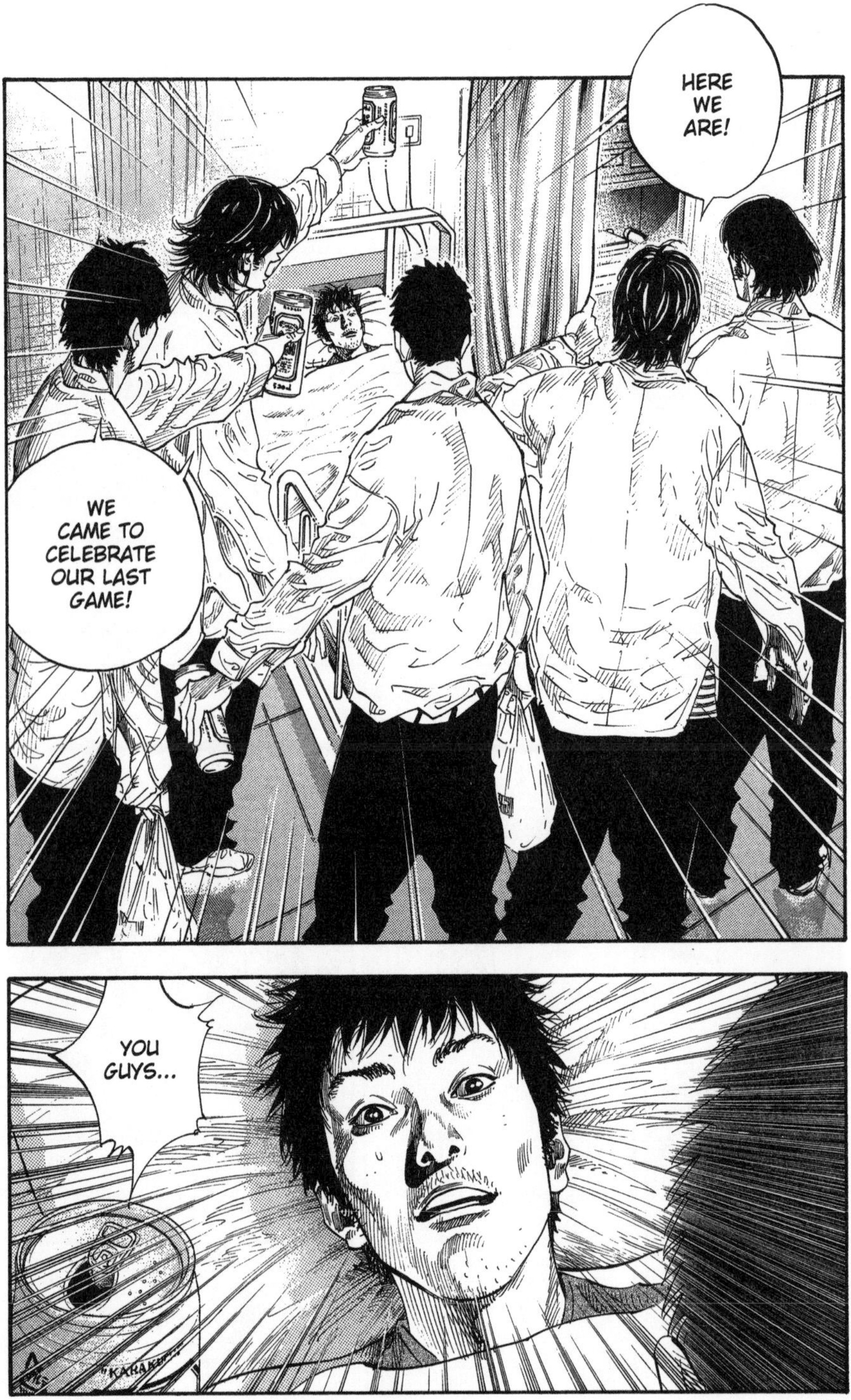
HERE WE ARE!
WE CAME TO CELEBRATE OUR LAST GAME!
YOU GUYS...

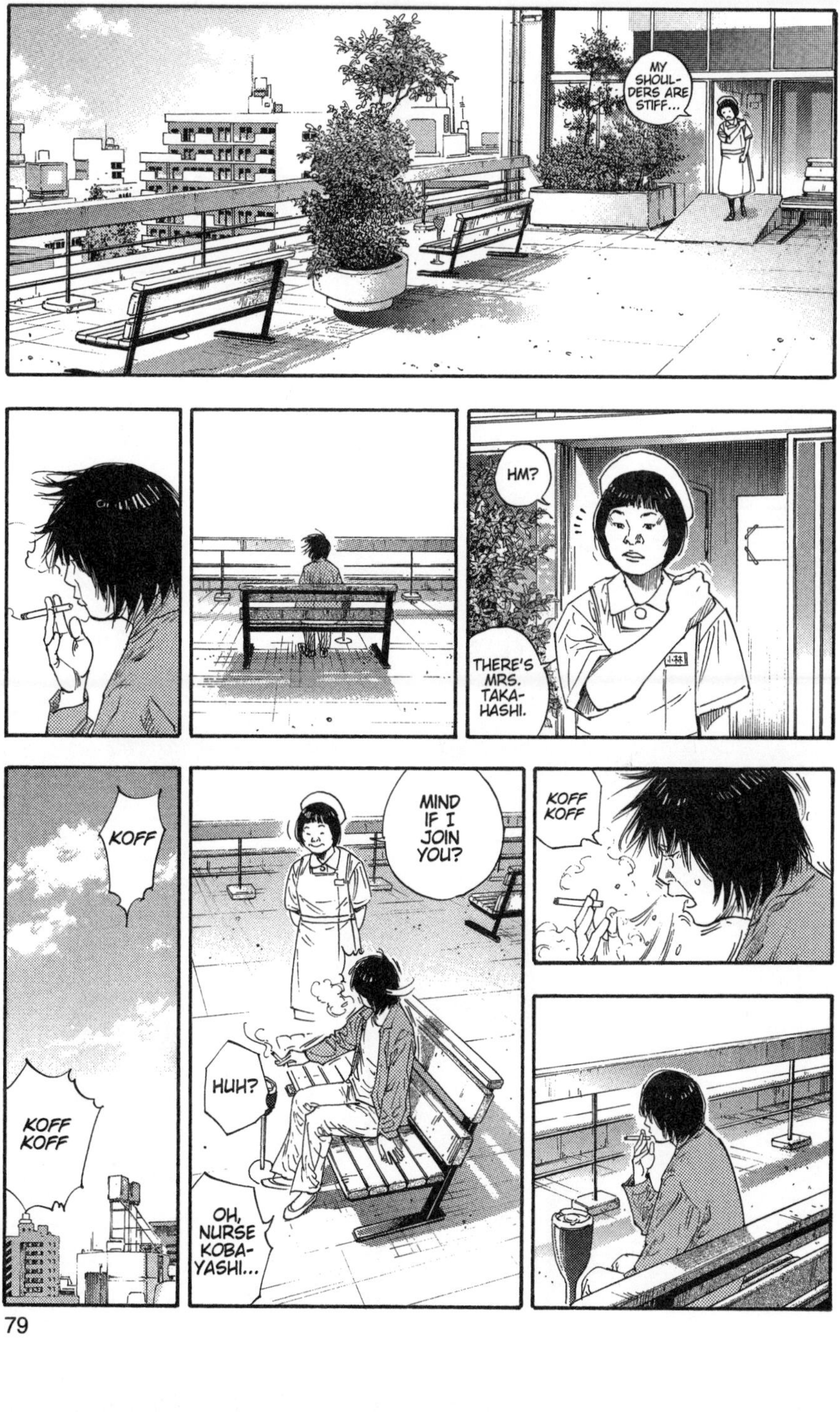
MY SHOUL-DERS ARE STIFF...
HM?
THERE'S MRS. TAKA-HASHI.
KOFF KOFF
MIND IF I JOIN YOU?
HUH?
OH, NURSE KOBA-YASHI...
KOFF
KOFF KOFF

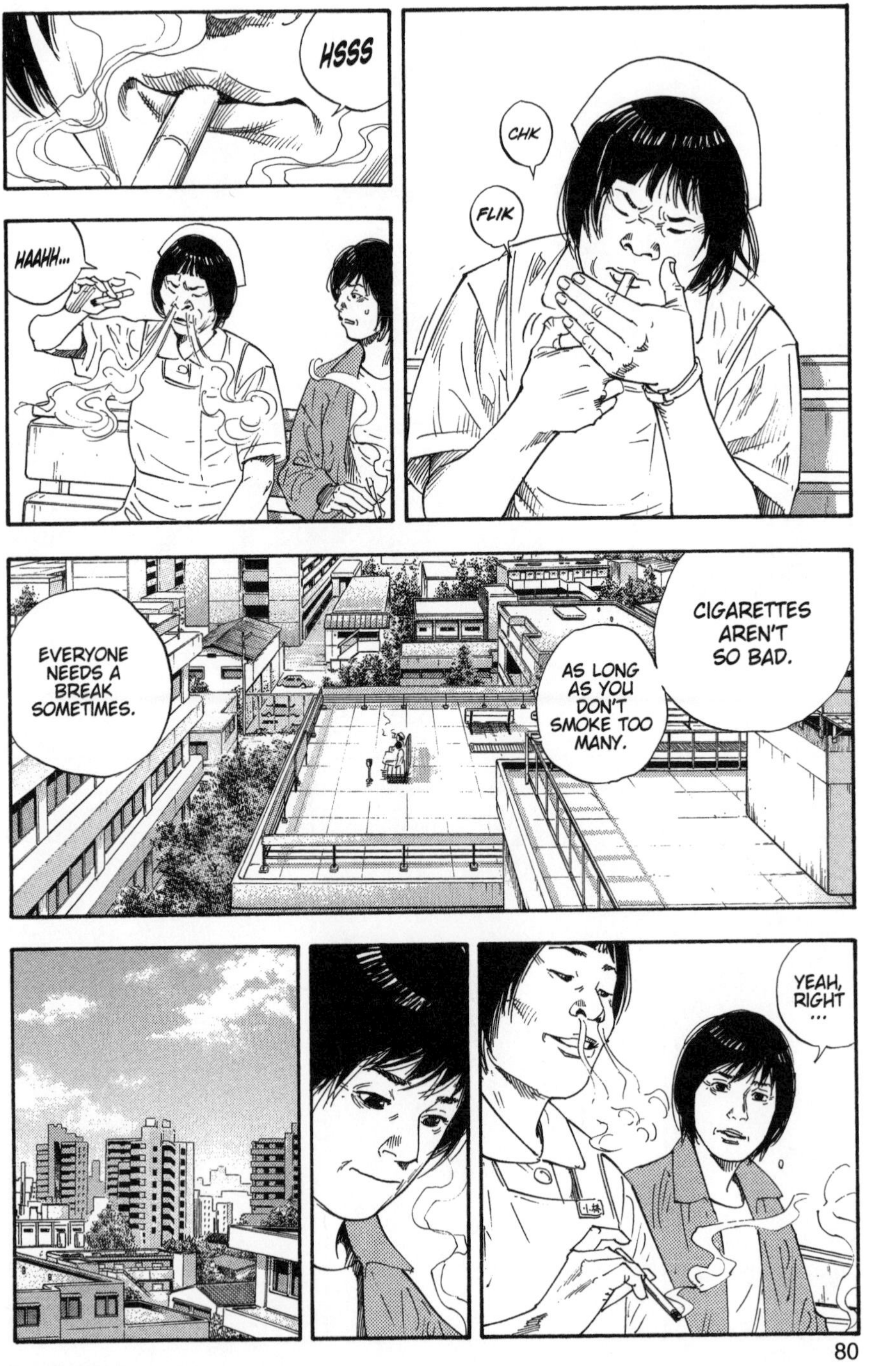
CHK
FLIK
HSSS
HAAHH...
CIGARETTES AREN'T SO BAD.
AS LONG AS YOU DON'T SMOKE TOO MANY.
EVERYONE NEEDS A BREAK SOMETIMES.
YEAH, RIGHT...

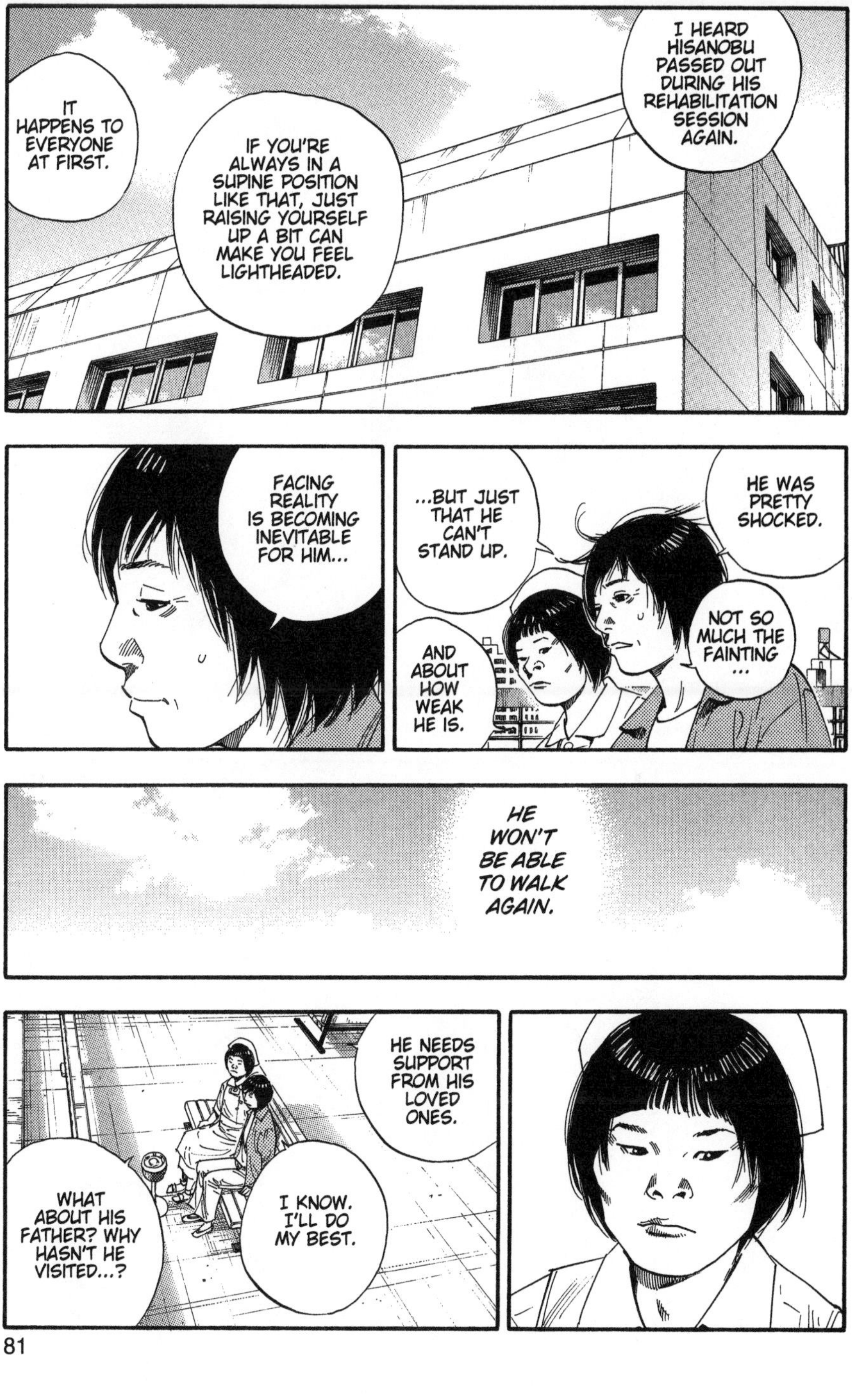
I HEARD HISANOBU PASSED OUT DURING HIS REHABILITATION SESSION AGAIN.
IF YOU'RE ALWAYS IN A SUPINE POSITION LIKE THAT, JUST RAISING YOURSELF UP A BIT CAN MAKE YOU FEEL LIGHTHEADED.
IT HAPPENS TO EVERYONE AT FIRST.
HE WAS PRETTY SHOCKED.
NOT SO MUCH THE FAINTING ...
...BUT JUST THAT HE CAN'T STAND UP.
AND ABOUT HOW WEAK HE IS.
FACING REALITY IS BECOMING INEVITABLE FOR HIM...
HE WON'T BE ABLE TO WALK AGAIN.
HE NEEDS SUPPORT FROM HIS LOVED ONES.
I KNOW. I'LL DO MY BEST.
WHAT ABOUT HIS FATHER? WHY HASN'T HE VISITED...?

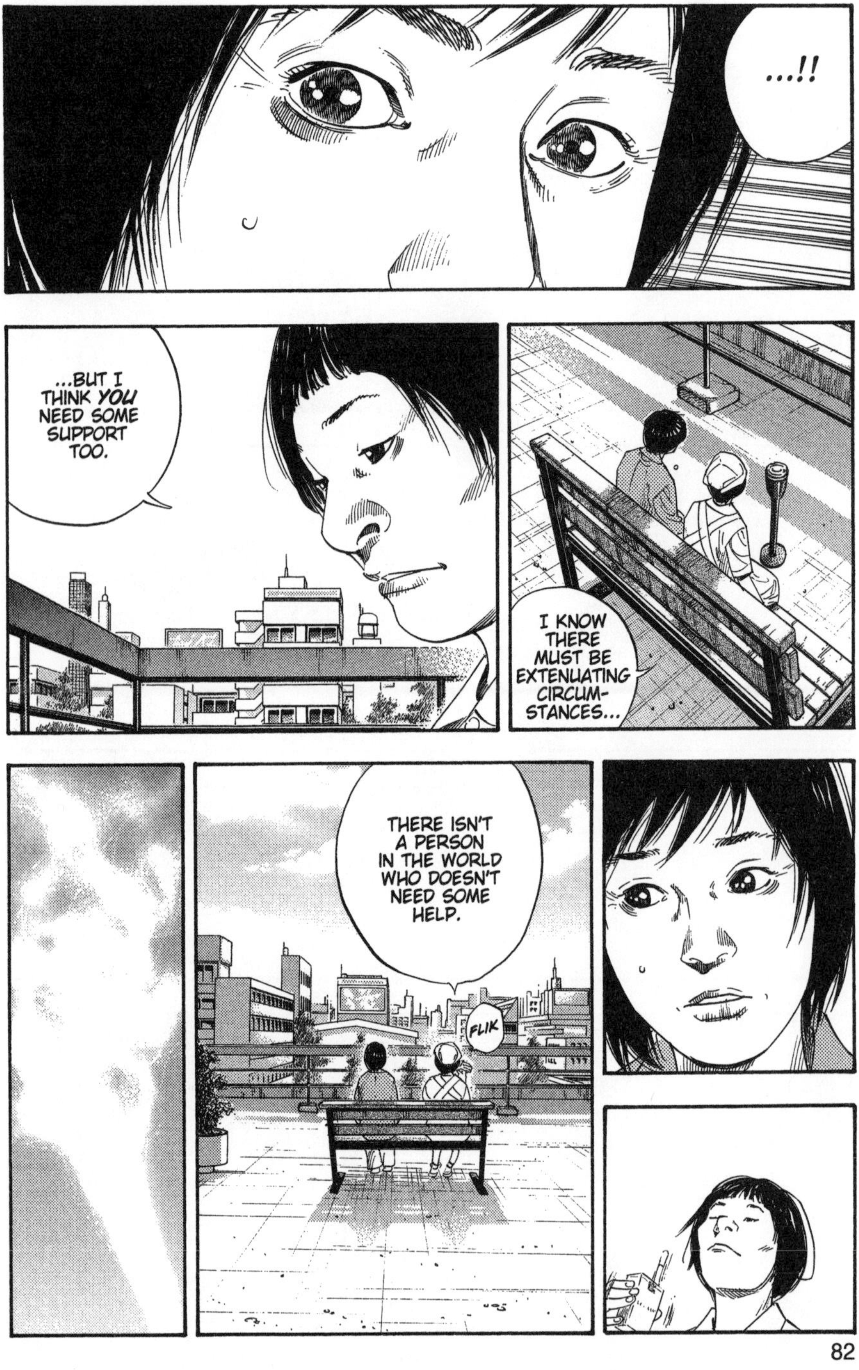
...!!
I KNOW THERE MUST BE EXTENUATING CIRCUM-STANCES...
...BUT I THINK *YOU* NEED SOME SUPPORT TOO.
THERE ISN'T A PERSON IN THE WORLD WHO DOESN'T NEED SOME HELP.
FLIK

HA HA HA HA!
WHAT'RE YOU TALKING ABOUT?!
THAT'S *YOU!*
NO WAY!
KEEP IT DOWN, YOU GUYS. THIS IS A HOSPITAL!
YOU'RE LOUDER THAN US!
HA HA!
...
WE MUST REALLY SUCK TO LOSE TO MIHARA!
THAT'S 'CAUSE FURUTA CAN'T SINK A THING!
SHUT UP!!

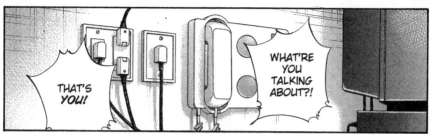

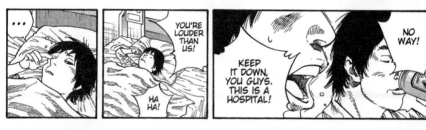

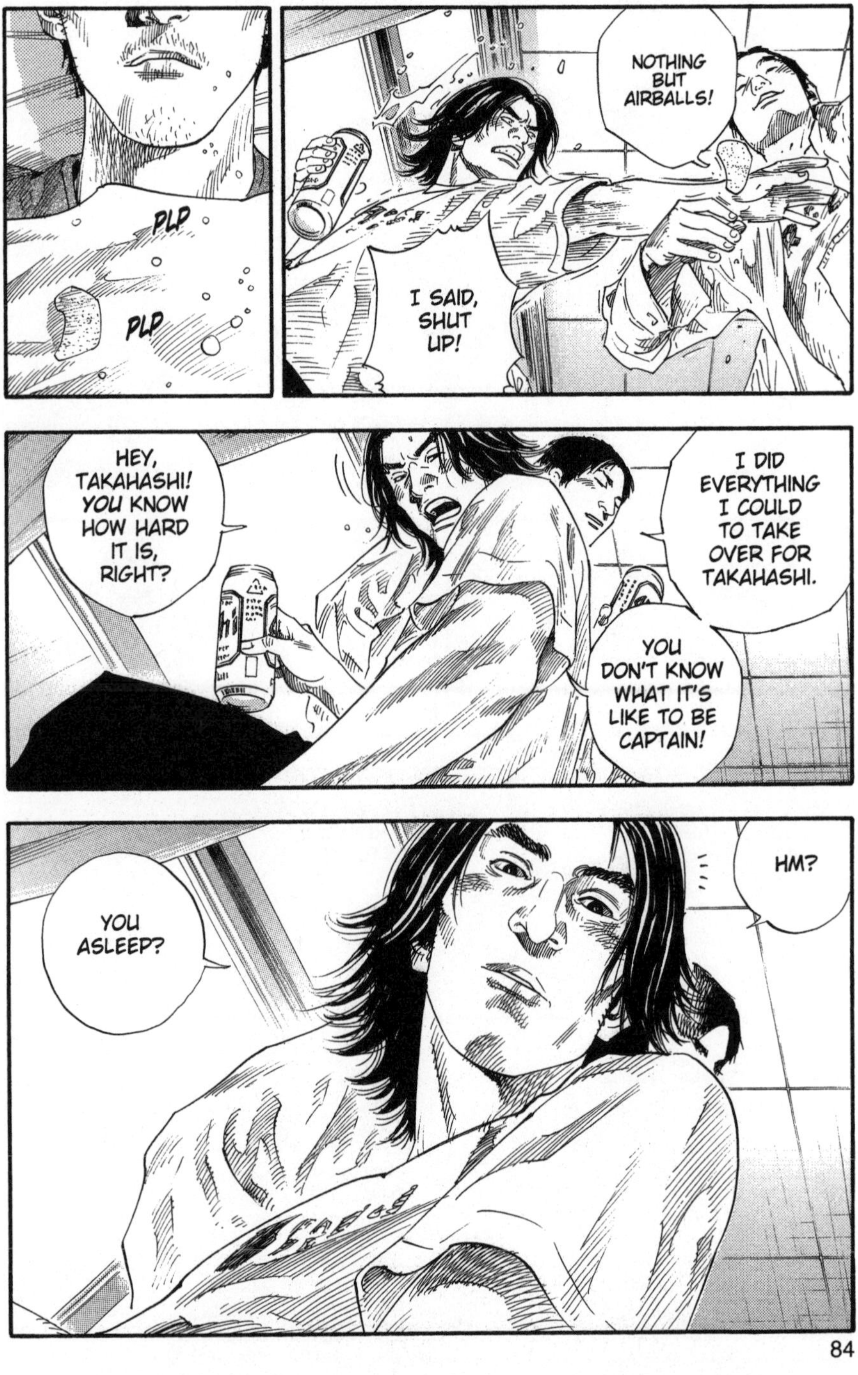
NOTHING BUT AIRBALLS!
I SAID, SHUT UP!
PLP
PLP
I DID EVERYTHING I COULD TO TAKE OVER FOR TAKAHASHI.
YOU DON'T KNOW WHAT IT'S LIKE TO BE CAPTAIN!
HEY, TAKAHASHI! YOU KNOW HOW HARD IT IS, RIGHT?
HM?
YOU ASLEEP?

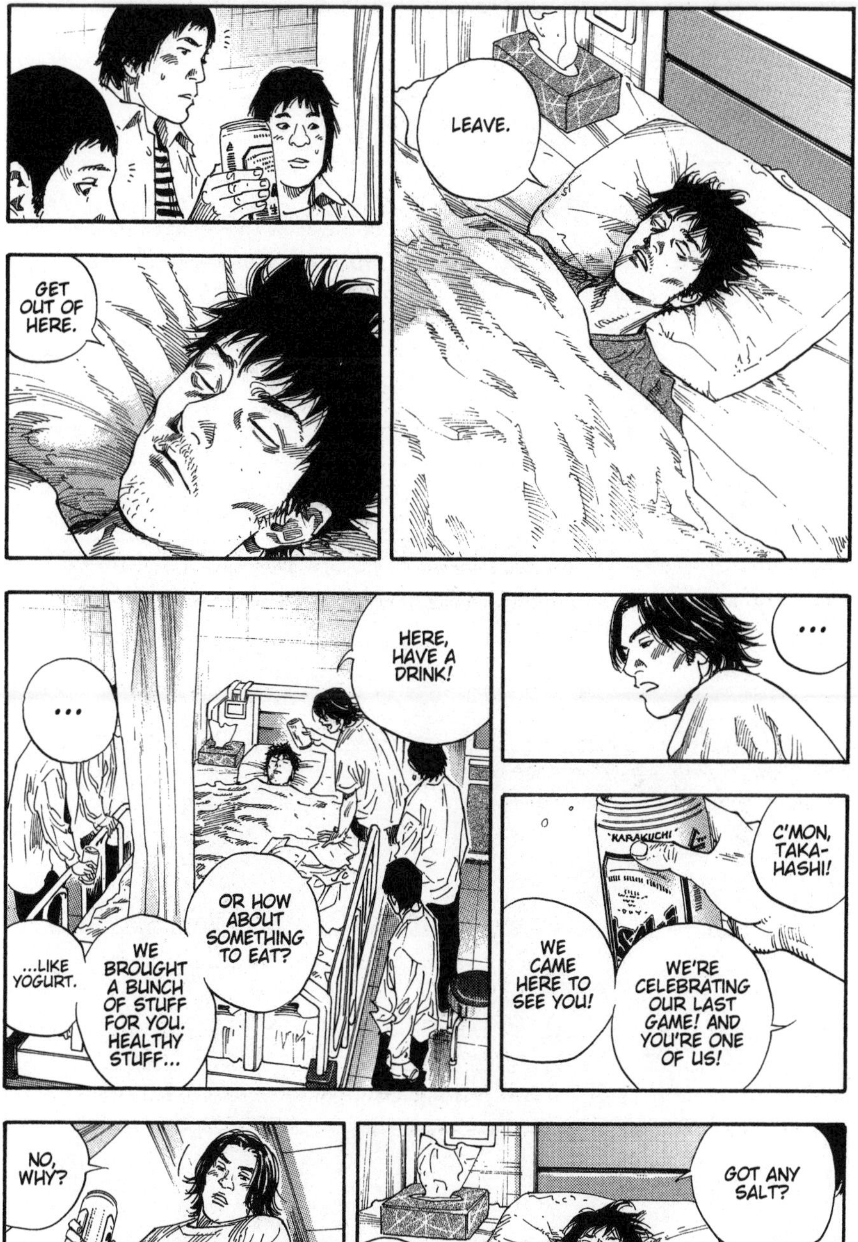
LEAVE.
GET OUT OF HERE.
...
C'MON, TAKA-HASHI!
WE'RE CELEBRATING OUR LAST GAME! AND YOU'RE ONE OF US!
WE CAME HERE TO SEE YOU!
HERE, HAVE A DRINK!
...
OR HOW ABOUT SOMETHING TO EAT?
WE BROUGHT A BUNCH OF STUFF FOR YOU. HEALTHY STUFF...
...LIKE YOGURT.
GOT ANY SALT?
SALT?
NO, WHY?

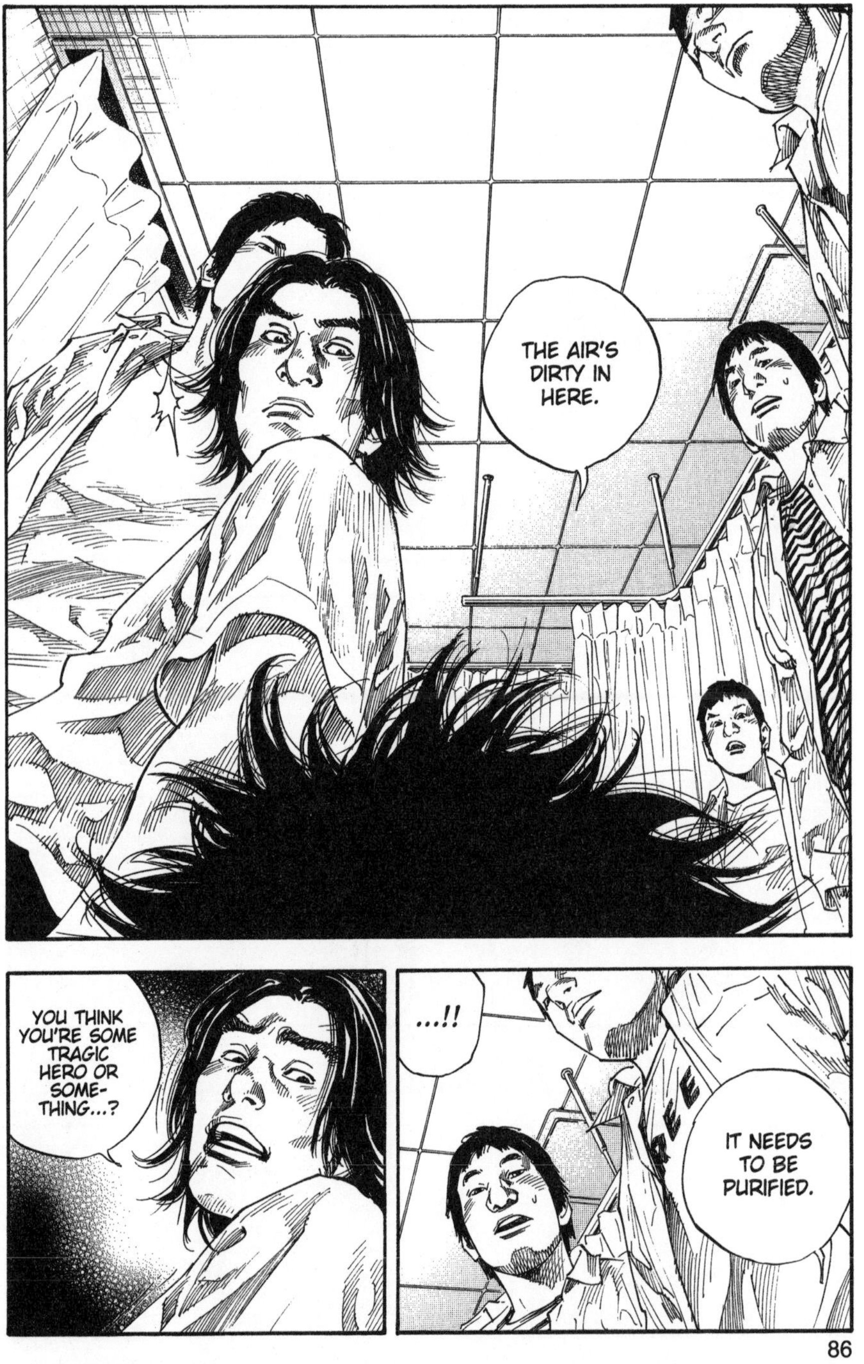
THE AIR'S DIRTY IN HERE.
IT NEEDS TO BE PURIFIED.
...!!
YOU THINK YOU'RE SOME TRAGIC HERO OR SOME-THING...?

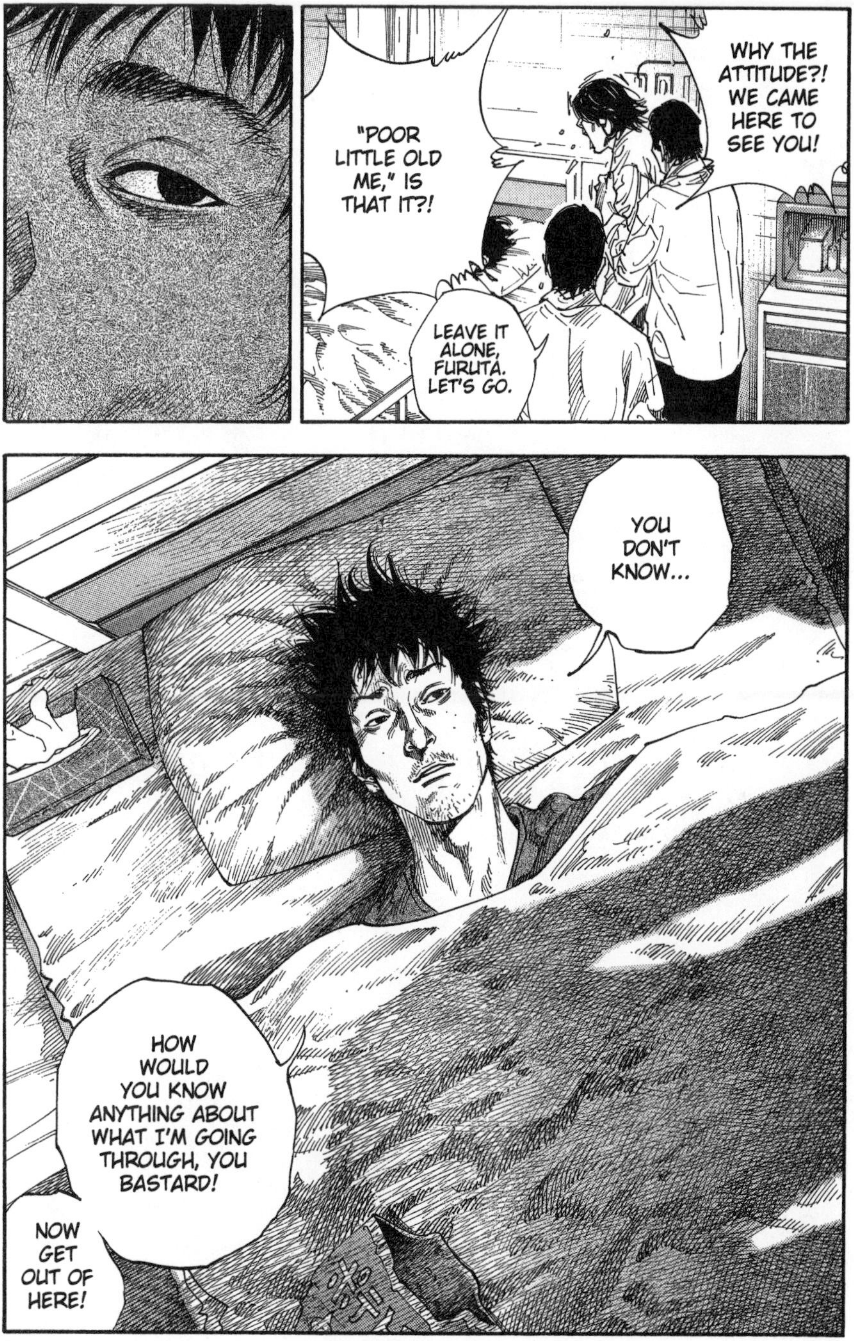
WHY THE ATTITUDE?! WE CAME HERE TO SEE YOU!
"POOR LITTLE OLD ME," IS THAT IT?!
LEAVE IT ALONE, FURUTA. LET'S GO.
YOU DON'T KNOW...
HOW WOULD YOU KNOW ANYTHING ABOUT WHAT I'M GOING THROUGH, YOU BASTARD!
NOW GET OUT OF HERE!

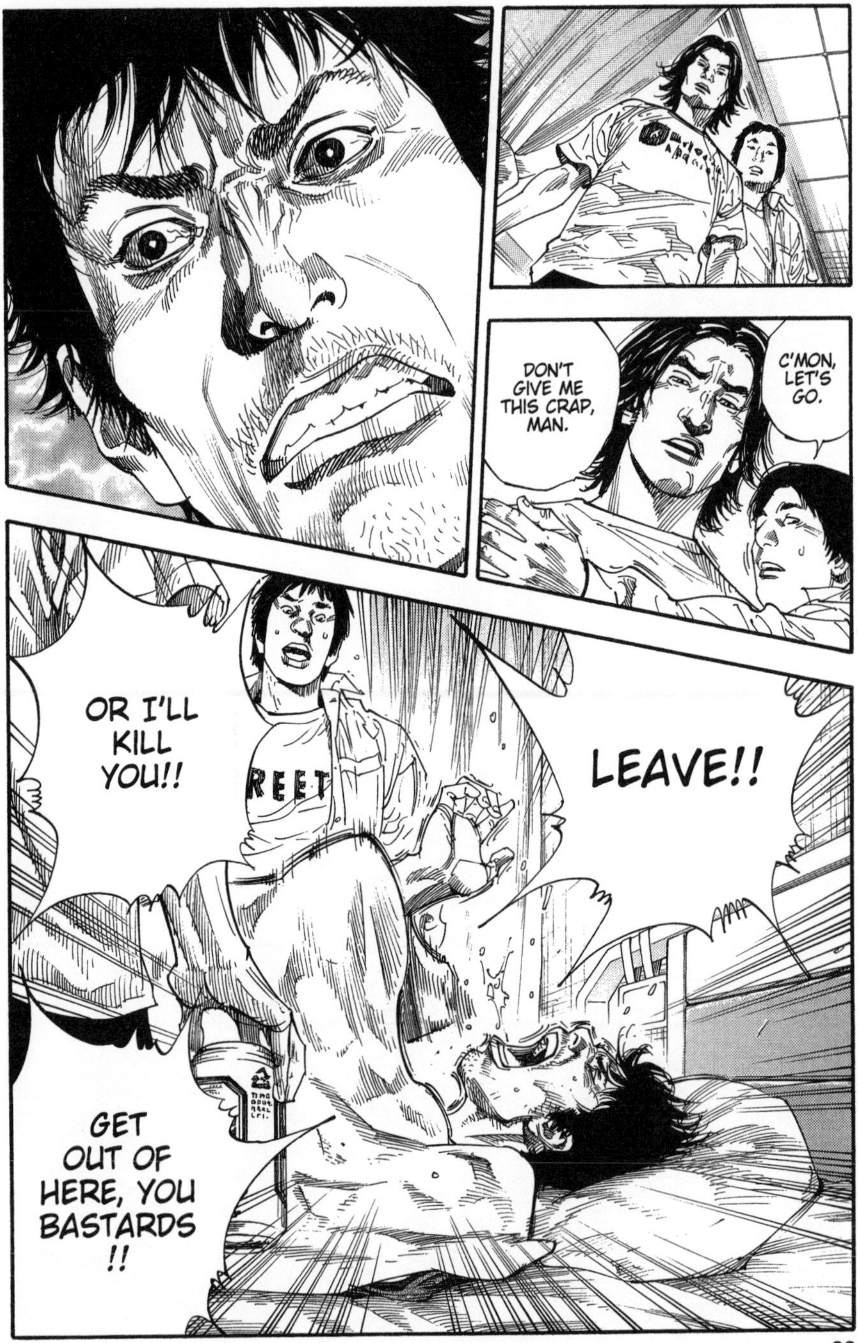
C'MON, LET'S GO.
DON'T GIVE ME THIS CRAP, MAN.
LEAVE!!
OR I'LL KILL YOU!!
GET OUT OF HERE, YOU BASTARDS !!

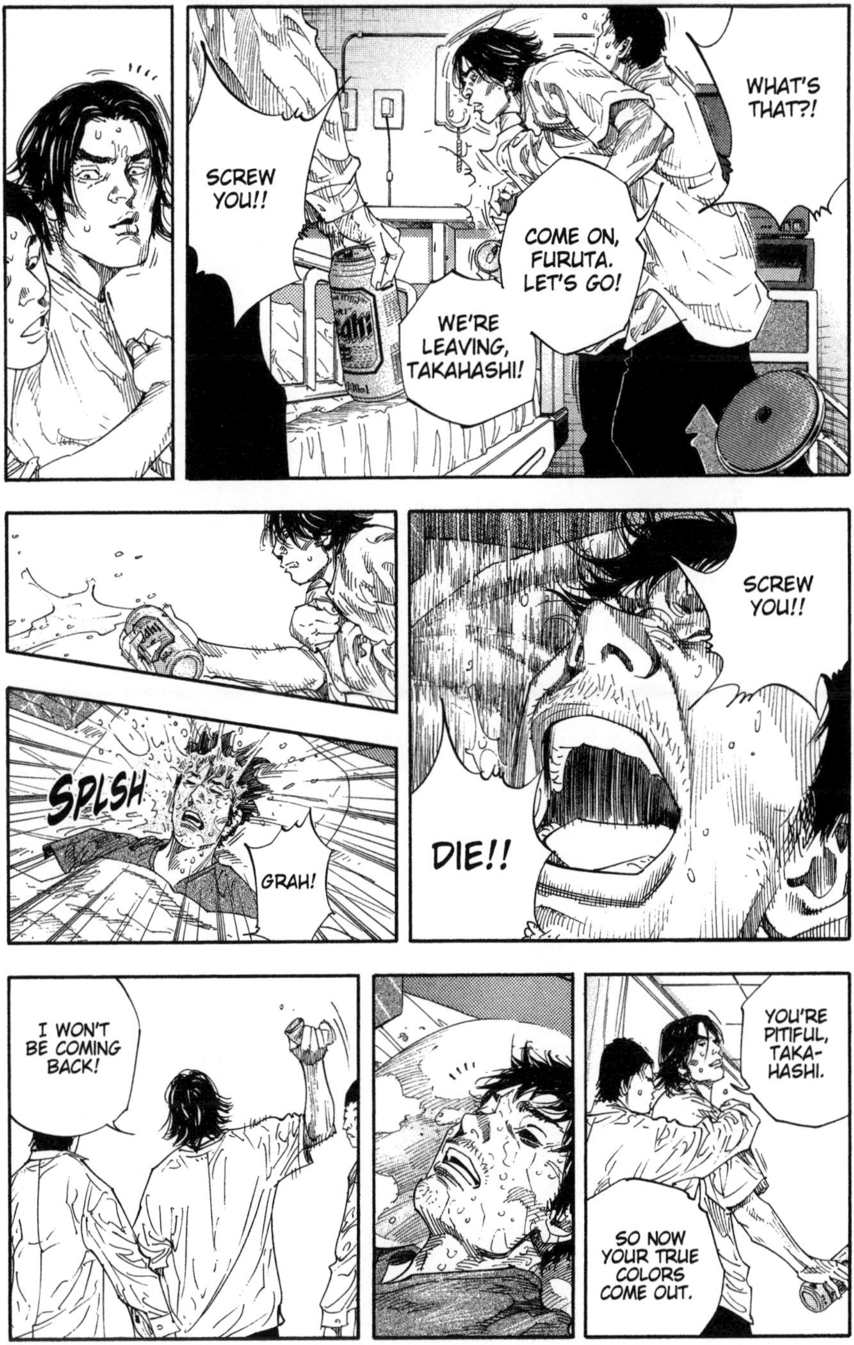
WHAT'S THAT?!
COME ON, FURUTA. LET'S GO!
WE'RE LEAVING, TAKAHASHI!
SCREW YOU!!
SCREW YOU!!
DIE!!
SPLSH
GRAH!
YOU'RE PITIFUL, TAKA-HASHI.
SO NOW YOUR TRUE COLORS COME OUT.
I WON'T BE COMING BACK!

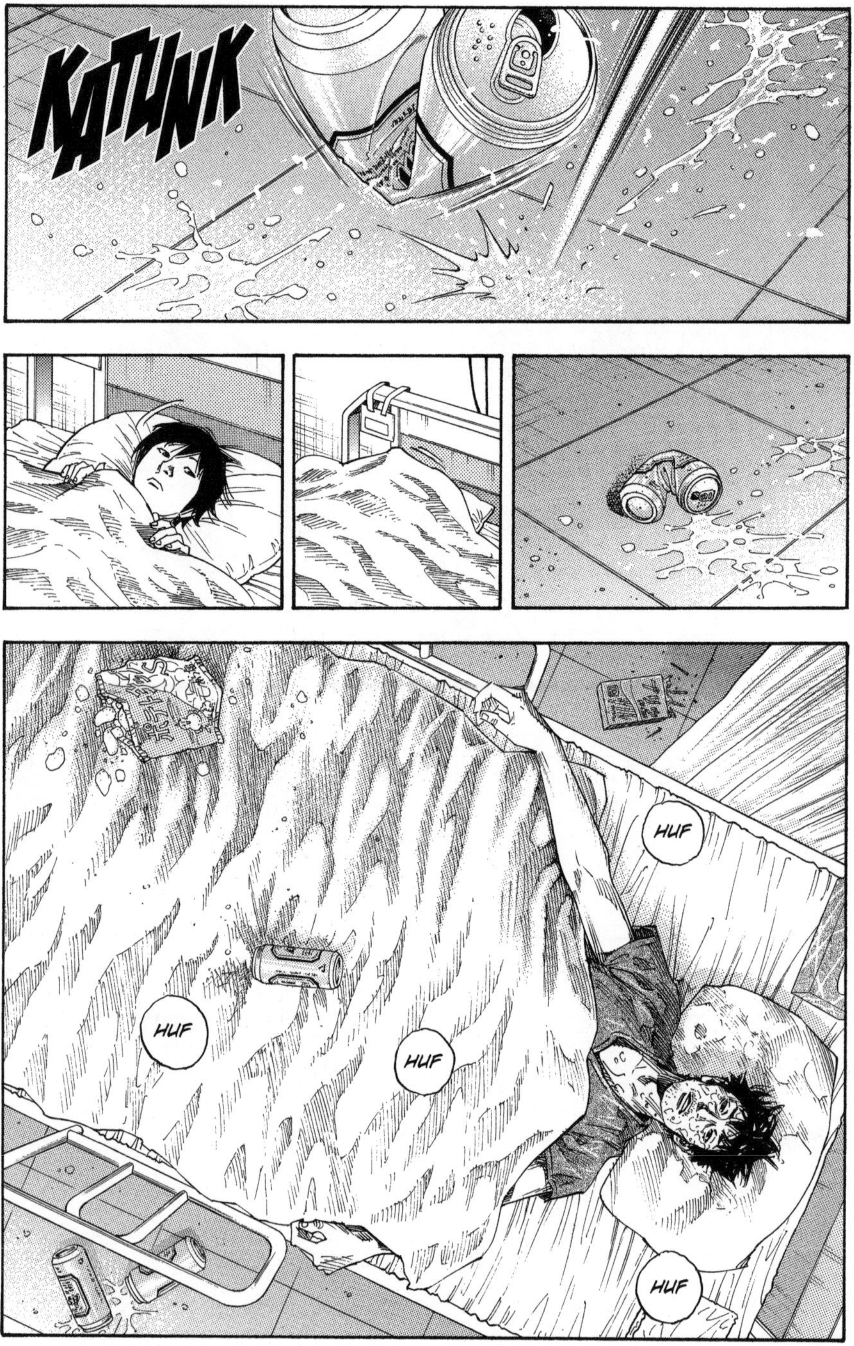
KATUNK
HUF
HUF
HUF
HUF

FMP
WIPE WIPE

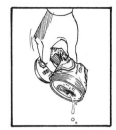

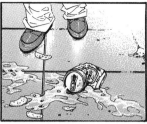

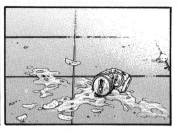

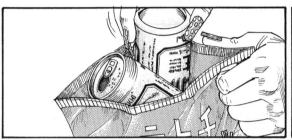

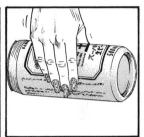

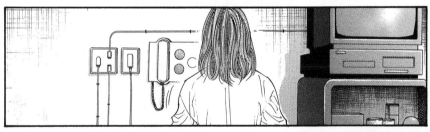

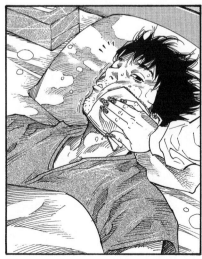

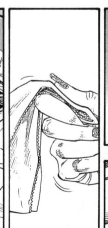

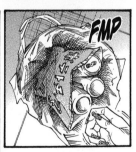

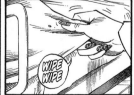

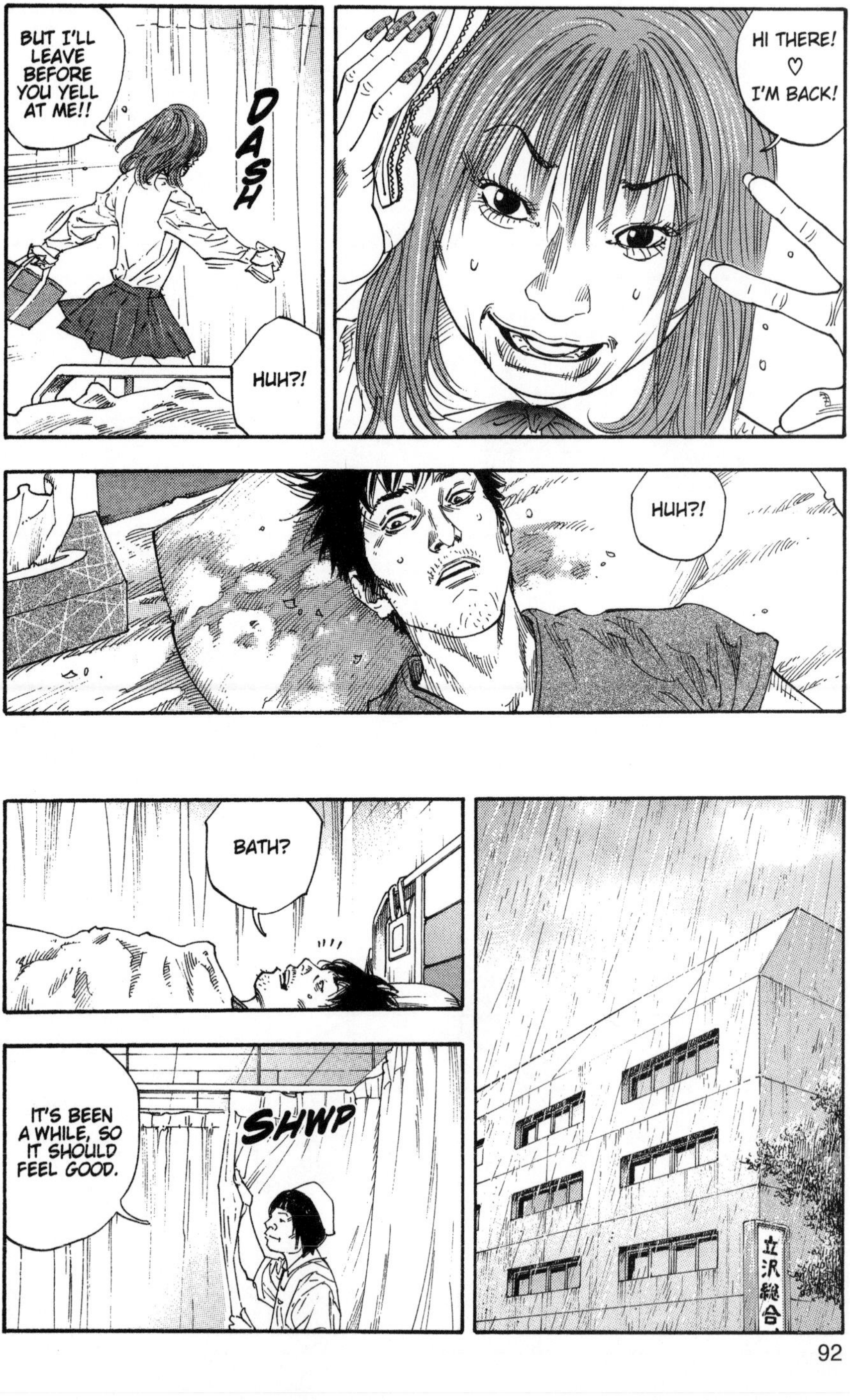
HI THERE! ♡ I'M BACK!
BUT I'LL LEAVE BEFORE YOU YELL AT ME!!
DASH
HUH?!
HUH?!
立沢総合
BATH?
SHWP
IT'S BEEN A WHILE, SO IT SHOULD FEEL GOOD.

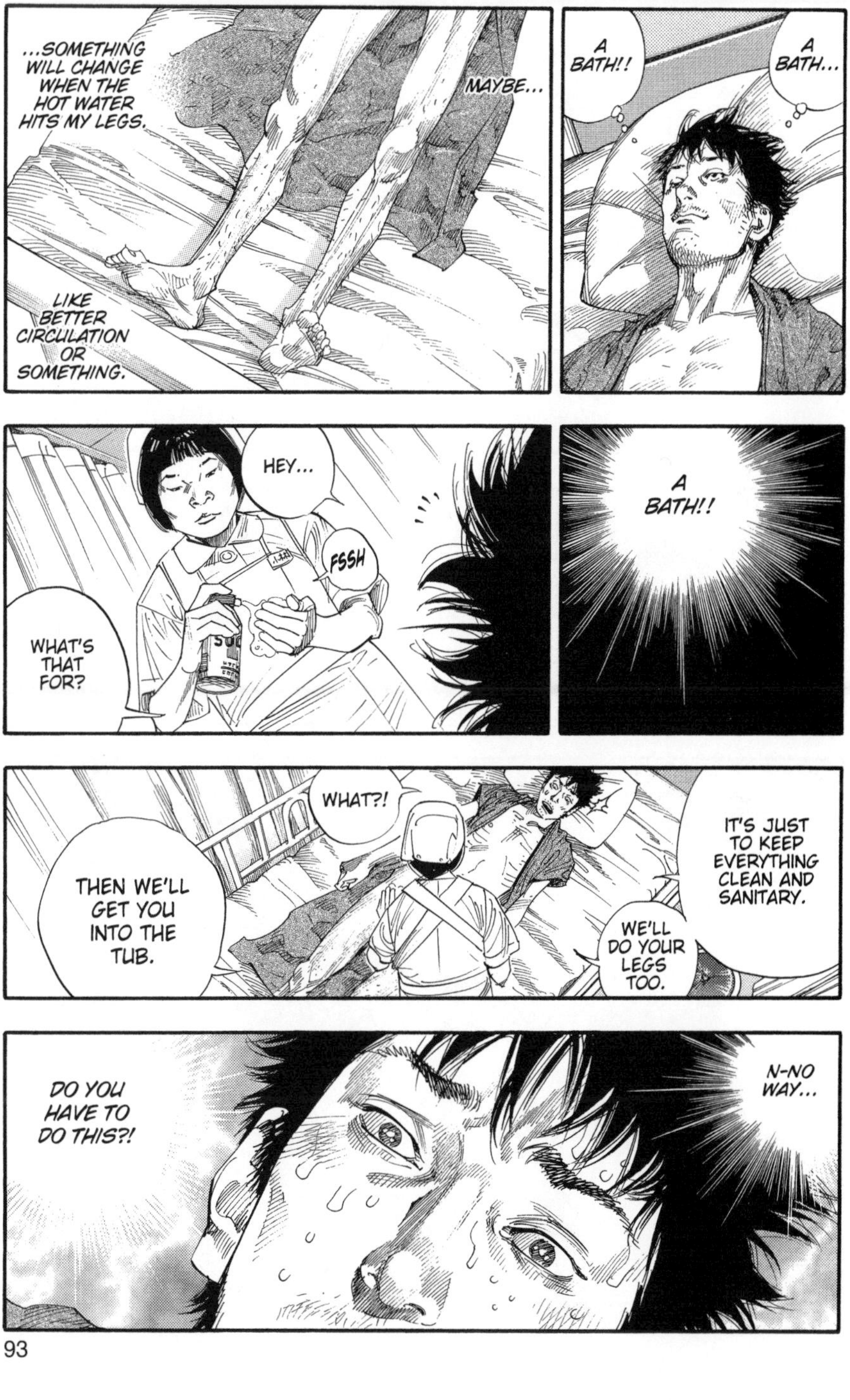
A BATH...
A BATH!!
MAYBE...
...SOMETHING WILL CHANGE WHEN THE HOT WATER HITS MY LEGS.
LIKE BETTER CIRCULATION OR SOMETHING.
A BATH!!
HEY...
FSSH
WHAT'S THAT FOR?
IT'S JUST TO KEEP EVERYTHING CLEAN AND SANITARY.
WE'LL DO YOUR LEGS TOO.
WHAT?!
THEN WE'LL GET YOU INTO THE TUB.
N-NO WAY...
DO YOU HAVE TO DO THIS?!

RATTA

RATTA

THEY DID IT...

RATTA

RATTA

RATTA

RATTA

RATTA

EVERY-THING SET?

RATTA

RATTA

CUTE NURSE NAKAMURA'S GONNA WASH ME?!

GASP!

ALL READY!

OKAY, LET'S GET YOU CLEANED UP!!

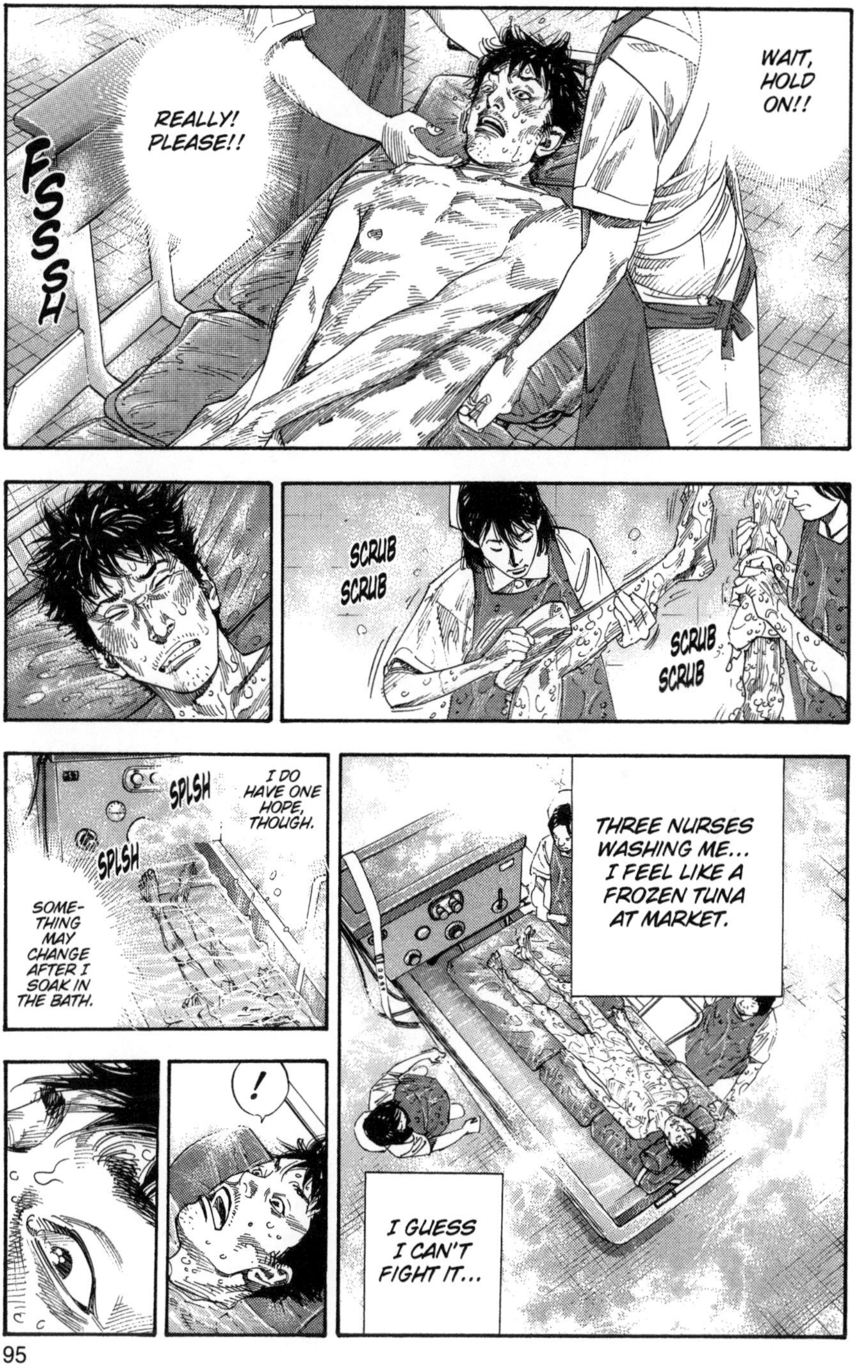
WAIT, HOLD ON!!
REALLY! PLEASE!!
FSSSH
SCRUB SCRUB
SCRUB SCRUB
THREE NURSES WASHING ME... I FEEL LIKE A FROZEN TUNA AT MARKET.
I GUESS I CAN'T FIGHT IT...
SPLSH
I DO HAVE ONE HOPE, THOUGH.
SPLSH
SOME-THING MAY CHANGE AFTER I SOAK IN THE BATH.
!

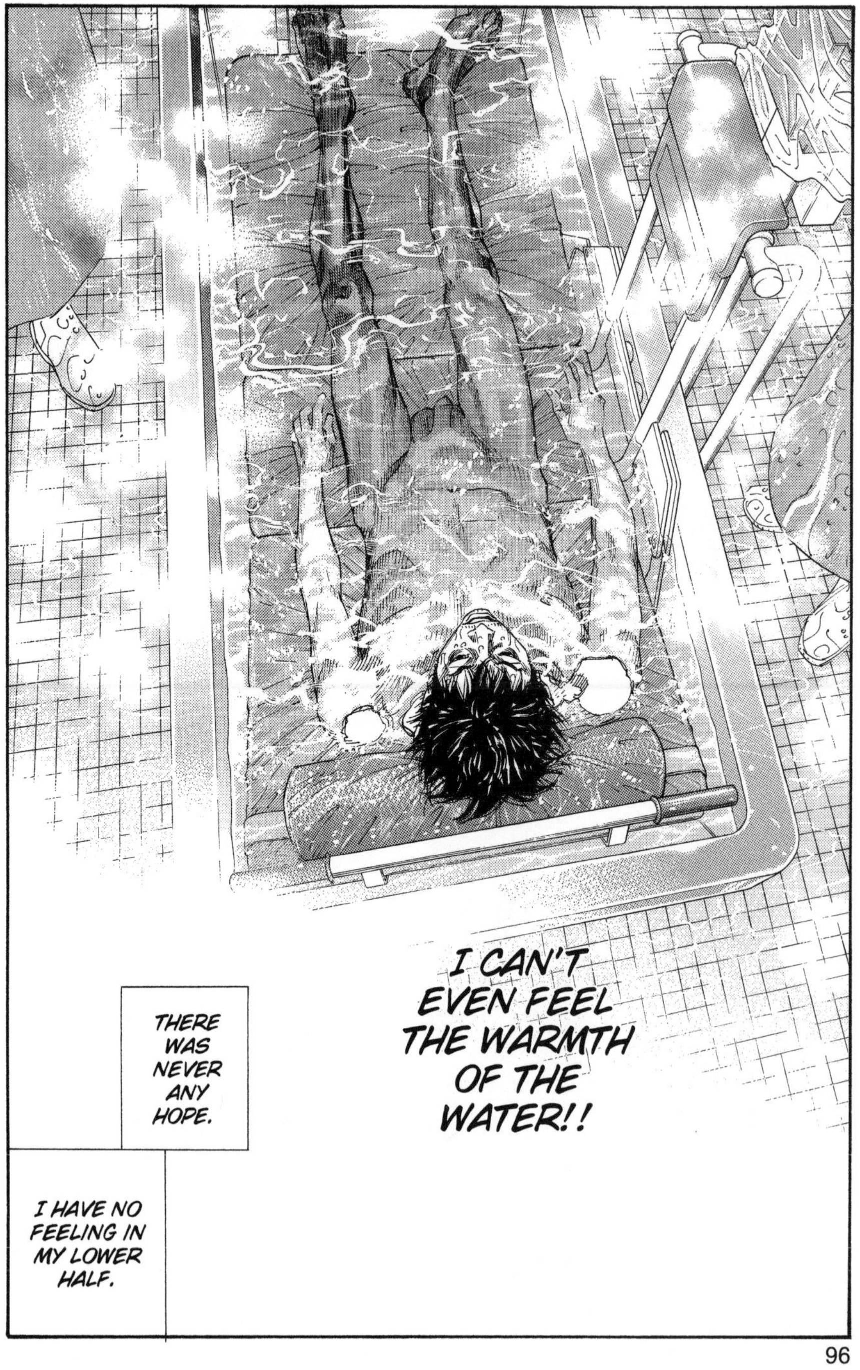
I CAN'T EVEN FEEL THE WARMTH OF THE WATER!!
THERE WAS NEVER ANY HOPE.
I HAVE NO FEELING IN MY LOWER HALF.

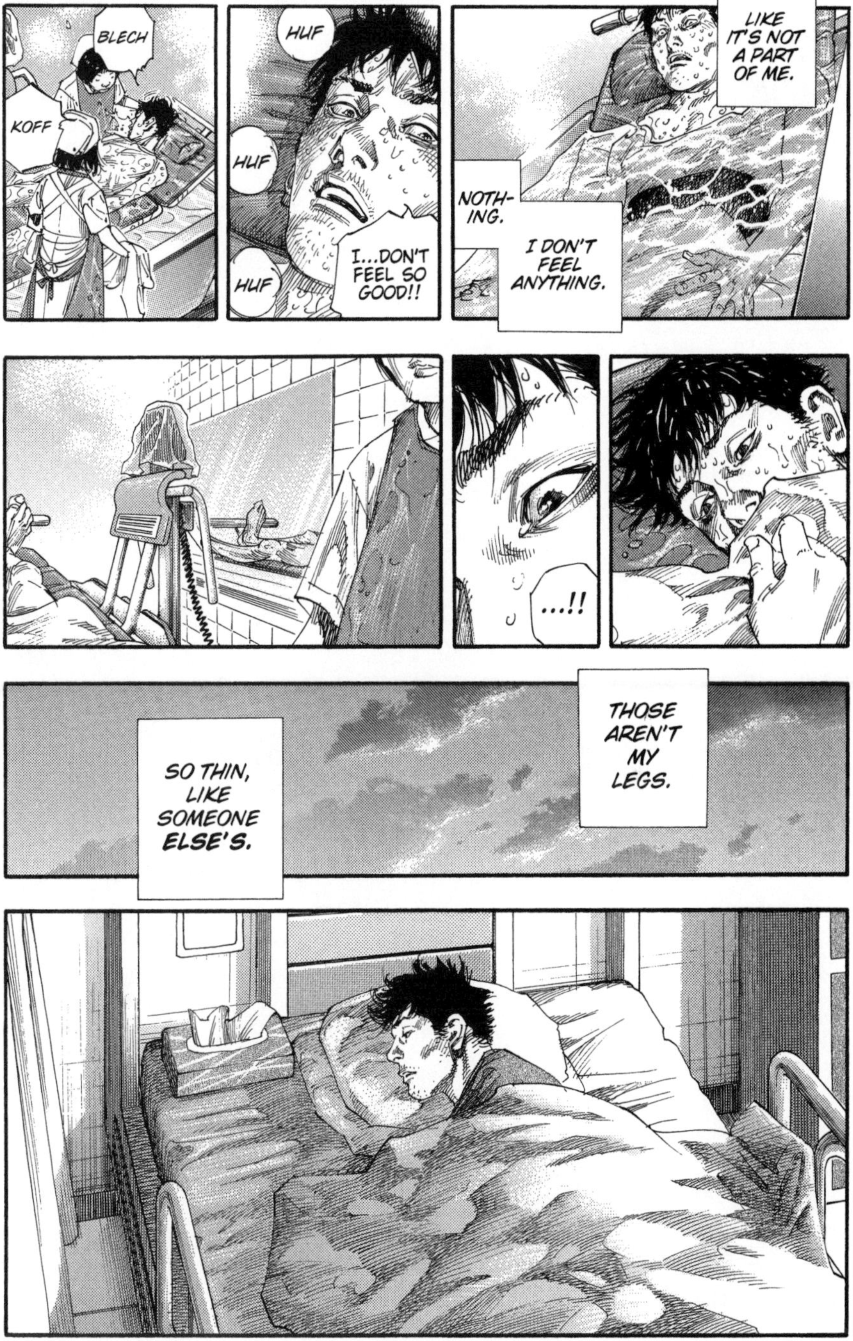
LIKE IT'S NOT A PART OF ME.
NOTH-ING.
I DON'T FEEL ANYTHING.
HUF
HUF
I...DON'T FEEL SO GOOD!!
HUF
BLECH
KOFF
...!!
THOSE AREN'T MY LEGS.
SO THIN, LIKE SOMEONE ELSE'S.

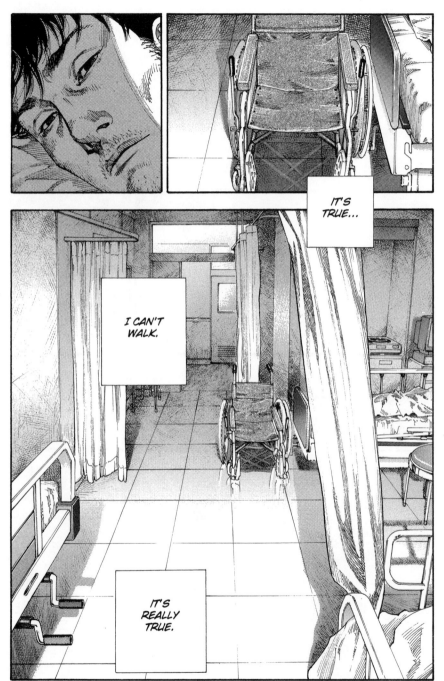

IT'S TRUE...

I CAN'T WALK.

IT'S REALLY TRUE.

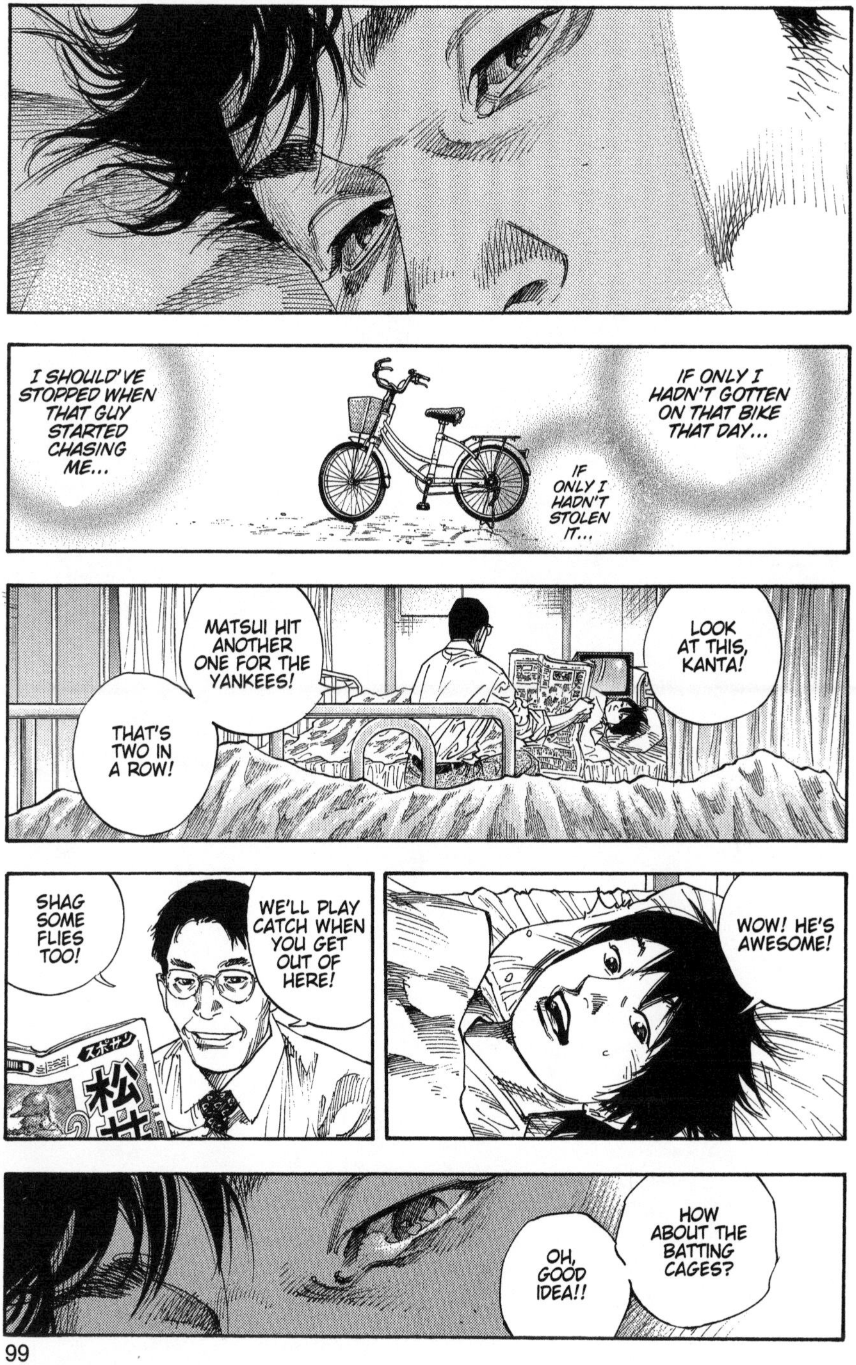
IF ONLY I HADN'T GOTTEN ON THAT BIKE THAT DAY...
IF ONLY I HADN'T STOLEN IT...
I SHOULD'VE STOPPED WHEN THAT GUY STARTED CHASING ME...
LOOK AT THIS, KANTA!
MATSUI HIT ANOTHER ONE FOR THE YANKEES!
THAT'S TWO IN A ROW!
WOW! HE'S AWESOME!
WE'LL PLAY CATCH WHEN YOU GET OUT OF HERE!
SHAG SOME FLIES TOO!
HOW ABOUT THE BATTING CAGES?
OH, GOOD IDEA!!

WHY
DID THIS
HAPPEN
TO ME...?

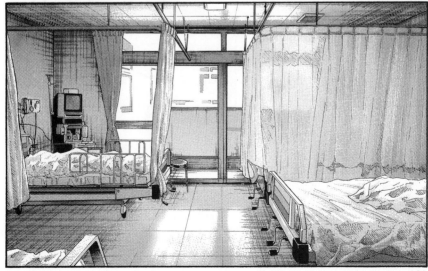

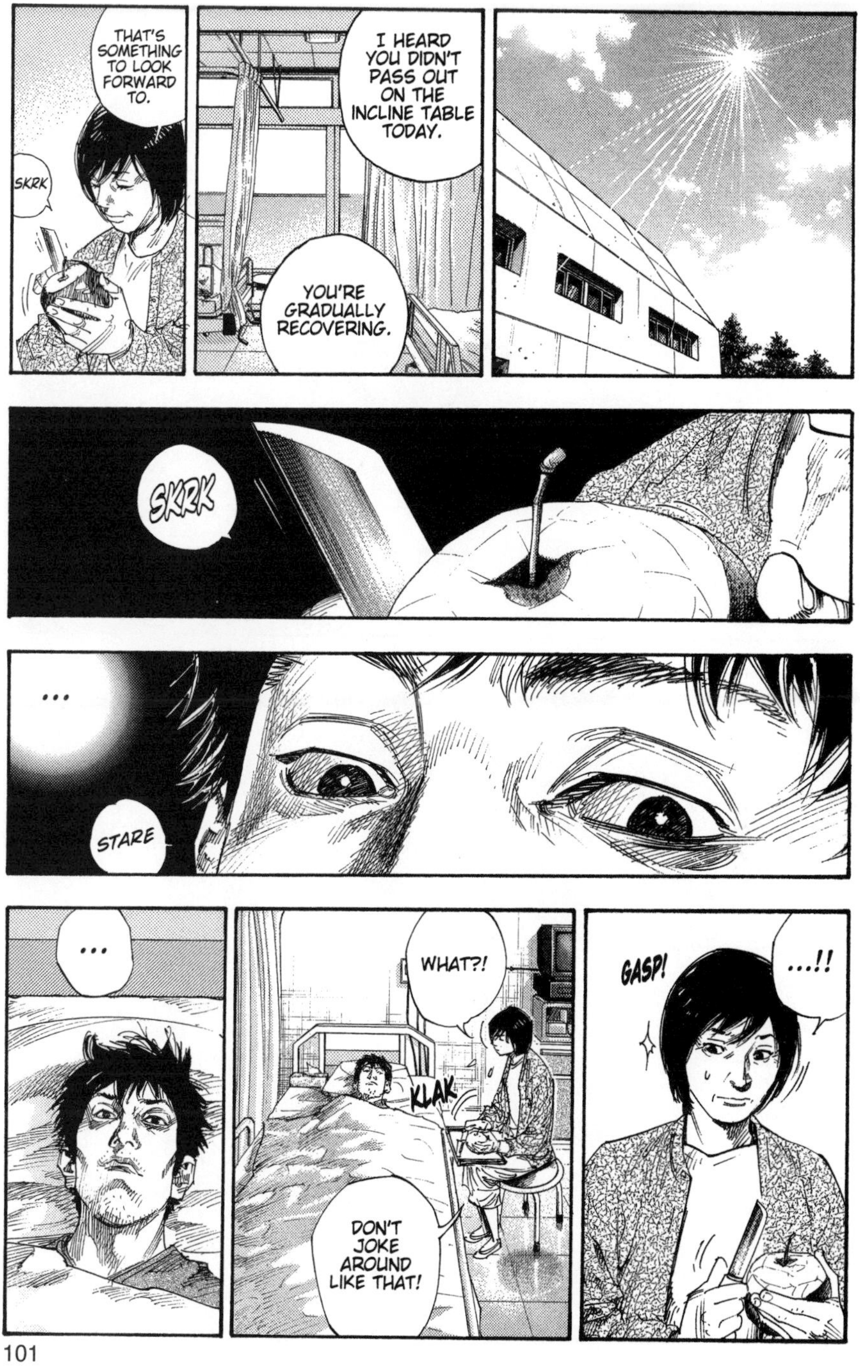
I HEARD YOU DIDN'T PASS OUT ON THE INCLINE TABLE TODAY.
YOU'RE GRADUALLY RECOVERING.
THAT'S SOMETHING TO LOOK FORWARD TO.
SKRK
SKRK
...
STARE
...!!
GASP!
WHAT?!
KLAK
DON'T JOKE AROUND LIKE THAT!
...

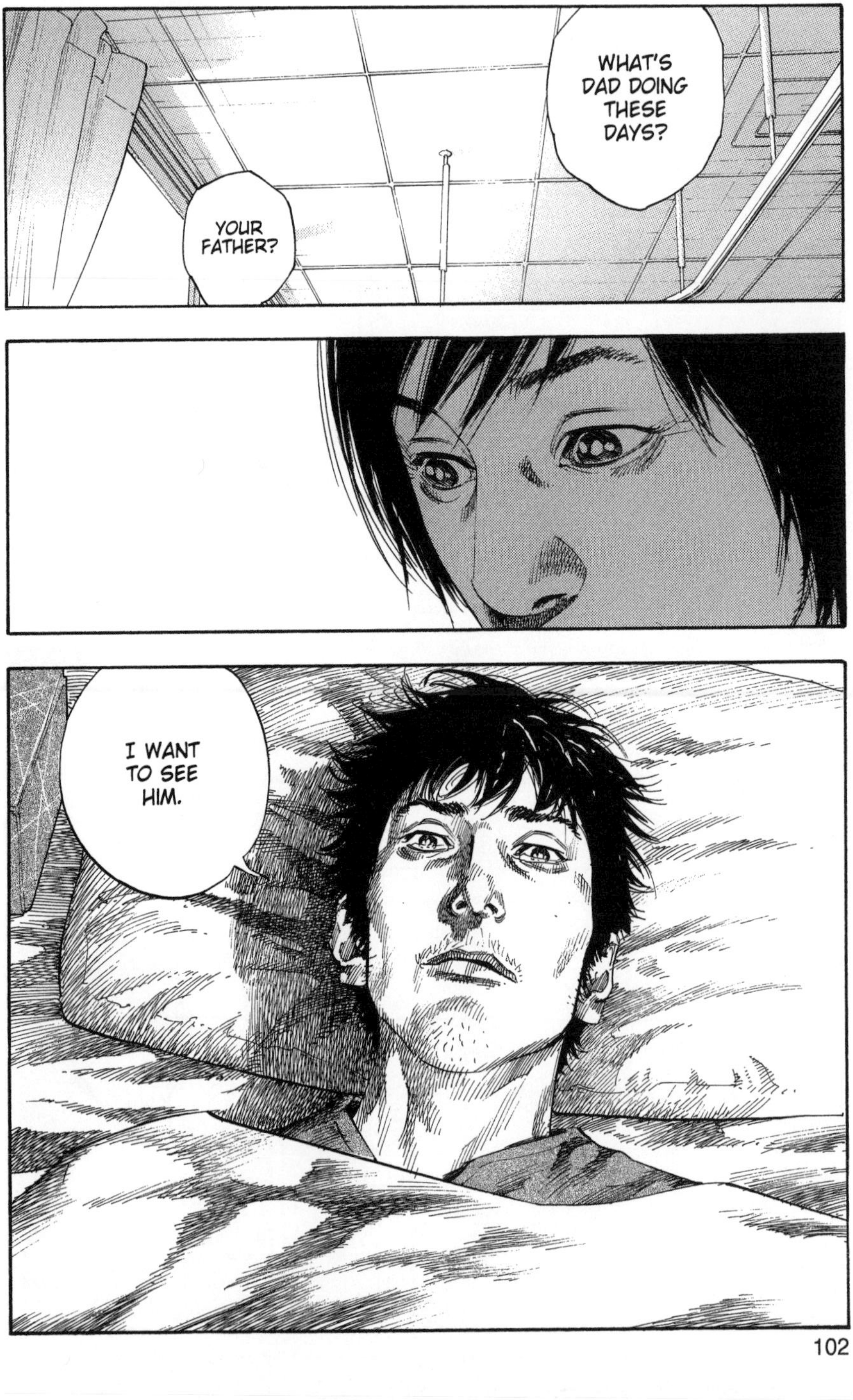
WHAT'S DAD DOING THESE DAYS?
YOUR FATHER?
I WANT TO SEE HIM.

REAL

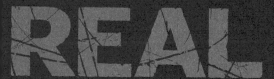

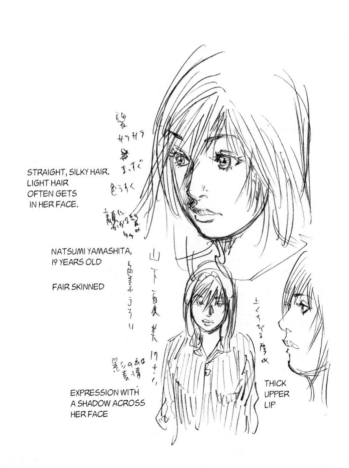

STRAIGHT, SILKY HAIR.
LIGHT HAIR
OFTEN GETS
IN HER FACE.

NATSUMI YAMASHITA,
19 YEARS OLD

FAIR SKINNED

EXPRESSION WITH
A SHADOW ACROSS
HER FACE

THICK
UPPER
LIP

I WANT TO SEE HIM...

*TACHIZAWA GENERAL HOSPITAL

...MY FATHER.

S K O O T

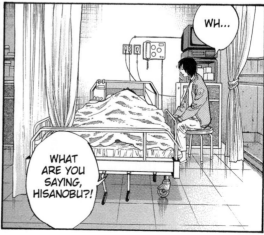

WH...

WHAT ARE YOU SAYING, HISANOBU?!

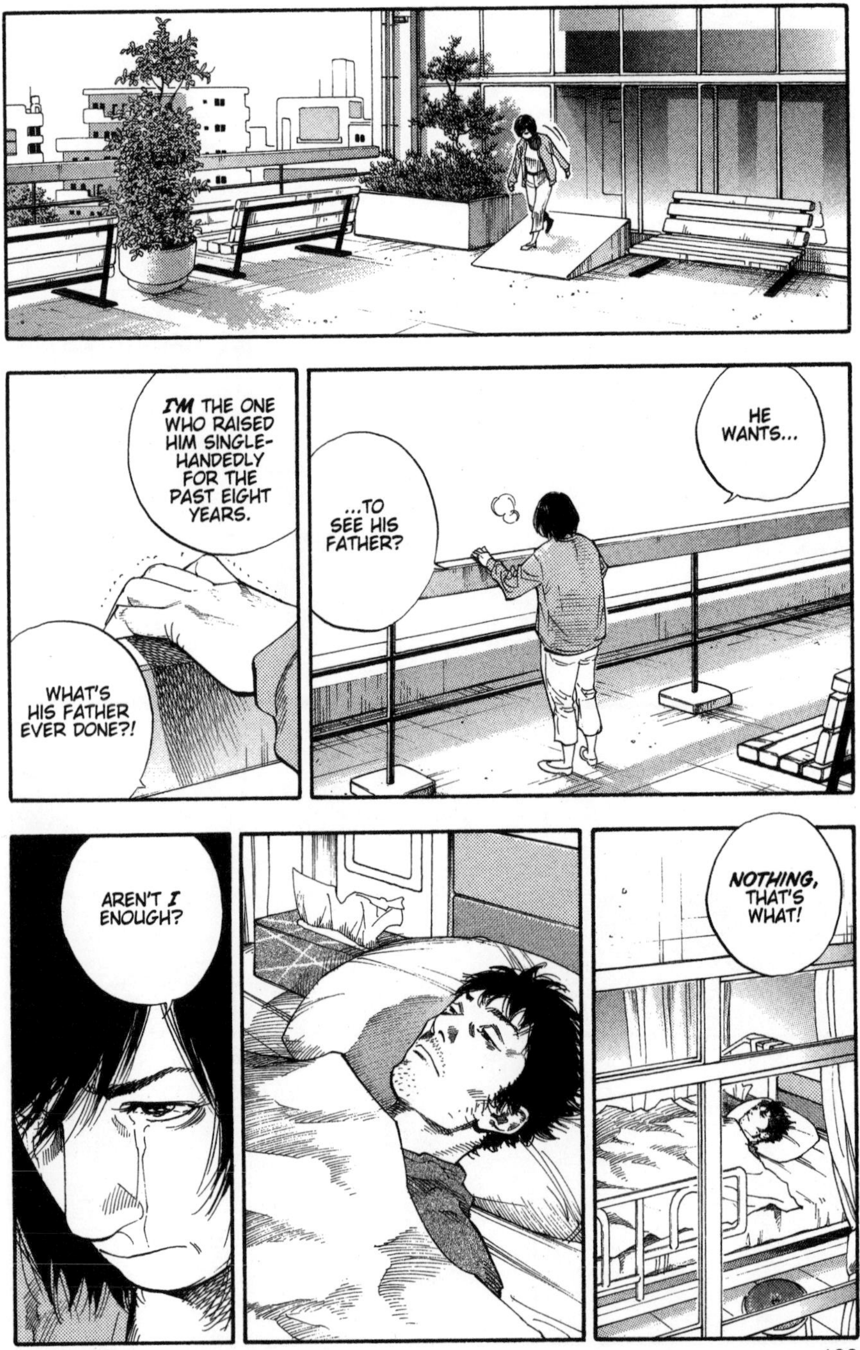
HE WANTS...
...TO SEE HIS FATHER?
I'M THE ONE WHO RAISED HIM SINGLE-HANDEDLY FOR THE PAST EIGHT YEARS.
WHAT'S HIS FATHER EVER DONE?!
NOTHING, THAT'S WHAT!
AREN'T *I* ENOUGH?

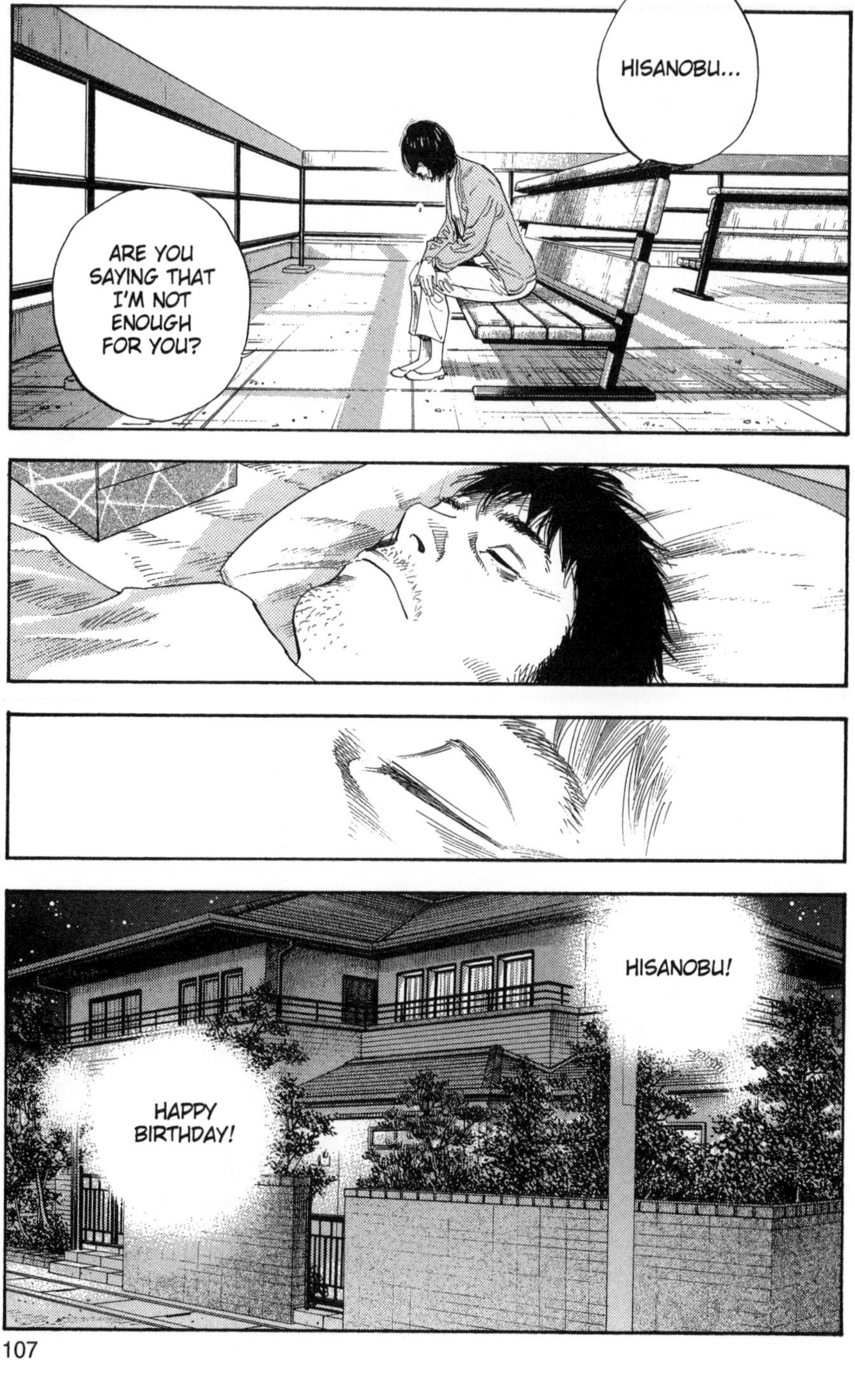
HISANOBU...
ARE YOU SAYING THAT I'M NOT ENOUGH FOR YOU?
HISANOBU!
HAPPY BIRTHDAY!

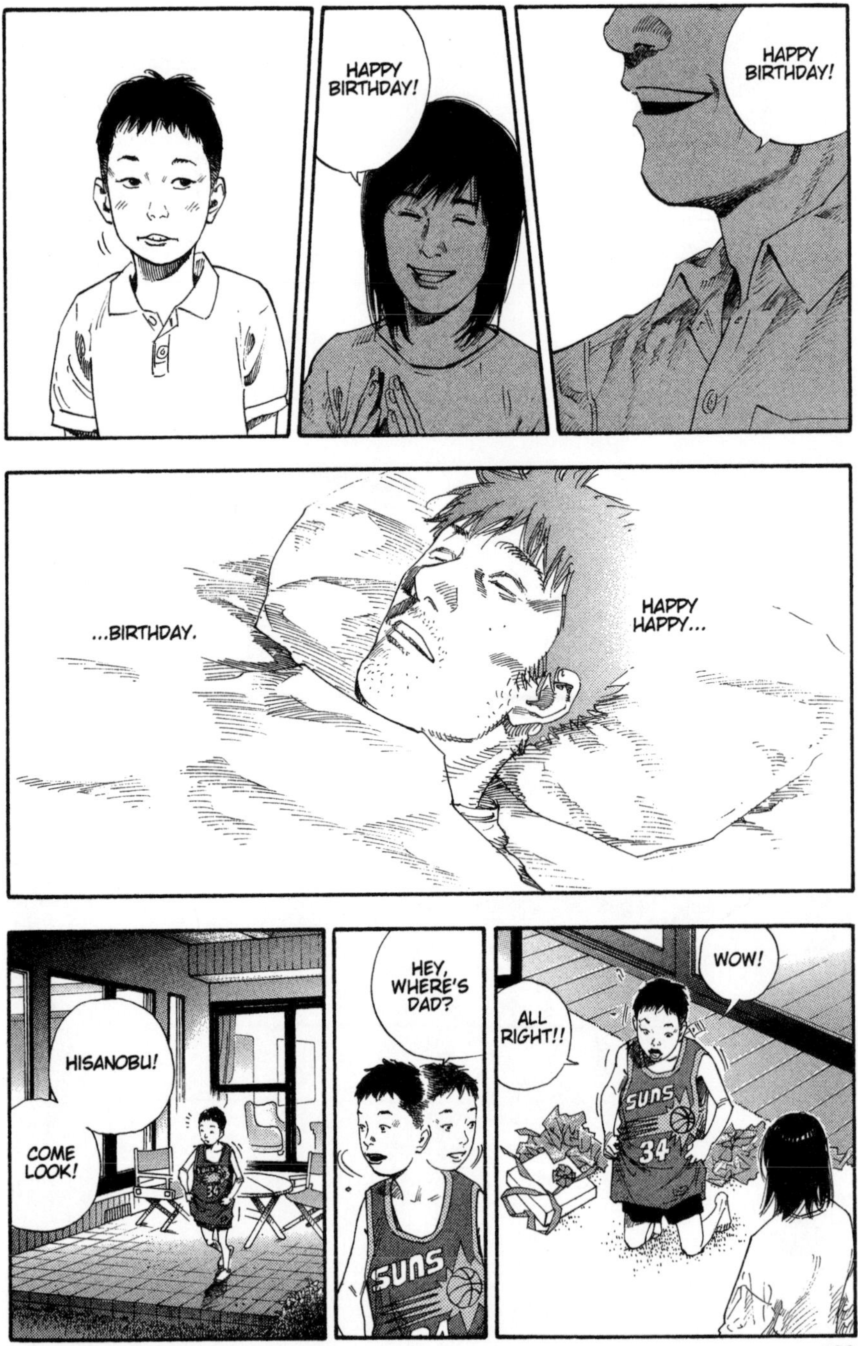
HAPPY BIRTHDAY!
HAPPY BIRTHDAY!
HAPPY HAPPY...
...BIRTHDAY.
WOW!
ALL RIGHT!!
HEY, WHERE'S DAD?
HISANOBU!
COME LOOK!

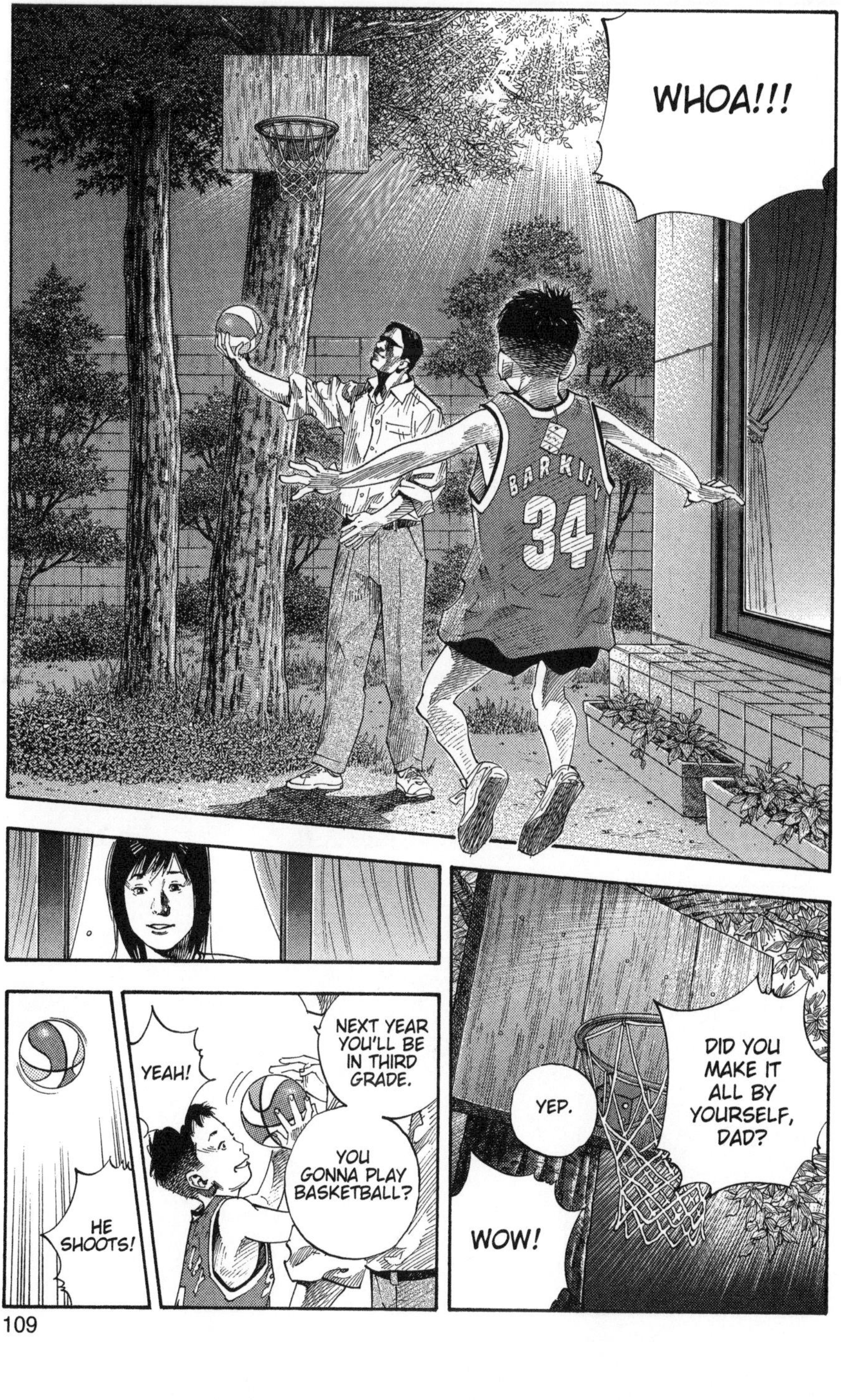
WHOA!!!
DID YOU MAKE IT ALL BY YOURSELF, DAD?
YEP.
WOW!
NEXT YEAR YOU'LL BE IN THIRD GRADE.
YEAH!
YOU GONNA PLAY BASKETBALL?
HE SHOOTS!

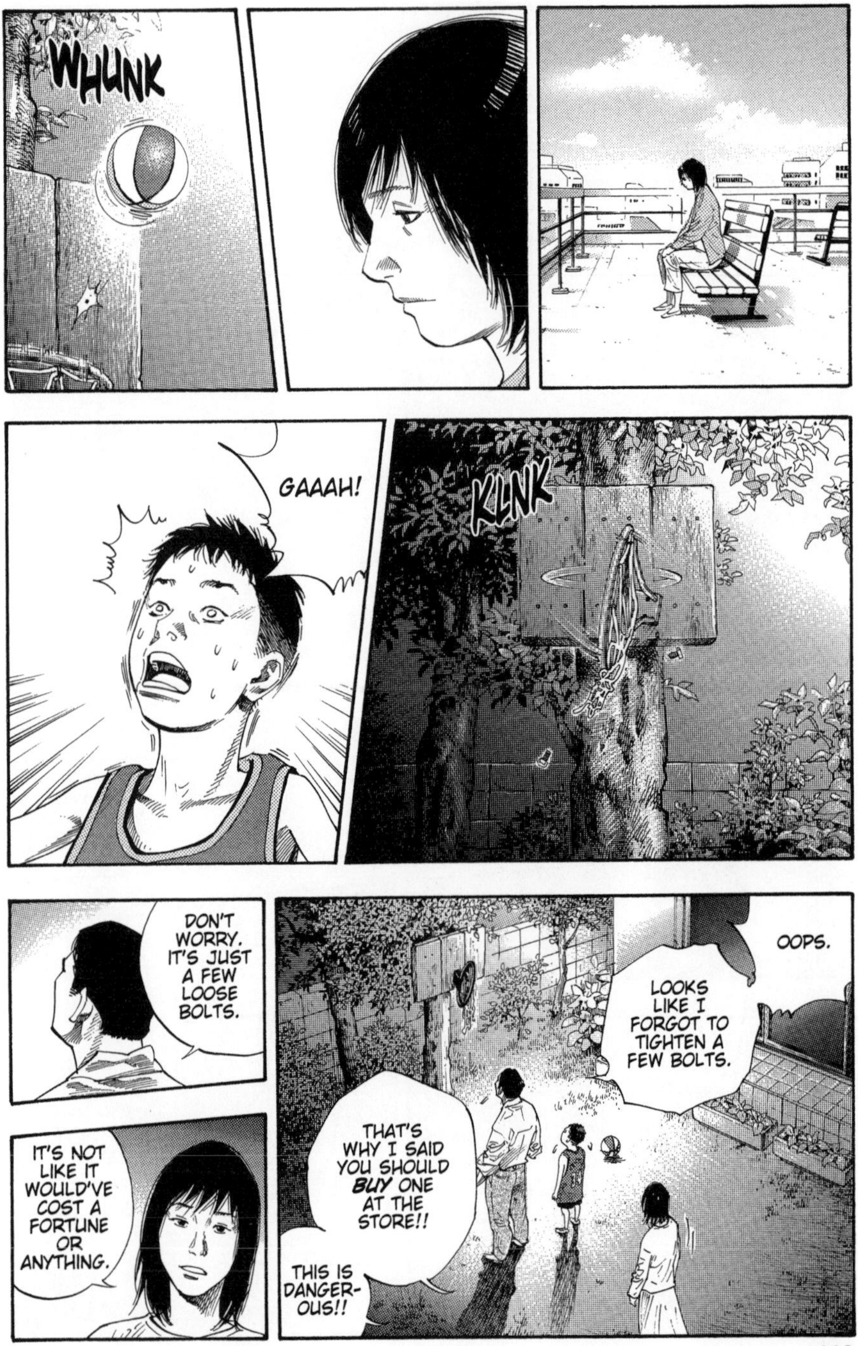
WHUNK
KLNK
GAAAH!
OOPS.
LOOKS LIKE I FORGOT TO TIGHTEN A FEW BOLTS.
THAT'S WHY I SAID YOU SHOULD BUY ONE AT THE STORE!!
THIS IS DANGER-OUS!!
DON'T WORRY. IT'S JUST A FEW LOOSE BOLTS.
IT'S NOT LIKE IT WOULD'VE COST A FORTUNE OR ANYTHING.

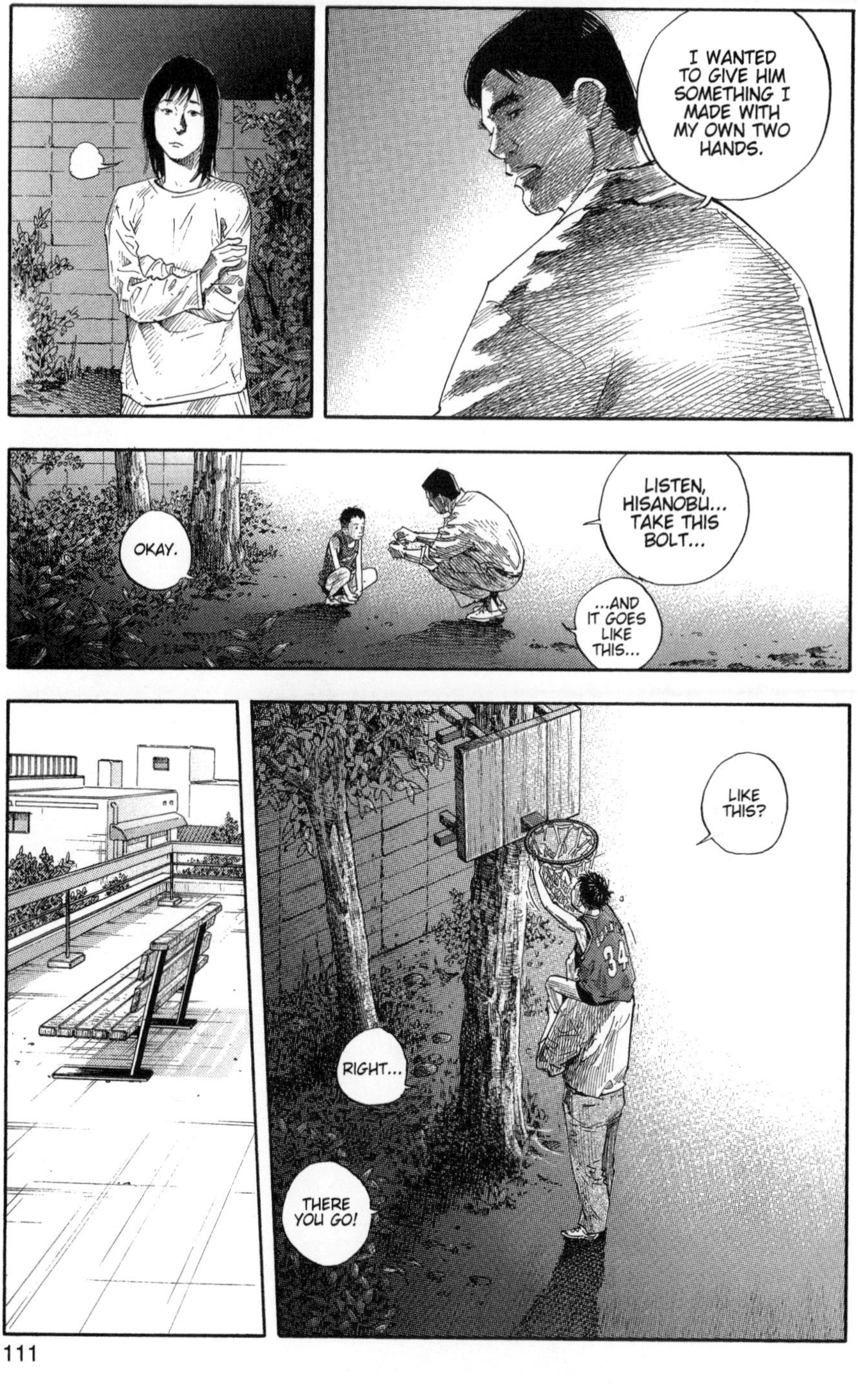
I WANTED TO GIVE HIM SOMETHING I MADE WITH MY OWN TWO HANDS.
LISTEN, HISANOBU... TAKE THIS BOLT...
...AND IT GOES LIKE THIS...
OKAY.
LIKE THIS?
RIGHT...
THERE YOU GO!

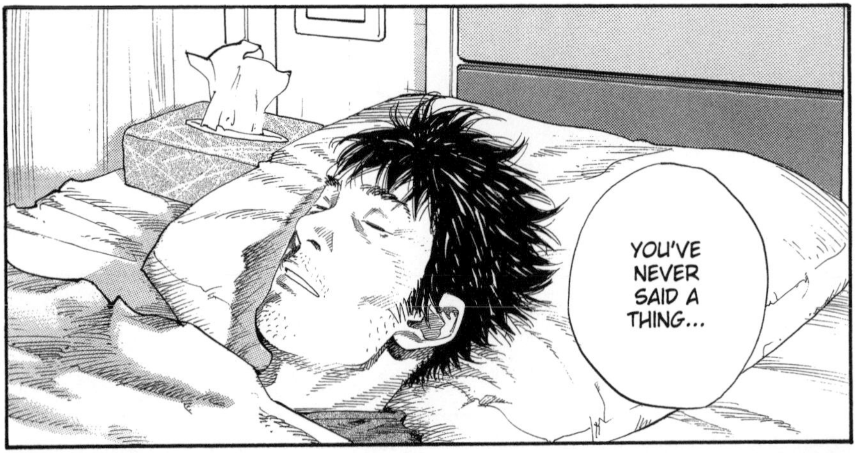
YOU'VE NEVER SAID A THING...
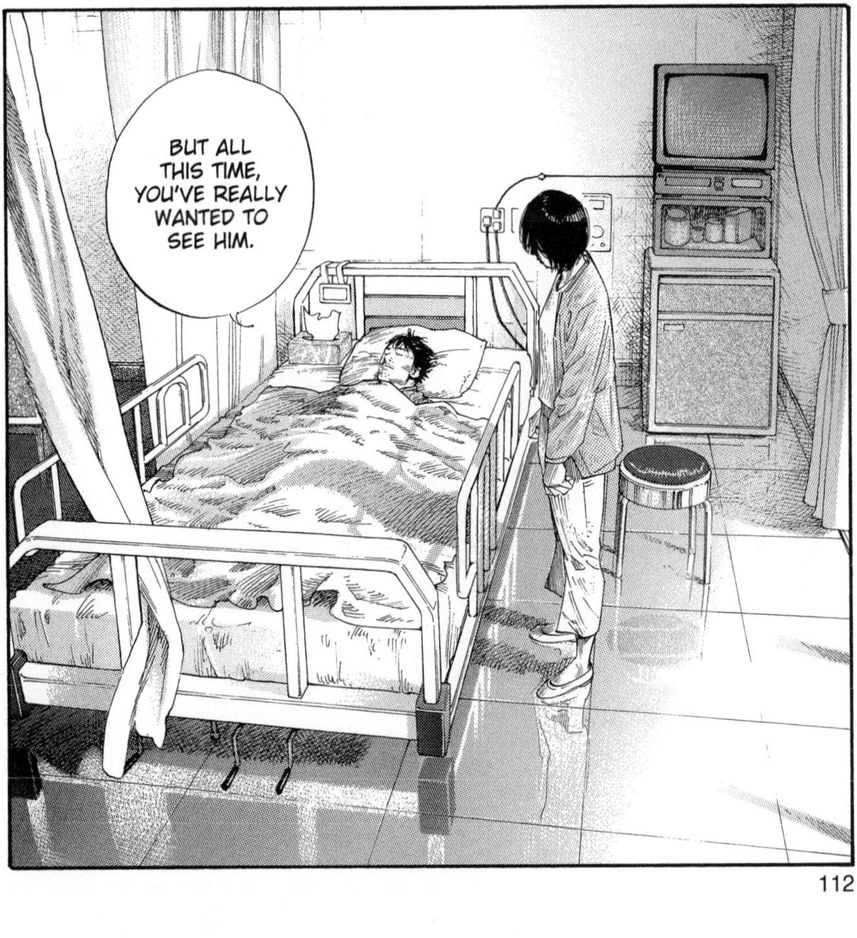
BUT ALL THIS TIME, YOU'VE REALLY WANTED TO SEE HIM.

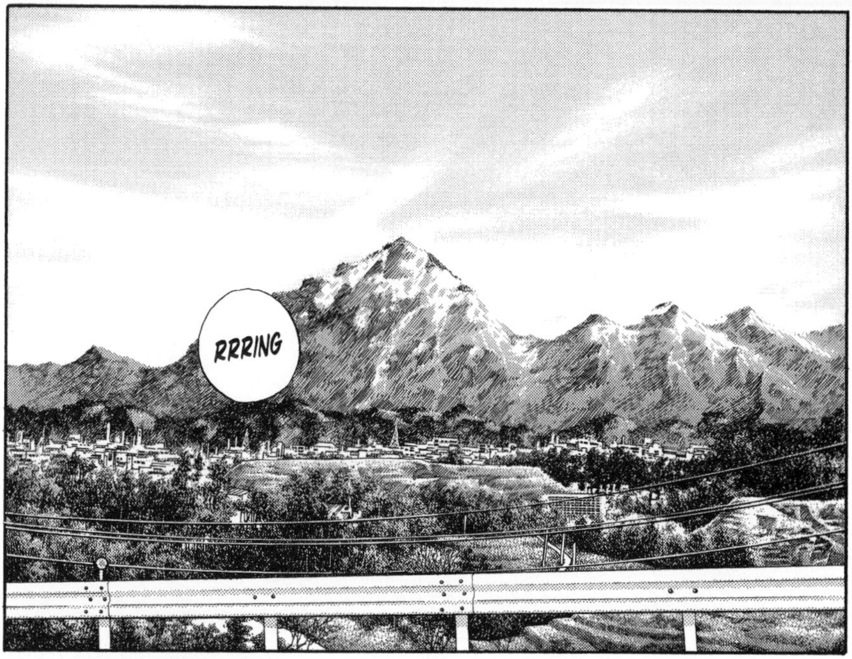
RRRING

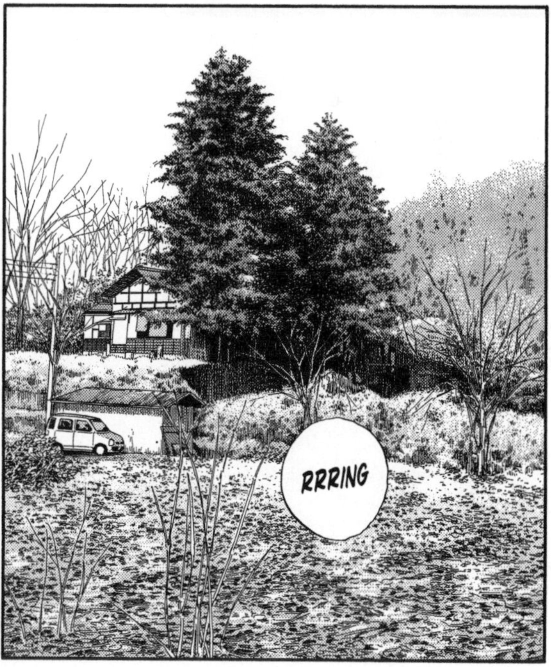
RRRING

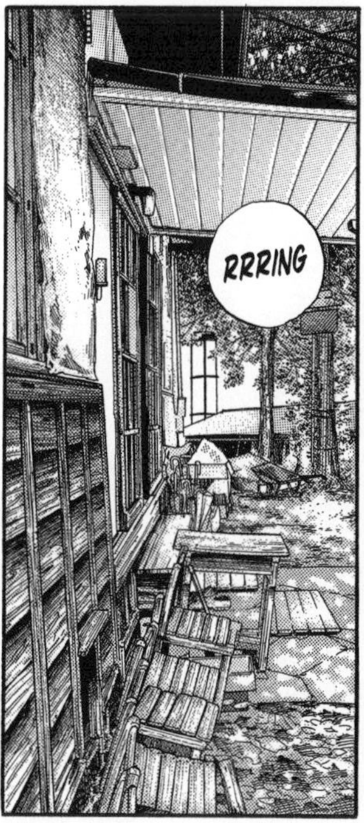
RRRING

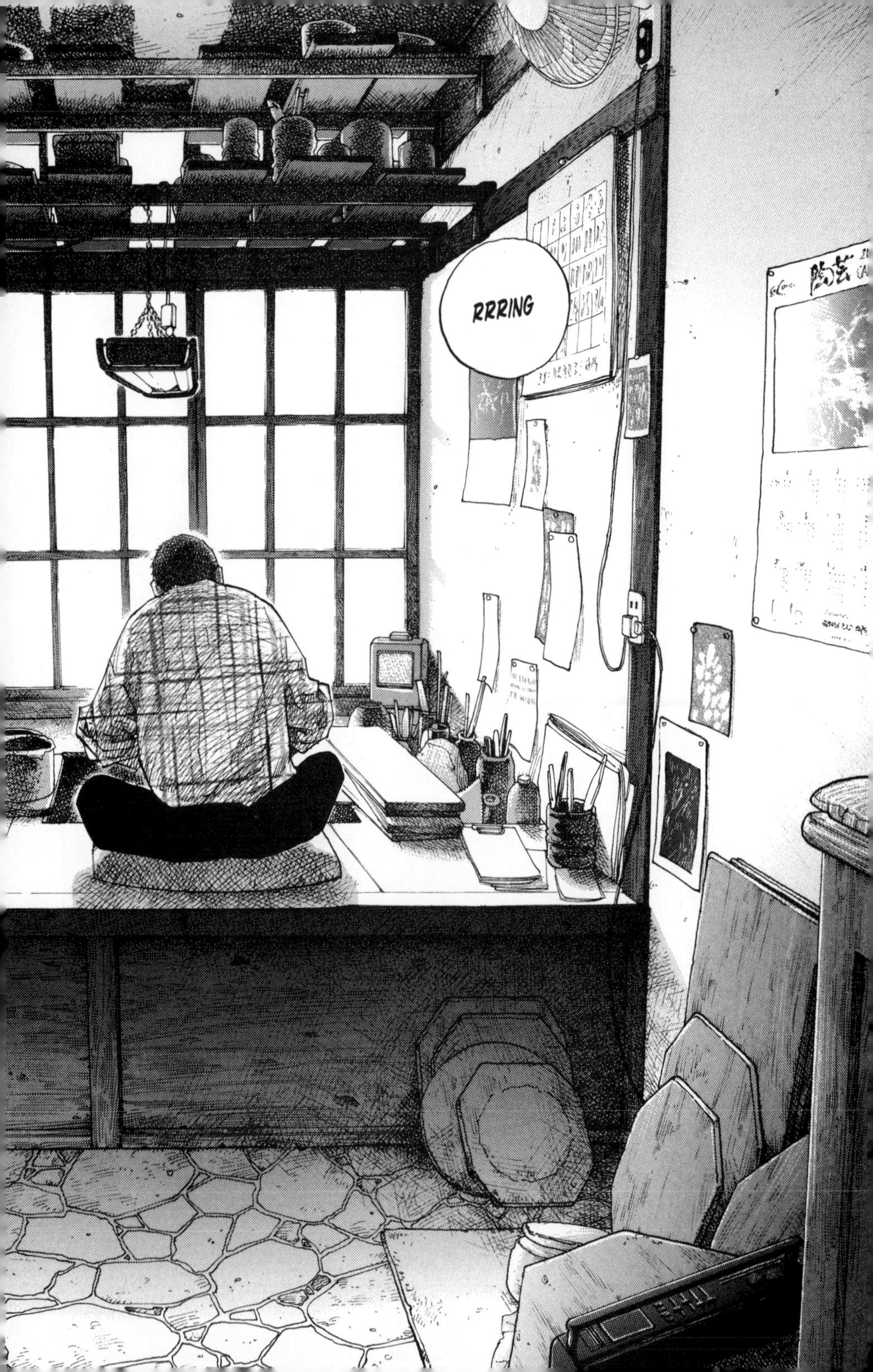
RRRING

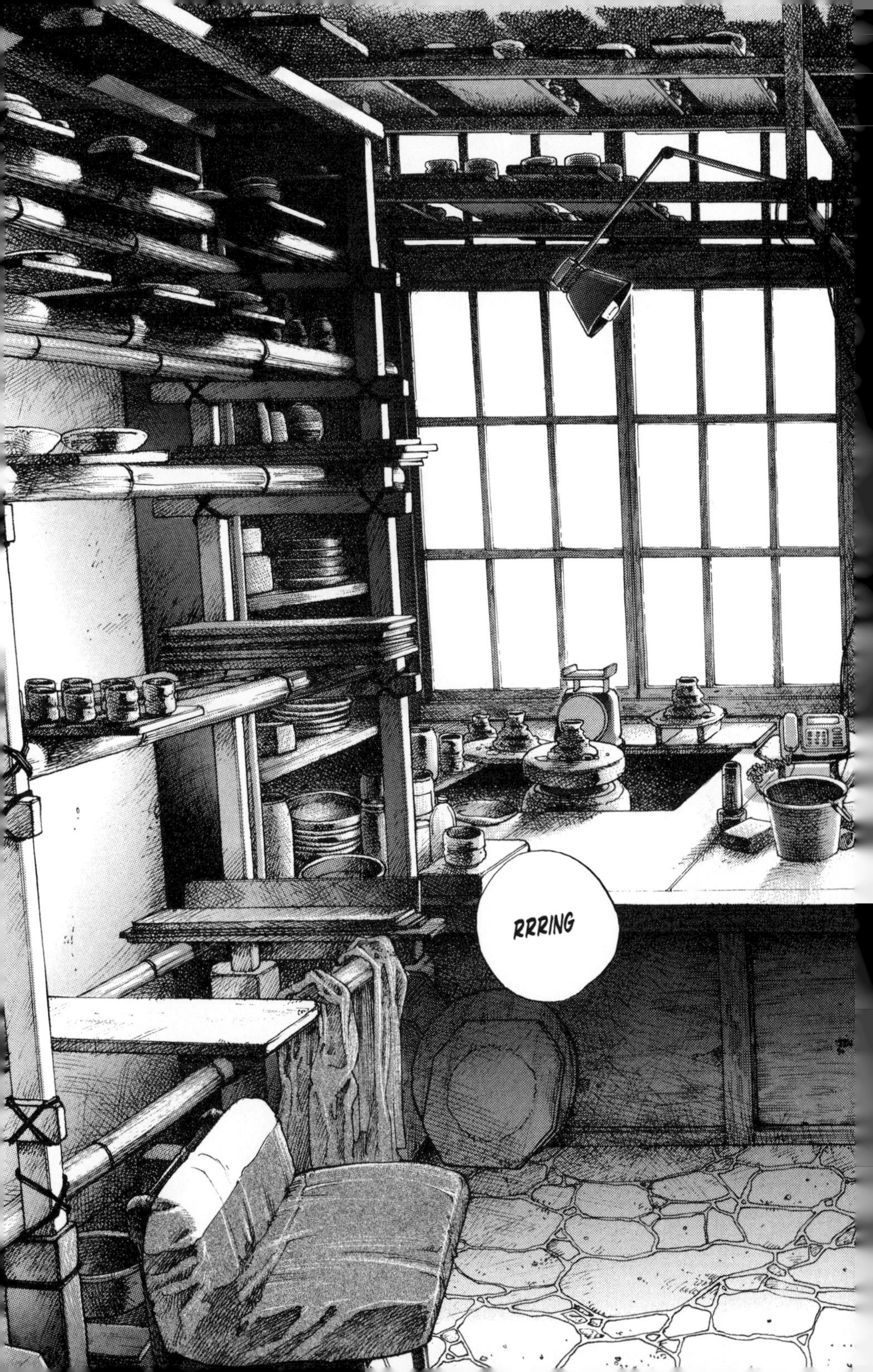
RRRING

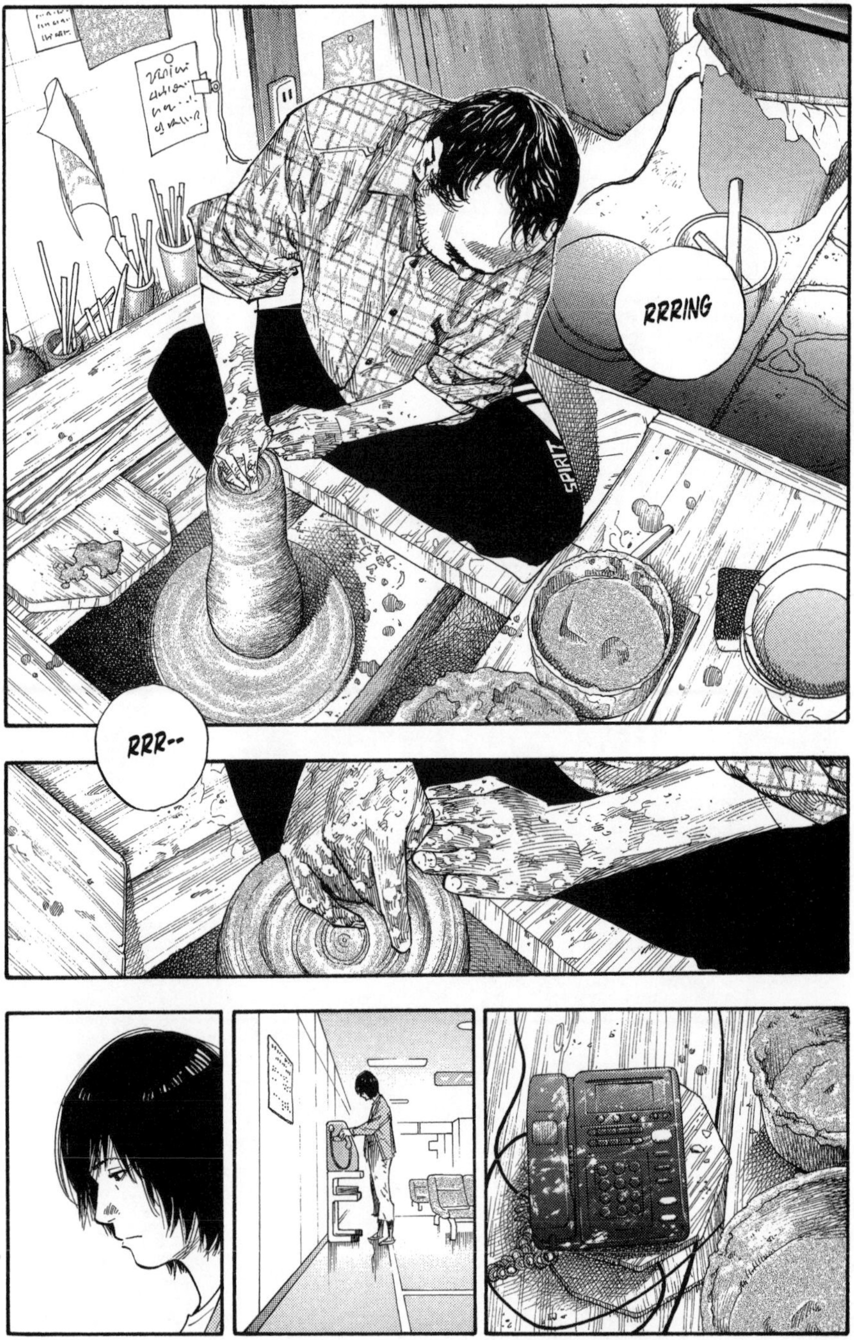
RRRING
RRR--

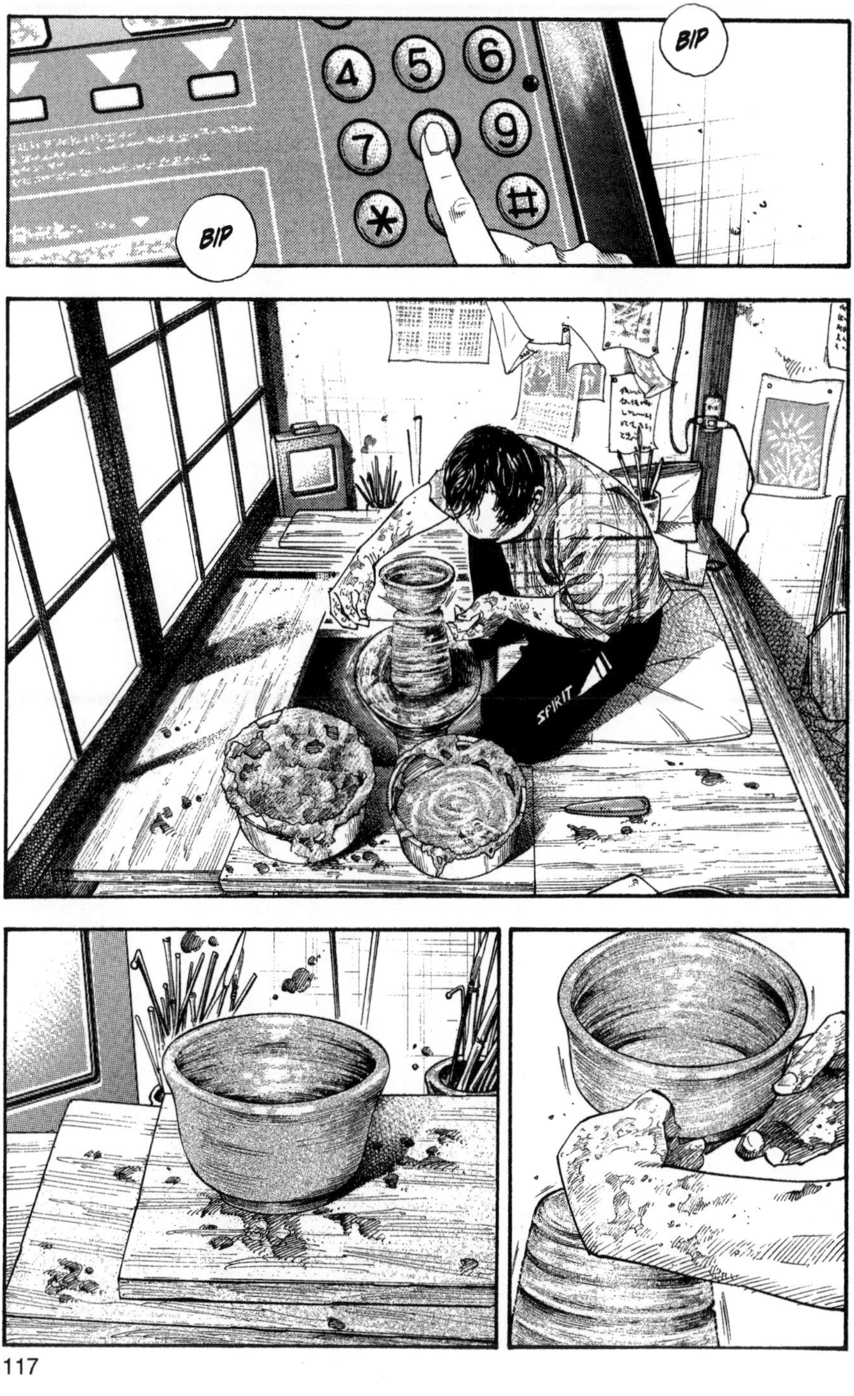
BIP
BIP
SPIRIT

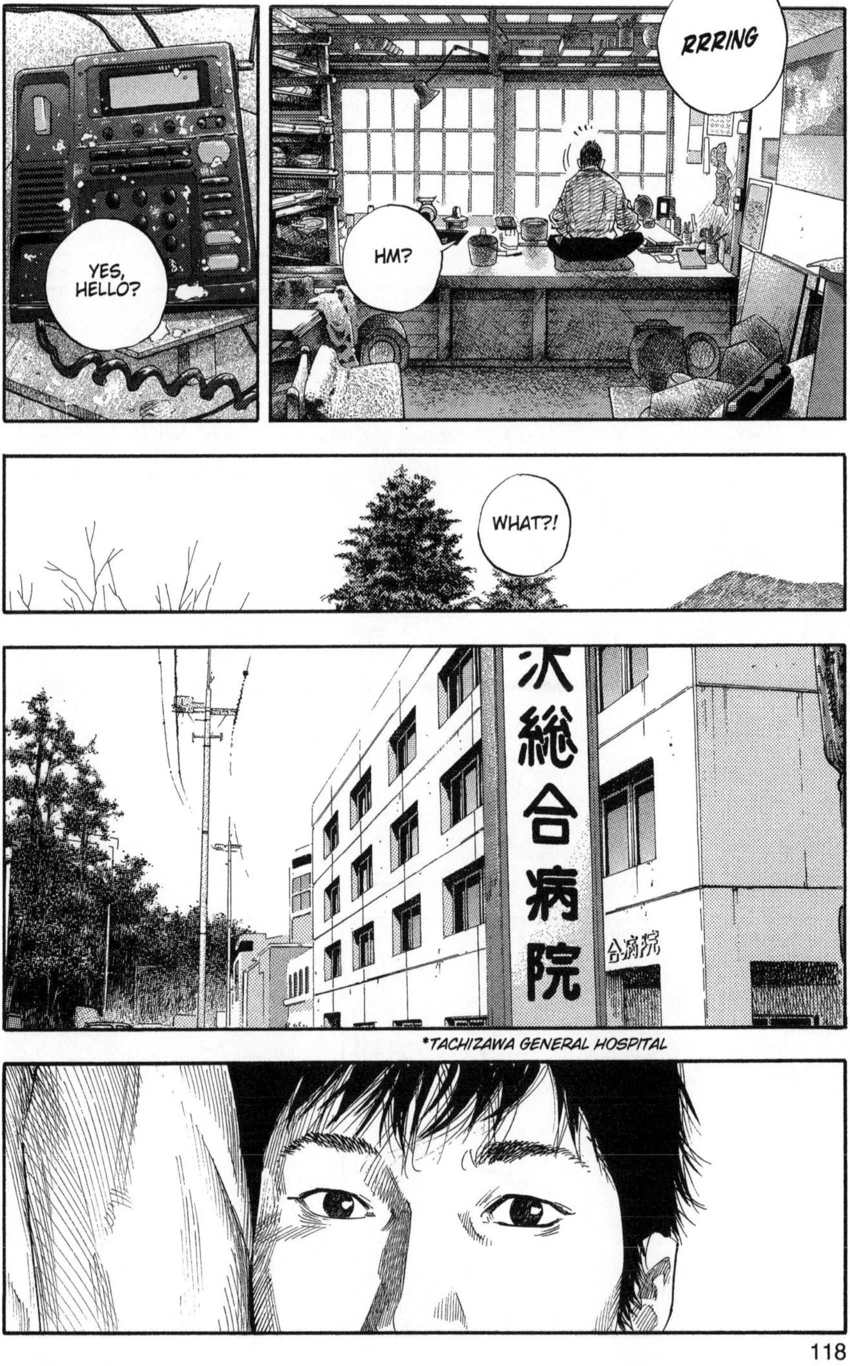
RRRING
HM?
YES, HELLO?
WHAT?!
沢総合病院
合病院
*TACHIZAWA GENERAL HOSPITAL

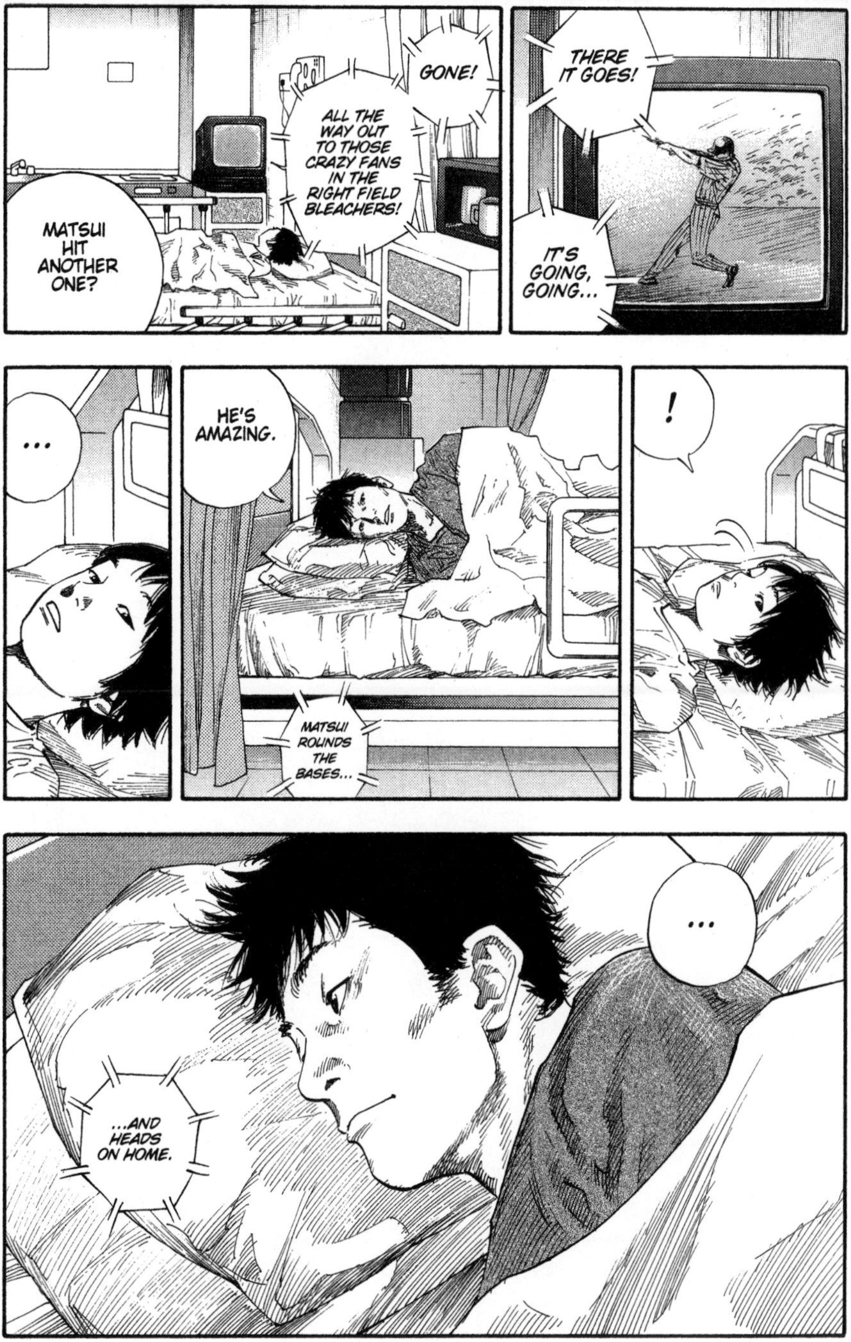
THERE IT GOES!
IT'S GOING, GOING...
GONE!
ALL THE WAY OUT TO THOSE CRAZY FANS IN THE RIGHT FIELD BLEACHERS!
MATSUI HIT ANOTHER ONE?
!
HE'S AMAZING.
MATSUI ROUNDS THE BASES...
...
...
...AND HEADS ON HOME.

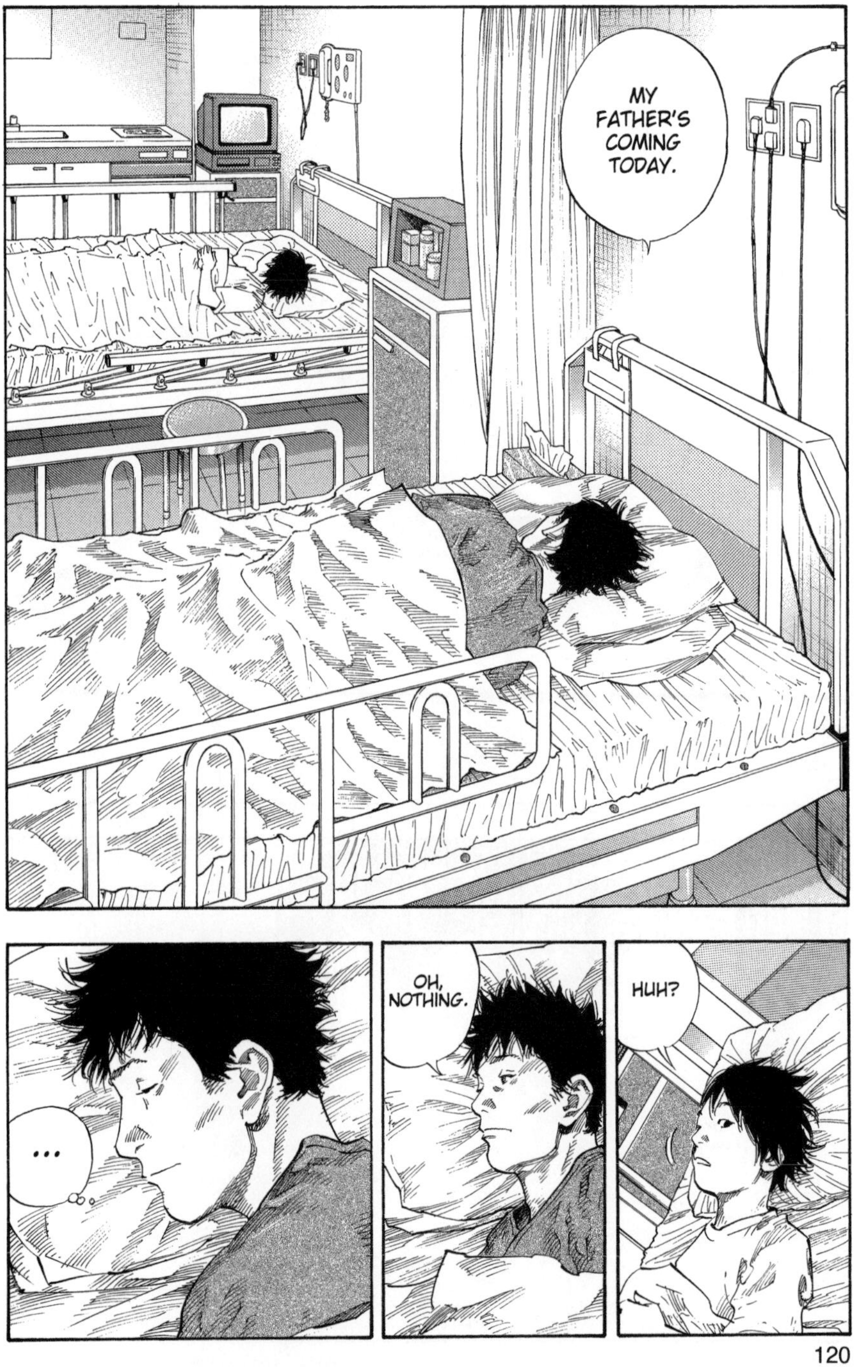
MY FATHER'S COMING TODAY.
HUH?
OH, NOTHING.
...

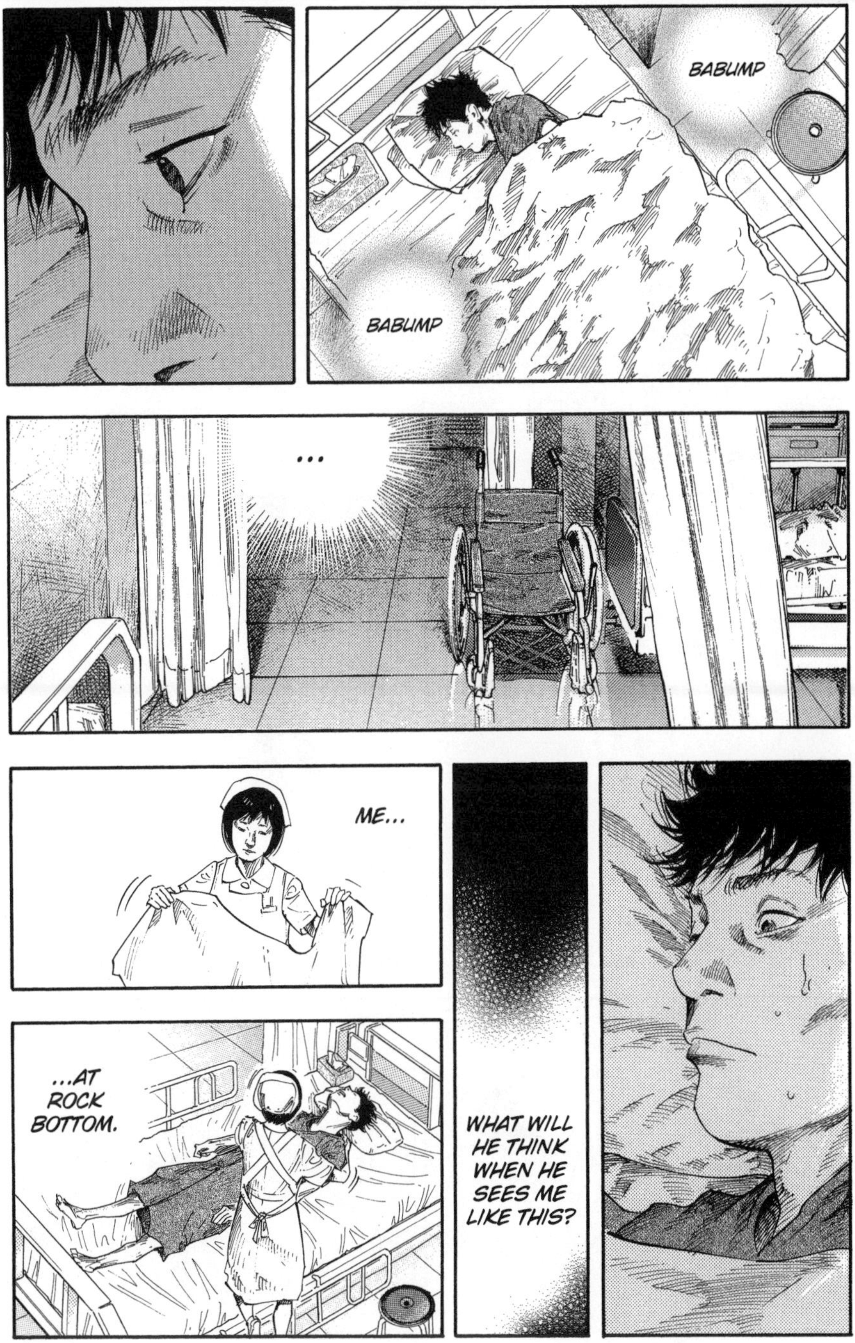
BABUMP
BABUMP
...
WHAT WILL HE THINK WHEN HE SEES ME LIKE THIS?
ME...
...AT ROCK BOTTOM.

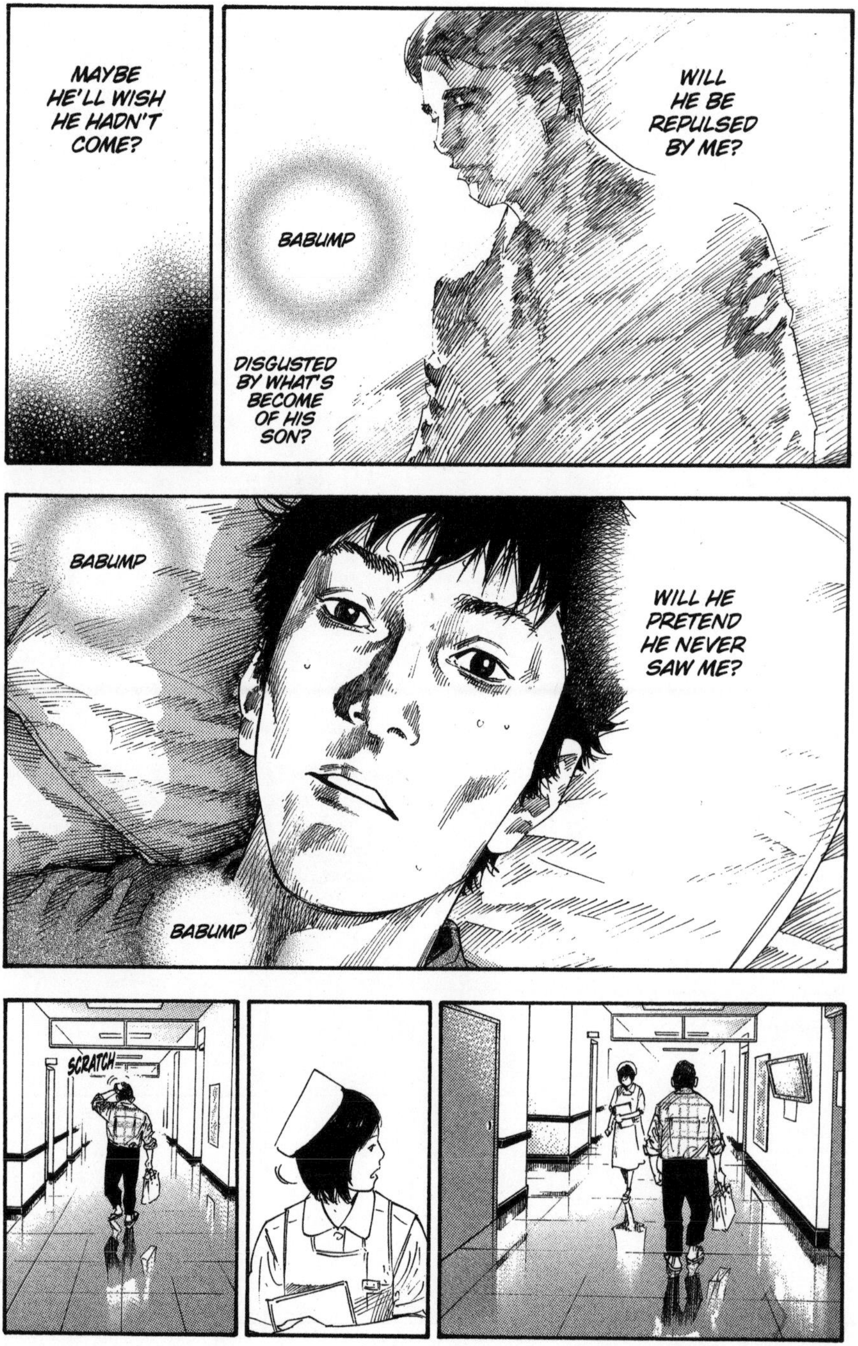
WILL HE BE REPULSED BY ME?
BABUMP
DISGUSTED BY WHAT'S BECOME OF HIS SON?
MAYBE HE'LL WISH HE HADN'T COME?
WILL HE PRETEND HE NEVER SAW ME?
BABUMP
BABUMP
SCRATCH

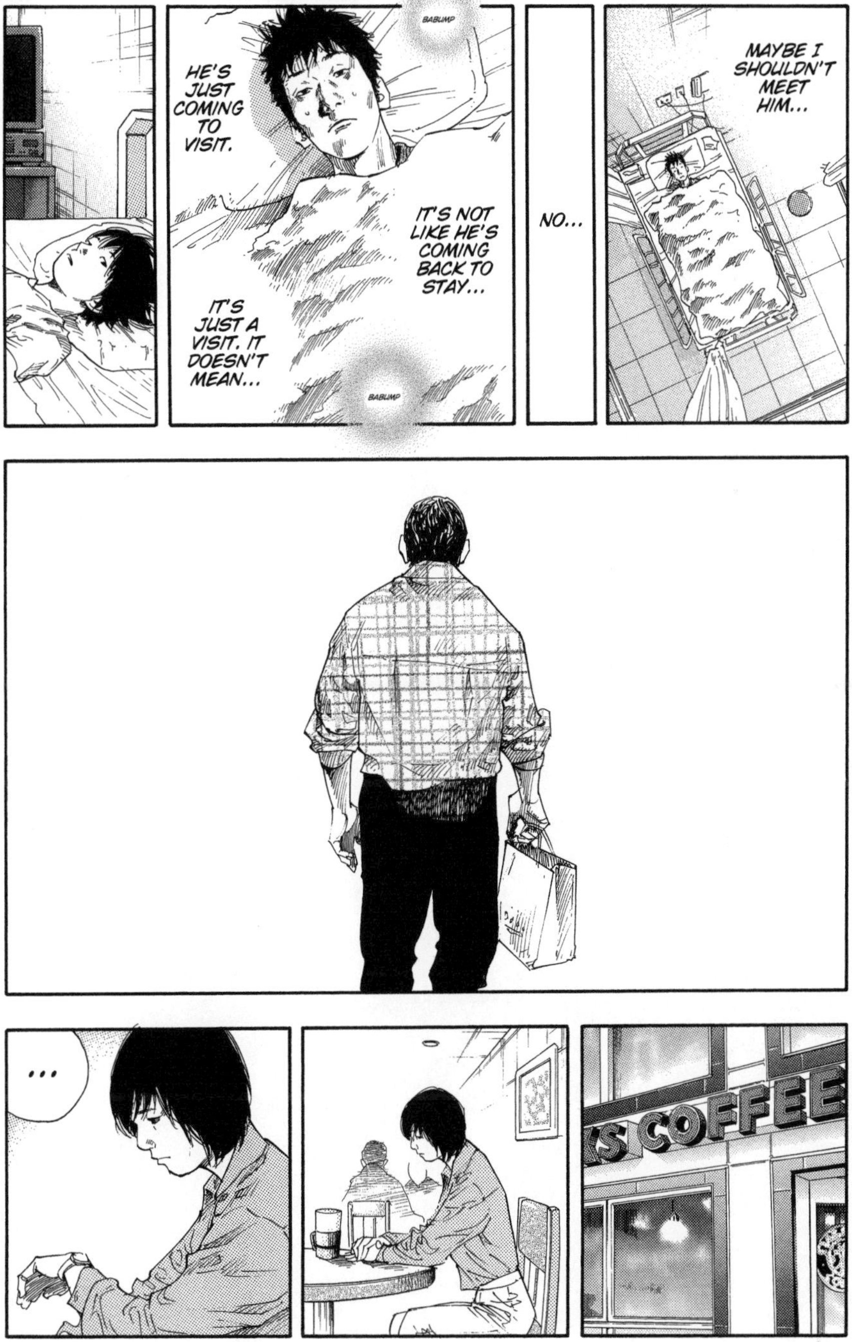
MAYBE I SHOULDN'T MEET HIM...
NO...
BABUMP
HE'S JUST COMING TO VISIT.
IT'S NOT LIKE HE'S COMING BACK TO STAY...
IT'S JUST A VISIT. IT DOESN'T MEAN...
BABUMP
COFFEE
...

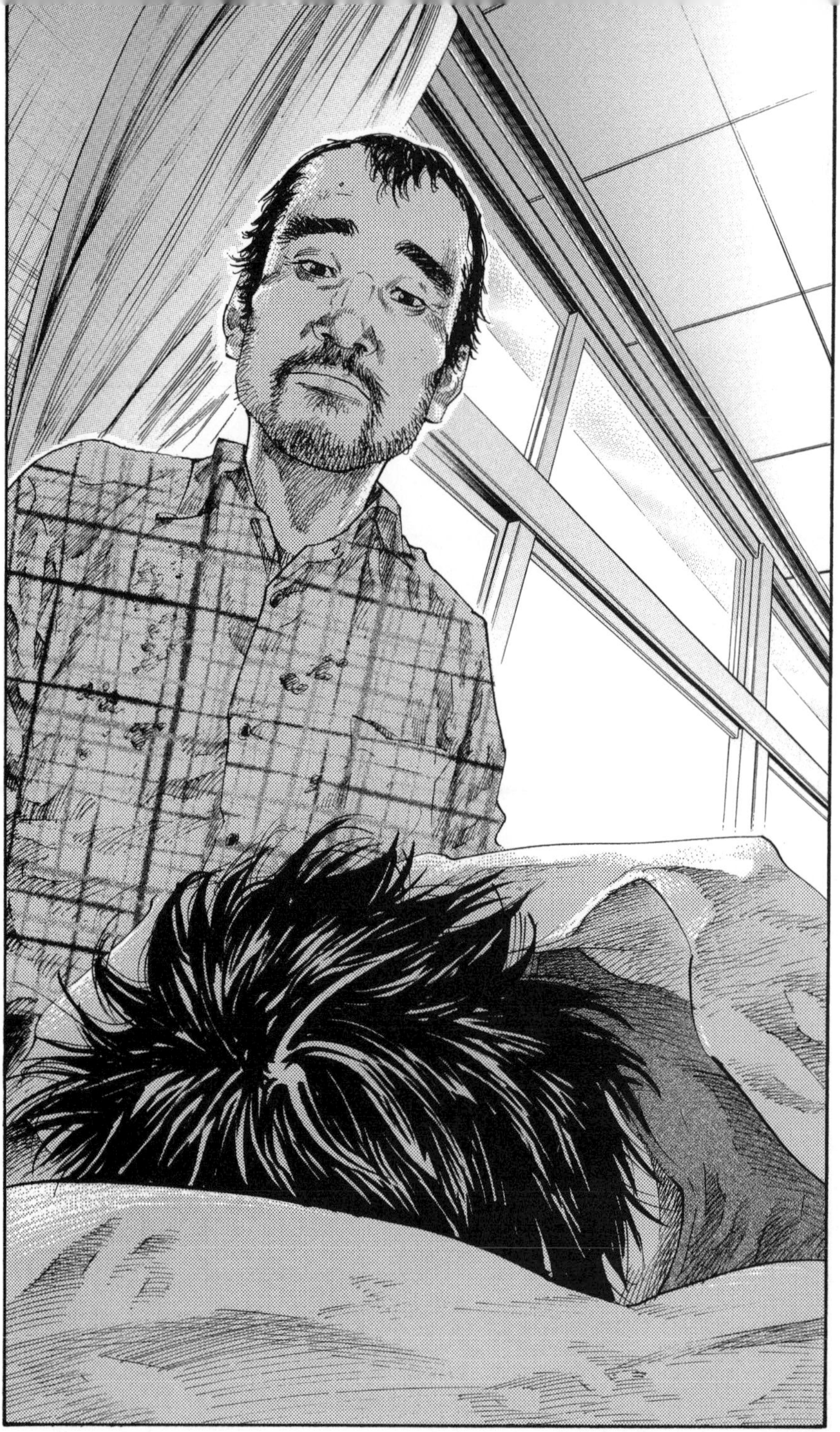

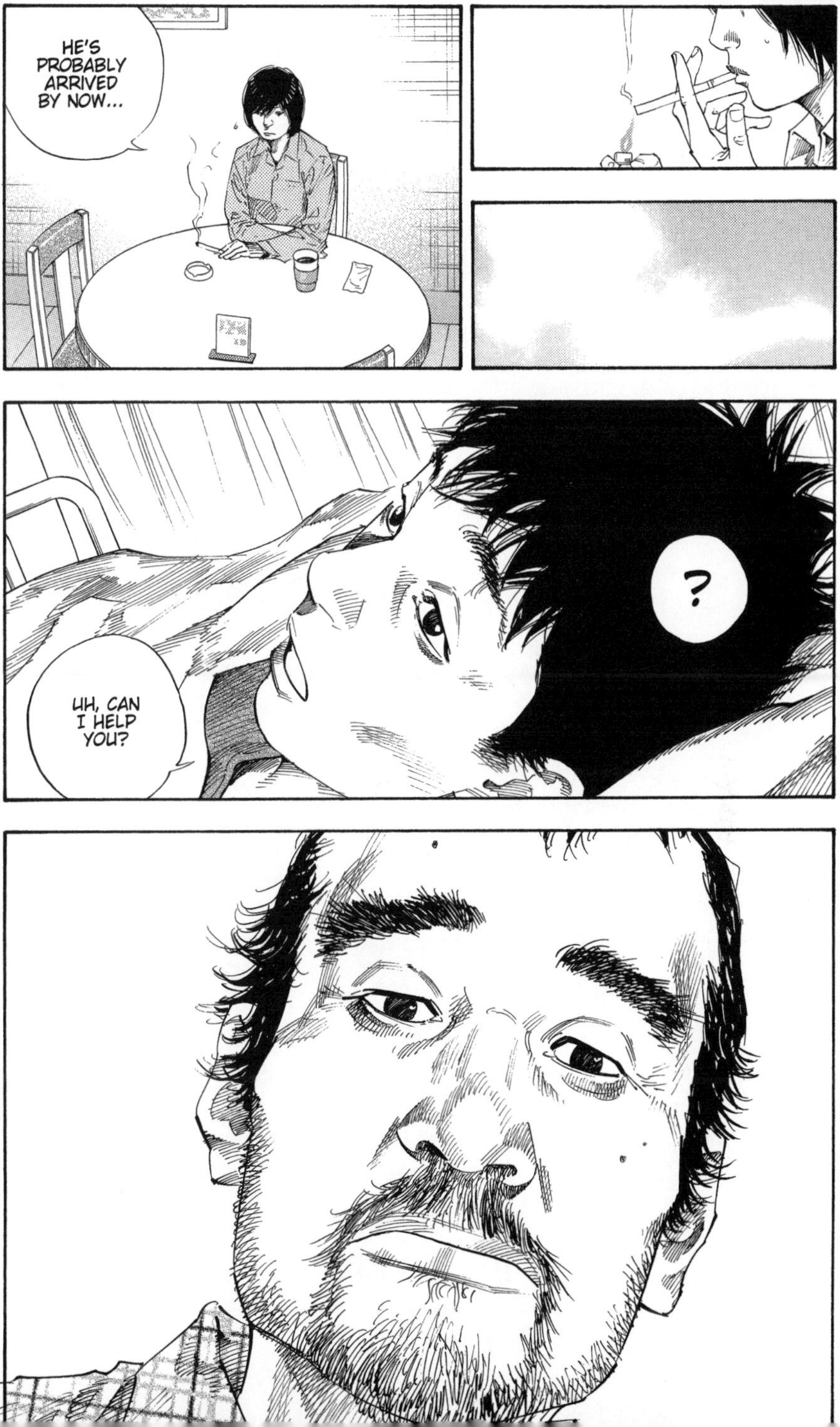
HE'S PROBABLY ARRIVED BY NOW...
?
UH, CAN I HELP YOU?

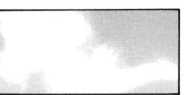

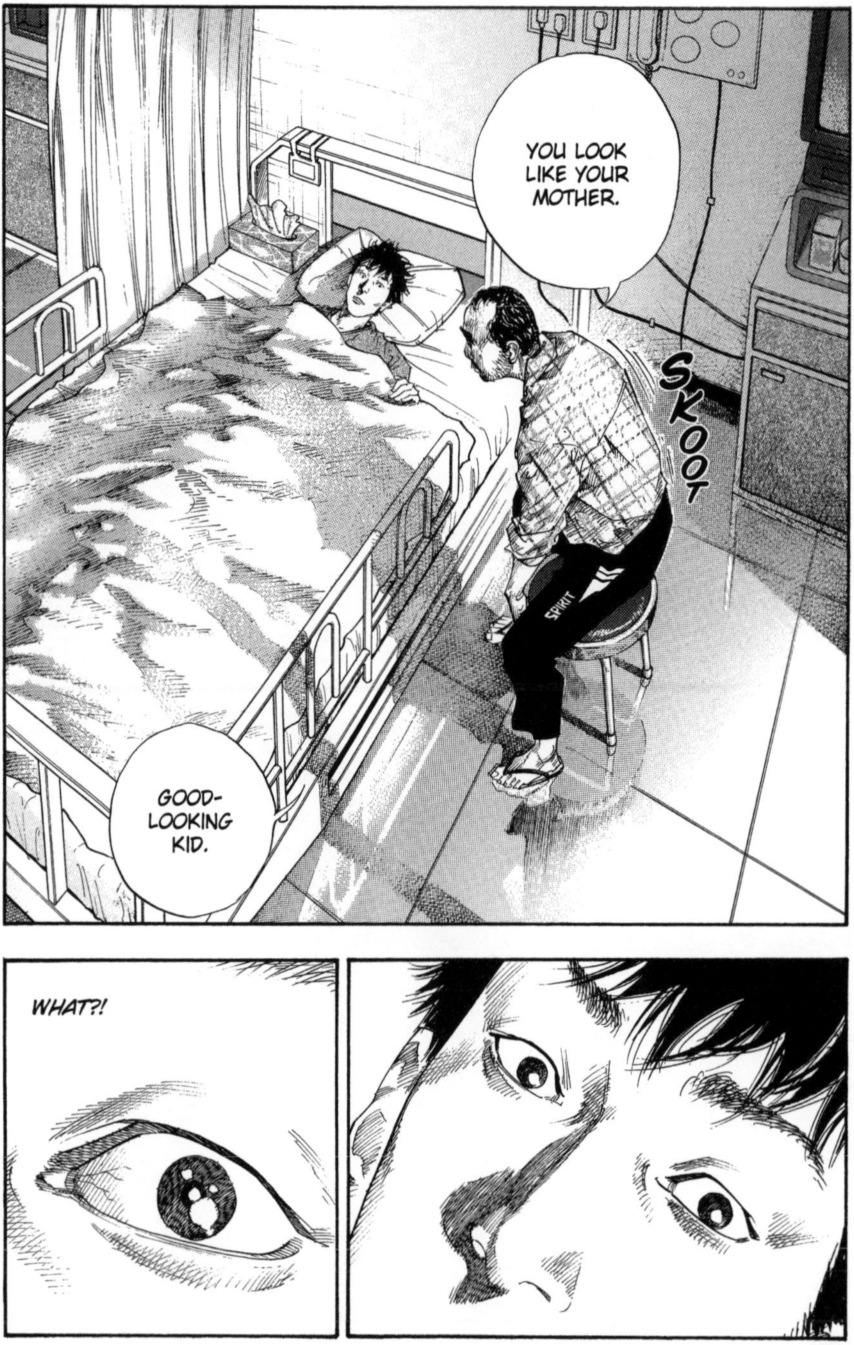
YOU LOOK LIKE YOUR MOTHER.
SKOOT
GOOD-LOOKING KID.
WHAT?!
SPIRIT

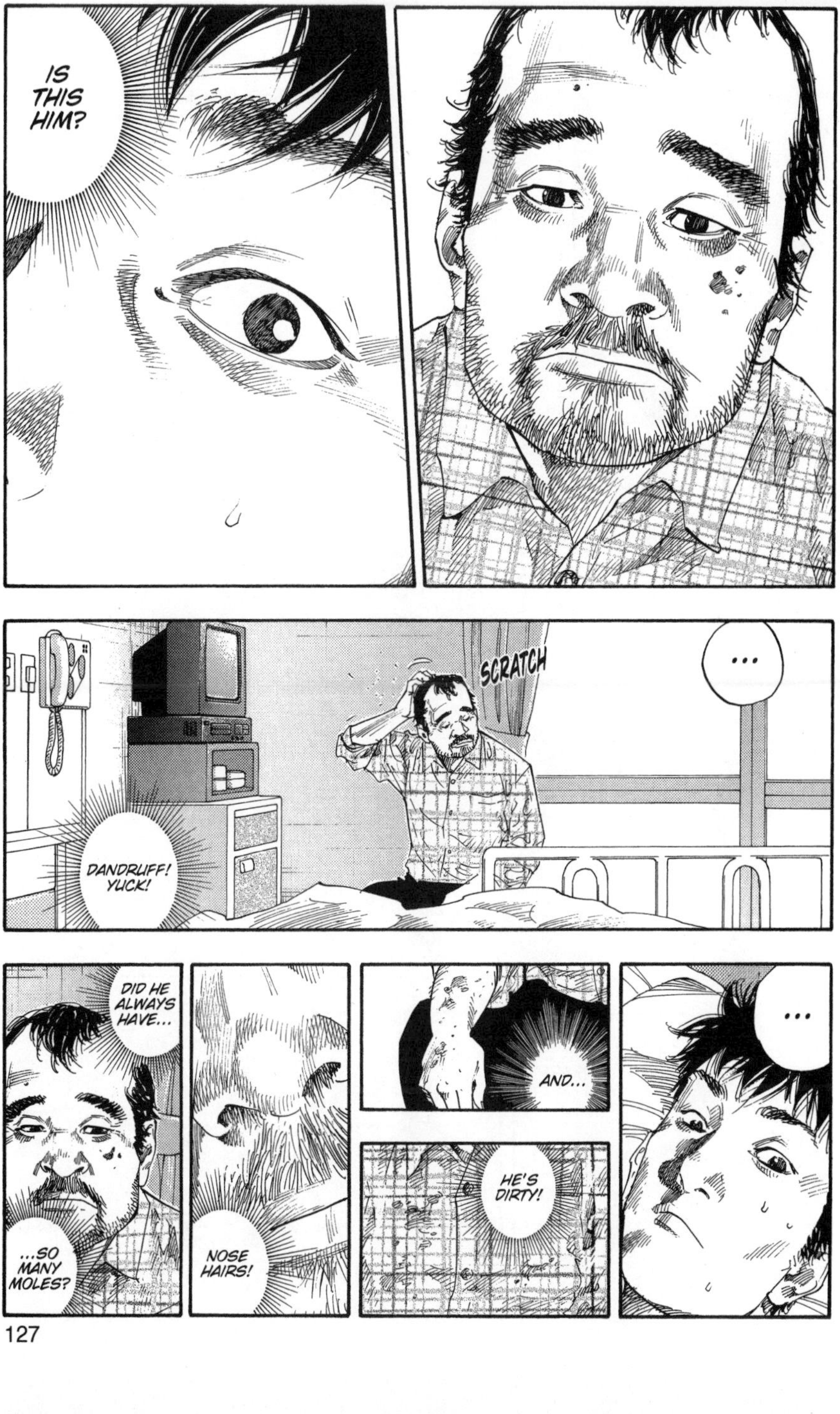
IS THIS HIM?
...
SCRATCH
DANDRUFF! YUCK!
...
AND...
HE'S DIRTY!
NOSE HAIRS!
DID HE ALWAYS HAVE...
...SO MANY MOLES?

WHAT THE--?!

SCRATCH SCRATCH

FLAKE FLAKE

HE'S THE ONE THAT'S HIT ROCK BOTTOM!

I HEARD YOU CAN'T WALK.

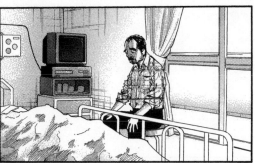

IT'S BEEN EIGHT YEARS...

I WON'T SAY ANYTHING TRITE.

...

...

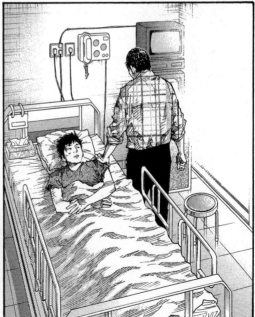

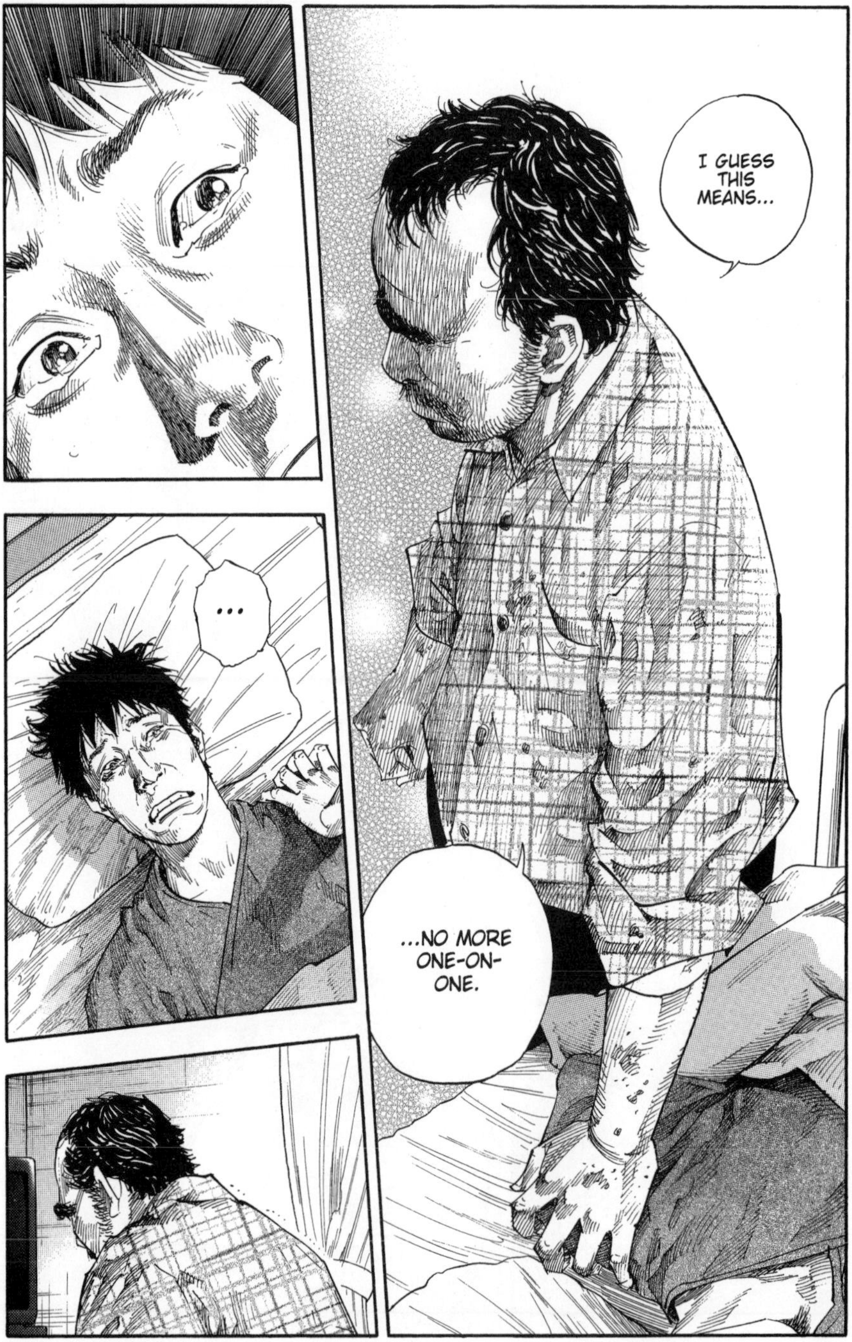
I GUESS THIS MEANS...
...NO MORE ONE-ON-ONE.
...

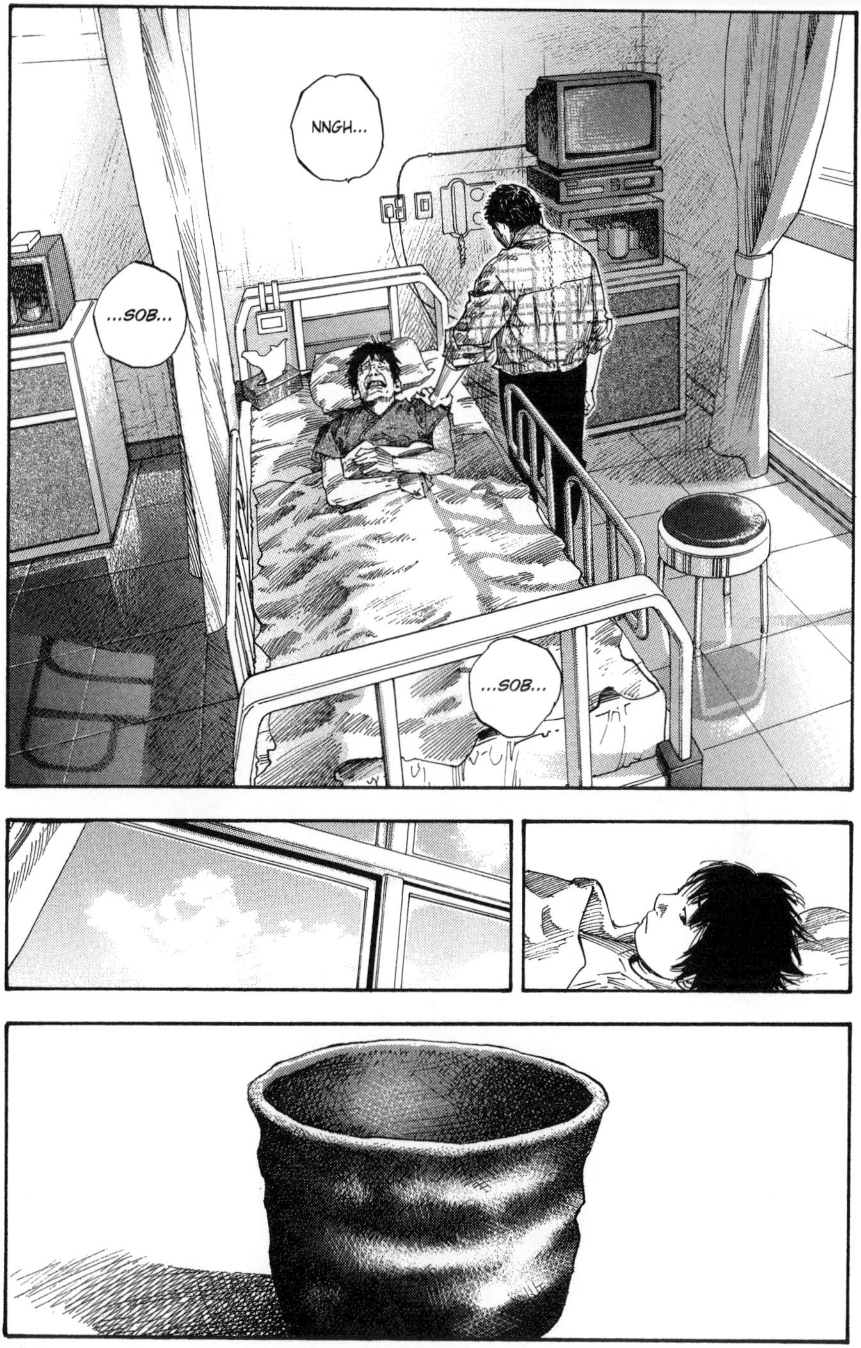
NNGH...
...SOB...
...SOB...

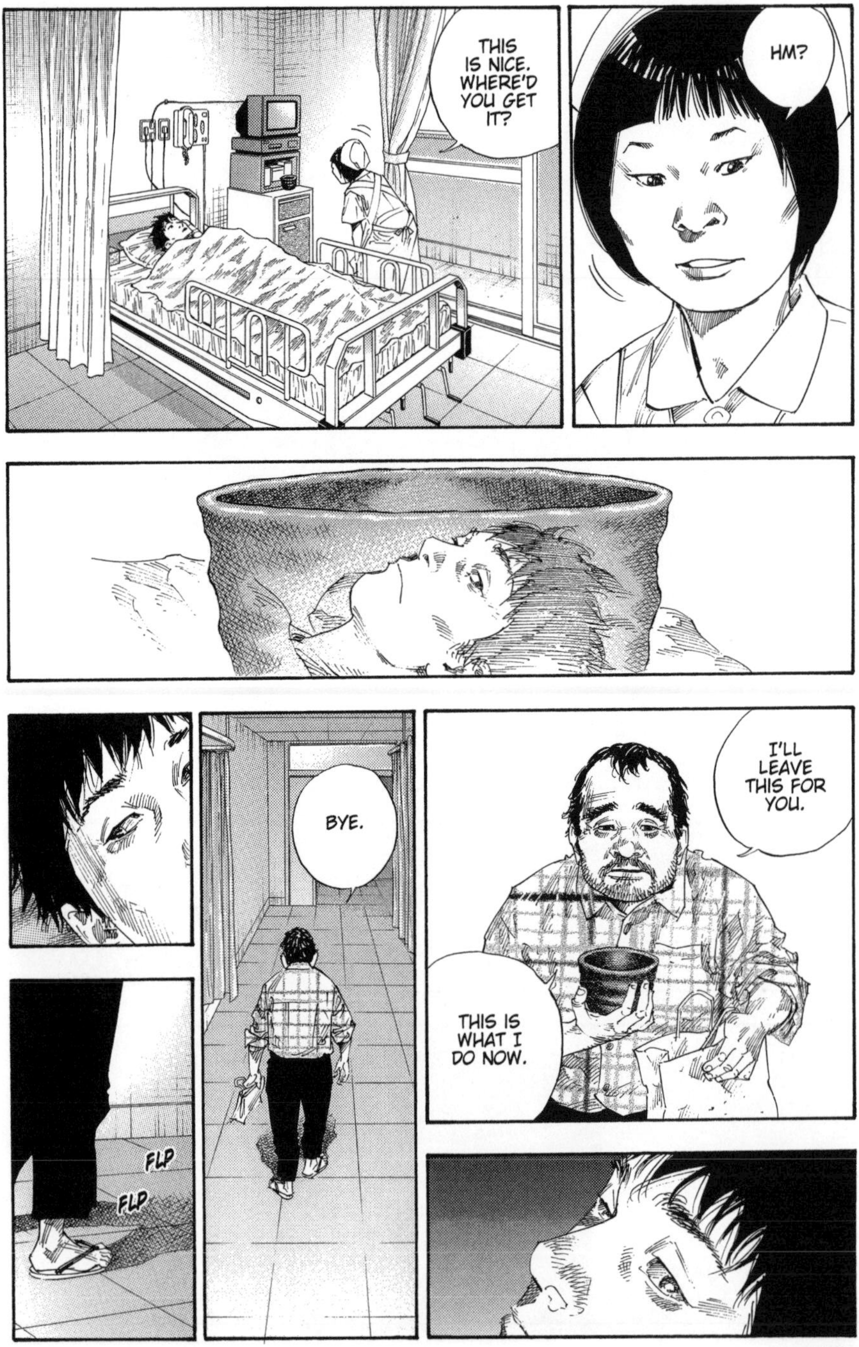
HM?
THIS IS NICE. WHERE'D YOU GET IT?
I'LL LEAVE THIS FOR YOU.
THIS IS WHAT I DO NOW.
BYE.
FLP
FLP

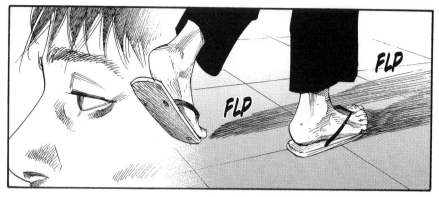

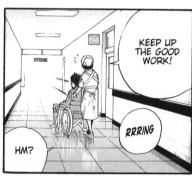

FLP
FLP
IT'S ALL THANKS TO THE INCLINE TABLE!
YOU CAN SIT UP NOW!
KEEP UP THE GOOD WORK!
RRRING
HM?
HMPH...
IT'S NO BIG DEAL.
LIKE FATHER LIKE SON...
...I GUESS WE WERE BOTH ALWAYS AT ROCK BOTTOM TO BEGIN WITH.

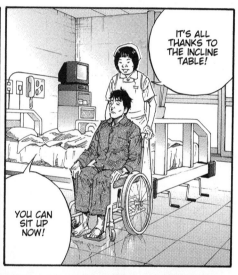

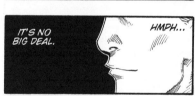

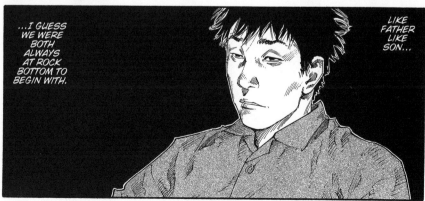

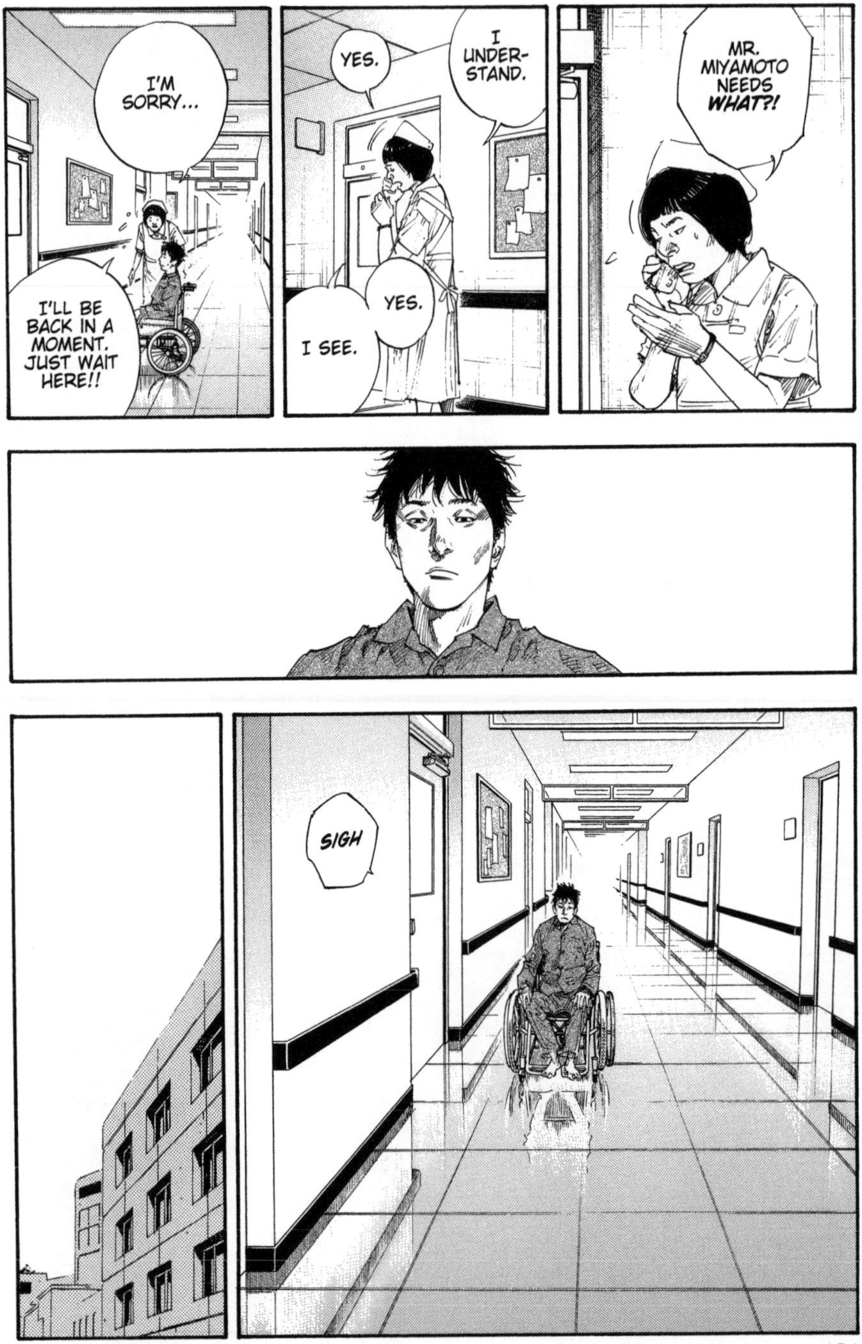
MR. MIYAMOTO NEEDS WHAT?!
I UNDERSTAND.
YES.
YES.
I SEE.
I'M SORRY...
I'LL BE BACK IN A MOMENT. JUST WAIT HERE!!
SIGH

HUF
HUF

SORRY ABOUT THAT--

WHAT'S ALL THE COMMOTION, NURSE KOBAYASHI?

DASH

DASH

CRASH!!

HISANOBU TAKAHASHI IS GONE?!

BUT HE CAN BARELY SIT UP!

AND HARDLY ANY TIME HAS...

I WAS CARELESS!!

ANYWAY, WE HAVE TO FIND HIM!

WHZZ

HMM...

...

CAN'T MOVE AN INCH, BUT I CAN STILL BLEED.

BLOOD...

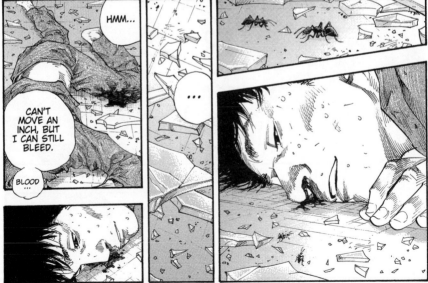

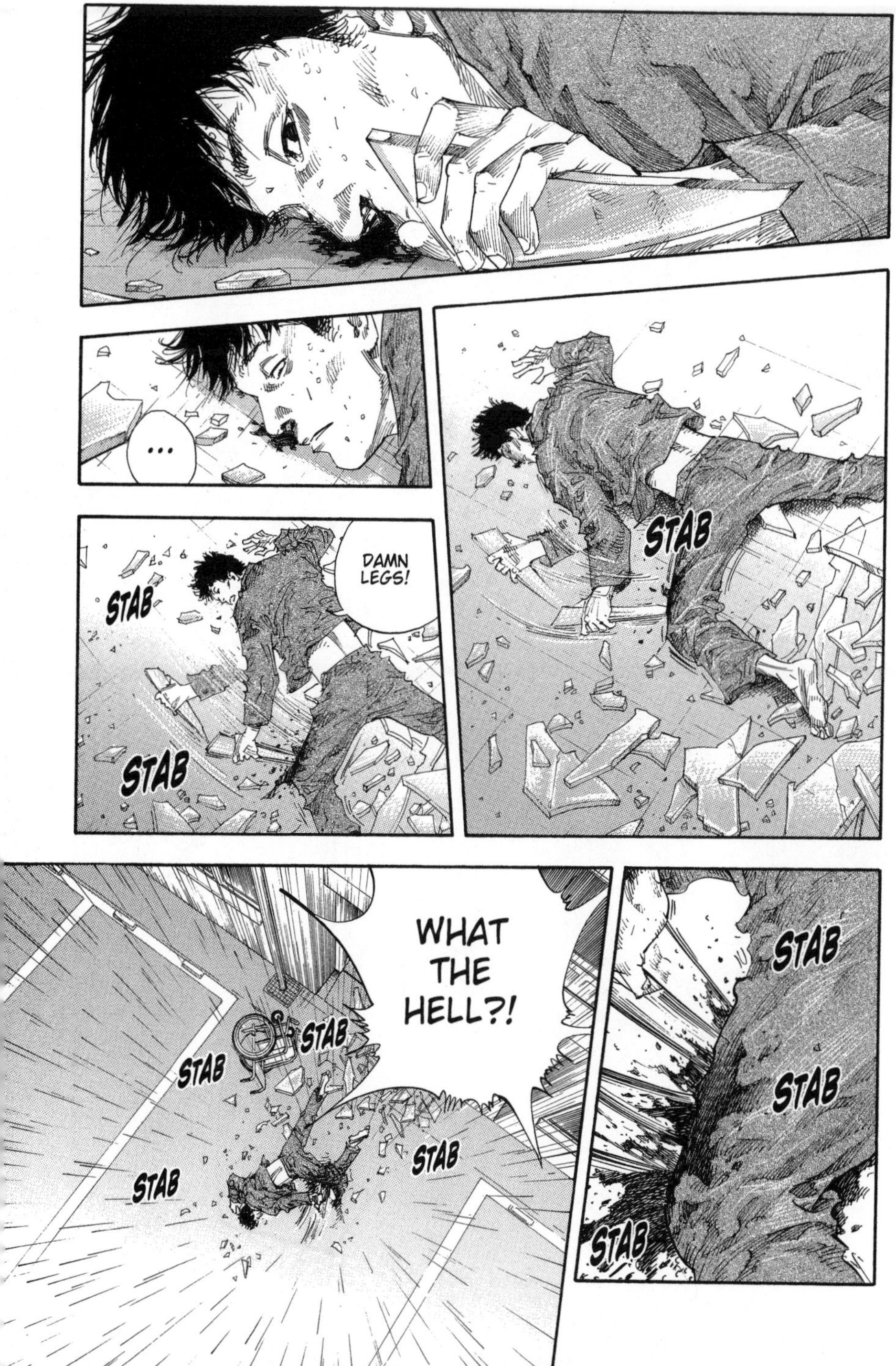
STAB
...
DAMN LEGS!
STAB
STAB
STAB
STAB
STAB
WHAT THE HELL?!
STAB
STAB
STAB
STAB

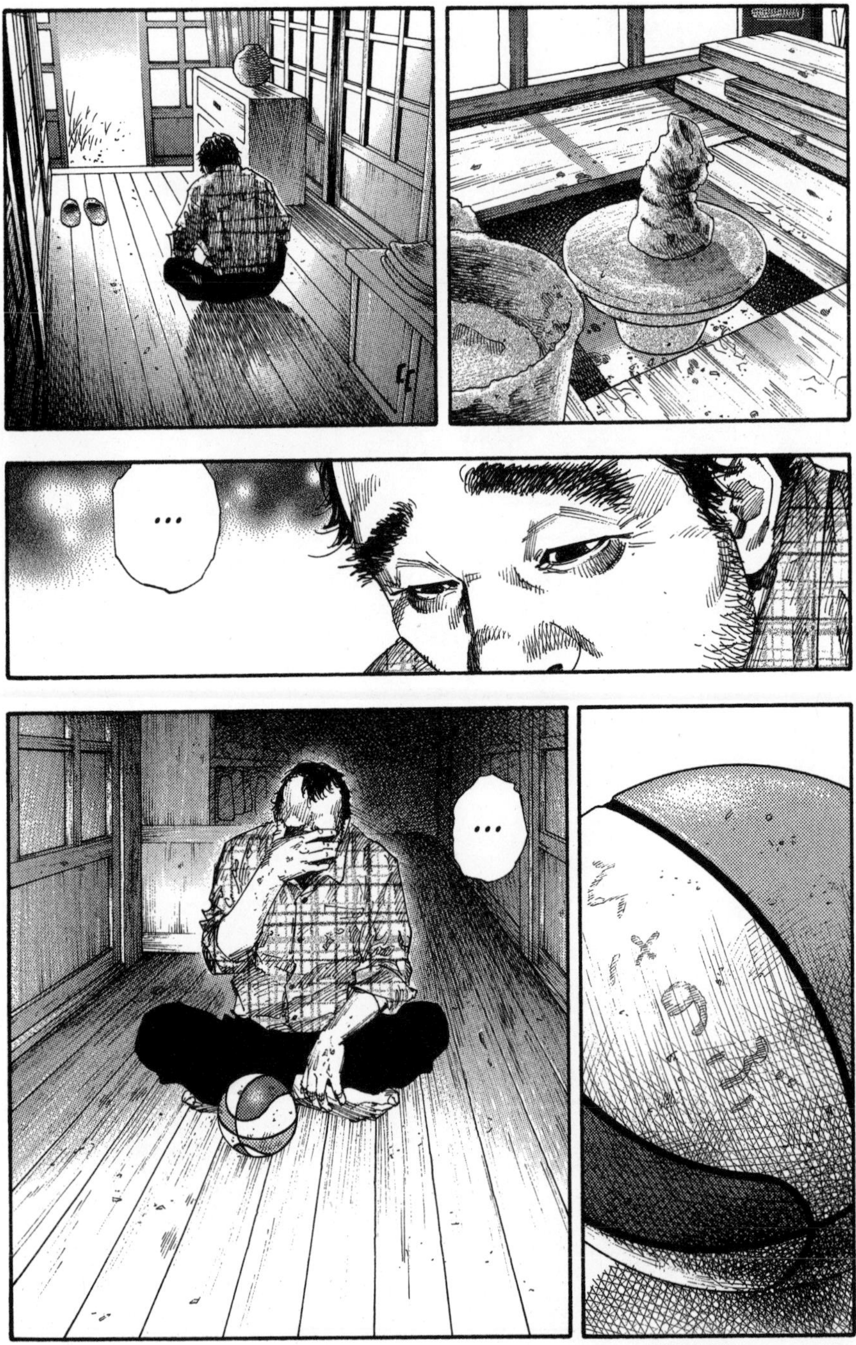
...
...

*HISANOBU

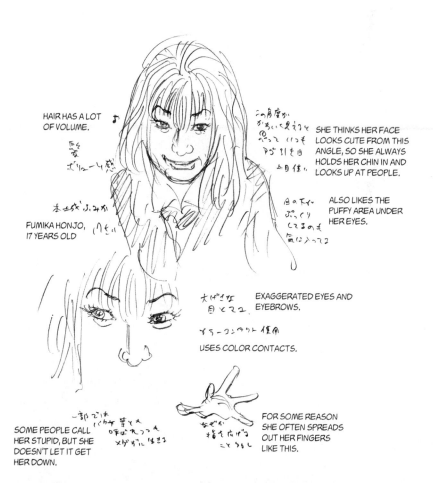

HAIR HAS A LOT OF VOLUME.
髪 ボリューム感
本城ふみか 17才
FUMIKA HONJO, 17 YEARS OLD
この角度がかわいく見えると思っていつもアゴ引き目上目使い
SHE THINKS HER FACE LOOKS CUTE FROM THIS ANGLE, SO SHE ALWAYS HOLDS HER CHIN IN AND LOOKS UP AT PEOPLE.
目の下がぷっくりしてるのも気に入ってる
ALSO LIKES THE PUFFY AREA UNDER HER EYES.
大げさな目とマユ
EXAGGERATED EYES AND EYEBROWS.
カラーコンタクト使用
USES COLOR CONTACTS.
一部ではバカ女等と呼ばれつつもメゲずに生きる
SOME PEOPLE CALL HER STUPID, BUT SHE DOESN'T LET IT GET HER DOWN.
なぜか指を広げることが多し
FOR SOME REASON SHE OFTEN SPREADS OUT HER FINGERS LIKE THIS.

REAL

17th

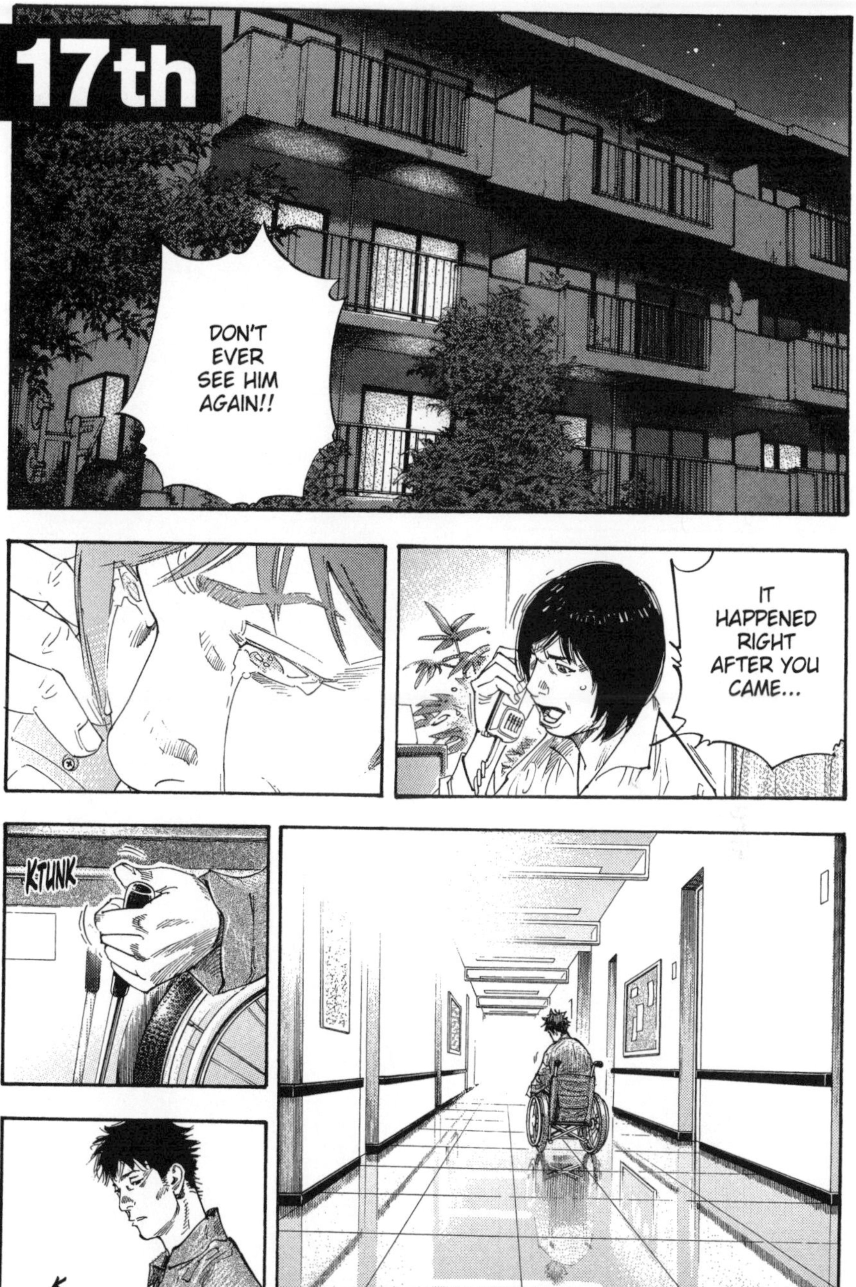
DON'T EVER SEE HIM AGAIN!!
IT HAPPENED RIGHT AFTER YOU CAME...
K-TUNK
KRK

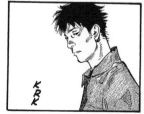

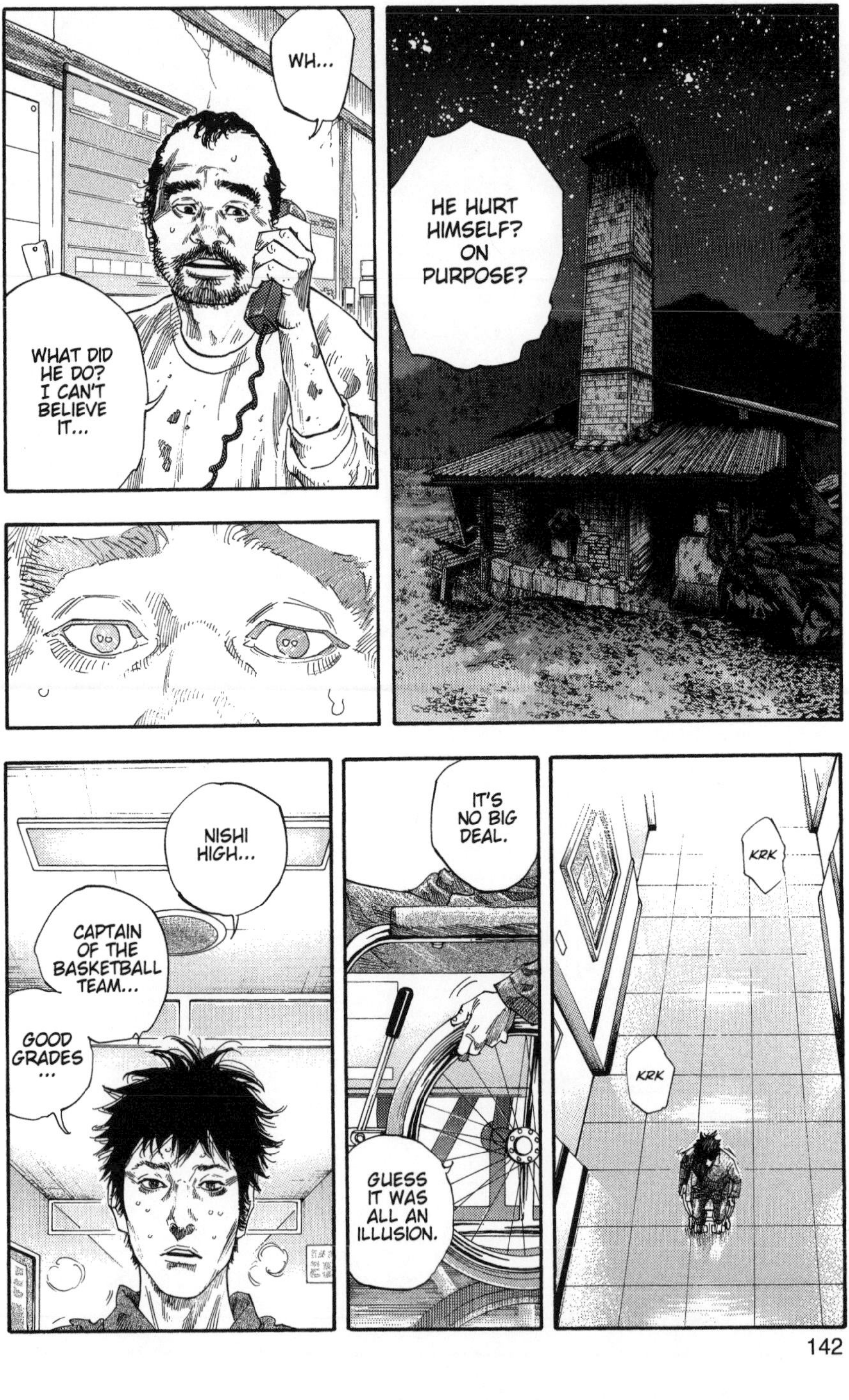
HE HURT HIMSELF? ON PURPOSE?
WH...
WHAT DID HE DO? I CAN'T BELIEVE IT...
KRK
KRK
IT'S NO BIG DEAL.
GUESS IT WAS ALL AN ILLUSION.
NISHI HIGH...
CAPTAIN OF THE BASKETBALL TEAM...
GOOD GRADES ...

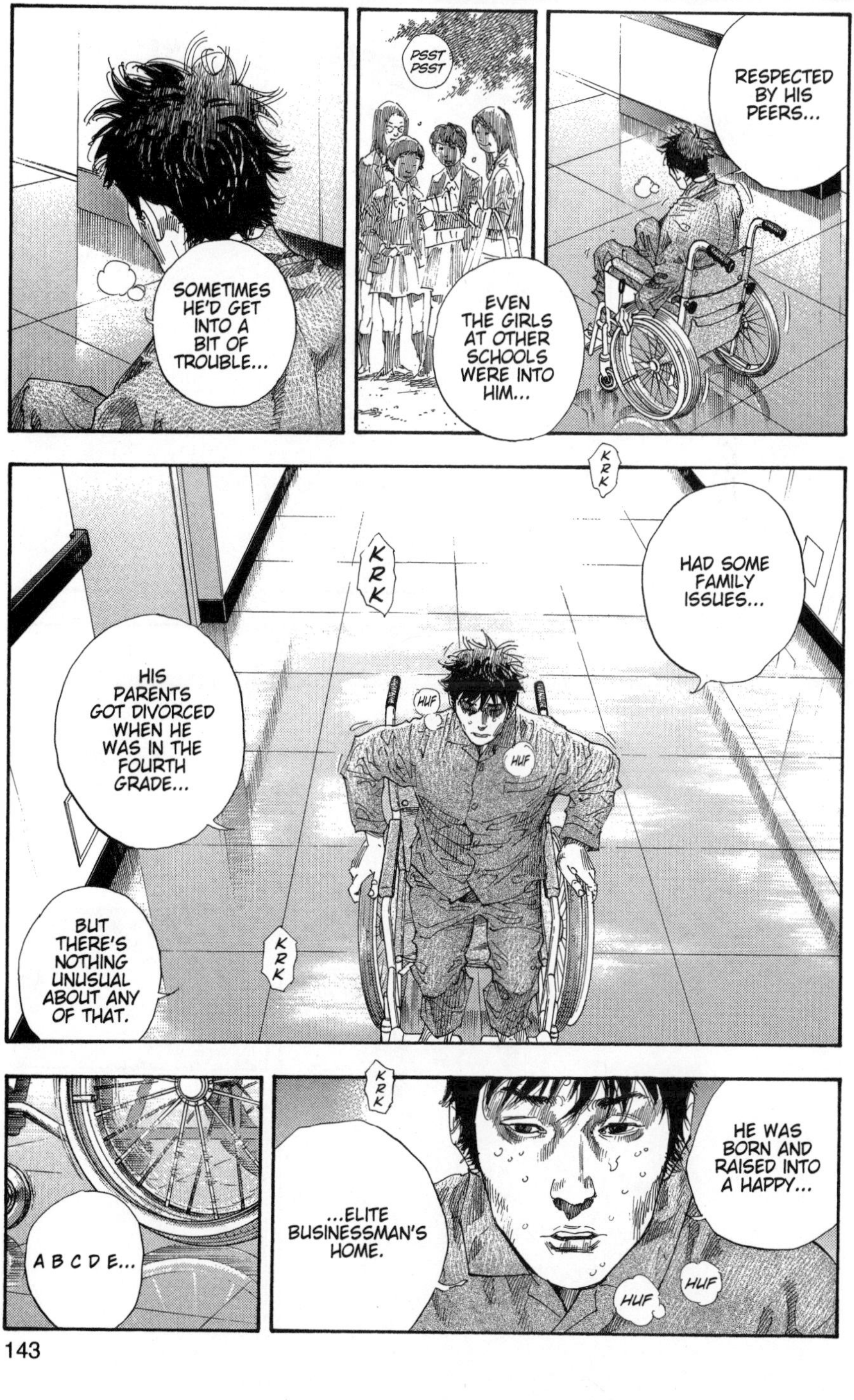
RESPECTED BY HIS PEERS...
PSST PSST
EVEN THE GIRLS AT OTHER SCHOOLS WERE INTO HIM...
SOMETIMES HE'D GET INTO A BIT OF TROUBLE...
KRK
HAD SOME FAMILY ISSUES...
KRK
HIS PARENTS GOT DIVORCED WHEN HE WAS IN THE FOURTH GRADE...
HUF
HUF
KRK
BUT THERE'S NOTHING UNUSUAL ABOUT ANY OF THAT.
KRK
HE WAS BORN AND RAISED INTO A HAPPY...
...ELITE BUSINESSMAN'S HOME.
HUF
HUF
A B C D E...

I WAS AT THE TOP --RANK A.

AT WORST, NO LOWER THAN B.

ALL OF THAT'S AN ILLUSION...

HUF

HUF

THIS IS THE *REAL* ME...

CAN'T EVEN STAND UP. NOT GOOD FOR ANYTHING.

DAZE

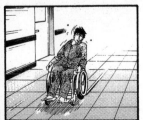

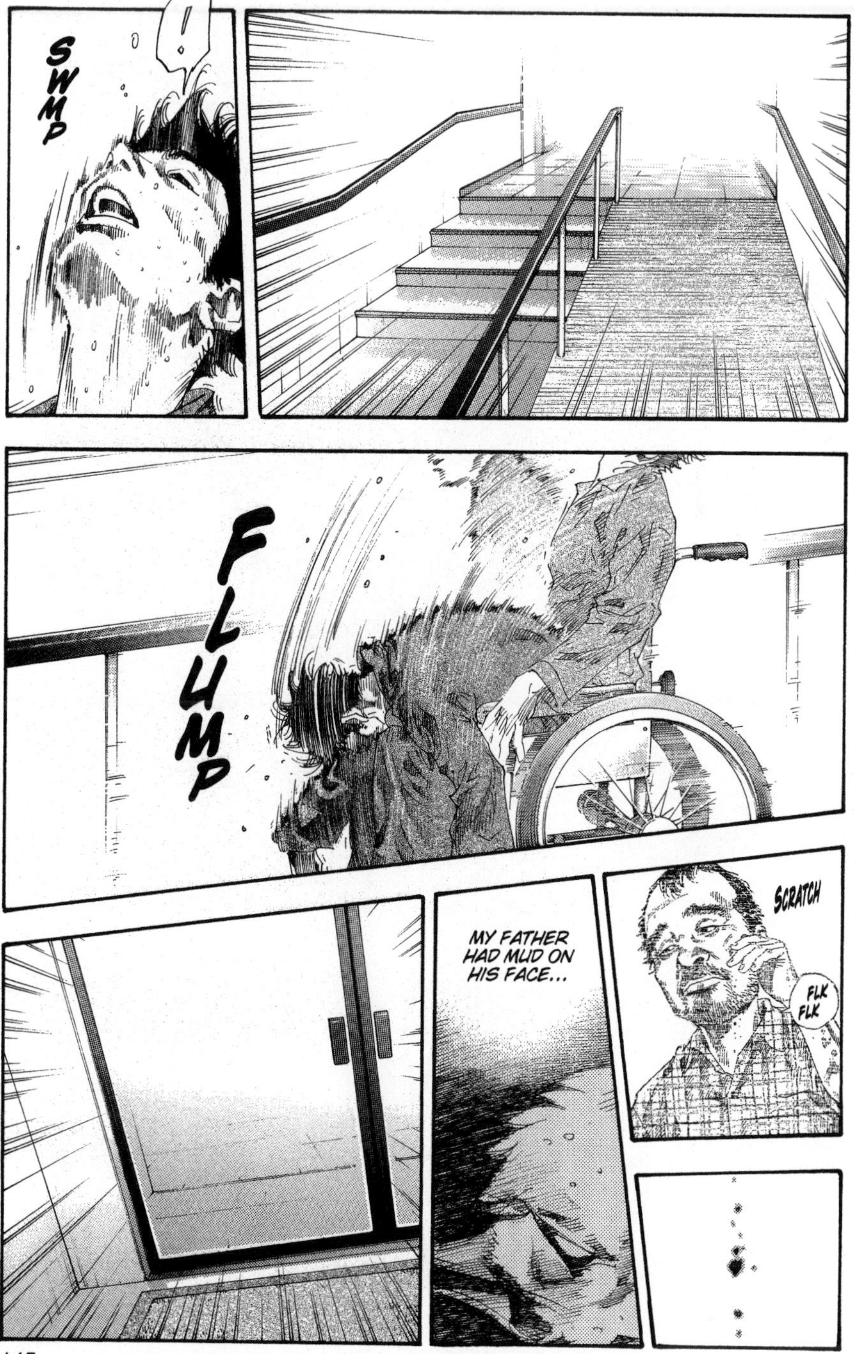
!
SWMP
FLUMP
SCRATCH
FLK FLK
MY FATHER HAD MUD ON HIS FACE...

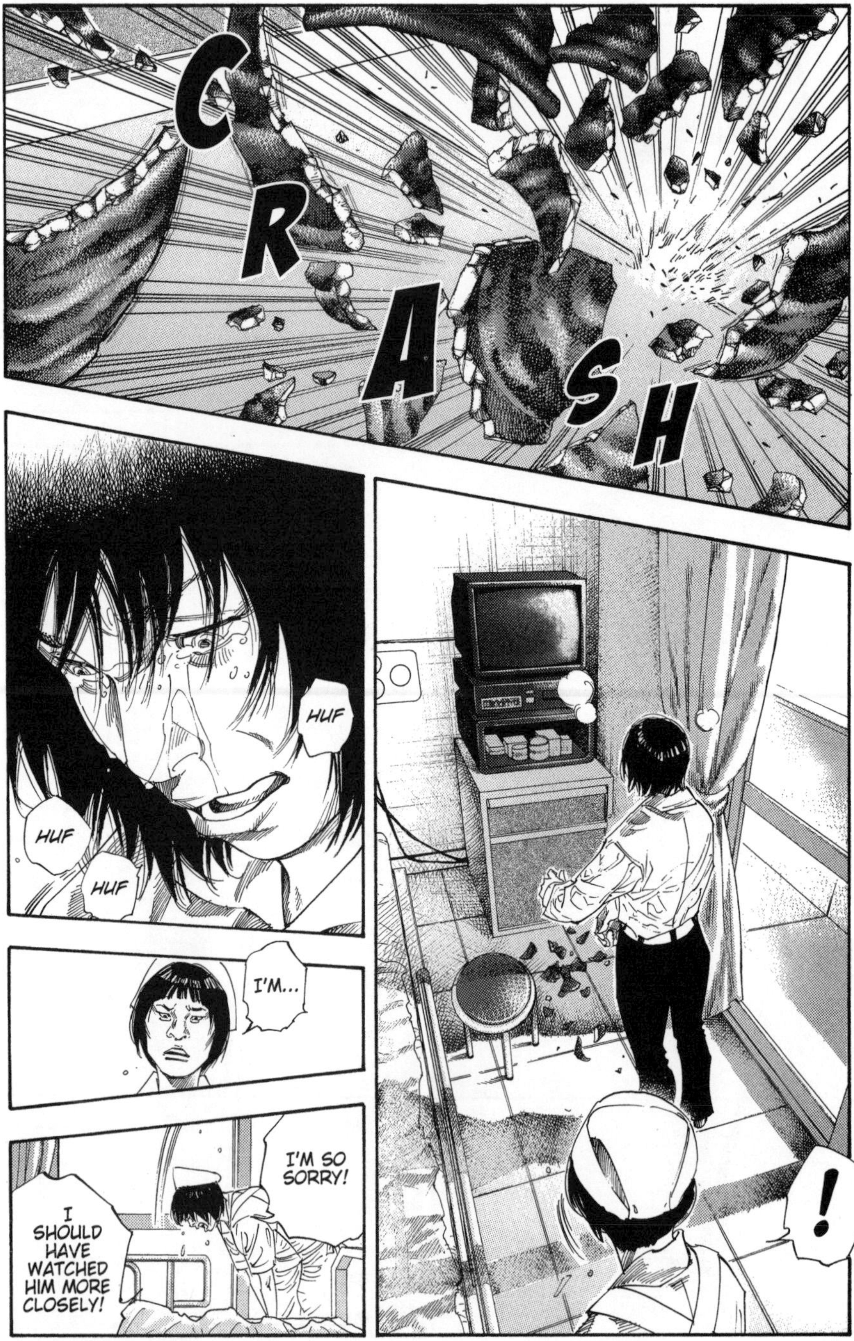
CRASH
!
HUF
HUF
HUF
I'M...
I'M SO SORRY!
I SHOULD HAVE WATCHED HIM MORE CLOSELY!

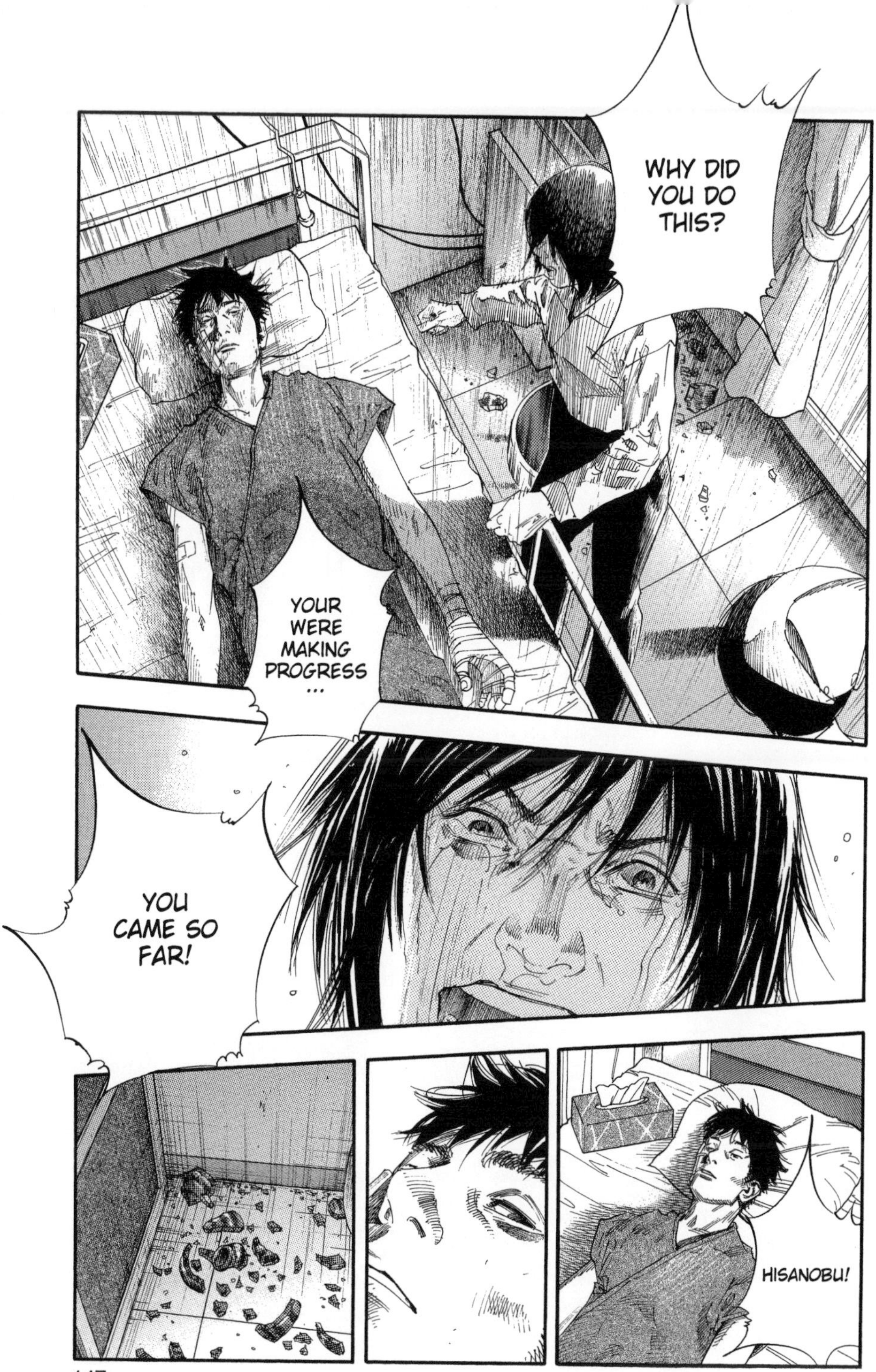
WHY DID YOU DO THIS?
YOUR WERE MAKING PROGRESS ...
YOU CAME SO FAR!
HISANOBU!

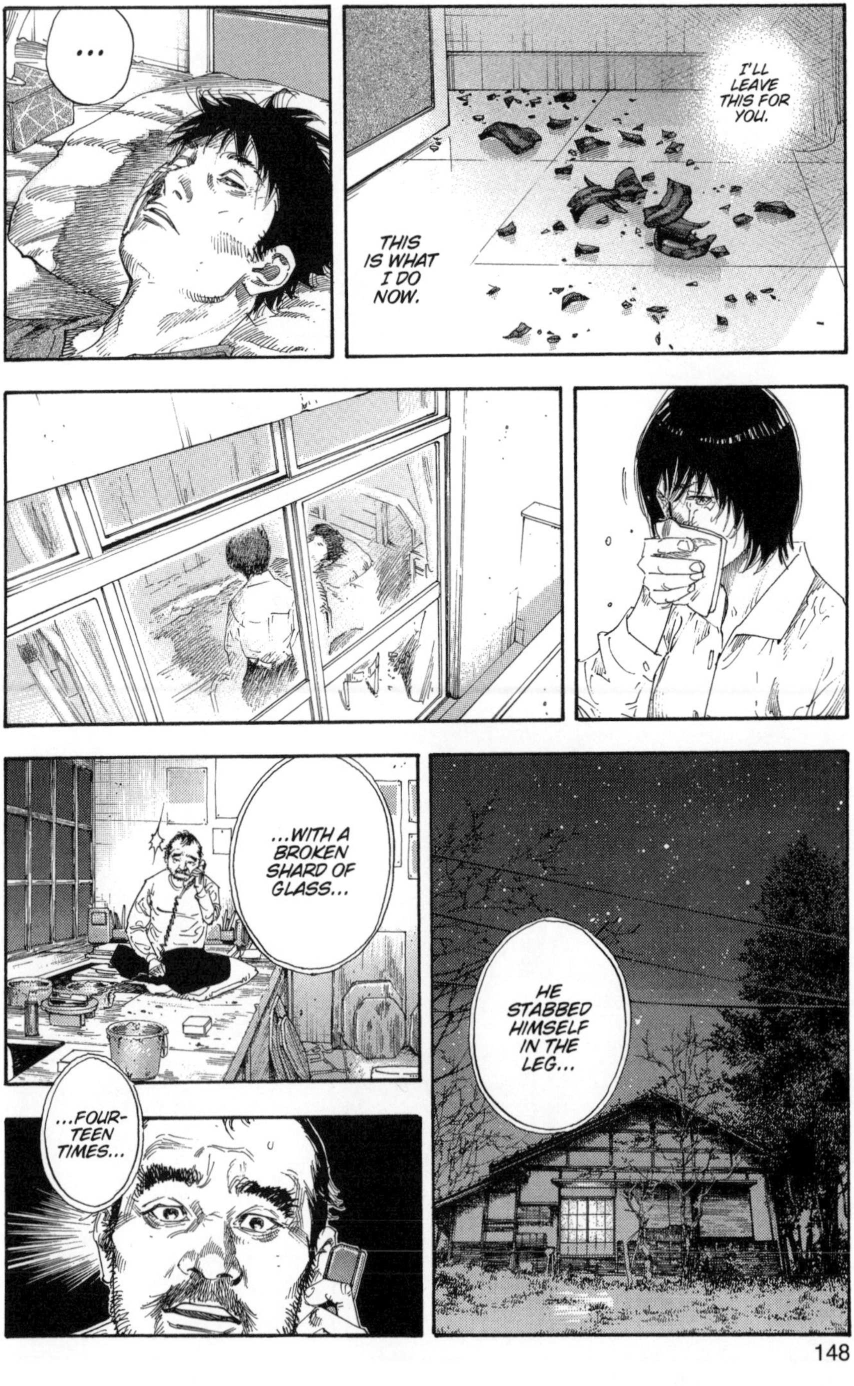
I'LL LEAVE THIS FOR YOU.
THIS IS WHAT I DO NOW.
...
HE STABBED HIMSELF IN THE LEG...
...WITH A BROKEN SHARD OF GLASS...
...FOUR-TEEN TIMES...

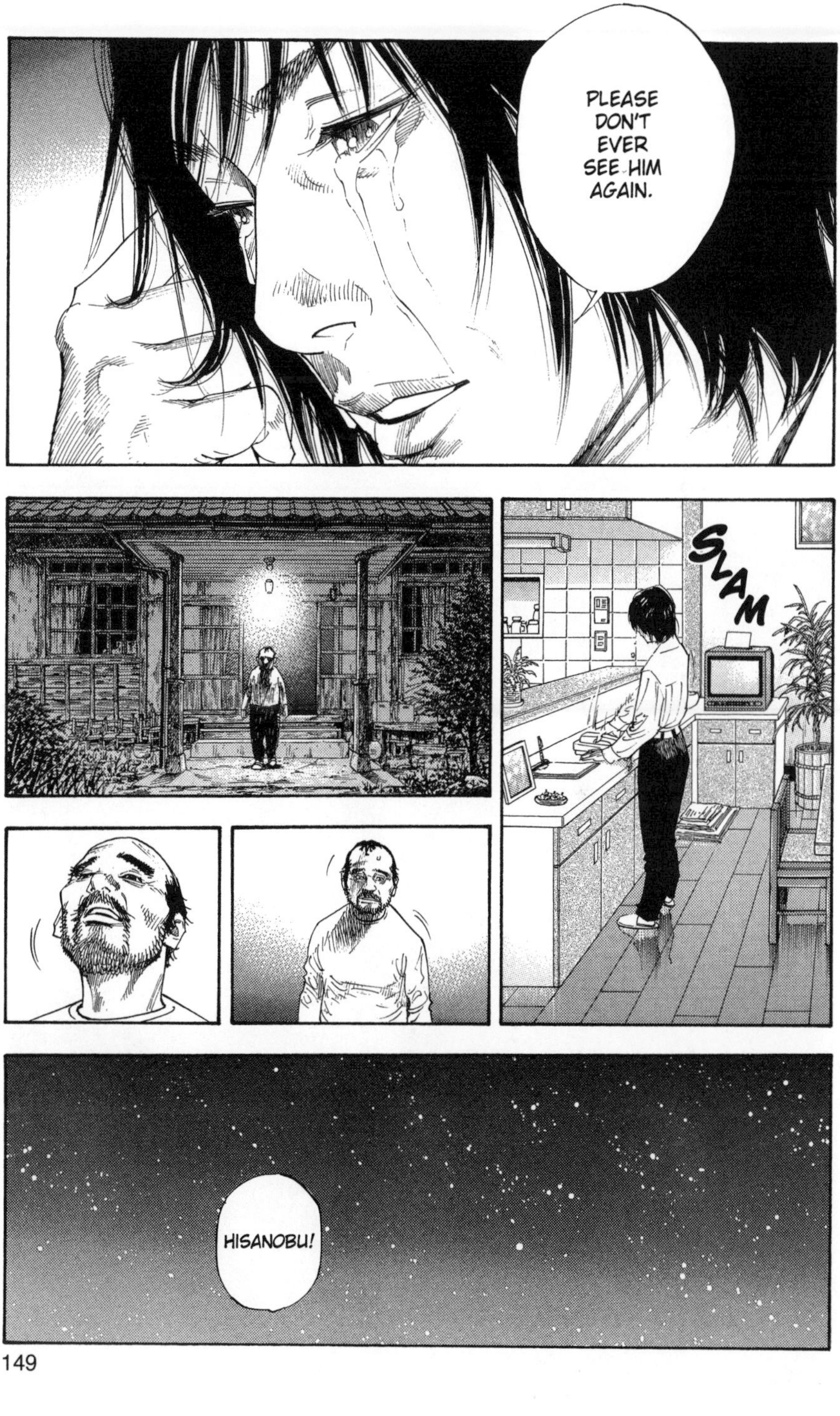
PLEASE DON'T EVER SEE HIM AGAIN.
SLAM
HISANOBU!

I GOT THOROUGHLY DISGUSTED WITH MYSELF...

...WHEN I WENT TO NAGANO TO SEE NATSUMI.

I WANT TO BECOME A BETTER PERSON.

JUST THINKING ABOUT IT WON'T CHANGE ANYTHING...

...SO I DECIDED TO TAKE ACTION.

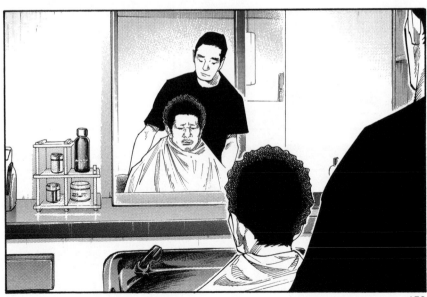

150

GLARE

RUSTLE

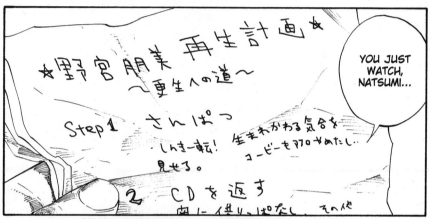

YOU JUST
WATCH,
NATSUMI...

☆野宮朋美 再生計画☆
〜更生への道〜

Step1 さんぱつ

・しんき一転！ 生まれかわる気合を
見せる。 コービーをアフロやめたし・・

2 CDを返す

肉に・借りっぱなし・その他

*TOMOMI NOMIYA'S PLAN FOR A NEW BEGINNING. STEP 1: HAIRCUT

OKAY,
DO IT.

RIGHT.

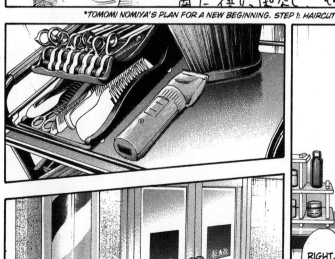

151

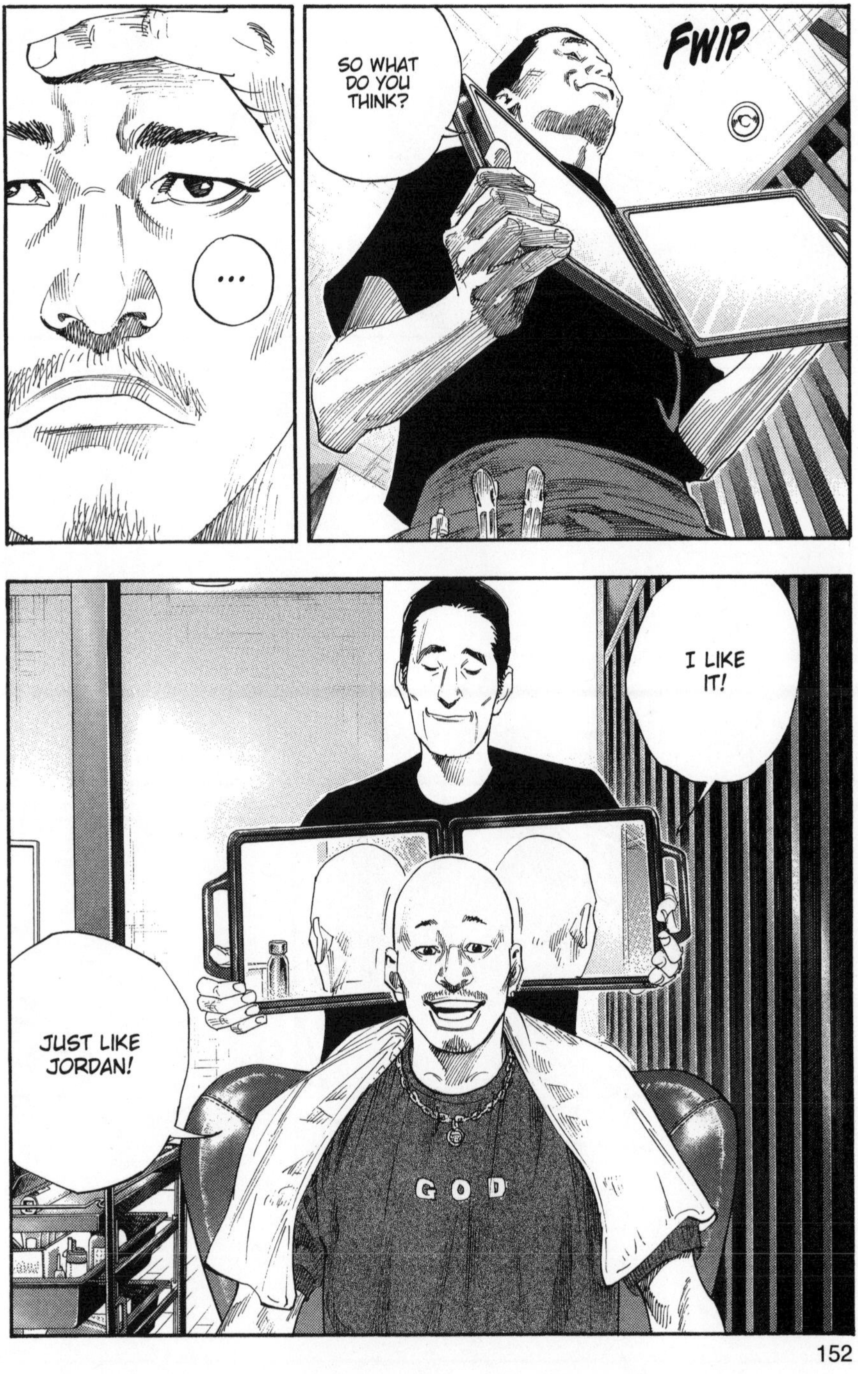
FWIP
SO WHAT DO YOU THINK?
...
I LIKE IT!
JUST LIKE JORDAN!
GOD

SHUF

SHUF

WHAT?

S-SORRY!

···

?

MURMUR

HM?

MURMUR

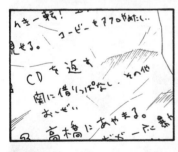

···

THIS JORDAN CUT WAS SUPPOSED TO BE A FRESH NEW START FOR ME, BUT IT'S SCARING PEOPLE OFF.

TSK!

JAPAN JUST AIN'T READY FOR THIS...

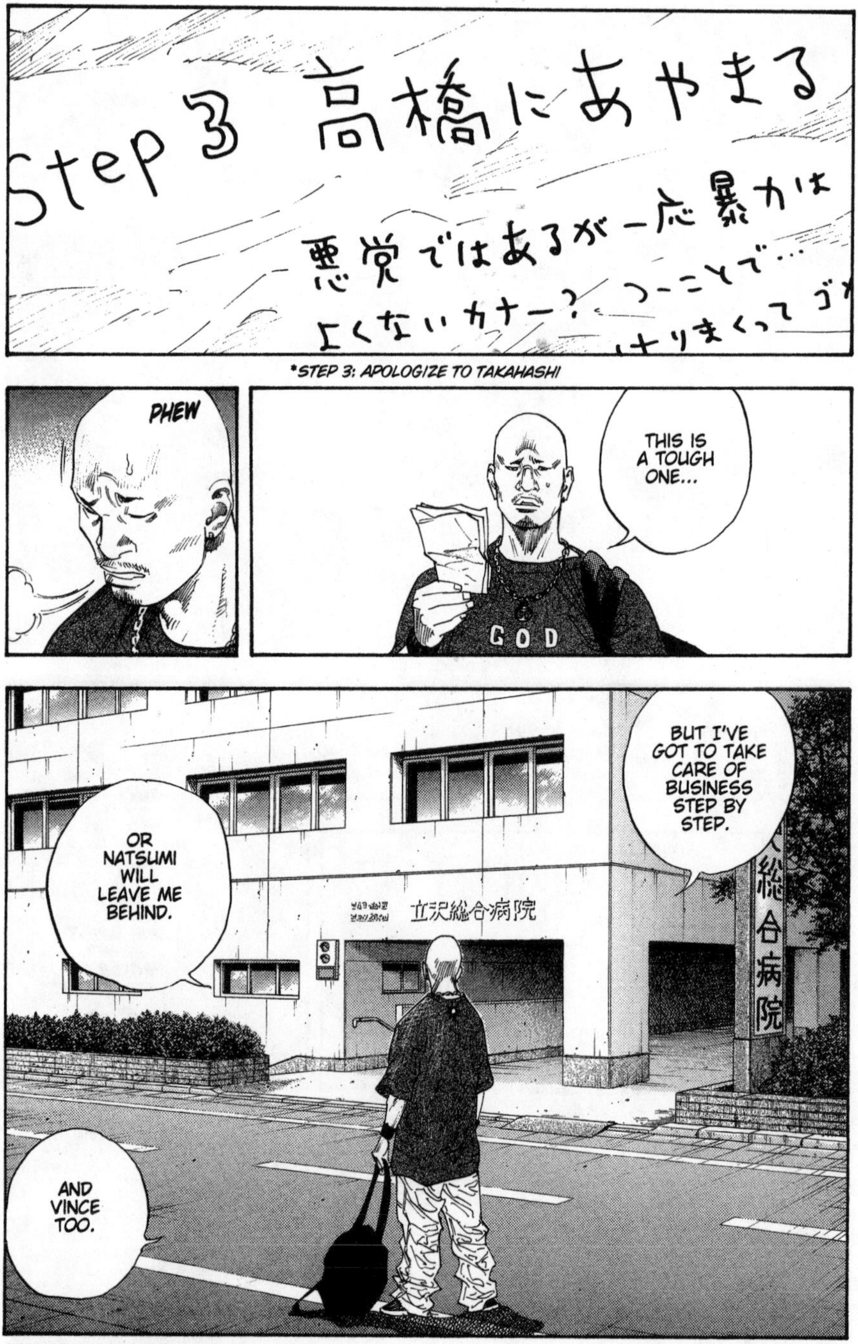
Step 3 高橋にあやまる
悪党ではあるが一応暴力は
よくないカナー? つーことで…
THIS IS A TOUGH ONE...
GOD
PHEW
BUT I'VE GOT TO TAKE CARE OF BUSINESS STEP BY STEP.
立沢総合病院
OR NATSUMI WILL LEAVE ME BEHIND.
AND VINCE TOO.
*STEP 3: APOLOGIZE TO TAKAHASHI

*TACHIZAWA GENERAL HOSPITAL

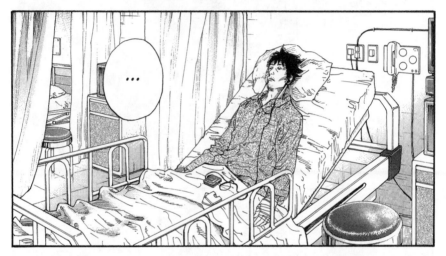

...

GASP!

I GUESS THIS MEANS...

...NO MORE ONE-ON-ONE.

155

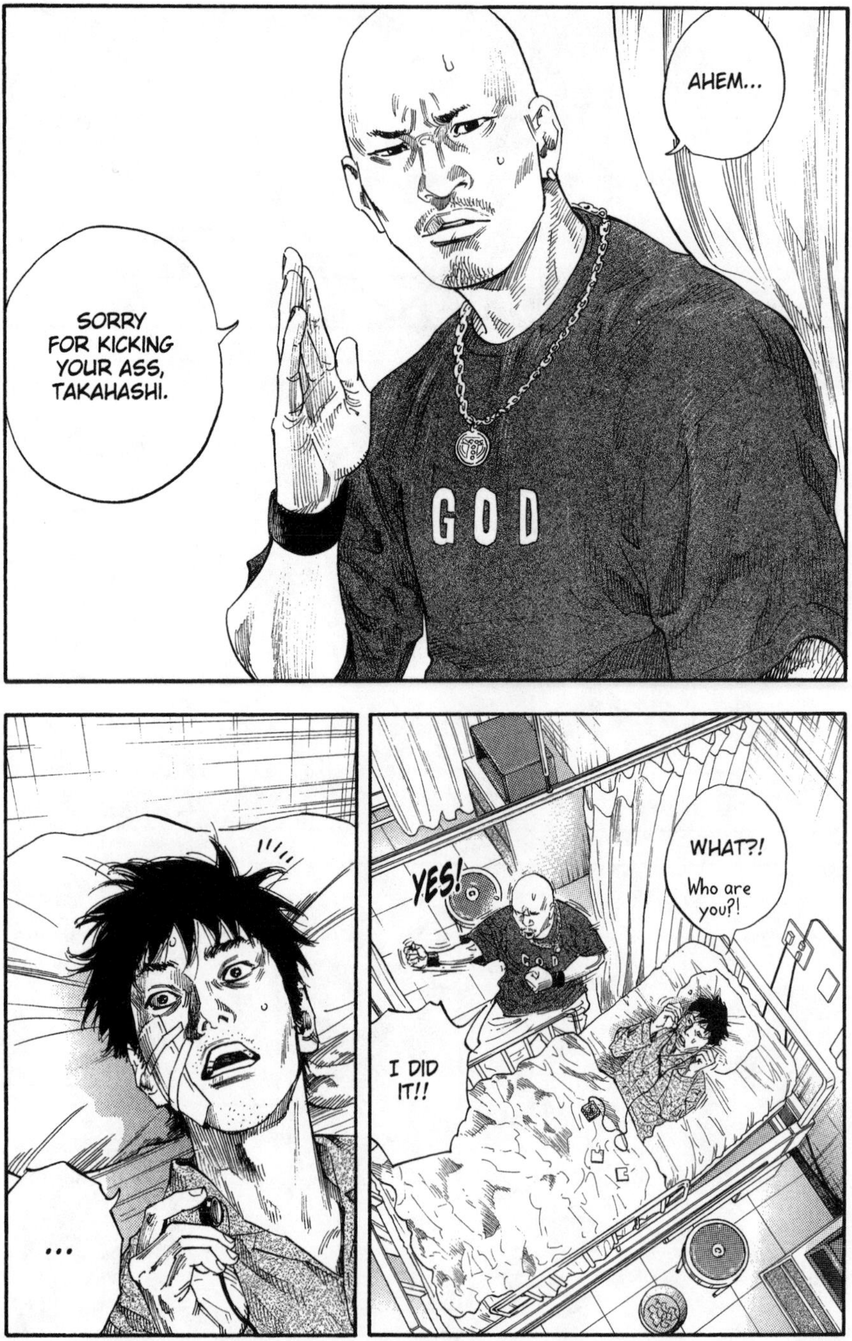
AHEM...
SORRY FOR KICKING YOUR ASS, TAKAHASHI.
WHAT?!
Who are you?!
YES!
I DID IT!!
...

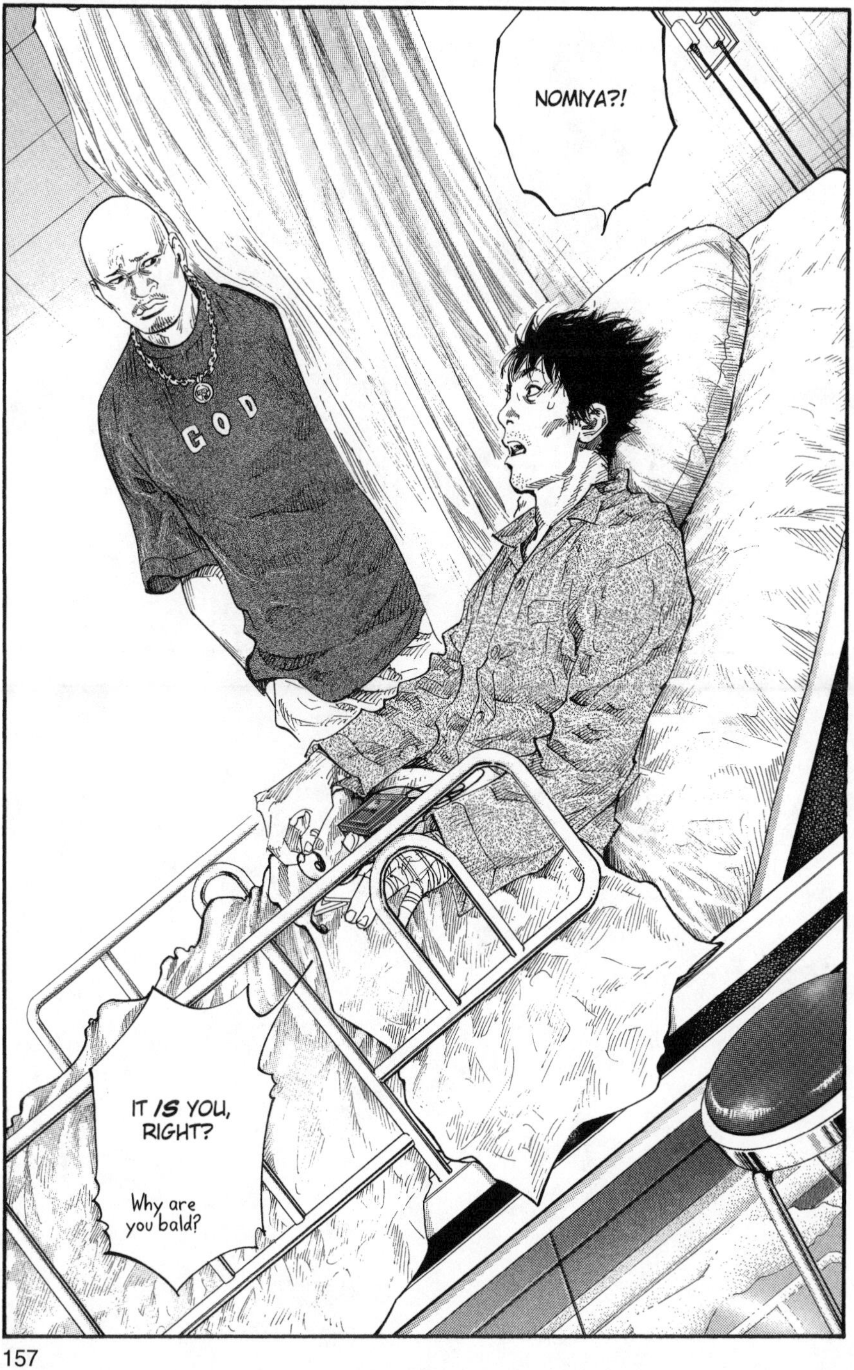
NOMIYA?!
IT *IS* YOU, RIGHT?
Why are you bald?

DAMN IT!
WHAT'S HE DOING HERE?
GOD
GET OUT OF HERE, YOU JERK!
STILL NOT DOING SO HOT, EH?

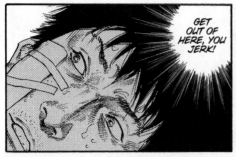

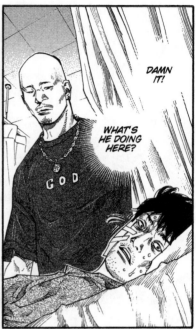

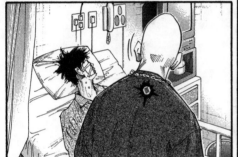

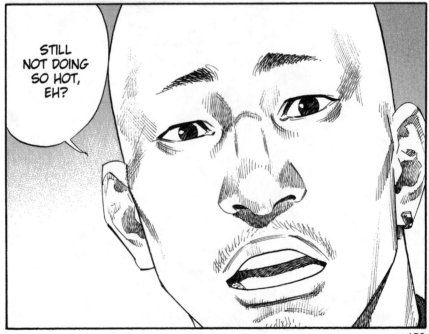

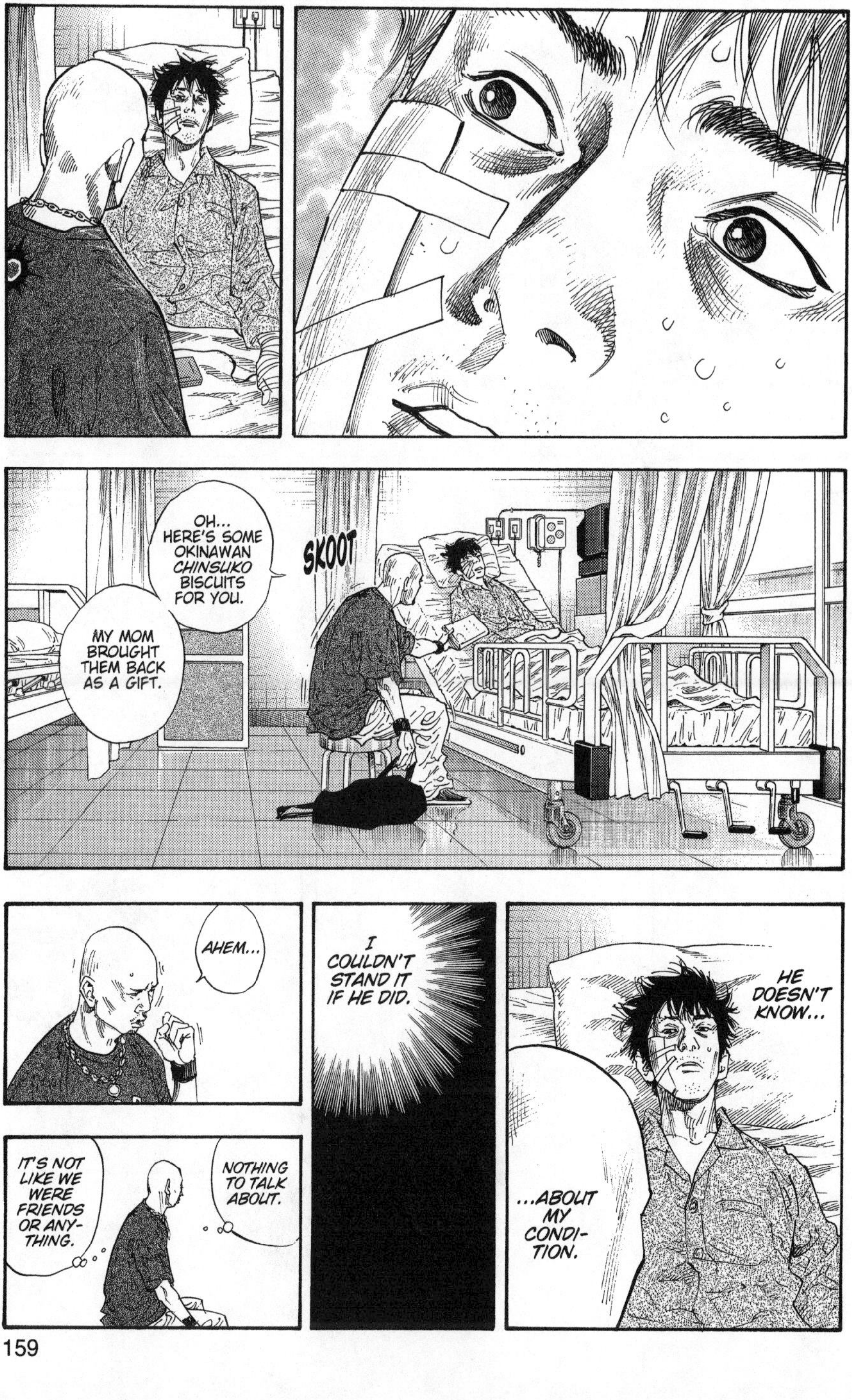
SKOOT
OH... HERE'S SOME OKINAWAN *CHINSUKO* BISCUITS FOR YOU.
MY MOM BROUGHT THEM BACK AS A GIFT.
HE DOESN'T KNOW...
...ABOUT MY CONDITION.
I COULDN'T STAND IT IF HE DID.
AHEM...
NOTHING TO TALK ABOUT.
IT'S NOT LIKE WE WERE FRIENDS OR ANY-THING.

OOPS.

TMP
TP

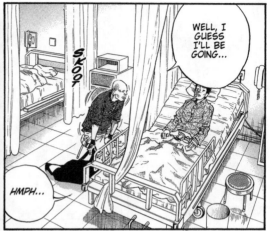

WELL, I GUESS I'LL BE GOING...

SKOOT

HMPH...

BMP

BMP

...!!

HEY...

...I WENT TO SEE NISHI HIGH'S LAST GAME.

!

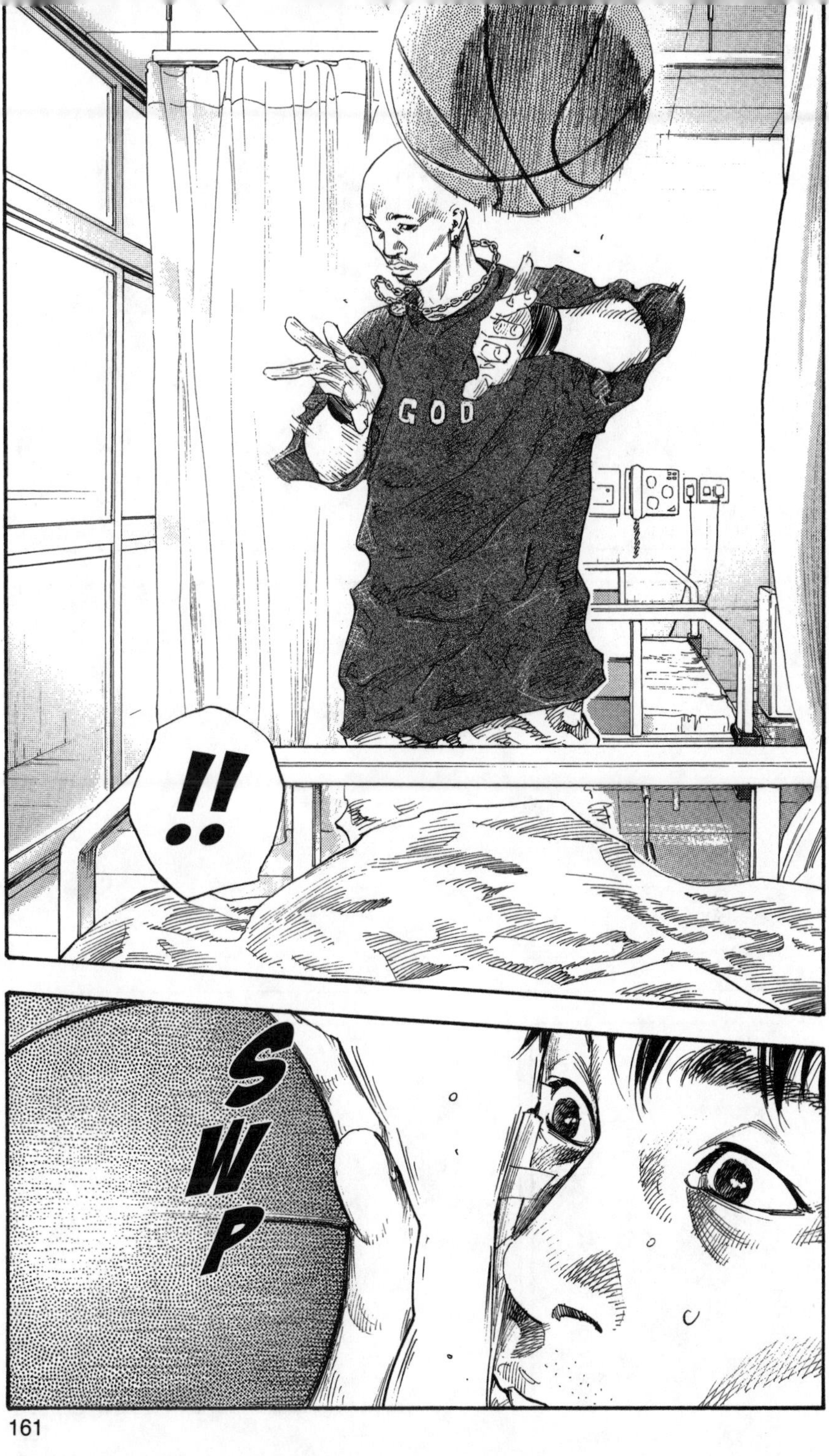
GOD
!!
SWP

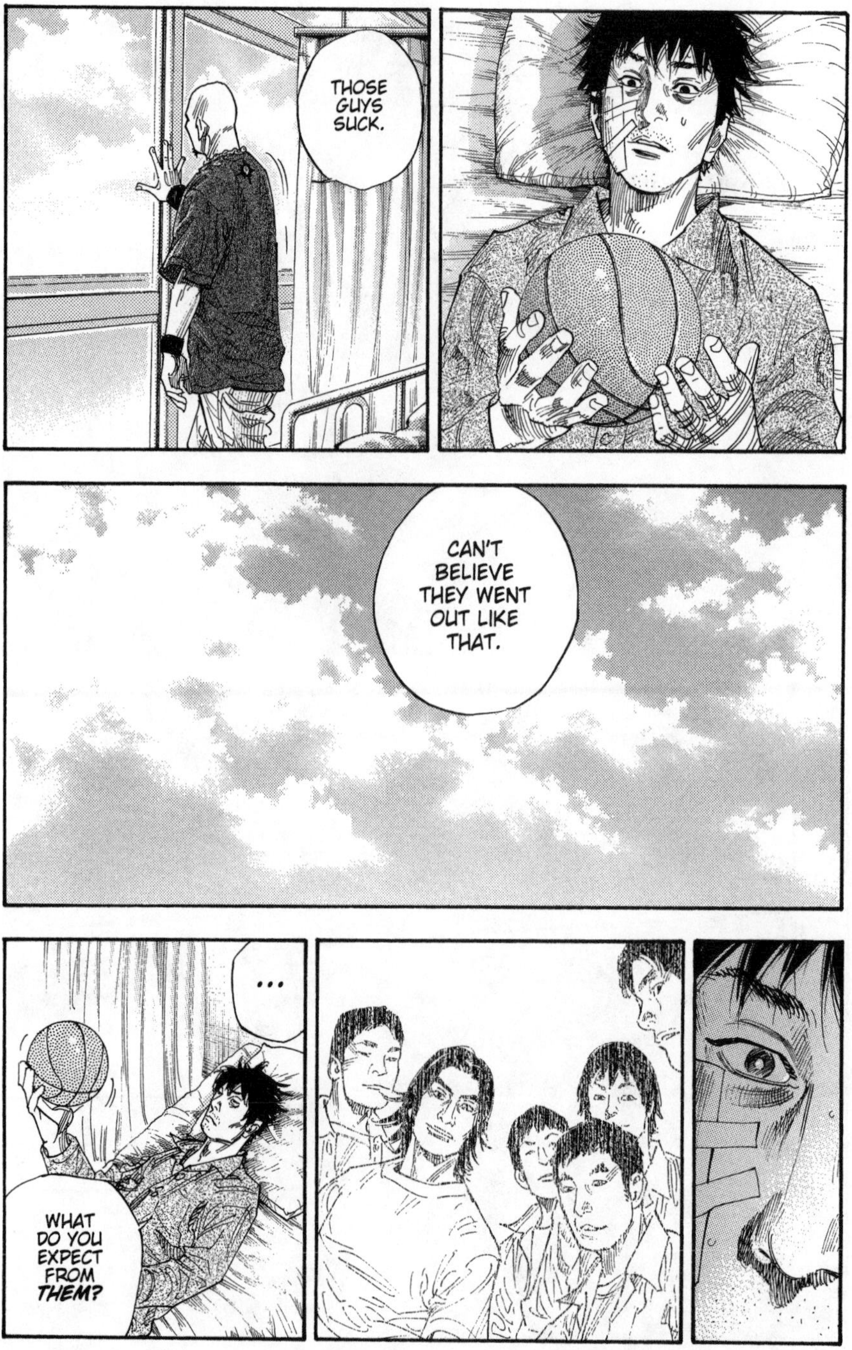
THOSE GUYS SUCK.
CAN'T BELIEVE THEY WENT OUT LIKE THAT.
...
WHAT DO YOU EXPECT FROM *THEM*?

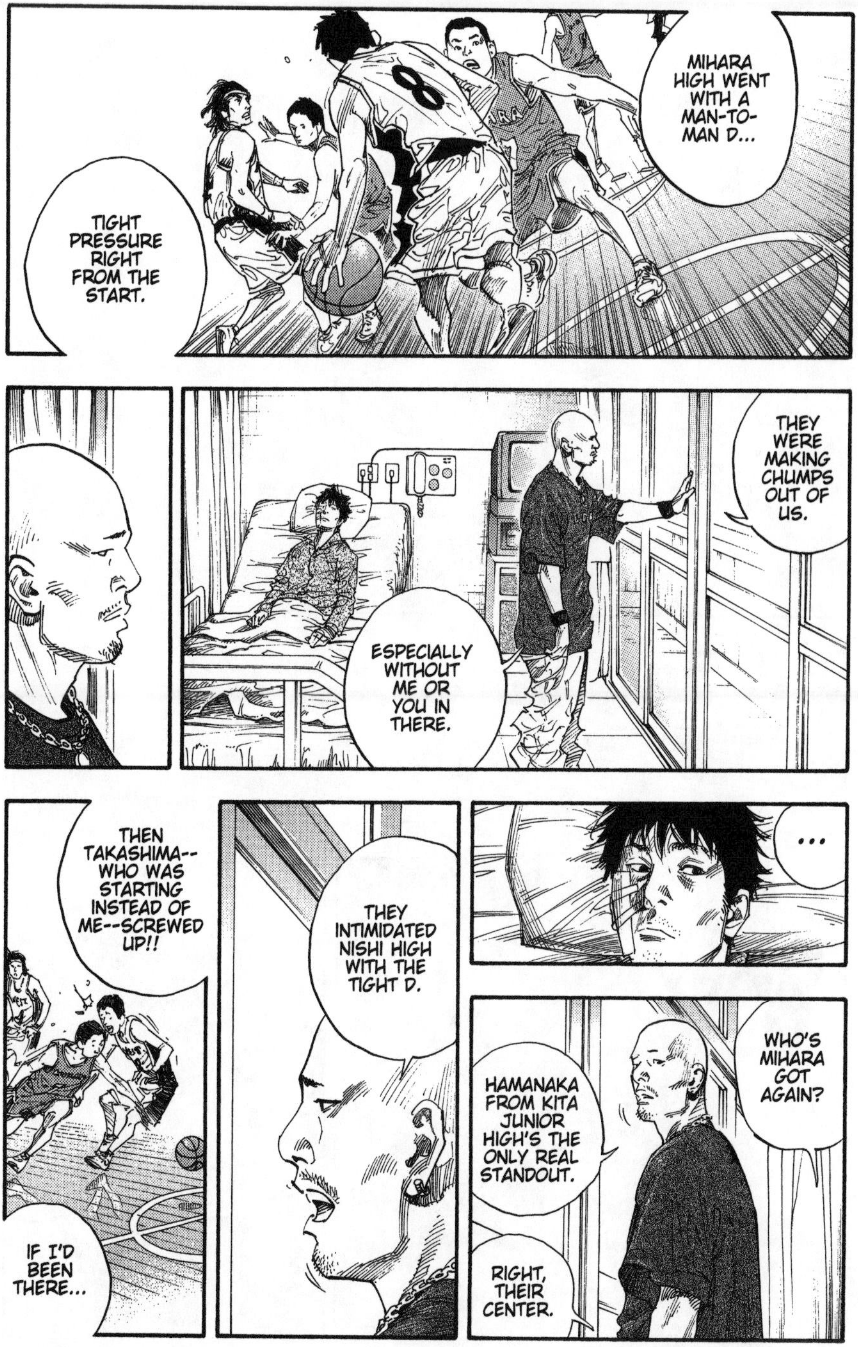
MIHARA HIGH WENT WITH A MAN-TO-MAN D...
TIGHT PRESSURE RIGHT FROM THE START.
THEY WERE MAKING CHUMPS OUT OF US.
ESPECIALLY WITHOUT ME OR YOU IN THERE.
...
WHO'S MIHARA GOT AGAIN?
HAMANAKA FROM KITA JUNIOR HIGH'S THE ONLY REAL STANDOUT.
RIGHT, THEIR CENTER.
THEY INTIMIDATED NISHI HIGH WITH THE TIGHT D.
THEN TAKASHIMA--WHO WAS STARTING INSTEAD OF ME--SCREWED UP!!
IF I'D BEEN THERE...

IF ONLY I'D BEEN THERE...
SKWK
SKWK
SKWK
YOU SURE YOU WANNA BE UP THIS CLOSE?!
SKWK
SKWK
BAM

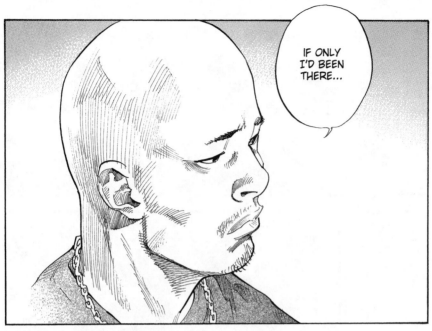

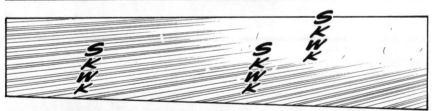

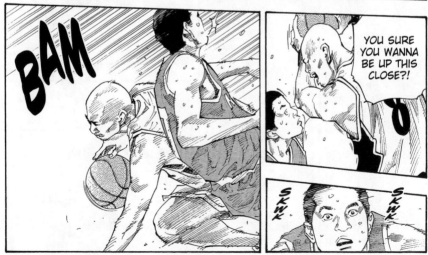

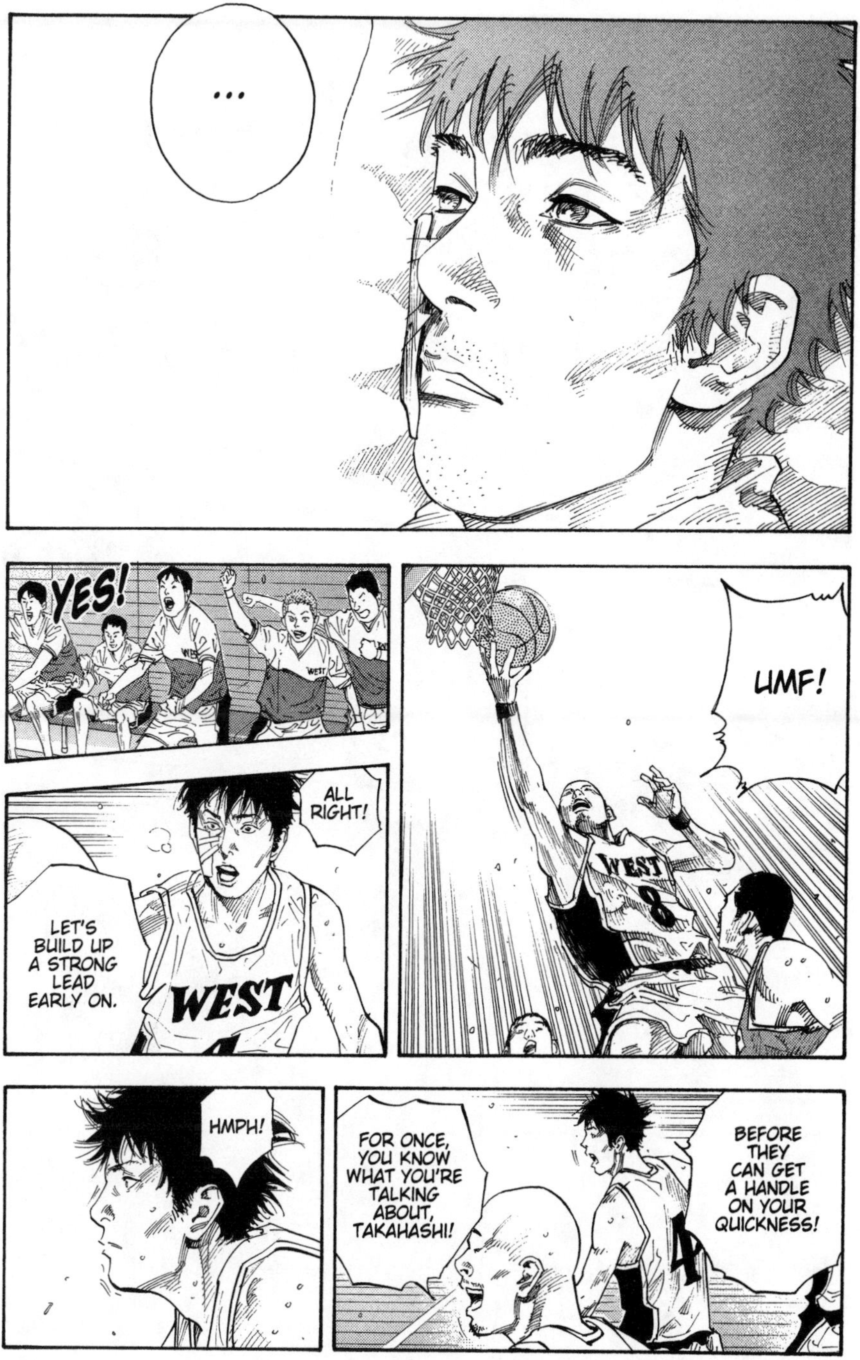
...
UMF!
YES!
ALL RIGHT!
LET'S BUILD UP A STRONG LEAD EARLY ON.
BEFORE THEY CAN GET A HANDLE ON YOUR QUICKNESS!
FOR ONCE, YOU KNOW WHAT YOU'RE TALKING ABOUT, TAKAHASHI!
HMPH!

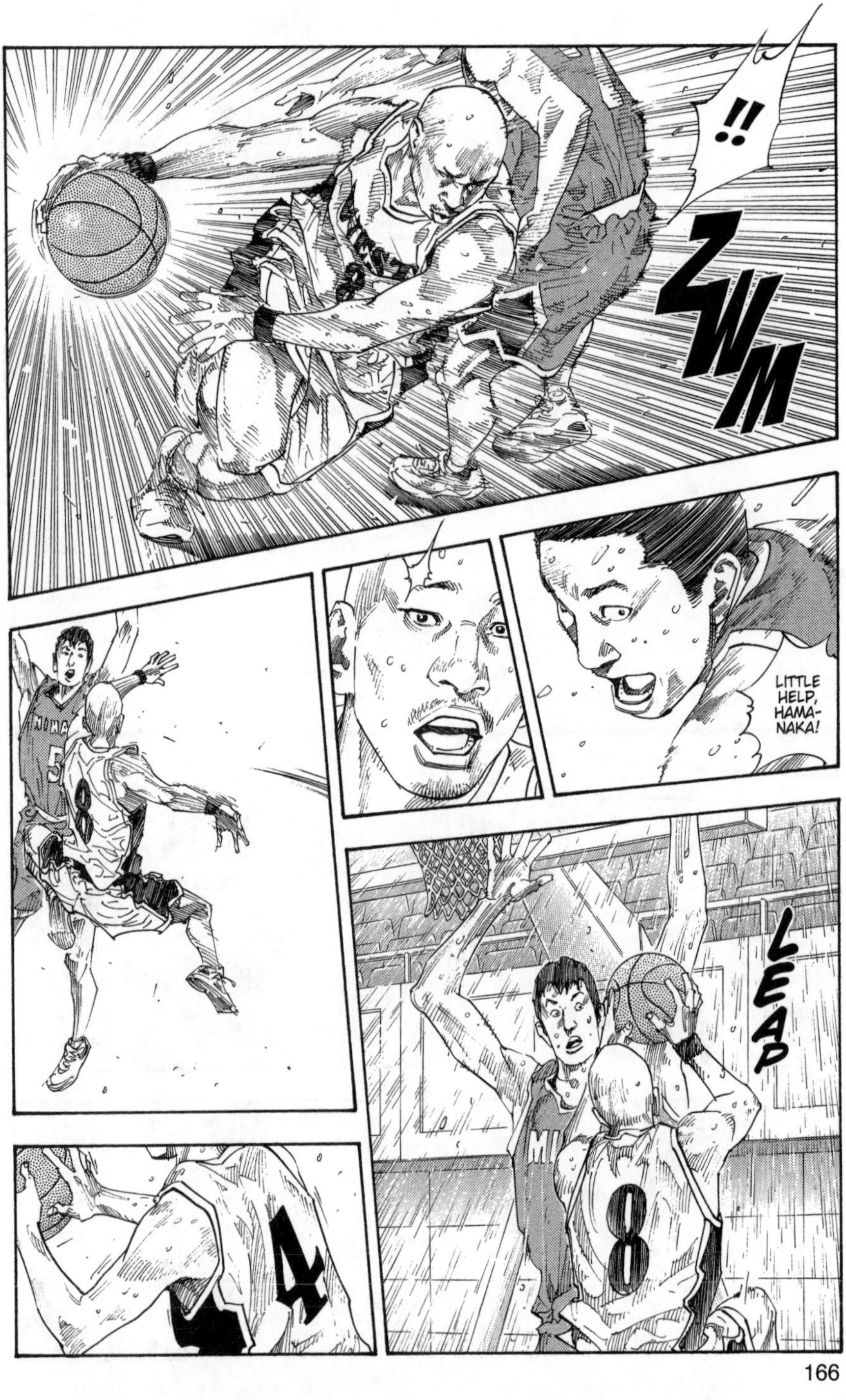
!!
ZWM
LITTLE HELP, HAMA-NAKA!
LEAP

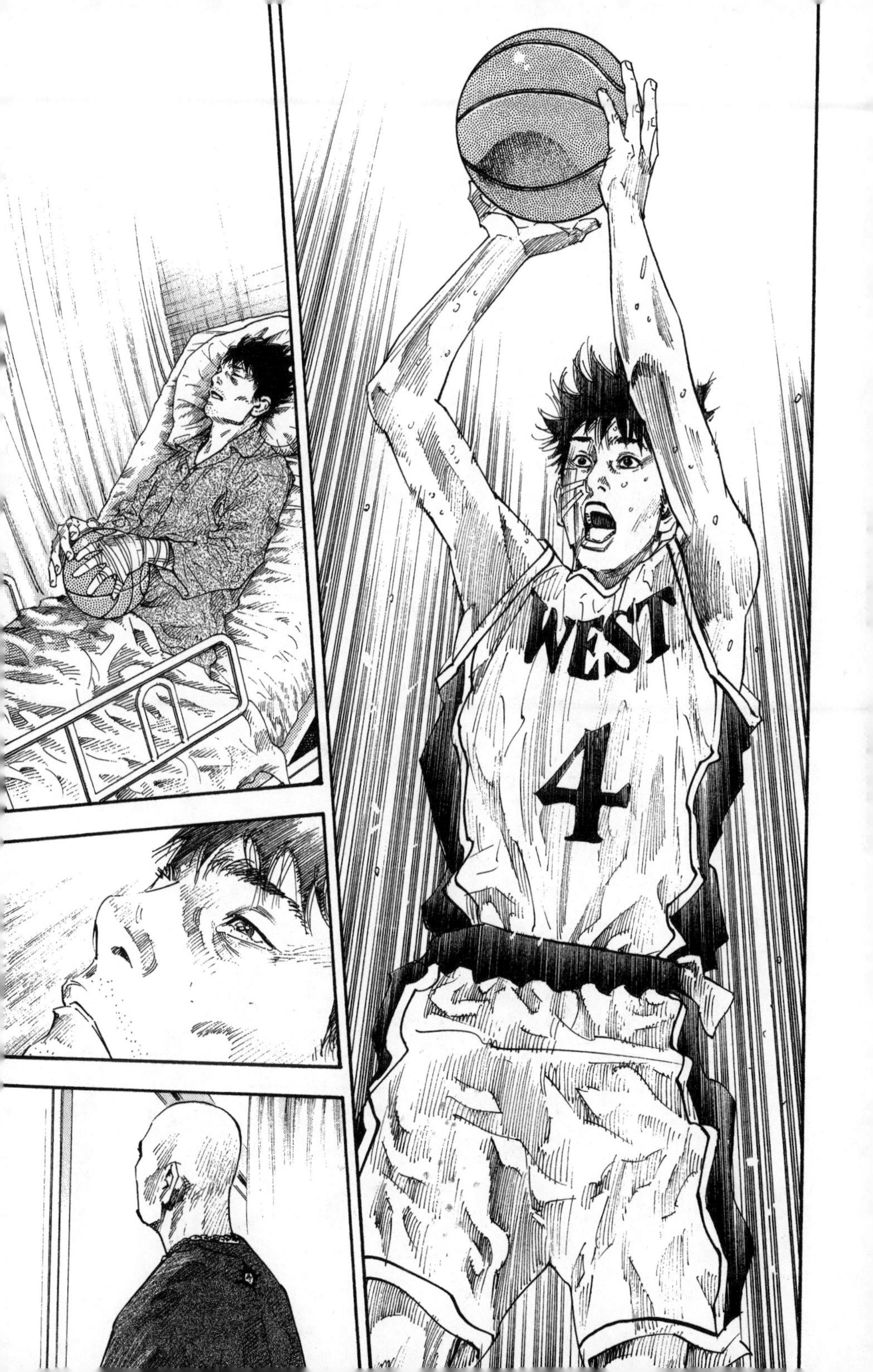
WEST
4

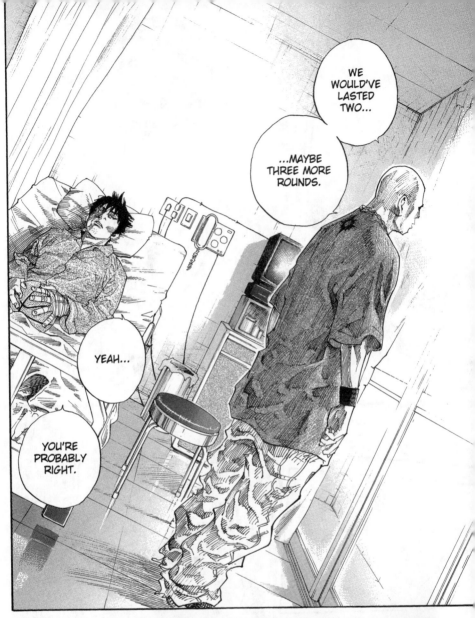

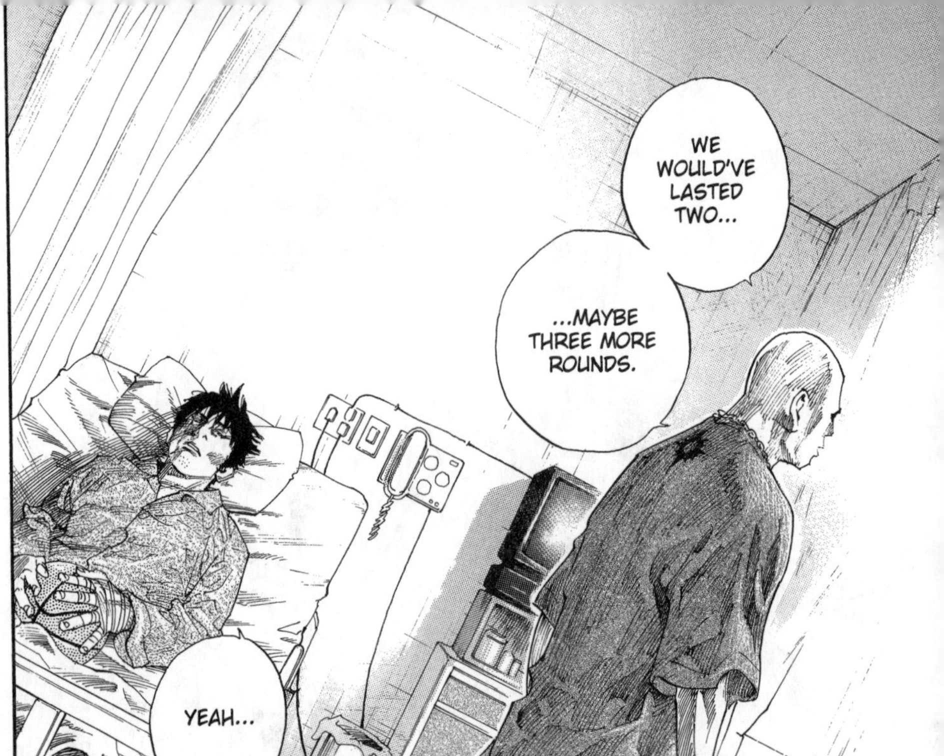
WE WOULD'VE LASTED TWO...
...MAYBE THREE MORE ROUNDS.
YEAH...
YOU'RE PROBABLY RIGHT.
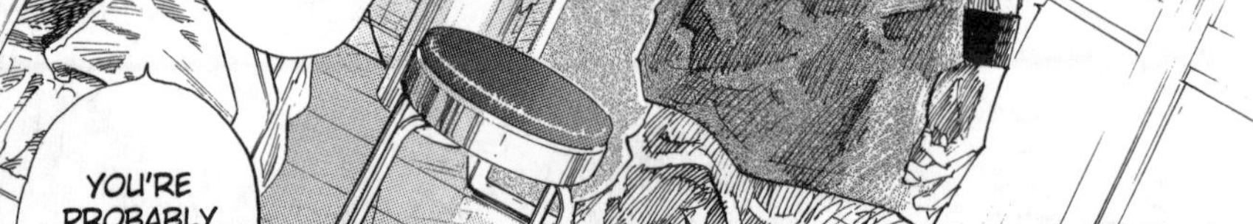

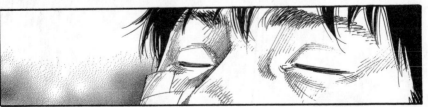

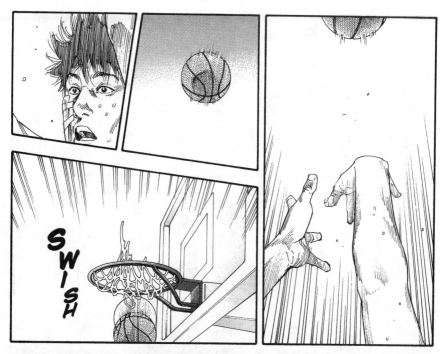

SWISH

I GUESS THIS MEANS...

...NO MORE ONE-ON-ONE.

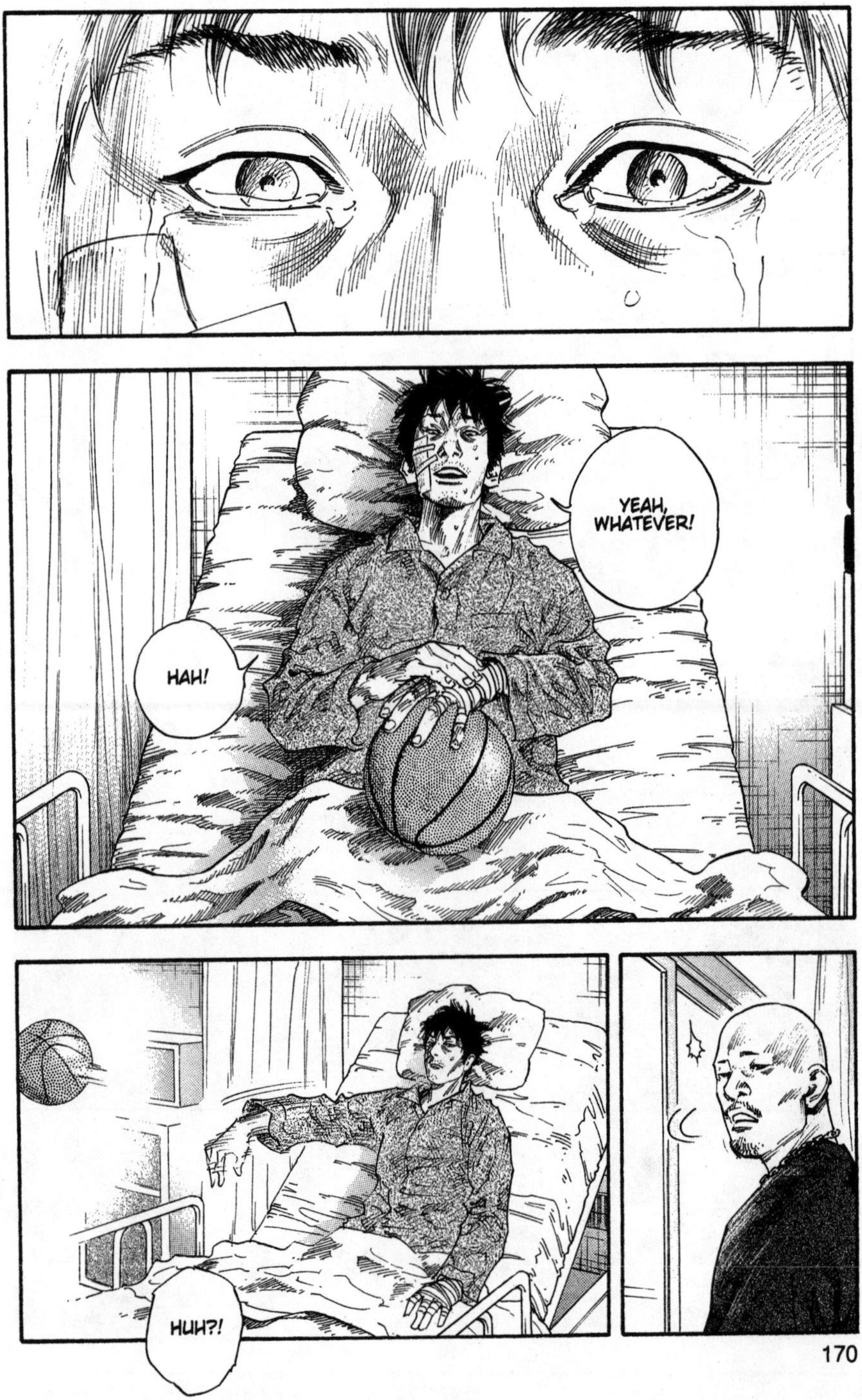
YEAH, WHATEVER!
HAH!
HUH?!

GET OUT OF HERE, NOMIYA.

WHAT'D YOU COME FOR ANYWAY?

BP

BAP

BAP

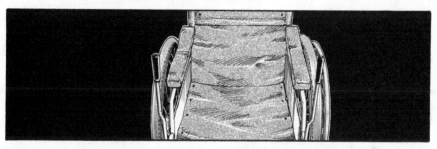

GET OUT!

HUH?

WHAT'S YOUR PROBLEM?

GOD

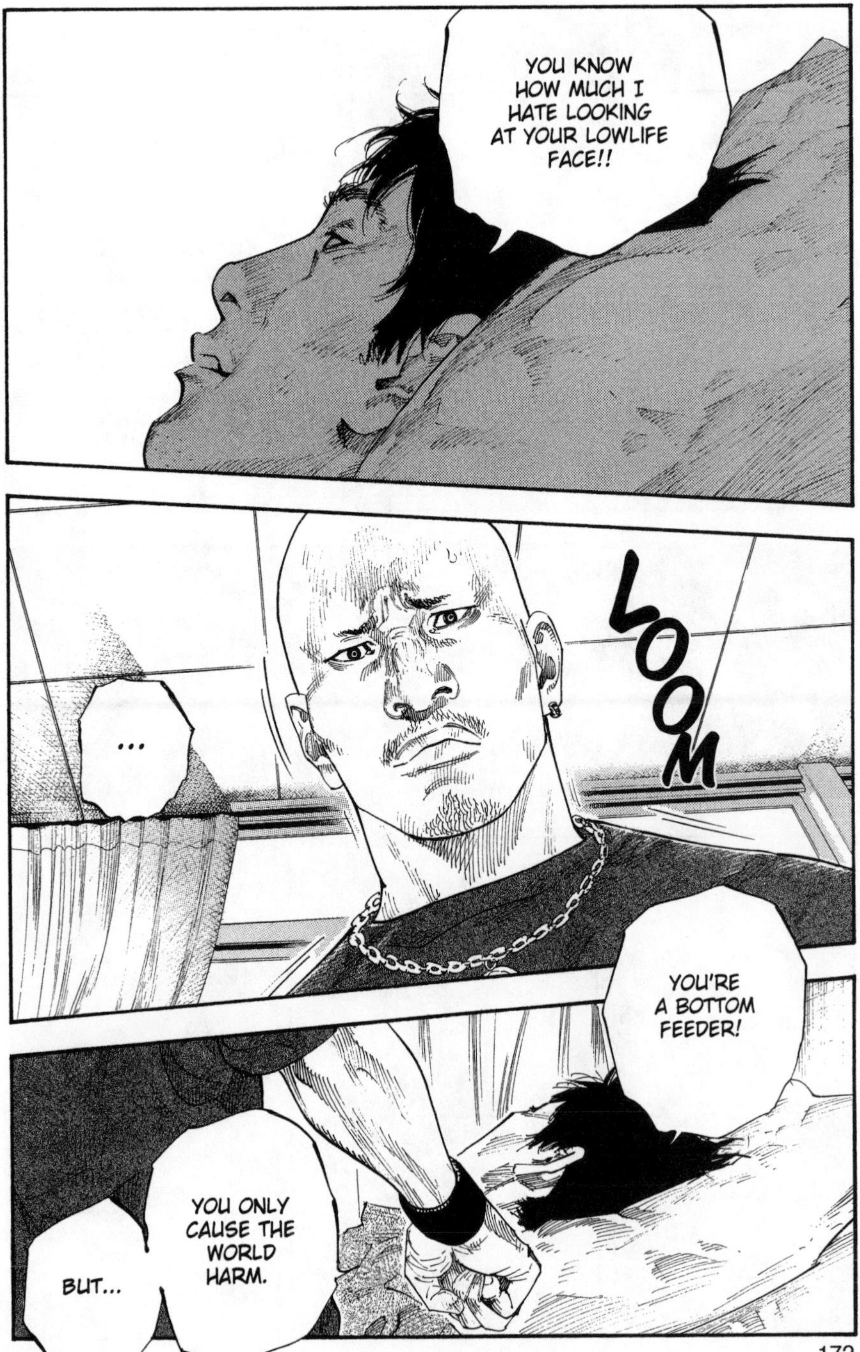
YOU KNOW HOW MUCH I HATE LOOKING AT YOUR LOWLIFE FACE!!
VOOM
...
YOU'RE A BOTTOM FEEDER!
YOU ONLY CAUSE THE WORLD HARM.
BUT...

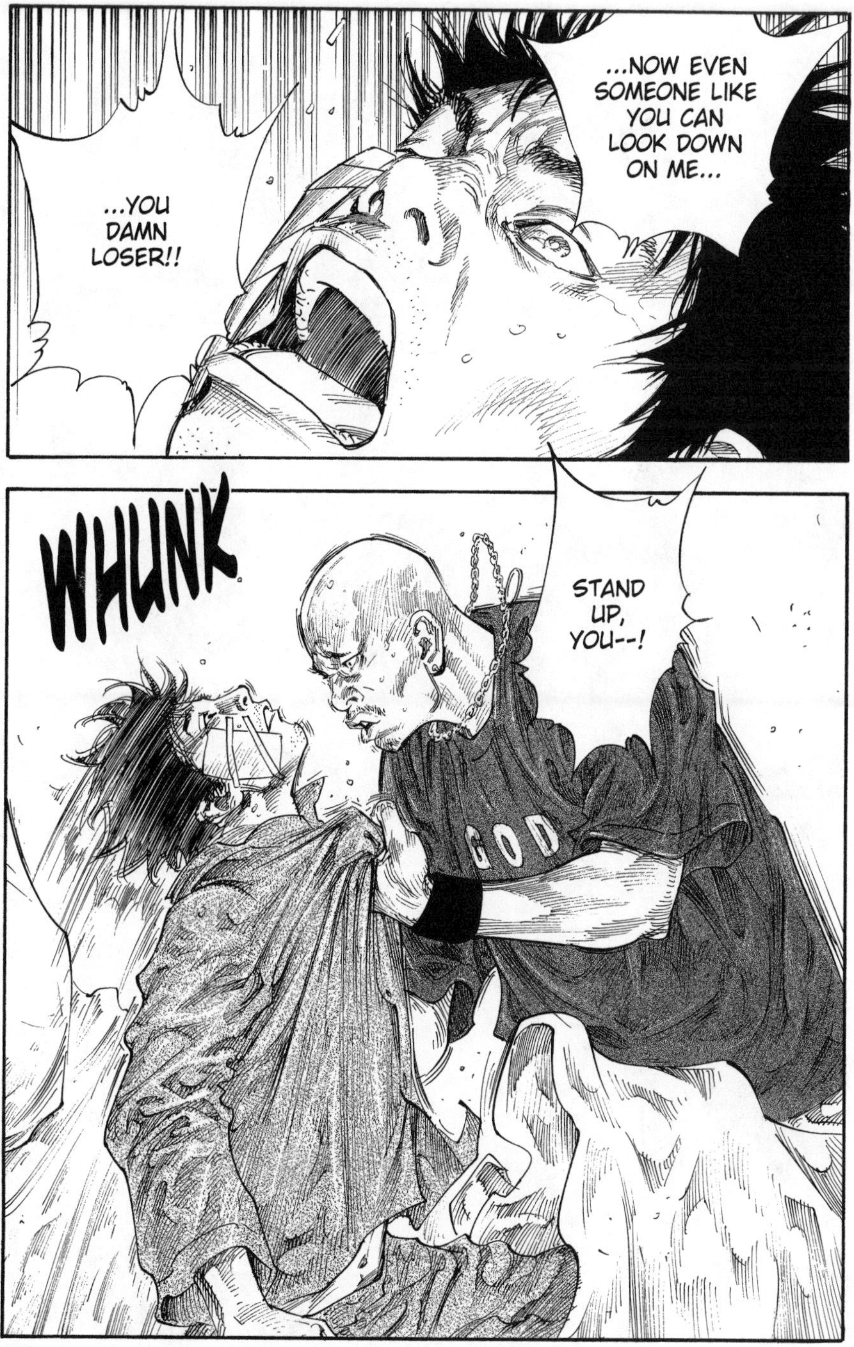
...NOW EVEN SOMEONE LIKE YOU CAN LOOK DOWN ON ME...
...YOU DAMN LOSER!!
STAND UP, YOU--!
WHUNK

?!

SLUMP

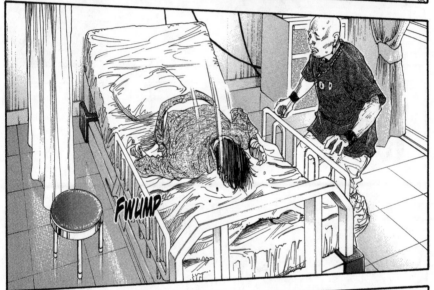
FWUMP

HAH...

HEH
HEH
HEH...

STAND
UP?

174

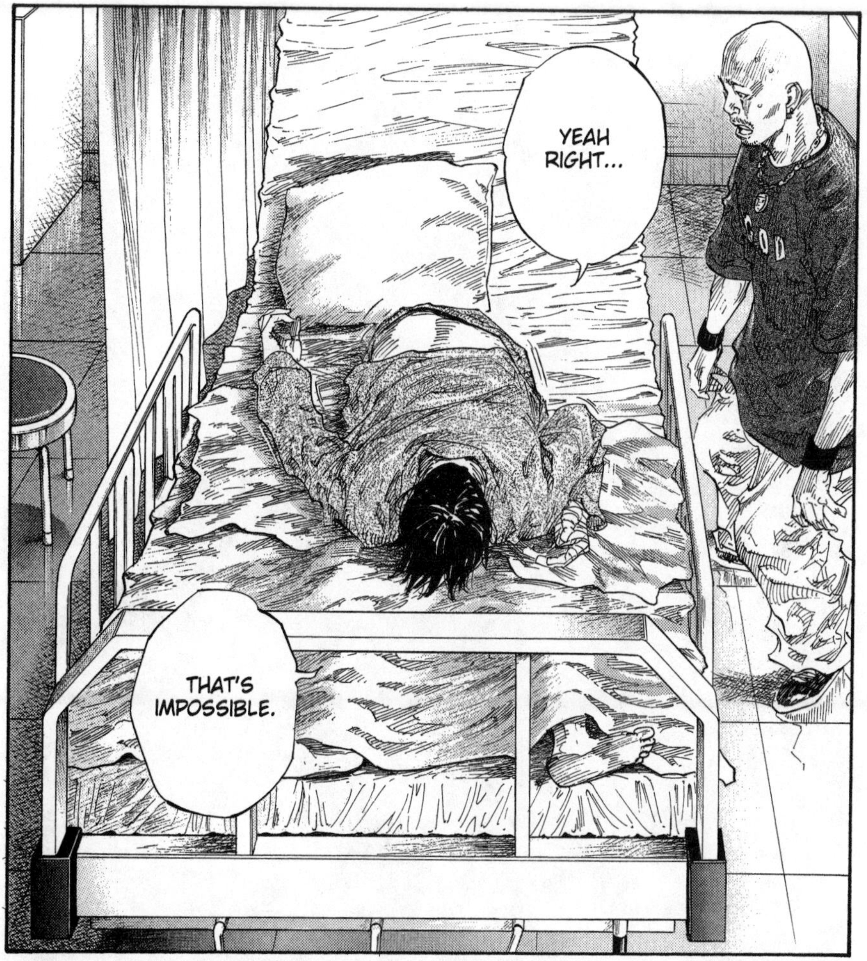
YEAH RIGHT...
THAT'S IMPOSSIBLE.

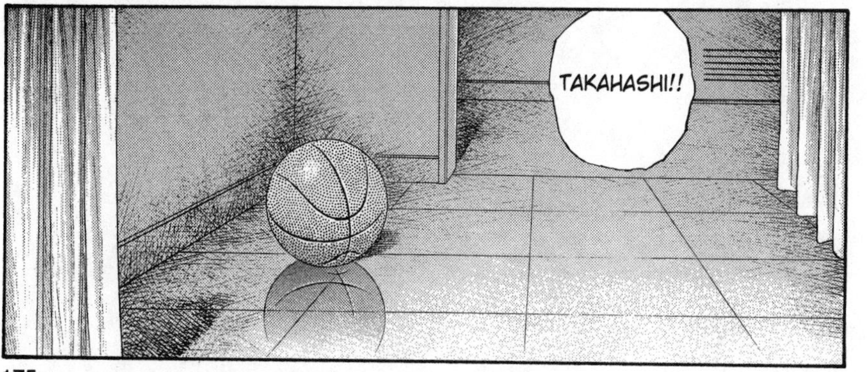
TAKAHASHI!!

REAL

18th

ARE YOU--?!

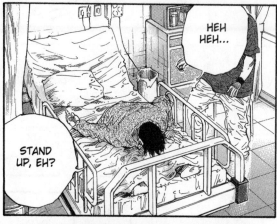

HEH HEH...

STAND UP, EH?

TAKAHASHI!

...

UMF

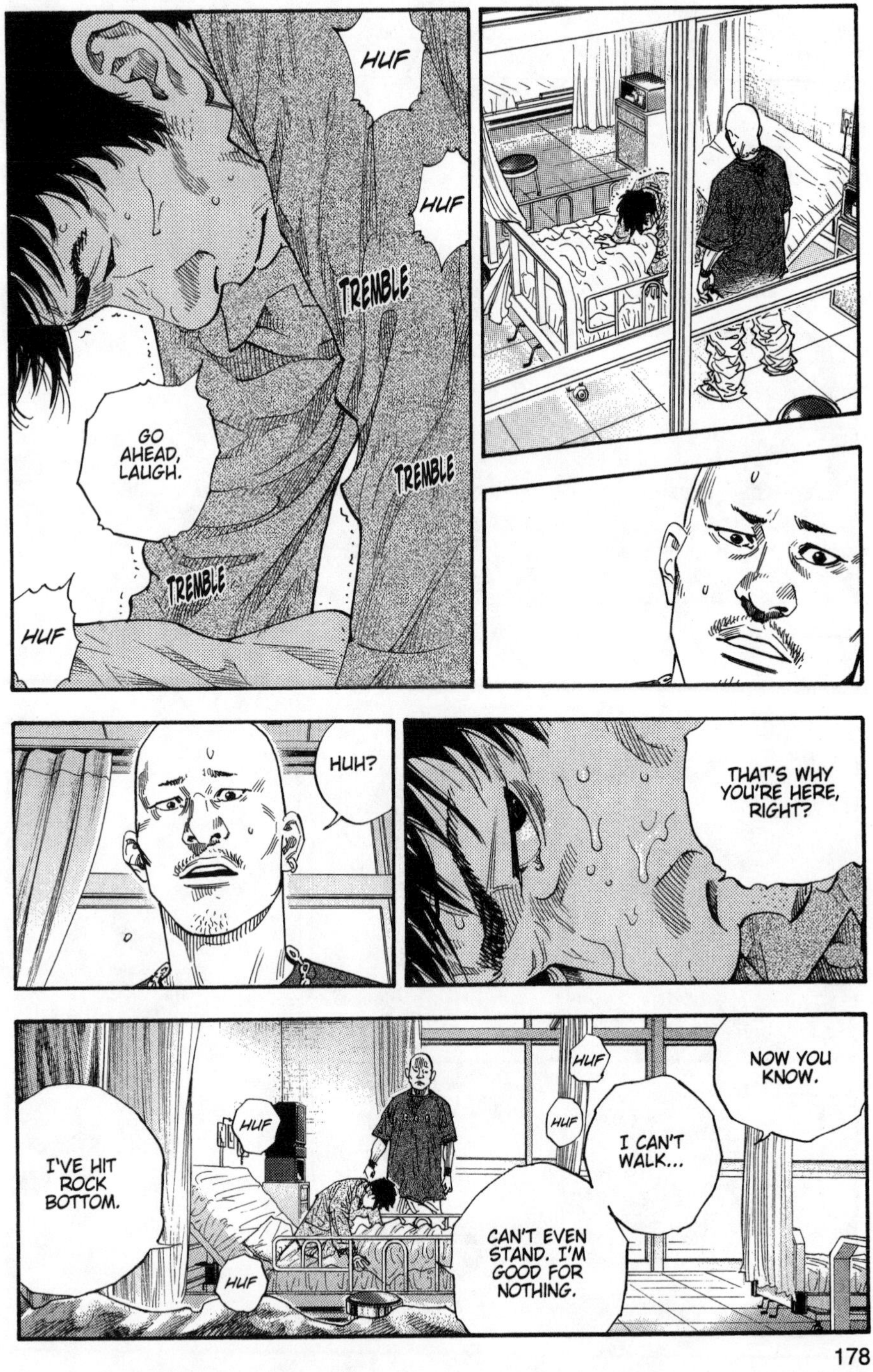
HUF
HUF
TREMBLE
GO AHEAD, LAUGH.
TREMBLE
TREMBLE
HUF
THAT'S WHY YOU'RE HERE, RIGHT?
HUH?
NOW YOU KNOW.
HUF
HUF
I CAN'T WALK...
CAN'T EVEN STAND. I'M GOOD FOR NOTHING.
HUF
I'VE HIT ROCK BOTTOM.
HUF

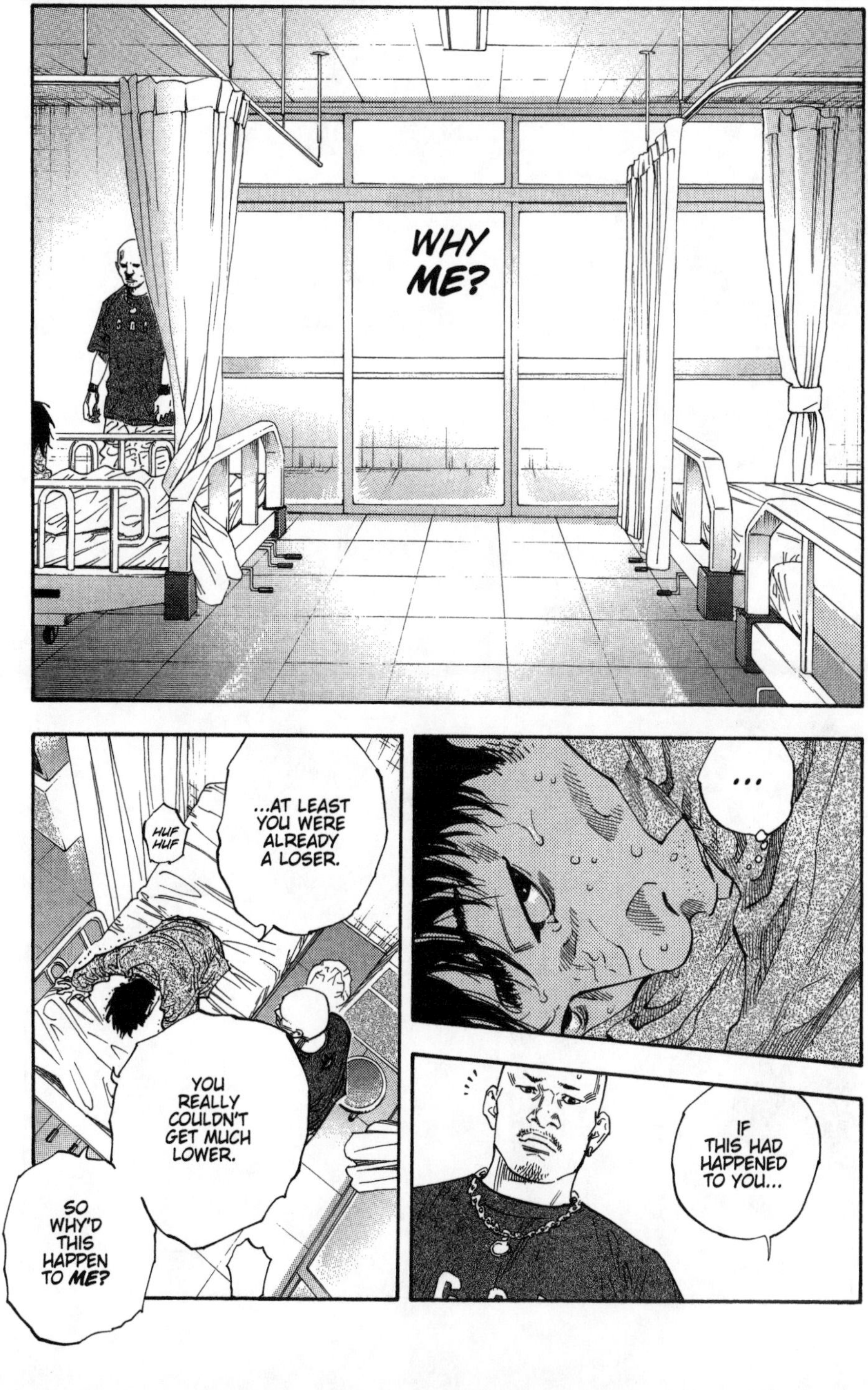
WHY ME?
...
IF THIS HAD HAPPENED TO YOU...
...AT LEAST YOU WERE ALREADY A LOSER.
HUF HUF
YOU REALLY COULDN'T GET MUCH LOWER.
SO WHY'D THIS HAPPEN TO *ME*?

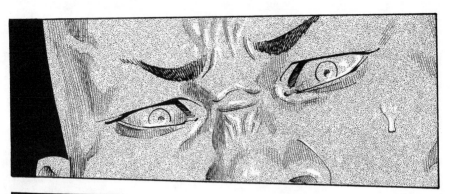

I WANT TO
BECOME A
BETTER
PERSON!

A BETTER
PERSON...

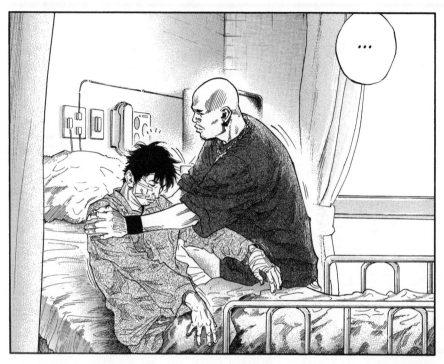

...
WHAP
DON'T TOUCH ME!
IS THAT PITY, NOMIYA?! YOU PITY ME?!
HUF
HUF
I MUST BE IN PRETTY BAD SHAPE TO BE PITIED BY A LOSER LIKE YOU!
HAH! THAT'S A LAUGH!
HUF
HAH!
I'M LOWER THAN LOW!
GOD

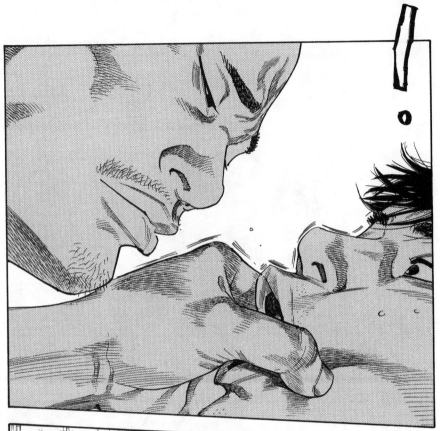

IT'S AGAINST MY PRINCIPLES TO HIT A MAN WHEN HE'S DOWN, BUT YOU'RE REALLY TRYING MY PATIENCE...

...!!

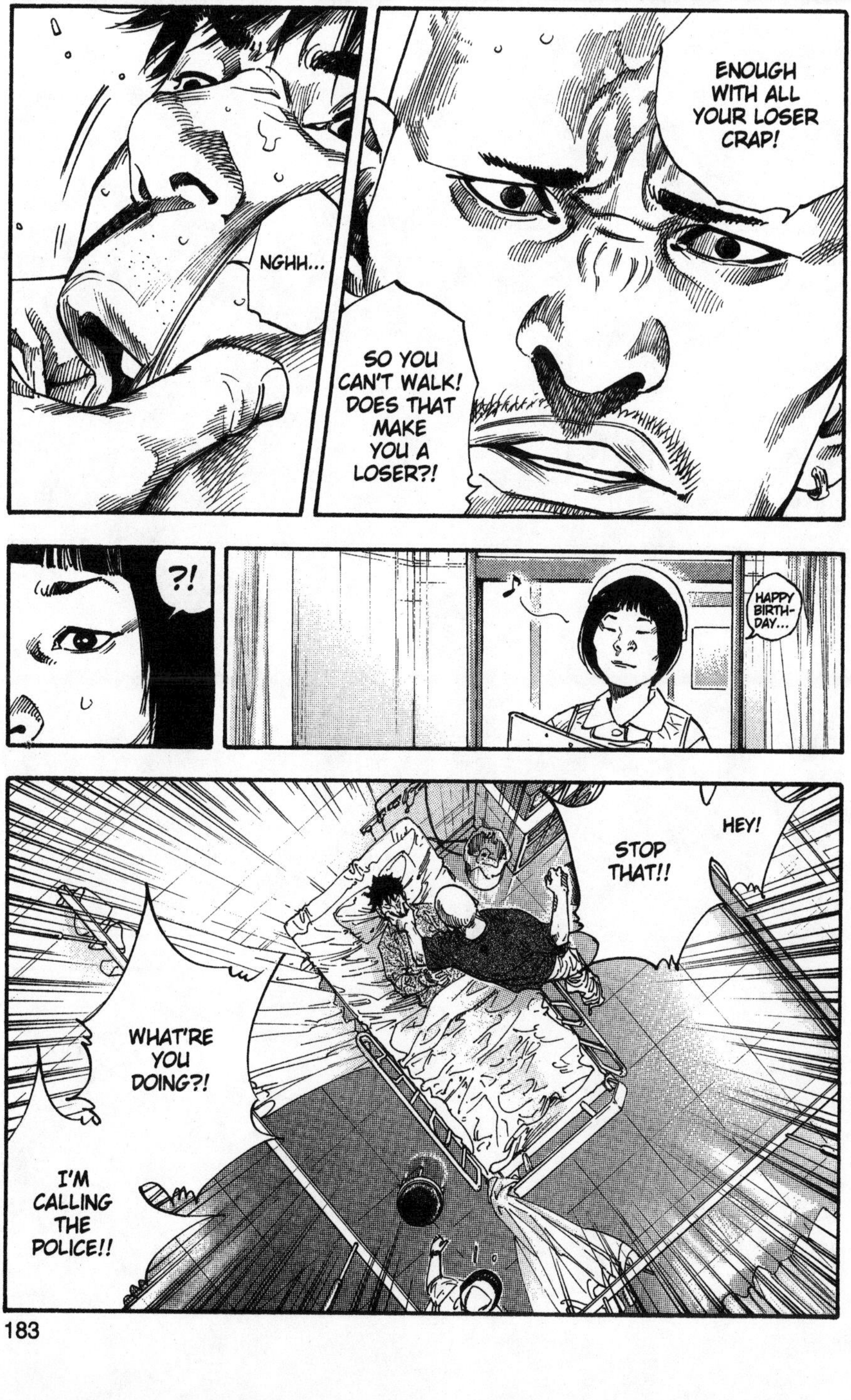
ENOUGH WITH ALL YOUR LOSER CRAP!
SO YOU CAN'T WALK! DOES THAT MAKE YOU A LOSER?!
NGHH...
HAPPY BIRTH-DAY...
?!
HEY!
STOP THAT!!
WHAT'RE YOU DOING?!
I'M CALLING THE POLICE!!

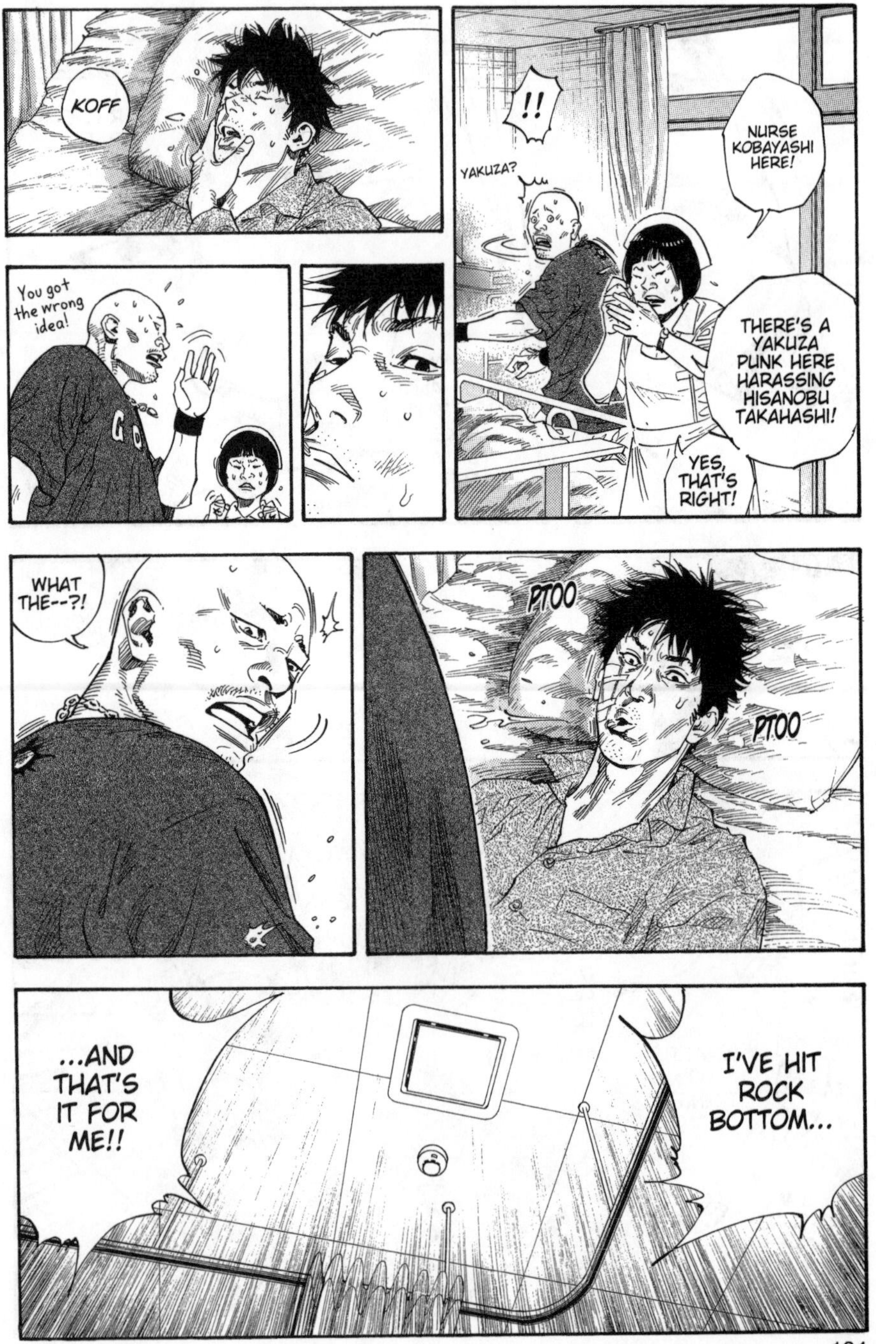
!!
NURSE KOBAYASHI HERE!
YAKUZA?
THERE'S A YAKUZA PUNK HERE HARASSING HISANOBU TAKAHASHI!
YES, THAT'S RIGHT!
KOFF
You got the wrong idea!
PTOO
PTOO
WHAT THE--?!
I'VE HIT ROCK BOTTOM...
...AND THAT'S IT FOR ME!!

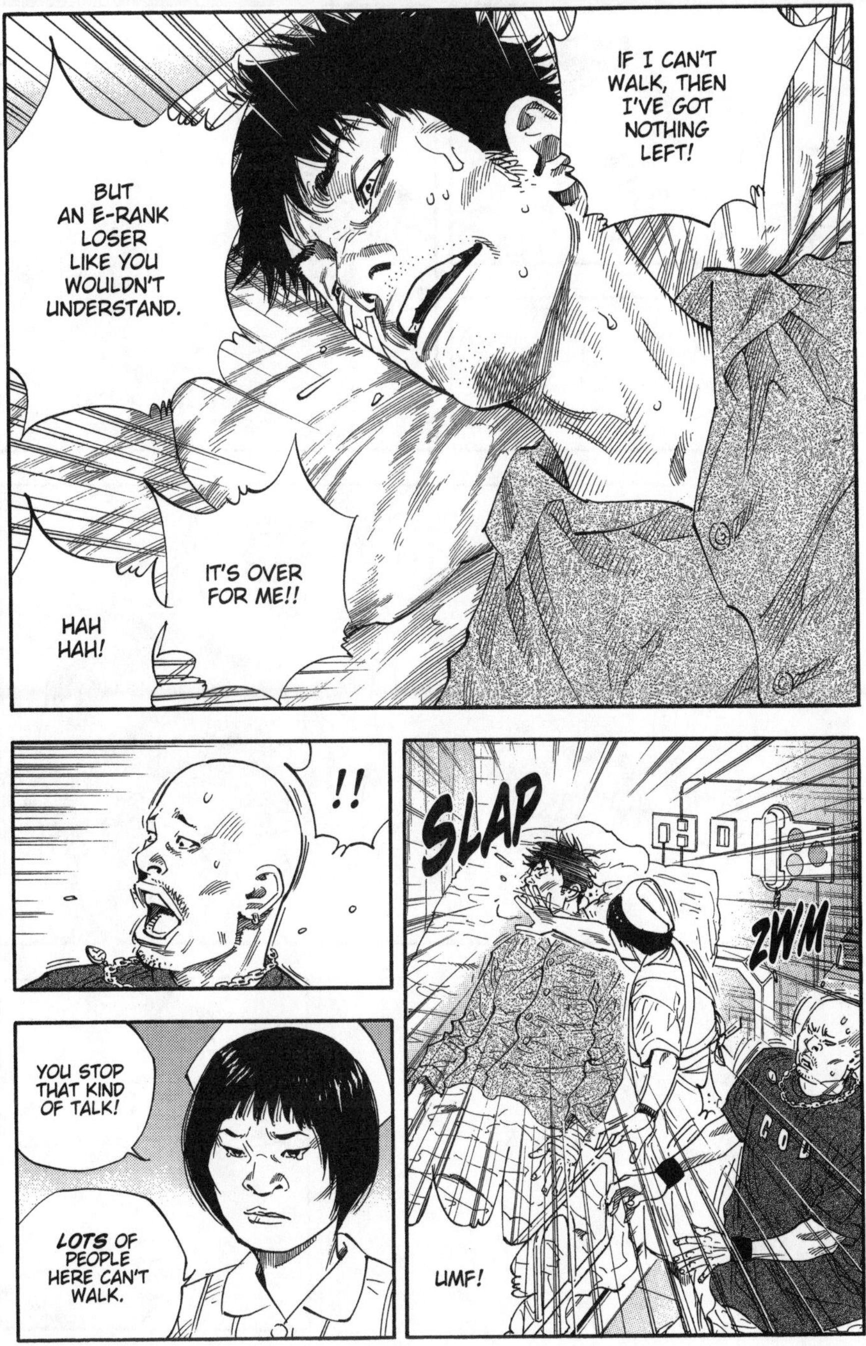
IF I CAN'T WALK, THEN I'VE GOT NOTHING LEFT!
BUT AN E-RANK LOSER LIKE YOU WOULDN'T UNDERSTAND.
IT'S OVER FOR ME!!
HAH HAH!
SLAP
ZWM
UMF!
!!
YOU STOP THAT KIND OF TALK!
LOTS OF PEOPLE HERE CAN'T WALK.

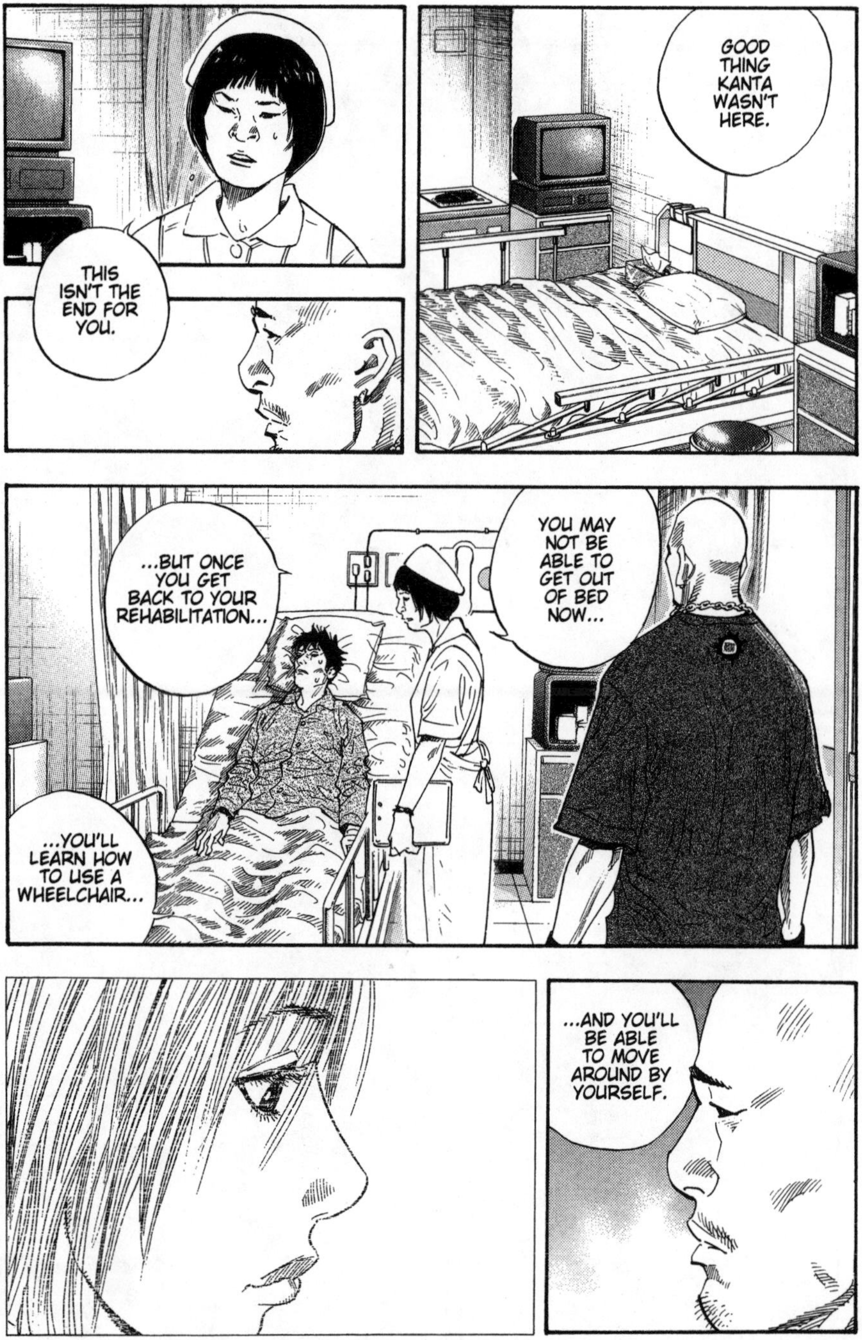
GOOD THING KANTA WASN'T HERE.
THIS ISN'T THE END FOR YOU.
YOU MAY NOT BE ABLE TO GET OUT OF BED NOW...
...BUT ONCE YOU GET BACK TO YOUR REHABILITATION...
...YOU'LL LEARN HOW TO USE A WHEELCHAIR...
...AND YOU'LL BE ABLE TO MOVE AROUND BY YOURSELF.

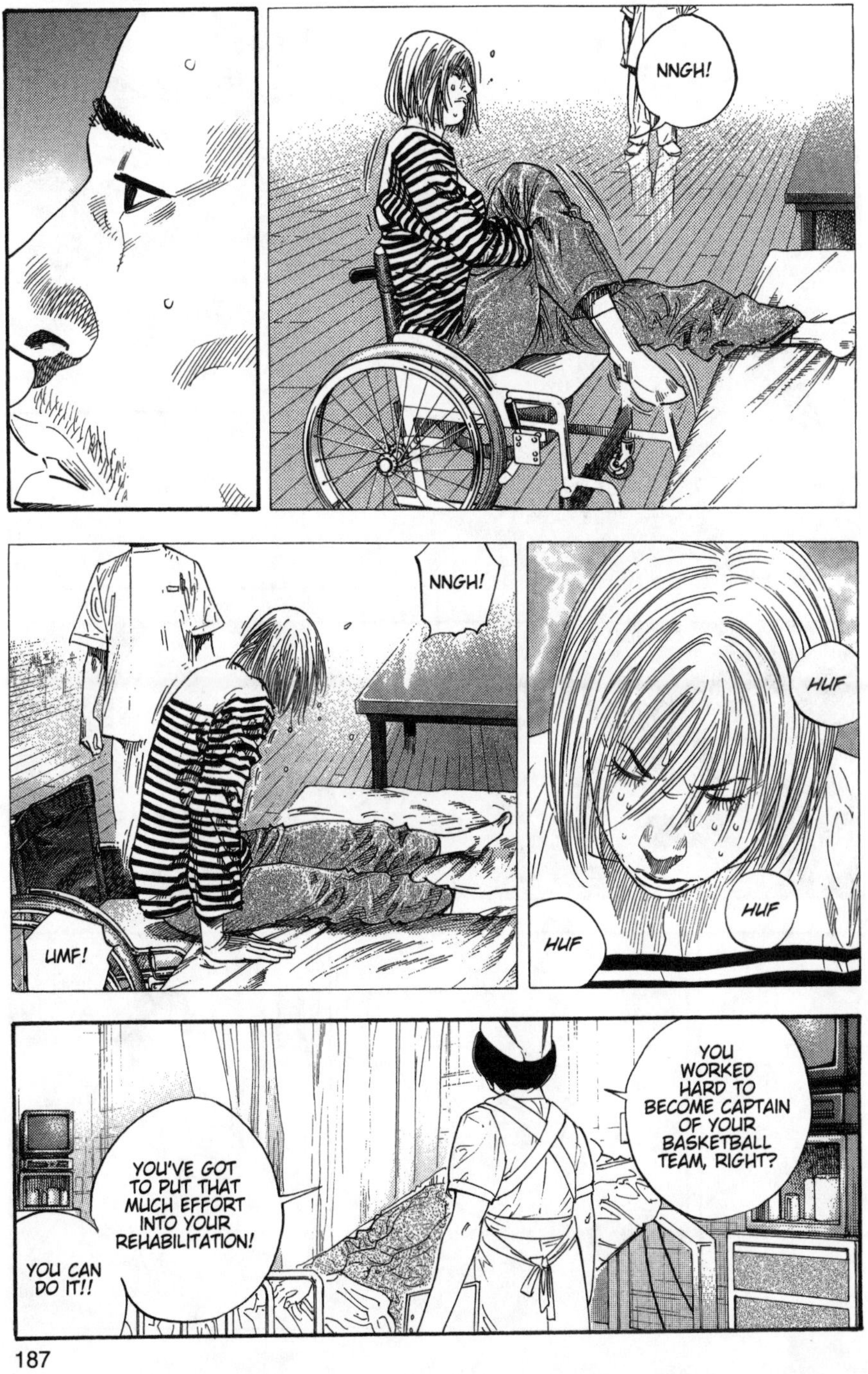
NNGH!
HUF
HUF
HUF
NNGH!
UMF!
YOU WORKED HARD TO BECOME CAPTAIN OF YOUR BASKETBALL TEAM, RIGHT?
YOU'VE GOT TO PUT THAT MUCH EFFORT INTO YOUR REHABILITATION!
YOU CAN DO IT!!

SLUMP

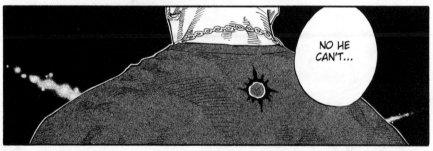

NO HE CAN'T...

IT'S JUST LIKE AT BASKETBALL PRACTICE.

TAKAHASHI...

HUH?

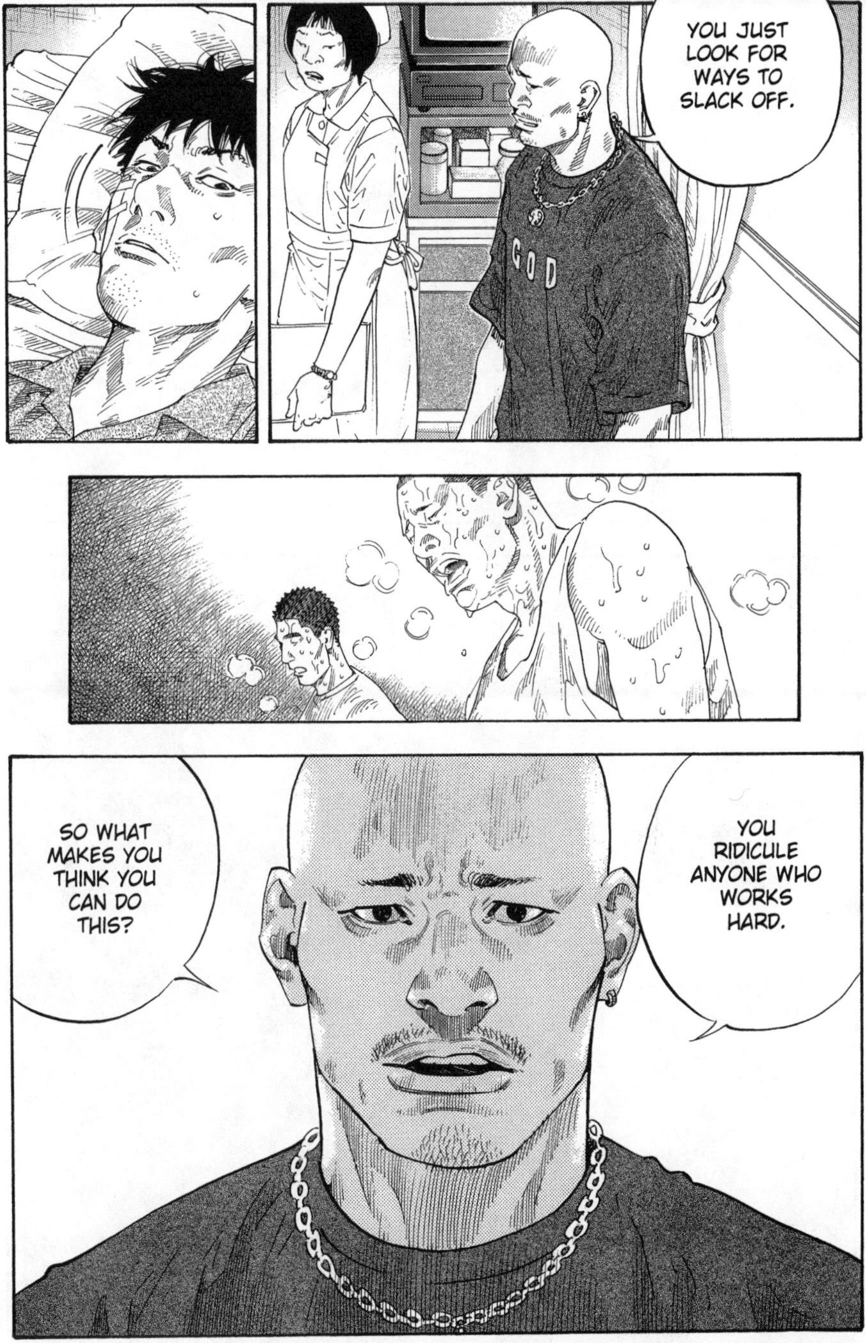
YOU JUST LOOK FOR WAYS TO SLACK OFF.
GOD
YOU RIDICULE ANYONE WHO WORKS HARD.
SO WHAT MAKES YOU THINK YOU CAN DO THIS?

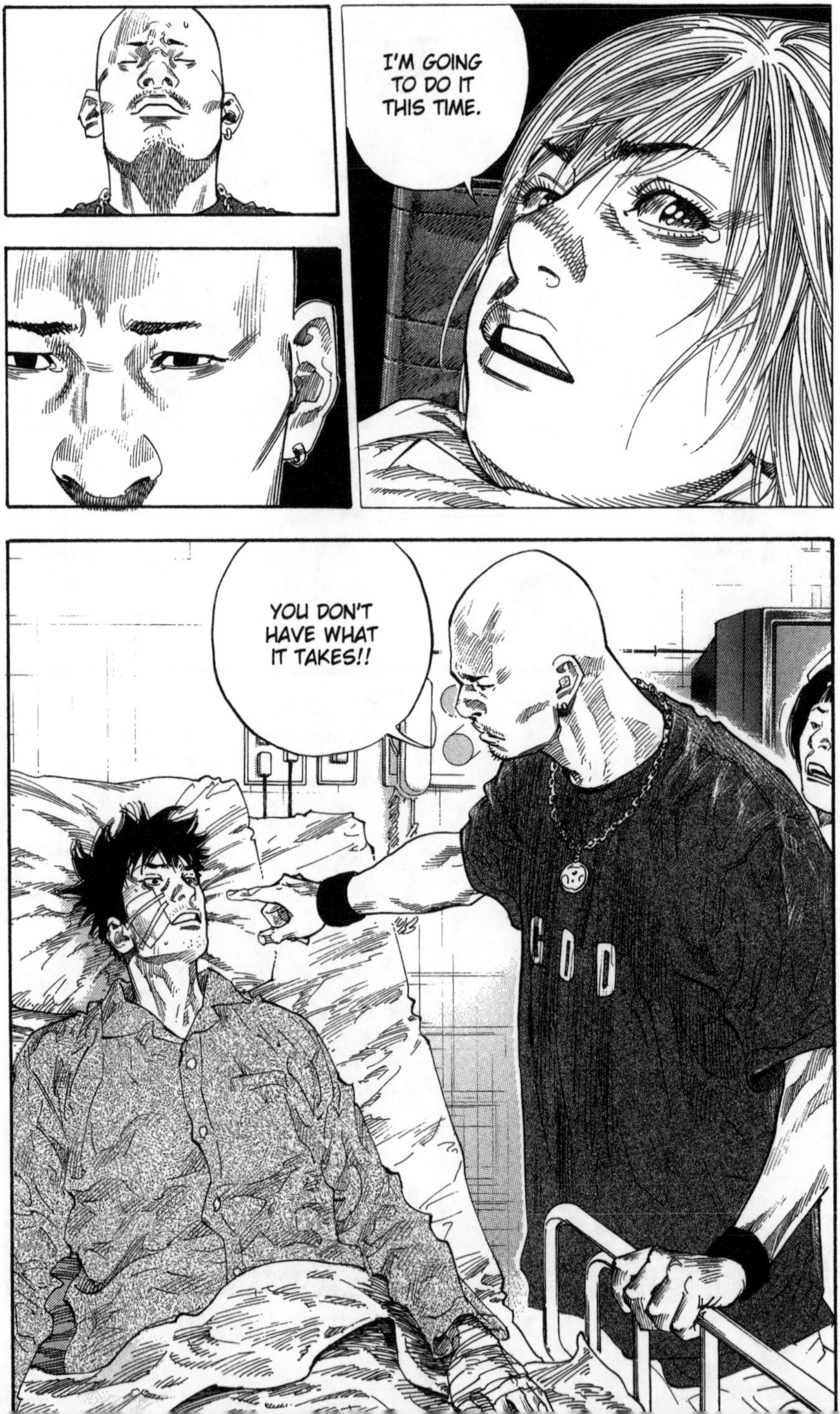
I'M GOING TO DO IT THIS TIME.
YOU DON'T HAVE WHAT IT TAKES!!

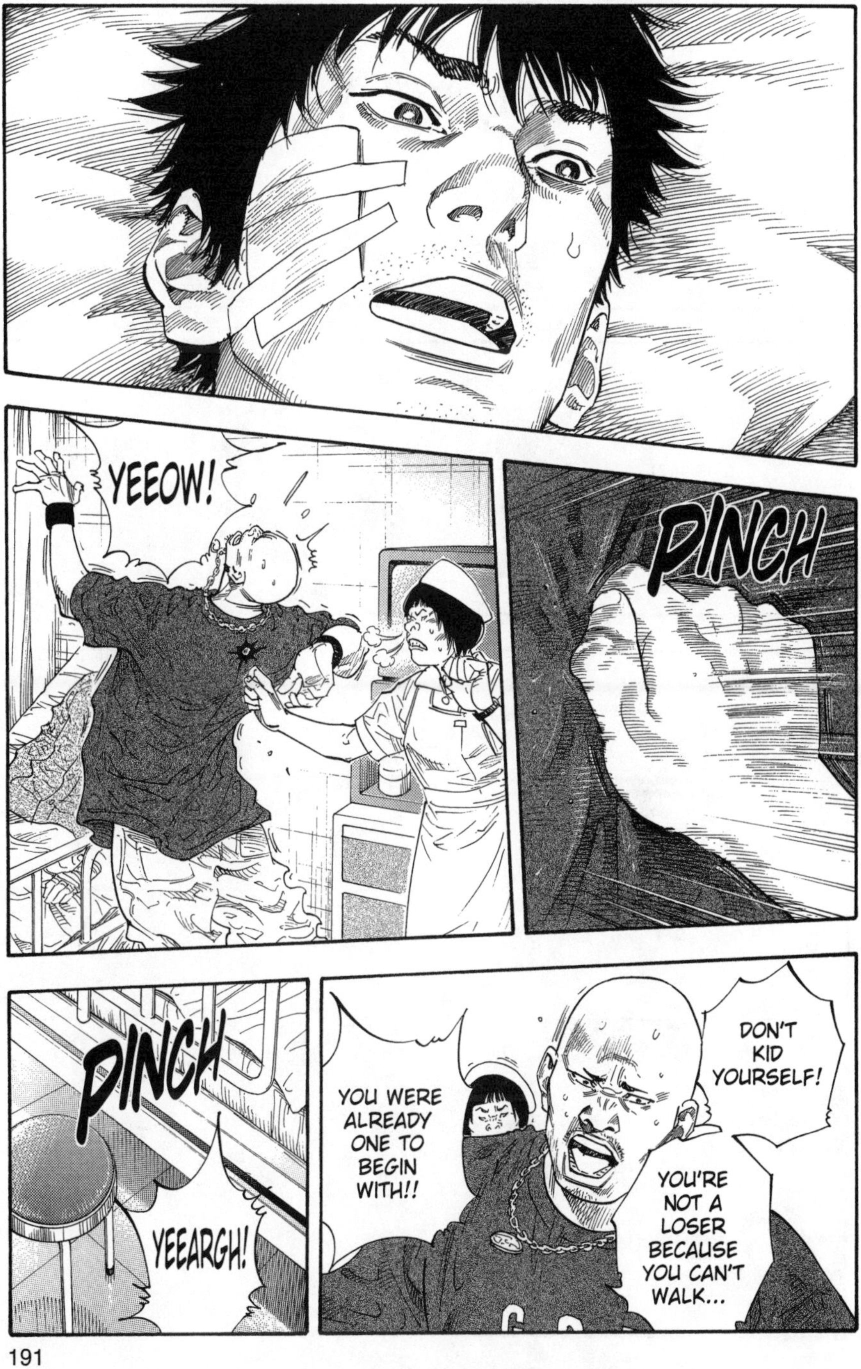
PINCH
YEEOW!
DON'T KID YOURSELF!
YOU'RE NOT A LOSER BECAUSE YOU CAN'T WALK...
YOU WERE ALREADY ONE TO BEGIN WITH!!
PINCH
YEEARGH!

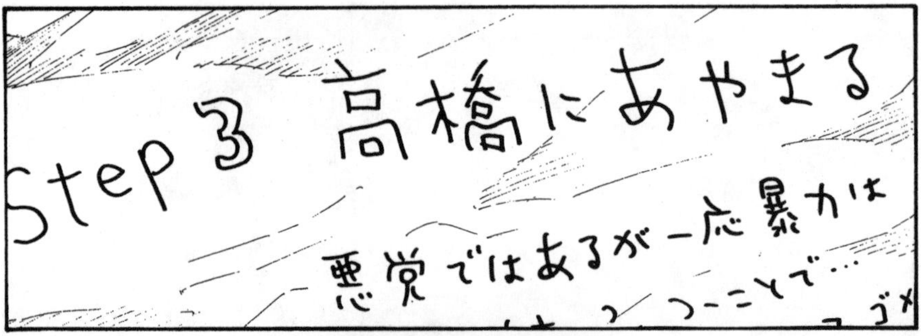
Step 3 高橋にあやまる
悪党ではあるが一応暴力は

*STEP 3: APOLOGIZE TO TAKAHASHI

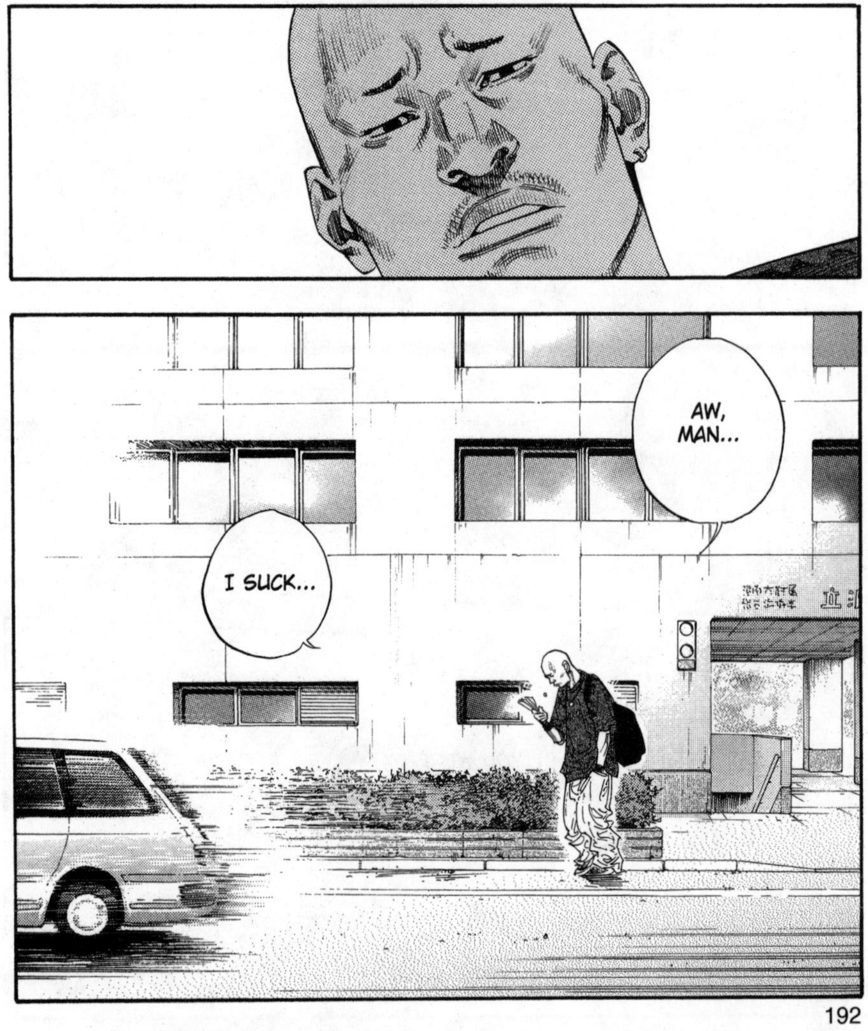
AW, MAN...
I SUCK...

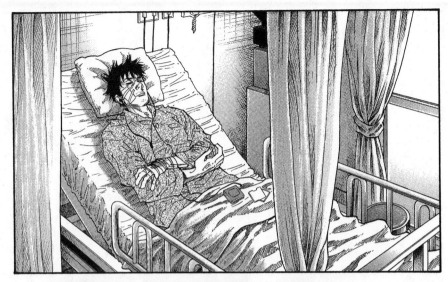

...

YOU DON'T HAVE WHAT IT TAKES!!

...BIRTHDAY! ♪

HAPPY... ♪

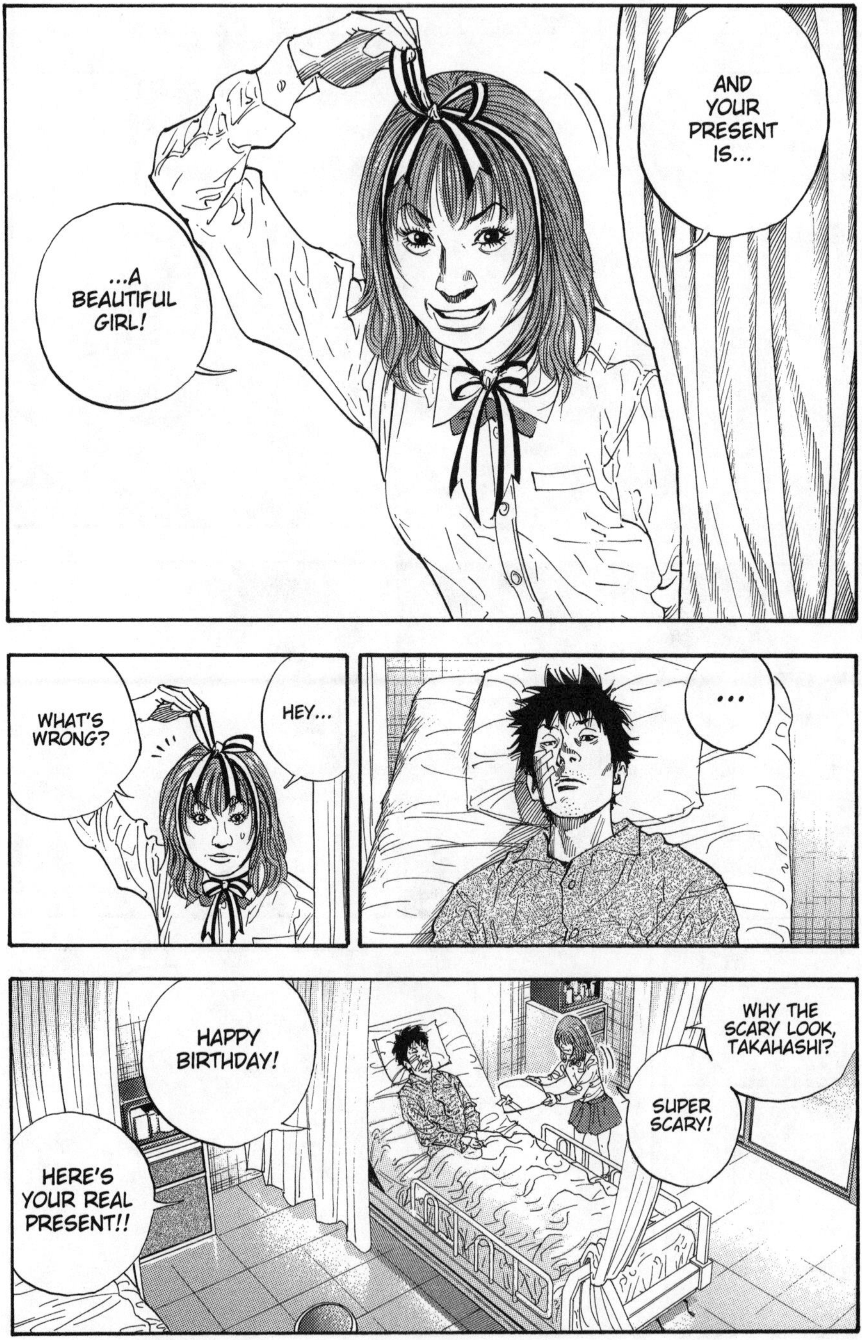
AND YOUR PRESENT IS...
...A BEAUTIFUL GIRL!
...
HEY...
WHAT'S WRONG?
WHY THE SCARY LOOK, TAKAHASHI?
SUPER SCARY!
HAPPY BIRTHDAY!
HERE'S YOUR REAL PRESENT!!

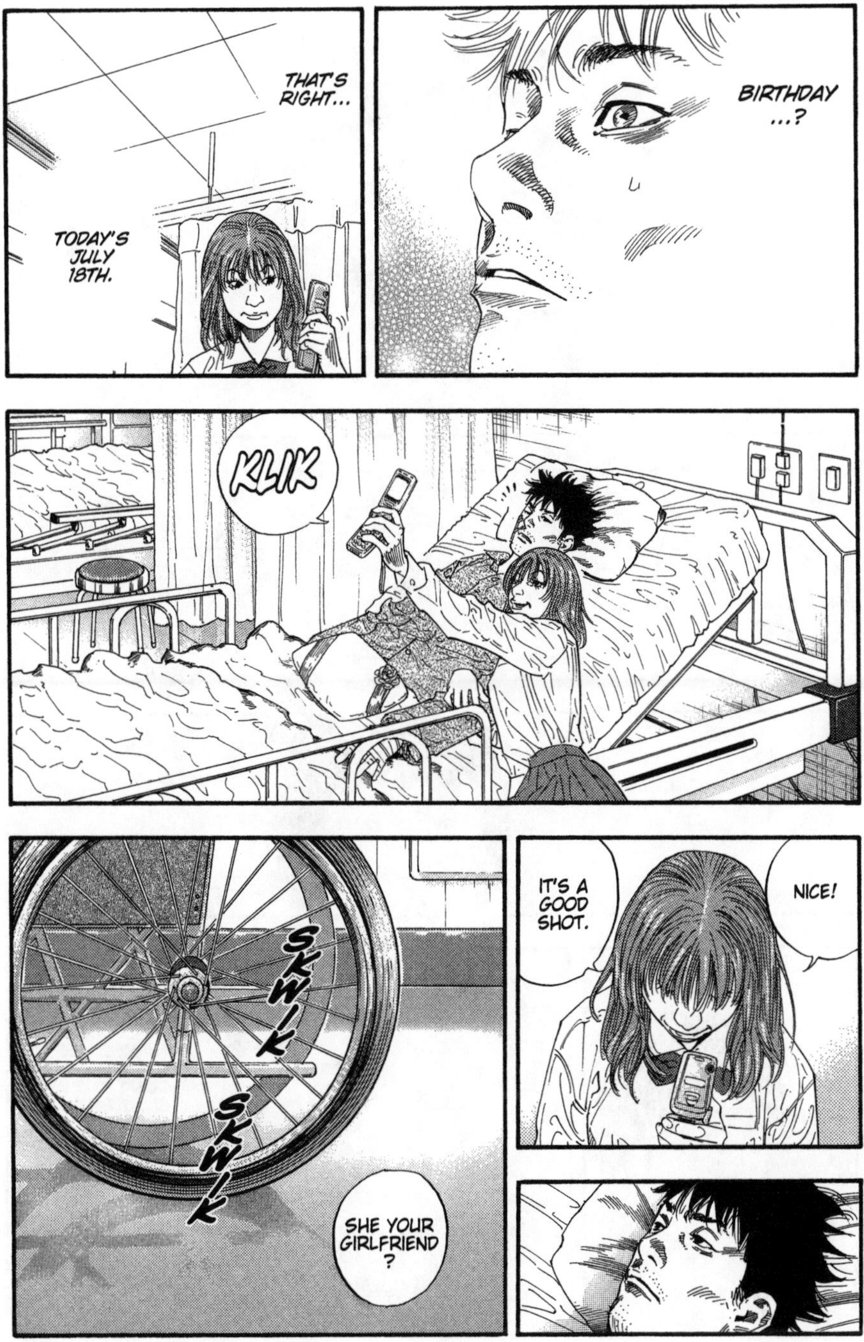
BIRTHDAY ...?
THAT'S RIGHT...
TODAY'S JULY 18TH.
KLIK
NICE!
IT'S A GOOD SHOT.
SKWIK
SKWIK
SHE YOUR GIRLFRIEND ?

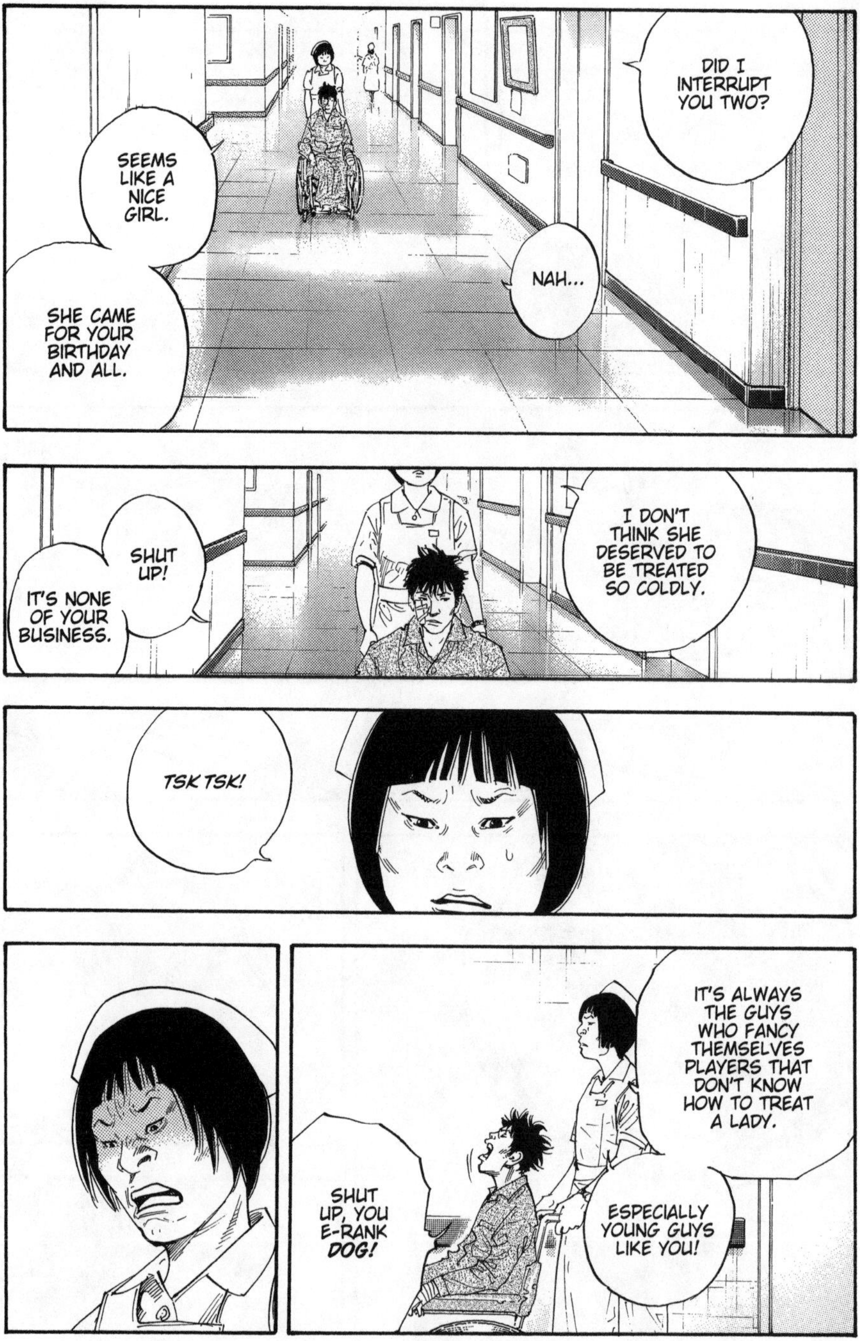
DID I INTERRUPT YOU TWO?
NAH...
SEEMS LIKE A NICE GIRL.
SHE CAME FOR YOUR BIRTHDAY AND ALL.
I DON'T THINK SHE DESERVED TO BE TREATED SO COLDLY.
SHUT UP!
IT'S NONE OF YOUR BUSINESS.
TSK TSK!
IT'S ALWAYS THE GUYS WHO FANCY THEMSELVES PLAYERS THAT DON'T KNOW HOW TO TREAT A LADY.
ESPECIALLY YOUNG GUYS LIKE YOU!
SHUT UP, YOU E-RANK DOG!

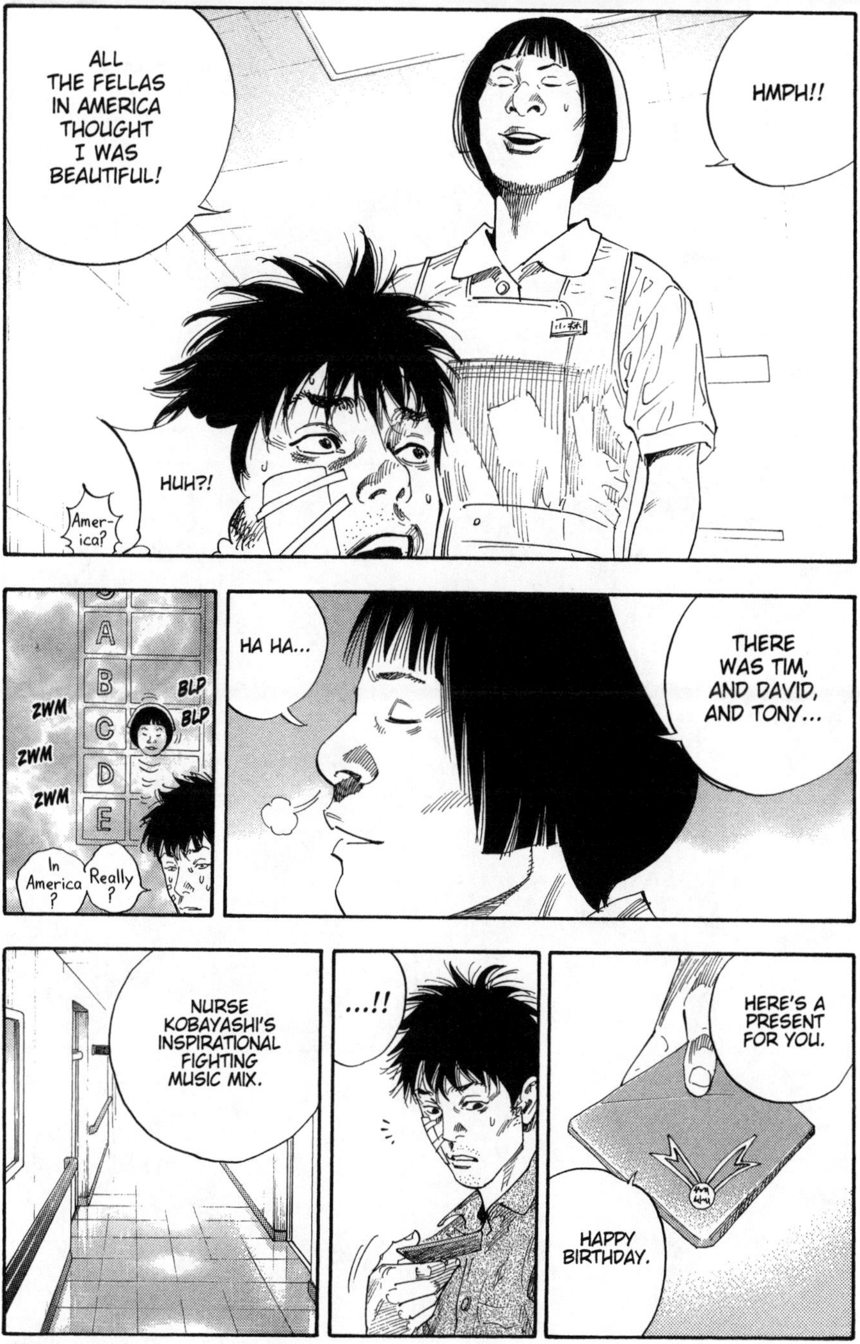
HMPH!!
ALL THE FELLAS IN AMERICA THOUGHT I WAS BEAUTIFUL!
HUH?!
America?
THERE WAS TIM, AND DAVID, AND TONY...
HA HA...
BLP BLP
ZWM ZWM ZWM
Really?
In America?
HERE'S A PRESENT FOR YOU.
HAPPY BIRTHDAY.
...!!
NURSE KOBAYASHI'S INSPIRATIONAL FIGHTING MUSIC MIX.

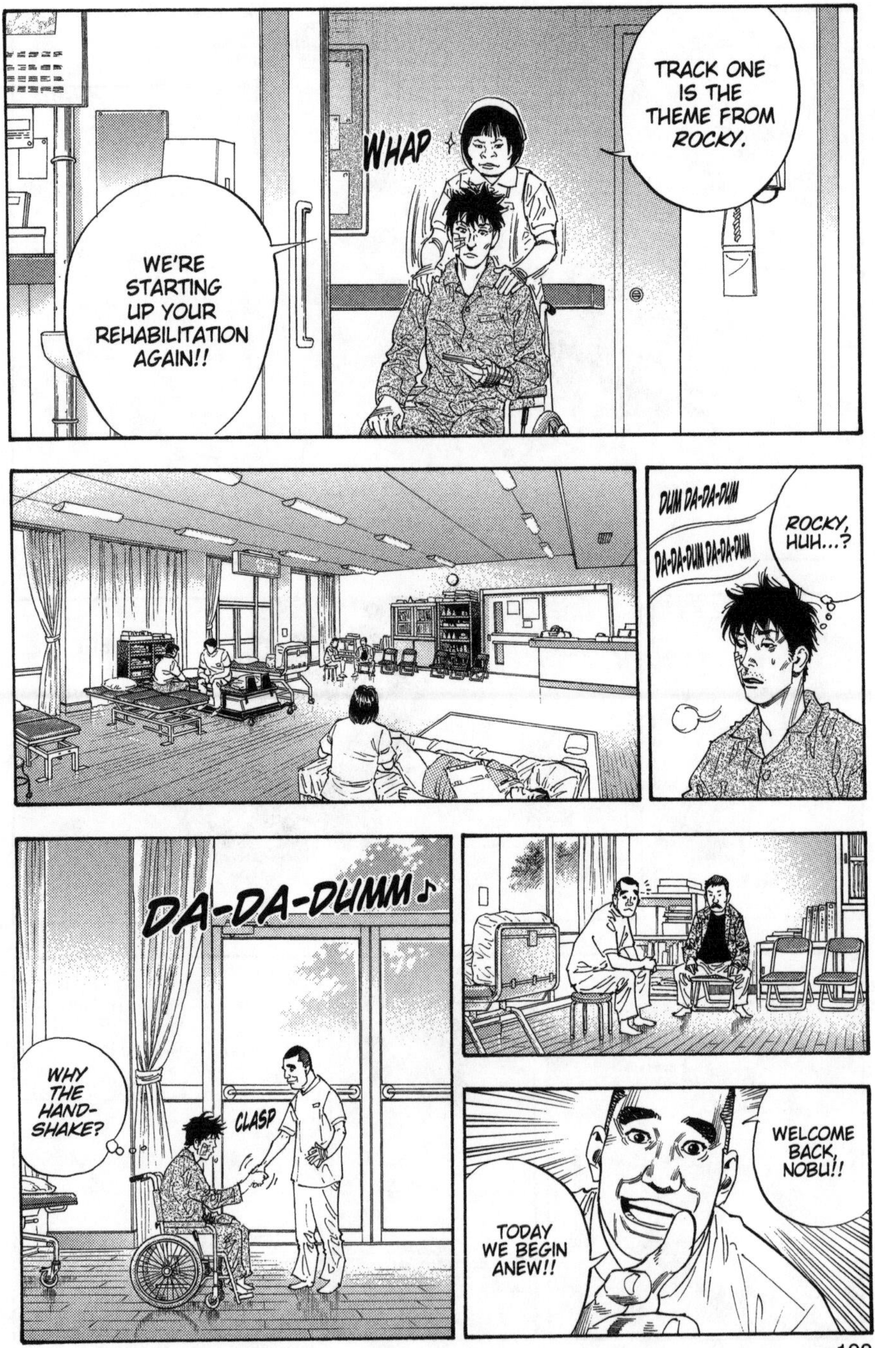
TRACK ONE IS THE THEME FROM *ROCKY.*
WHAP
WE'RE STARTING UP YOUR REHABILITATION AGAIN!!
ROCKY, HUH...?
DUM DA-DA-DUM
DA-DA-DUM DA-DA-DUM
WELCOME BACK, NOBU!!
TODAY WE BEGIN ANEW!!
DA-DA-DUMM♪
CLASP
WHY THE HAND-SHAKE?

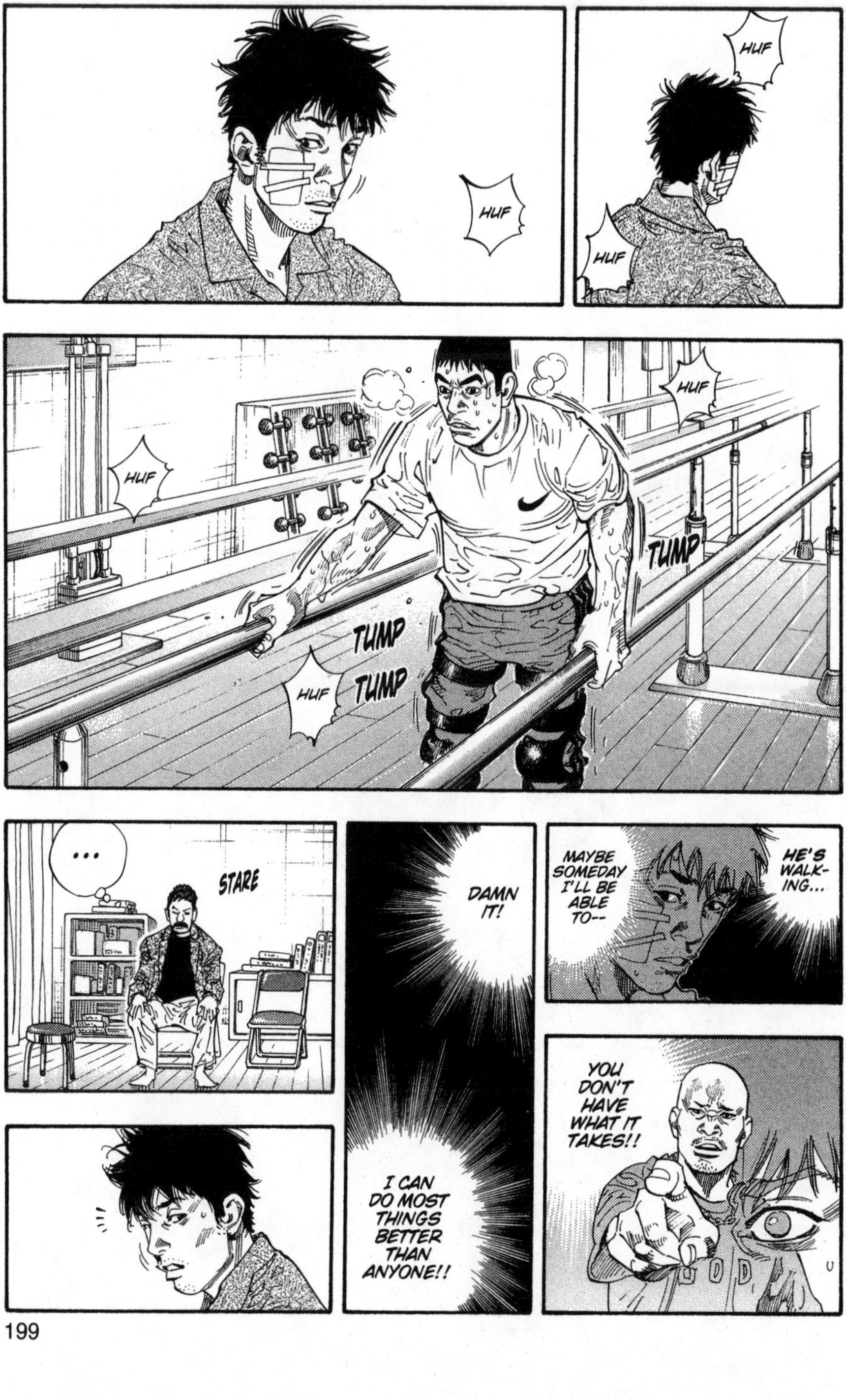
HUF
HUF
HUF
HUF
TUMP
HUF
TUMP
TUMP
HUF
HE'S WALKING...
MAYBE SOMEDAY I'LL BE ABLE TO--
YOU DON'T HAVE WHAT IT TAKES!!
DAMN IT!
I CAN DO MOST THINGS BETTER THAN ANYONE!!
STARE
...

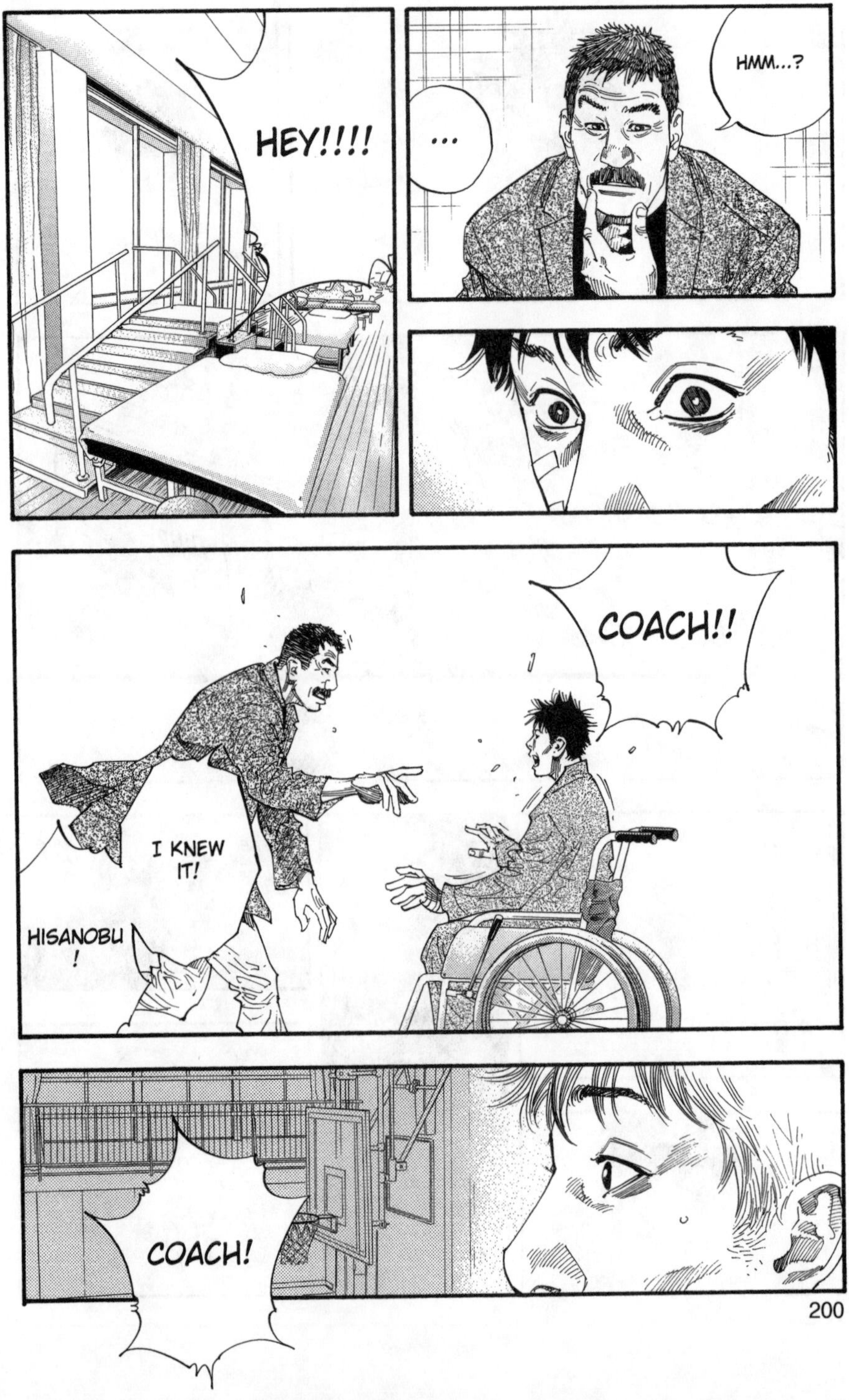
HMM...?
...
HEY!!!!
COACH!!
I KNEW IT!
HISANOBU!
COACH!

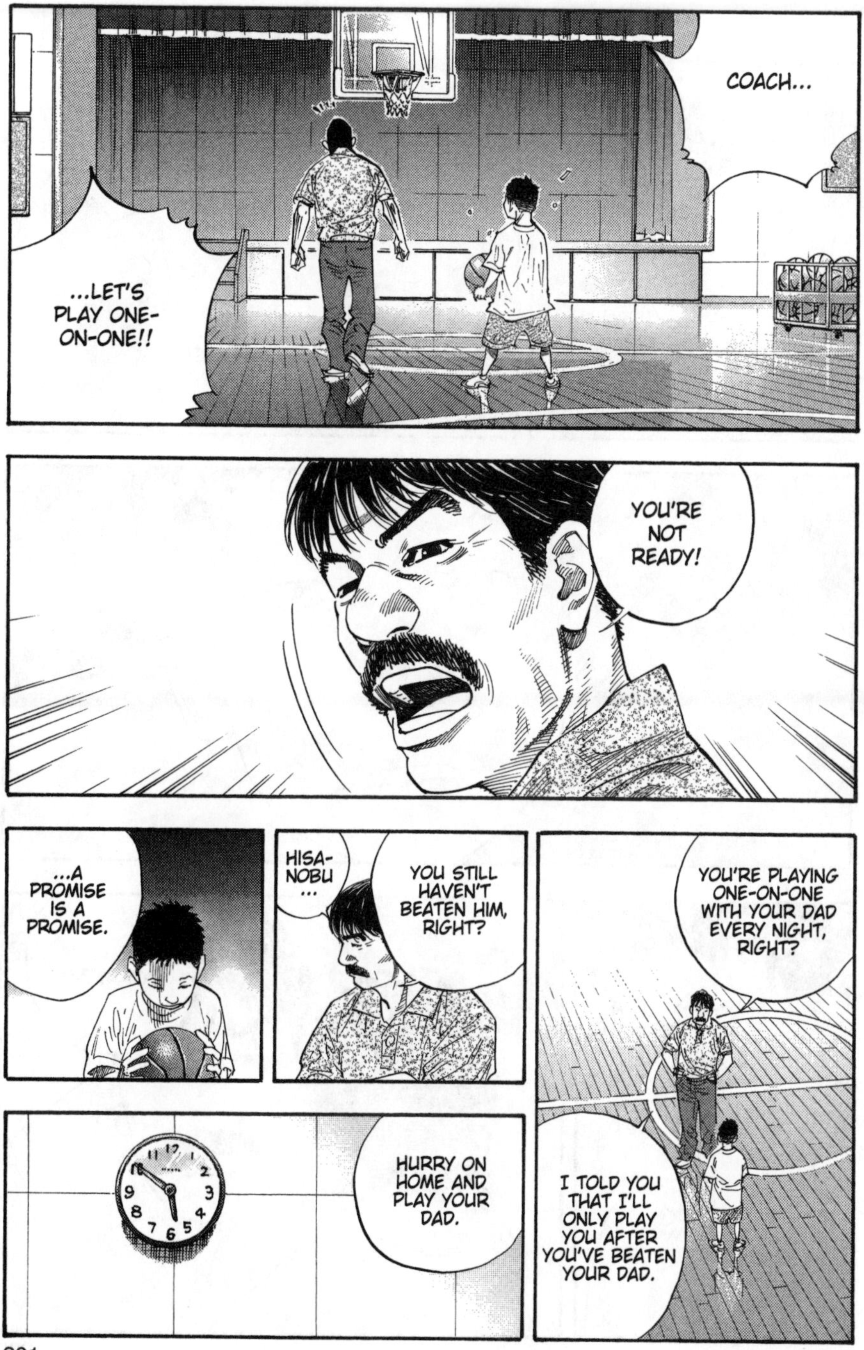
COACH...
...LET'S PLAY ONE-ON-ONE!!
YOU'RE NOT READY!
YOU'RE PLAYING ONE-ON-ONE WITH YOUR DAD EVERY NIGHT, RIGHT?
I TOLD YOU THAT I'LL ONLY PLAY YOU AFTER YOU'VE BEATEN YOUR DAD.
YOU STILL HAVEN'T BEATEN HIM, RIGHT?
HISA-NOBU...
...A PROMISE IS A PROMISE.
HURRY ON HOME AND PLAY YOUR DAD.

HISA-
NOBU...

PLEASE,
COACH!

PLEASE!!

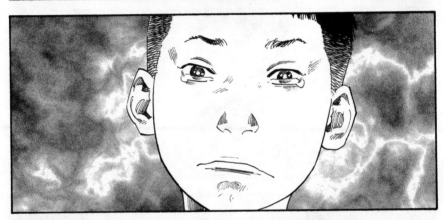

SOB

SOB

SOB

ARE YOU
OKAY?

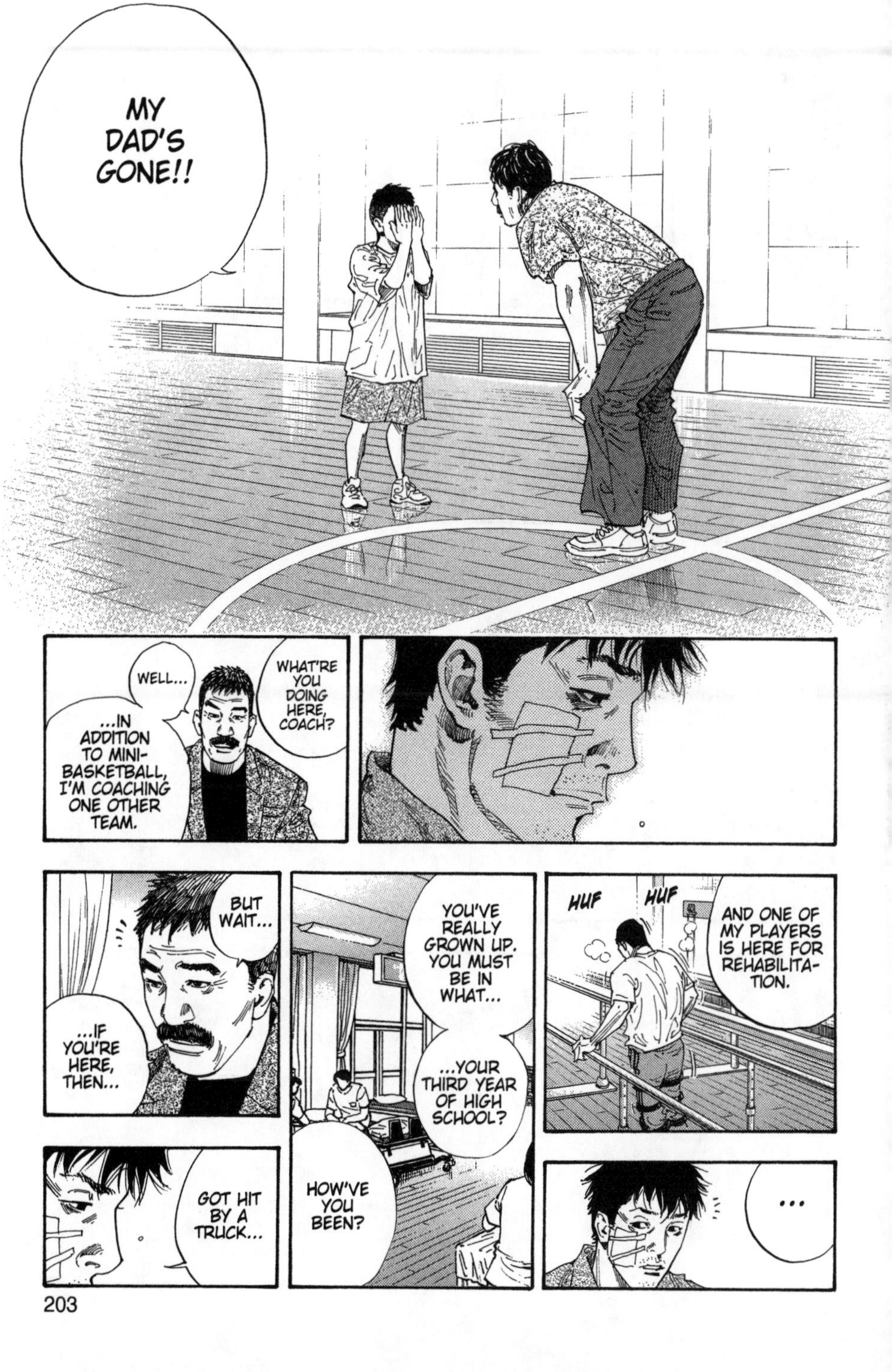
MY DAD'S GONE!!
WHAT'RE YOU DOING HERE, COACH?
WELL...
...IN ADDITION TO MINI-BASKETBALL, I'M COACHING ONE OTHER TEAM.
HUF HUF
AND ONE OF MY PLAYERS IS HERE FOR REHABILITATION.
...
YOU'VE REALLY GROWN UP. YOU MUST BE IN WHAT...
...YOUR THIRD YEAR OF HIGH SCHOOL?
HOW'VE YOU BEEN?
BUT WAIT...
...IF YOU'RE HERE, THEN...
GOT HIT BY A TRUCK...

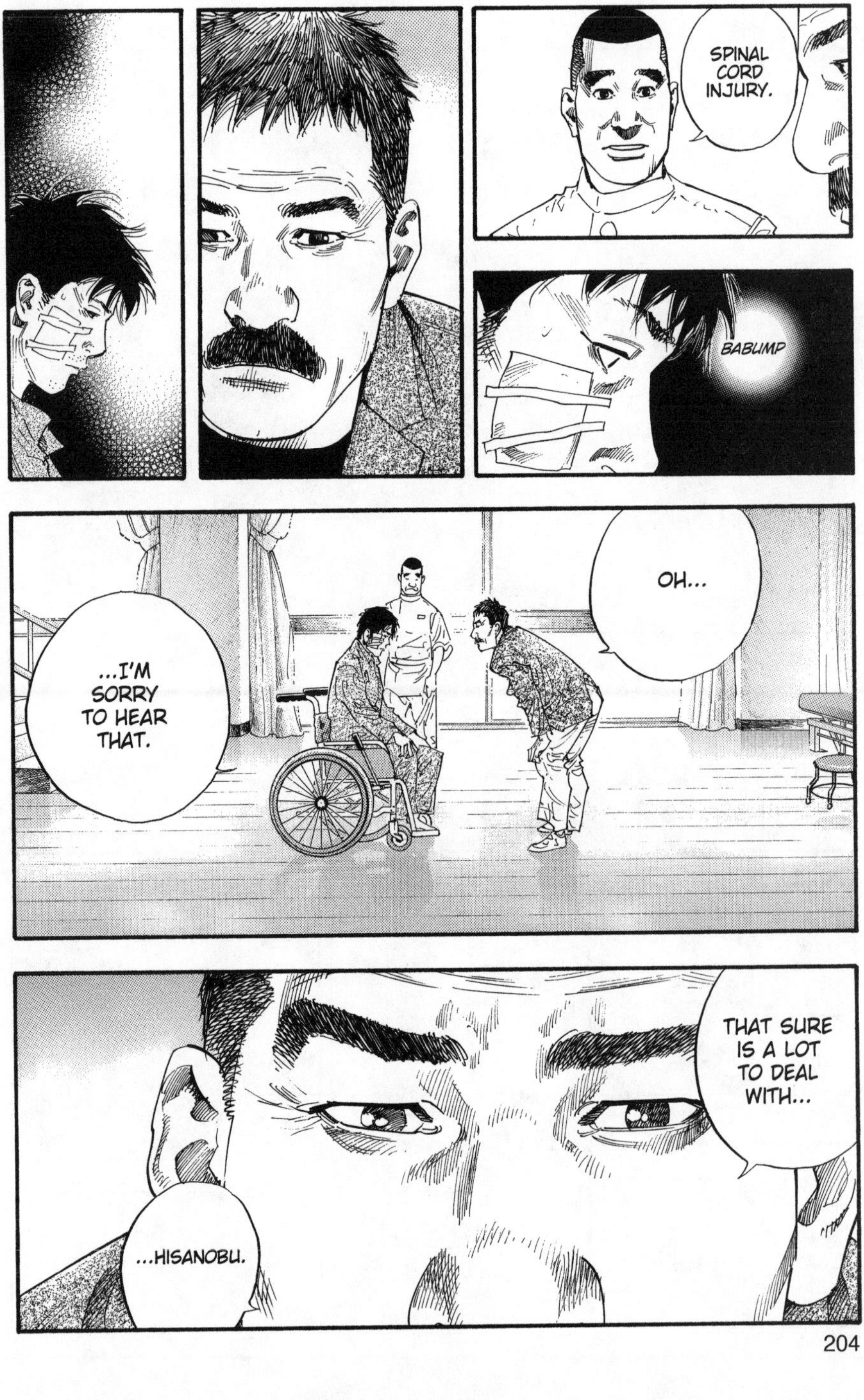
SPINAL CORD INJURY.
BABUMP
OH...
...I'M SORRY TO HEAR THAT.
THAT SURE IS A LOT TO DEAL WITH...
...HISANOBU.

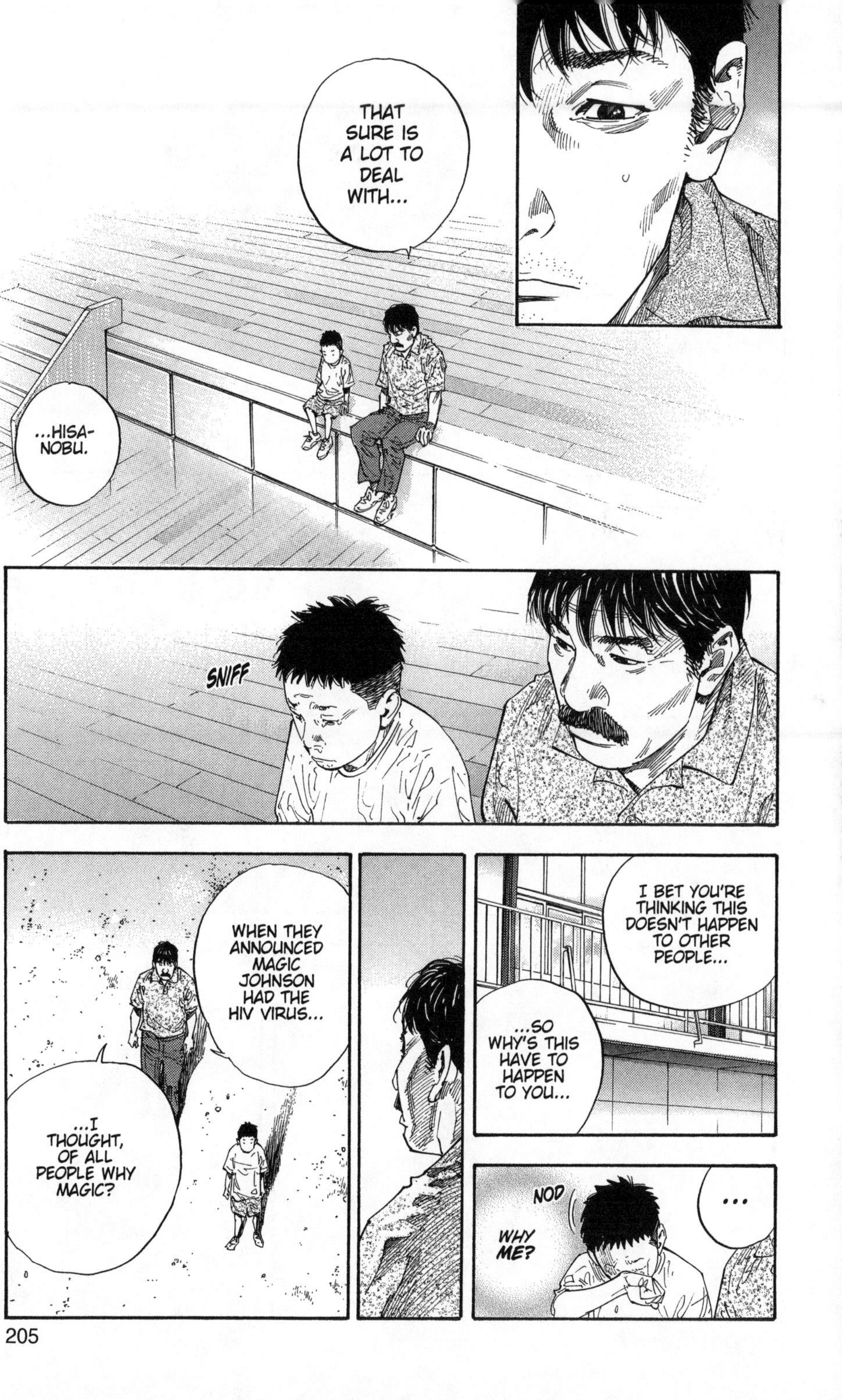
THAT SURE IS A LOT TO DEAL WITH...
...HISA-NOBU.
SNIFF
I BET YOU'RE THINKING THIS DOESN'T HAPPEN TO OTHER PEOPLE...
...SO WHY'S THIS HAVE TO HAPPEN TO YOU...
...
NOD
WHY ME?
WHEN THEY ANNOUNCED MAGIC JOHNSON HAD THE HIV VIRUS...
...I THOUGHT, OF ALL PEOPLE WHY MAGIC?

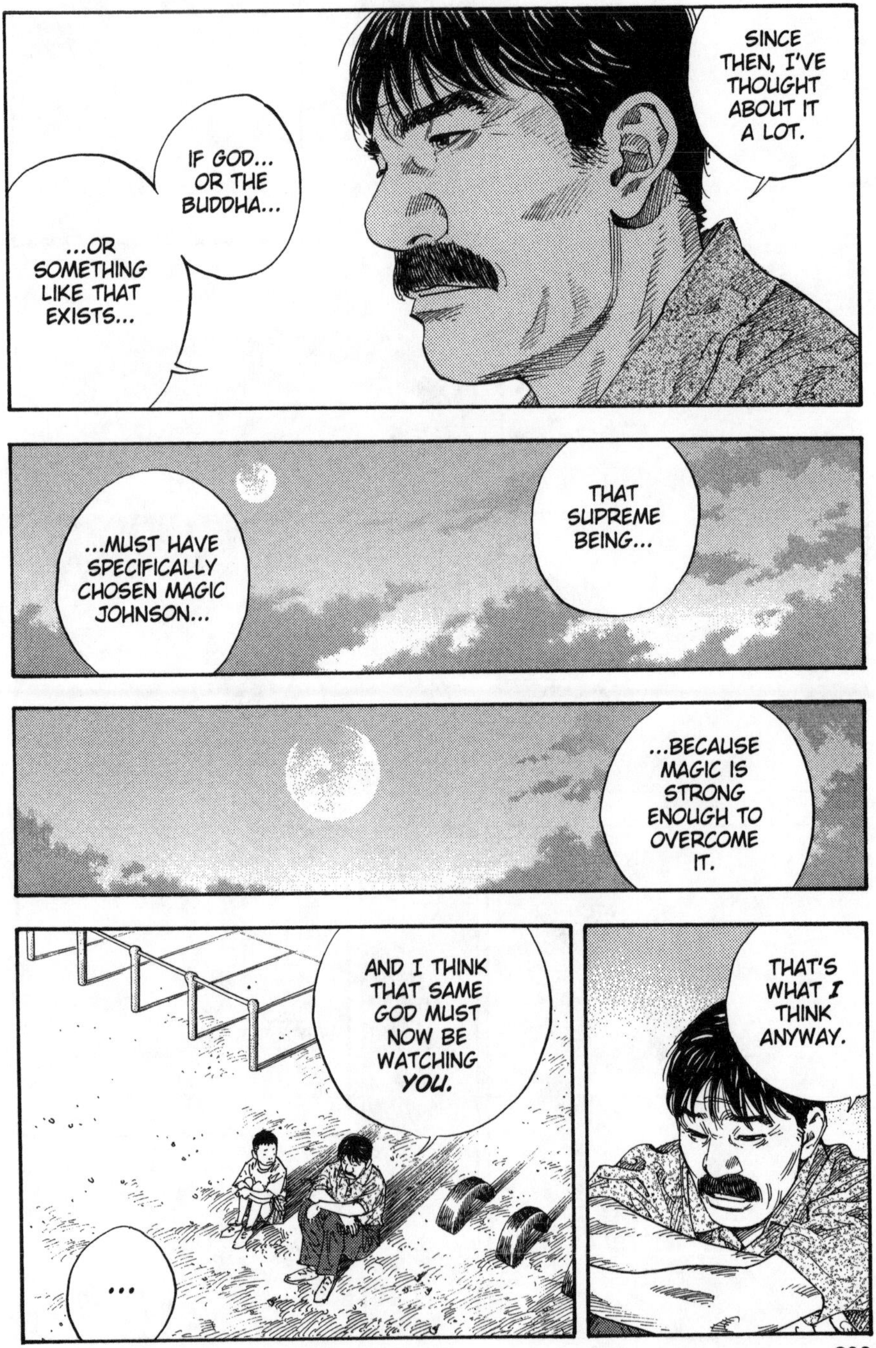
SINCE THEN, I'VE THOUGHT ABOUT IT A LOT.
IF GOD... OR THE BUDDHA...
...OR SOMETHING LIKE THAT EXISTS...
THAT SUPREME BEING...
...MUST HAVE SPECIFICALLY CHOSEN MAGIC JOHNSON...
...BECAUSE MAGIC IS STRONG ENOUGH TO OVERCOME IT.
THAT'S WHAT *I* THINK ANYWAY.
AND I THINK THAT SAME GOD MUST NOW BE WATCHING ***YOU.***
...

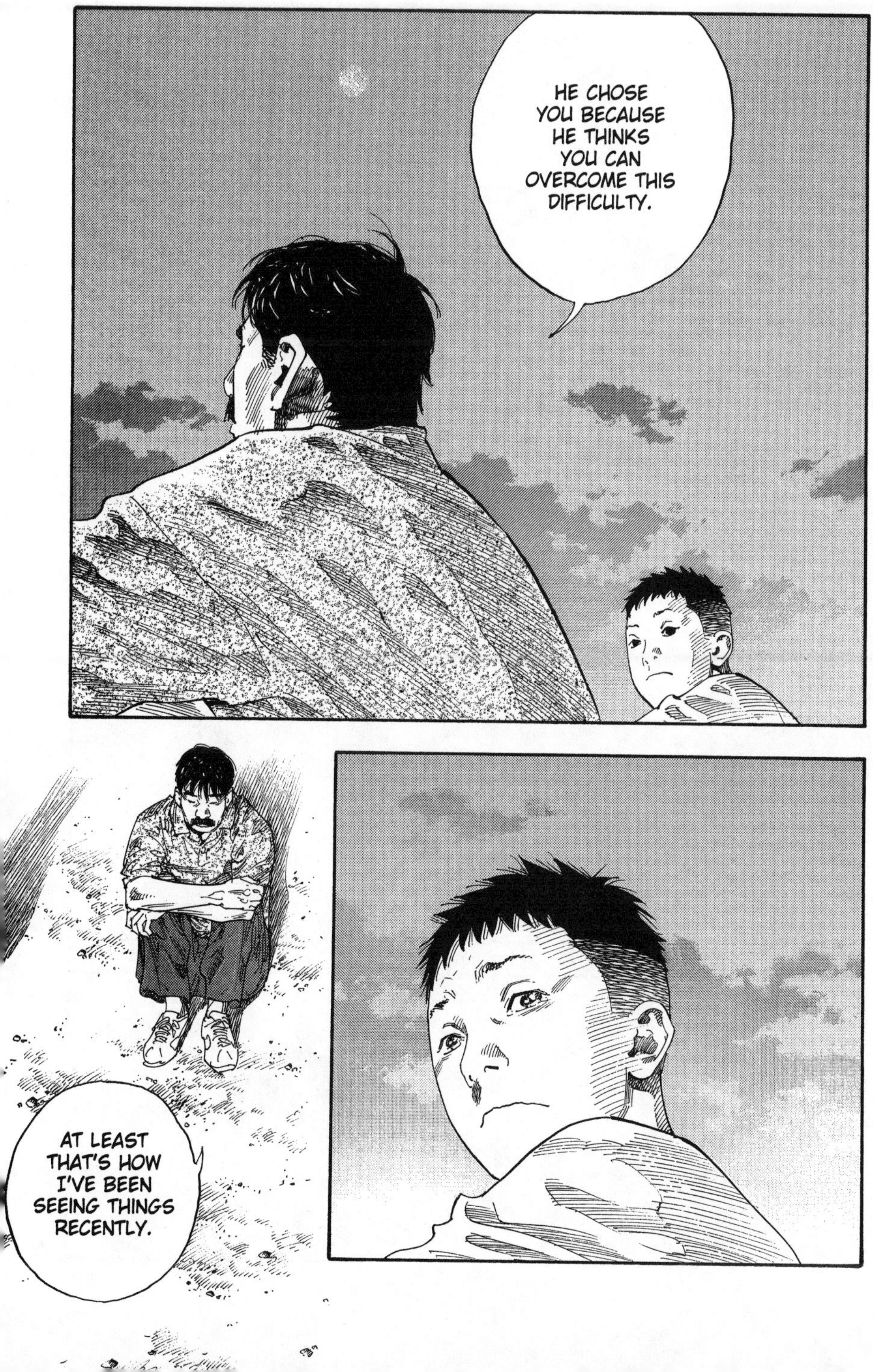
HE CHOSE YOU BECAUSE HE THINKS YOU CAN OVERCOME THIS DIFFICULTY.
AT LEAST THAT'S HOW I'VE BEEN SEEING THINGS RECENTLY.

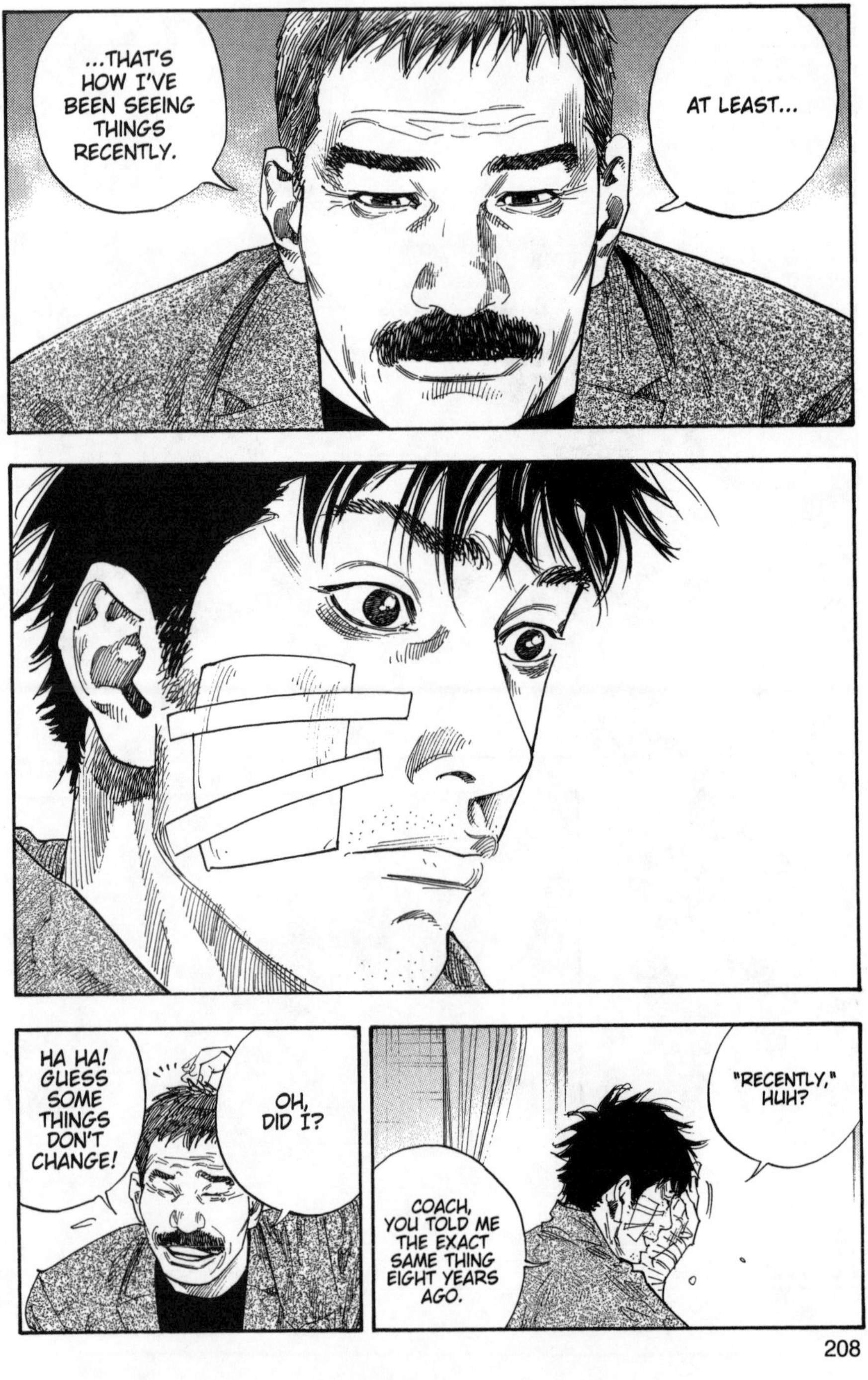
AT LEAST...
...THAT'S HOW I'VE BEEN SEEING THINGS RECENTLY.
"RECENTLY," HUH?
COACH, YOU TOLD ME THE EXACT SAME THING EIGHT YEARS AGO.
OH, DID I?
HA HA! GUESS SOME THINGS DON'T CHANGE!

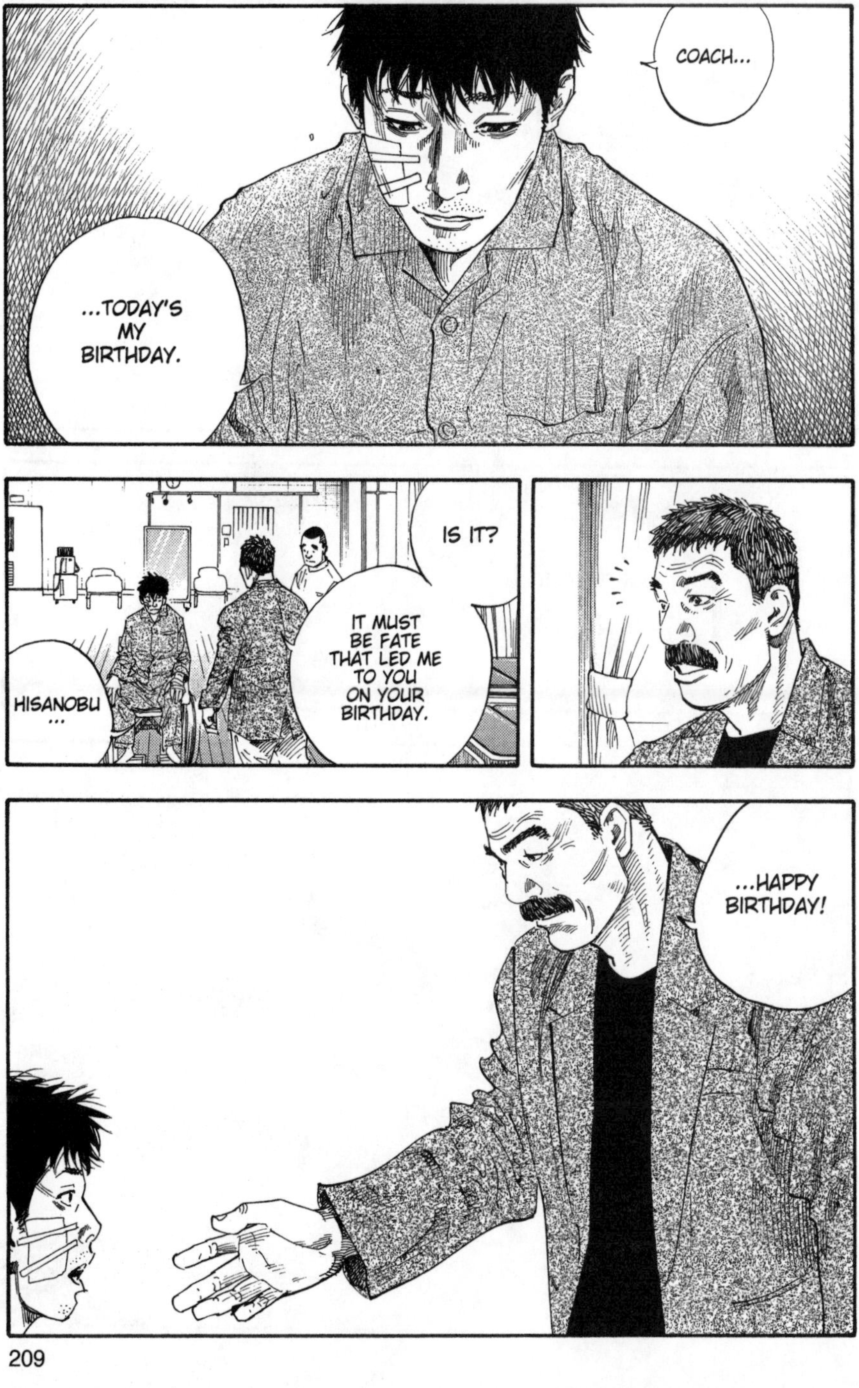
COACH...
...TODAY'S MY BIRTHDAY.
IS IT?
IT MUST BE FATE THAT LED ME TO YOU ON YOUR BIRTHDAY.
HISANOBU ...
...HAPPY BIRTHDAY!

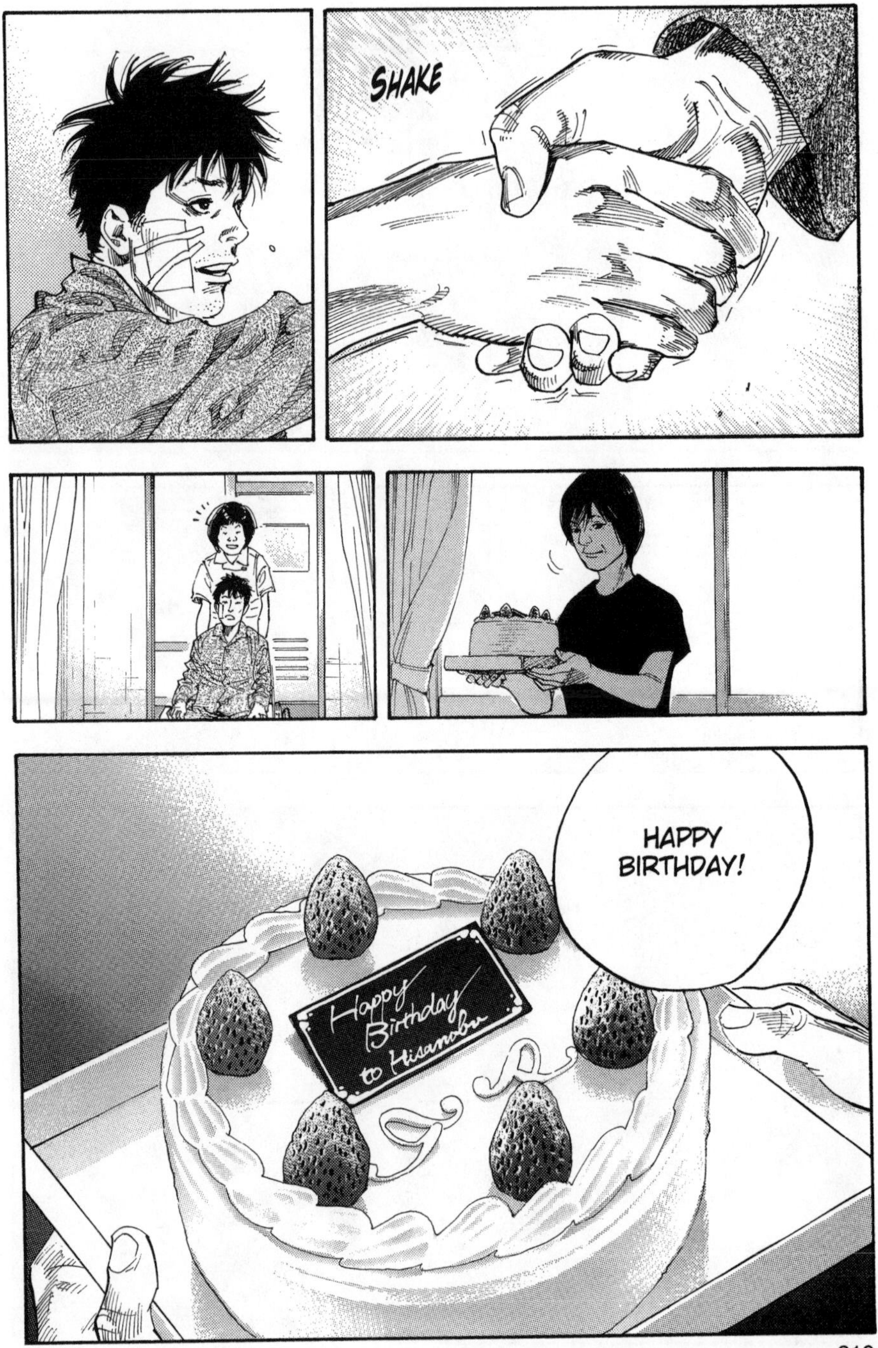
SHAKE
HAPPY BIRTHDAY!
Happy Birthday to Hisanobu

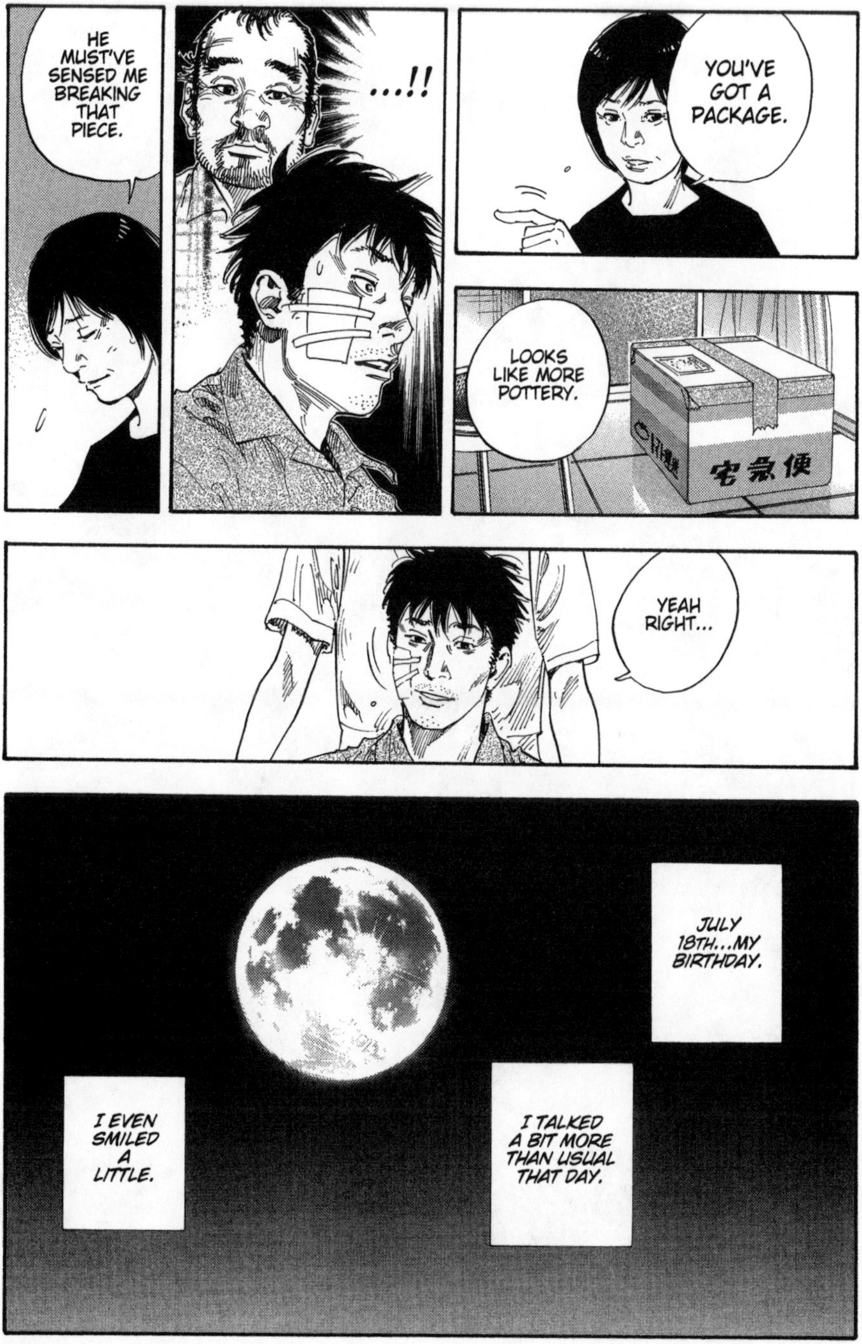
YOU'VE GOT A PACKAGE.
LOOKS LIKE MORE POTTERY.
宅急便
...!!
HE MUST'VE SENSED ME BREAKING THAT PIECE.
YEAH RIGHT...
JULY 18TH...MY BIRTHDAY.
I TALKED A BIT MORE THAN USUAL THAT DAY.
I EVEN SMILED A LITTLE.

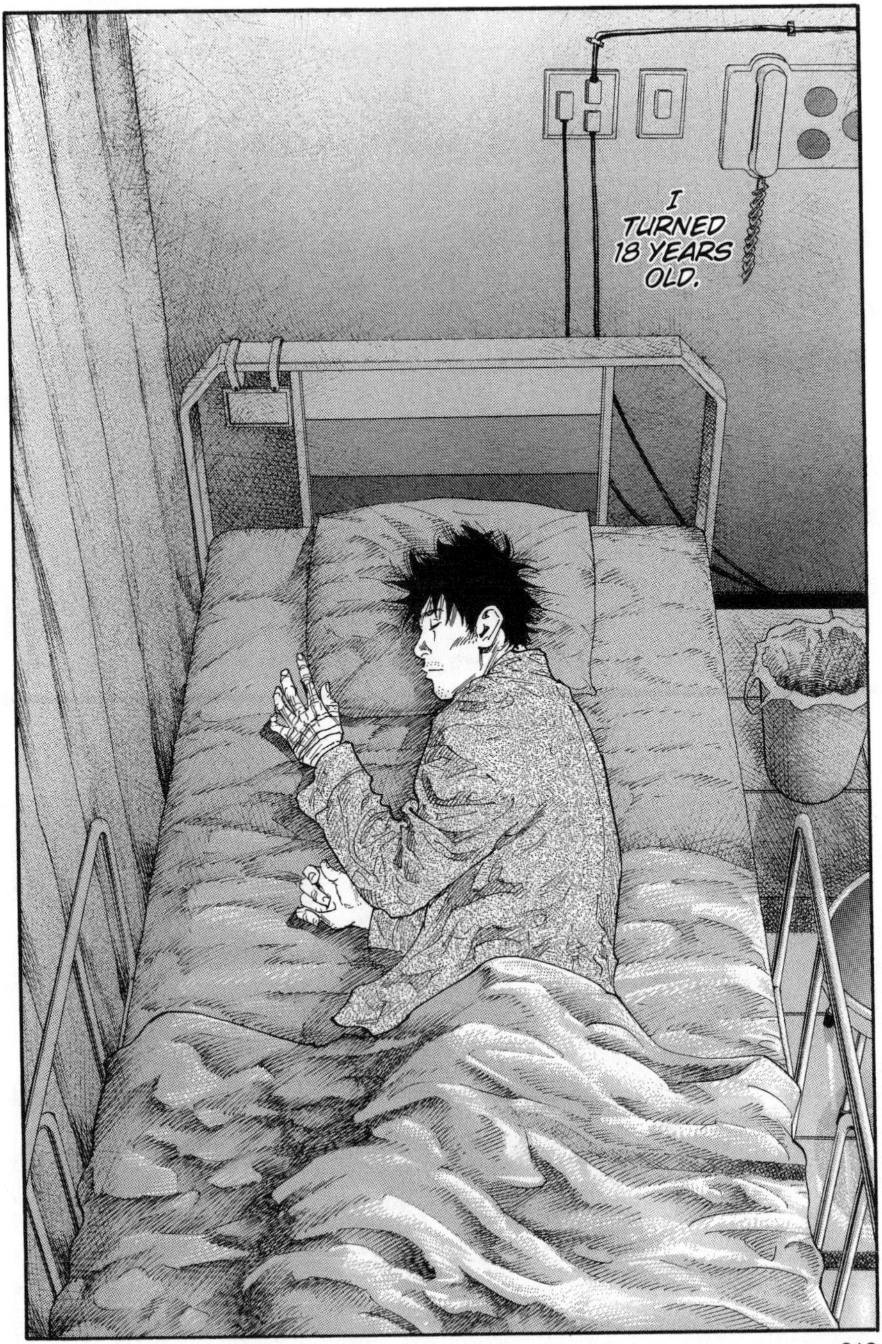
I TURNED 18 YEARS OLD.

REAL

Editorial Notes

This series follows Western name order convention, with given name followed by surname. For example, with Tomomi Nomiya, Tomomi is the first name and Nomiya is the last name. In addition, because the editor felt information about any given character's relationship to another can be gleaned from dialogue and other narrative clues, honorifics such as *-san* and *-kun* have been dropped. On occasion, however, an honorific has been retained for added effect.

Signs and other background text have been left in the original Japanese to retain the integrity of Inoue's artwork. This series takes place in Japan, so it makes sense that store signs and other background material are in Japanese. Translations will be provided in footnotes placed in between panels when such information is necessary to drive the narrative flow and when it is not graphically intrusive. Otherwise, translations will appear here in the Editorial Notes.

Page 85-86: Throwing salt after an unwelcome guest has been in your home is a superstitious practice with roots based in the Shinto belief that salt is a purifying agent.

Page 151, panel 3; 153, panel 6; 154, panel 1; 192, panel 1: translation of Nomiya's note:

> *Tomomi Nomiya's Rebirth Plan*
> ~The path to reform~
>
> Step 1: Haircut
> A complete change! Show how motivated you are to change.
> Even Kobe got rid of his afro.
>
> Step 2: Return CDs
> Had Seki's CDs for a while. Return everybody else's too.
>
> Step 3: Apologize to Takahashi.
> He's evil, but I guess violence isn't good?
> So…apologize to him for kicking his ass.

Real Vol. 3

VIZ Signature Edition

Story & Art by

Takehiko Inoue

Translation/John Werry
Touch-up & Lettering/Steve Dutro
Cover & Graphic Design/Yukiko Kamematsu Whitley
Editor/Andy Nakatani

Editor in Chief, Books/Alvin Lu
Editor in Chief, Magazines/Marc Weidenbaum
VP, Publishing Licensing/Rika Inouye
VP, Sales & Product Marketing/Gonzalo Ferreyra
VP, Creative/Linda Espinosa
Publisher/Hyoe Narita

Printed in the U.S.A.

Published by VIZ Media, LLC
P.O. Box 77010
San Francisco, CA 94107

10 9 8 7 6 5 4 3 2 1
First printing, January 2009

www.viz.com
store.viz.com

RATED T+ FOR OLDER TEEN

PARENTAL ADVISORY
REAL is rated T+ for Older Teen and is recommended for ages 16 and up. This volume contains strong language and mature themes.
ratings.viz.com